In Search

Reimagining What it Means to be a Teacher

Daniel Shindler
(Foreword by Jeffrey Boakye)

Grosvenor House
Publishing Limited

IN SEARCH: REIMAGINING WHAT IT MEANS TO BE A TEACHER

'In Search is right. I'm in! I've been swimming in the best possible sense. Swimming is the word – there are tides and pulls and undercurrents to the writing, and depths in which I find myself swimming. It's exhilarating, I mean that. Daniel Shindler is defying form, too (like water), and it requires focus and energy to engage in. The depths and connections are deeply immersive and so rich – Daniel is articulating something very profound.'

Jeffrey Boakye, bestselling author of
Black, Listed and *Hold Tight*

'Daniel Shindler's very frank, and personal, growth and development shows the reader he's not asking anything of them (or his students or his colleagues) he hasn't asked of himself, too. What Daniel's offering is a master showing the way and a kalyana mitra (noble friend) walking the path alongside him, offering support, provocation, perspective, and inspiration. A big part of what makes it such an enjoyable encounter is the clarity of Daniel's voice. For someone who doesn't know him will read it and will feel like they've made a new friend or acquired a mentor by the time they finish reading it. I do feel what Daniel is offering is a friendship of sorts, and the use of the invitation to play away and conversational tone amplifies this.'

Dr Ehpriya Matharu, writer/artist

'I loved its scope, the depth of thinking, the range of references, the way public and private, school and life, cross over. It got me thinking differently about things. It's also the perfect antidote to all the books around that reduce teaching to chunks, or a series of moves and techniques.'

Peter Hyman, Co-Director of Big Education,
Co-founder of School 21

'Shindler's aim as a teacher is to help students live in the present in a way which is informed by the future they want, rather than the difficulties of their past. I thought this was a very powerful idea and definitely one that is relevant beyond the classroom.'

Clare Carson, novelist

'It's a truly generous outpouring of knowledge and learning gathered over years from teaching and from life. It's amazing how Shindler has managed to bring together and curate ideas of his own, and of such a diverse range of sources to really provide a book that both stands alone, and a reference that can be used as a base for much more exploration.'

Rayne Wiselman, Senior Content Developer, Microsoft

'Rich, multi-layered, erudite, personal; it's like a manual, a memoir, and educational philosophy, as well as a commentary on how to live a rich life.'

Simon Misso-Veness, Deputy Principal,
German Swiss International School, Hong Kong

The right of Daniel Shindler to be identified as the author of this
work has been asserted in accordance with Section 78
of the Copyright, Designs and Patents Act 1988

The book cover is copyright to Daniel Shindler
Cover photograph of some of my students taken at a production of
Macbeth during The Shakespeare Schools Festival in 2004.

This book is published by
Grosvenor House Publishing Ltd
Link House
140 The Broadway, Tolworth, Surrey, KT6 7HT.
www.grosvenorhousepublishing.co.uk

A CIP record for this book
is available from the British Library

ISBN 978-1-83975-020-5

To my angels, Jo, Ellie and Rosa

'Most people come to know only one corner of their room, one spot near the window, one narrow strip on which they keep walking back and forth'

Rainer Maria Rilke

'I go out into the world in order to come back with a self'

Mikhaïl Bakhtin

'Let the beauty of what you love be what you do'

Rumi

CONTENTS

*All names of the students have been changed as have some, but not all, of the adults mentioned

FOREWORD

Before I get into it, here's something that nobody ever said to a new teacher:

You'll never be a great teacher.

They never say it because of how brutal and cruel it would be; to whip away the belief that there is some kind of bulletproof level of competence you can reach as an educator, a skill threshold beyond which you will never feel that knot of anxiety again.

Next, here's something that nobody ever said to a retired teacher:

You were never a great teacher.

Because it's a devastating thought; that you might have spent a lifetime in the classroom trying to perfect the unperfectable craft. That you never got to that place of expertise you thought you were always striving towards.

And finally, here are two things I'm telling you now:

1) There's no such thing as a new teacher.
2) There's no such thing as a retired teacher.

Let me explain.

I know this somewhat cryptic opening is suspiciously wise-sounding, with its Yoda-like rejection of linear thinking. I can only apologise if I've put a whiff of arrogance in the air. It isn't like that. See, when I first met Daniel, I was very close to being a 'new' teacher (having only really worked at the one school I qualified at) and I think it's fair to say he was very close to being a 'retired' teacher (entering the school at which he would draw his career to a close).

So, there we were, two ends of the teaching spectrum, horseshoed into collaboration in the mission to create something new in East London. I had no idea at the time I was entering into a phase of my career, and a relationship, that would have a profound impact on my whole outlook on life. If I'd known, I might have marked the occasion with some kind of farewell party, saying goodbye to all those weird myths you get fed as a young teacher about becoming 'outstanding' and not having to plan lessons anymore.

In Search. The title says it all. Teaching isn't a ladder, or a series of challenges, or a pro forma, or 'continued professional development', whatever that's supposed to mean. It's an act of curiosity. What will connect? What's the context? What's the subtext? What's the matter? What's the text? What's next? Who are you, who are we, who am I? It's a search. It's the effort to walk towards, not forward, or upwards, but inwards towards the self and outwards towards others, at the same time.

The more I got to know Daniel, working with him, problem solving, exploring new ideas and sharing our experiences, the more I realised that this is the space in which a teacher lives, ice on the hotplate, living, *being*, in the truest sense of the word. It's a mindset that comes with its own set of physics. It's the venn diagram of deep craft, human engagement and the expressive arts. It's relational and its relationships and it's as messy and fluid and challenging and ultimately as rewarding as life itself. Big words I know, but why else teach, if not to live? Believe me, with *In Search*, you're about to connect with a mind that fully appreciates how to live in teaching.

The book you're holding in your hands is not a how to, or even a why do. It's a dip in the waves that makes you come up for air. Which is exactly what any teacher, new, retired, or anywhere in between, will tell you teaching is like. Hence those first two things I said nobody ever said at the start of this foreword. You'll find yourself in these pages. It's a rich tapestry woven thick with experiences, episodes of a life lived in teaching.

Whether we realise it or not, teachers draw from this palimpsest with every interaction, every decision, every scheme of work, every curriculum unit, every triumph, every failure or frustration, because these are the embers that spark. It's a journey that came to life all over again as I read this book. We've all got a search in us and trust me, *In Search* is 100% a jumping off point for your own journey, whatever that may be.

Get ready.

Jeffrey Boakye

INTRODUCTION

Play away; techniques; strategies; concepts in this chapter that can be used in different contexts:

Ikigai

The never –ending dialogue

The walk toward

The public and the private self

Starting out as a 23-year-old, I really was the teacher in Roger McGough's poem where, 'Chaos ruled OK in the classroom As bravely the teacher walked in'.[1] 33 years later, having stepped into some of the most challenging environments, this embattled approach is still in me. Above my desk hangs a huge poster with Taylor Mali's *What Teachers Make* colourfully emboldened on it.[2] A lawyer at a dinner party famously asked Mali, a teacher and a poet, 'What's a kid going to learn from someone who decided his best option in life was to become a teacher?' I won't spoil the fun, watch Taylor's reply on YouTube and yell as you applaud his 'kick-arse' reply. But perhaps the lawyer did ask the right question. What does it mean to be an educator? Of course, such a question inevitably leads a good Jewish boy like me to the world of clinical practice. The Hungarian-born physician, Gabor Mate might have turned to Mali's dinner guest and explained teaching is, 'Not only so that others might hear me but so that I could hear myself'.[3] Vonnegut would have joined in,

'If you want to really hurt your parents, and you don't have the nerve to be gay, the least you can do is go into the arts. I'm not kidding. The arts are not a way to make a living. They are a very human way of making life more bearable. Practicing an art, no matter how well or badly, is a way to make your soul grow, for heaven's sake. Sing in the shower. Dance to the radio. Tell stories. Write a poem to a friend, even a lousy poem. Do it as well as you possibly can. You will get an enormous reward. You will have created something.'[4]

That's what I did, probably first to hurt my parents but then, once I got (or didn't get) over that, I tried to practice my craft well. In doing so, I've created a life in which the private and public self become inseparable. It's in the intersection of the private and public that this book lives. We will dance around many private and historical figures who will give us a context in which we can examine the deepest encounters I experienced with my students, the heartbeat of the search. It's an optimistic approach. At its core has been finding a way of creating infinite contexts that have allowed both my students and me to live in a present informed by the future rather than the past.

Of course, this kind of reimagining takes us beyond the classroom, so allow a small digression. Like others, I dream of cooking for a living. I'm not sure why. I hope it isn't as Houellebecq's narrator cruelly tells his reader, 'Gourmandise entered their lives as a new interest, brought on by their growing indifference to the flesh, like the passion of priests who, deprived of carnal joys, quiver before delicate viands and old wines.'[5]; Or even worse, 'You have to take an interest in something in life, I told myself. I wondered what could interest me, now that I was finished with love. I could take a course in wine tasting, maybe, or start collecting model aeroplanes.'[6] However, I spend a considerable amount of my time watching cooking programmes, or when I travel, hunting down places where the late Anthony Bourdain had eaten. Not because I particularly like what he himself once described on his Twitter feed as, 'the meathead culture'[7] but I do like the food he ate. When asked where he'd eat his last meal on earth, Bourdain replied in a way that drew me to him, 'I think I'd prefer to die like an old lion—to crawl away into the bushes where no-one can see me draw my last breath. But in this case, I'd crawl away to a seat in front of this beautiful hinoki wood sushi bar, where three-Michelin starred Jiro Ono would make me a 22- or 23-course omakase tasting menu.'[8] Tragically it wasn't to be.[9] In death as in life, Bourdain's search led me to the lifelong craft of Jiro Ono. Ono is often credited as 'the greatest sushi craftsman alive'.[10] He started working in a kitchen at the age of 7, and is still cooking in his 90s in the tiny basement of his three-Michelin-starred Tokyo restaurant. In the beautiful film, *Jiro Dreams of Sushi*, Ono articulates what I have felt about the art of teaching, 'Once you decide on your occupation... you must immerse yourself in your work. You have to fall in love with your work. Never complain about your job. You must dedicate your life to mastering your skill. That's the secret of success... and is the key to being regarded honourably.'[11] There are key themes here in the search for a life worth living. It's getting close to the Bakhtinian notion of the 'never-ending' dialogue. In such a dialogue there's no distinction between work and what you do outside, as 'everything feeds the work'.(12) In Japan they call this straddling of the private and the public, 'ikigai'. 'Ikigai' has no literal translation. 'Iki' means 'life' and 'gai' is often used to describe value or worth. It's the joining of what you love + what you are good at + what you feel the world needs + what you can get paid for. There's challenge and growth in these overlapping circles as you commit to learning a craft over a long period of time, forming your physical and emotional wellbeing. This notion of self-worth is close to the 'never-ending' dialogue to which Ono alludes. It's the lifelong search to 'become what one is'.(13)

But I digress. For me, the deepest, most immersive, educational experience is to take a cohort of students through from Year 7 to Year 11. Apologies to the post-16 teachers, but I never learnt the craft needed at this level. The 'never-ending' dialogue, the search to 'become what one is', starts when the eleven-year-old child enters my drama studio, often uncertain and apprehensive, often excited and expectant. Here's another core theme we will unpack. For this kind of dialogue will need to nurture, 'A spirit in which we are certain by not being certain of our certainties. To the extent that we are not quite sure about our certainties, we begin to "walk toward" certainties.'(14) We often like to talk about experiences as a journey. The sign, 'Life is a journey not a destination', stands proudly above the desk in my drama studio. However, dig deeper. There's something that resonates if we redefine the journey as a search, viewing the process as a 'walk toward'. For the students and me, it's been a social process over an extended period of time in which we have learnt to let go notions of certainty in order to discover anything long-lasting. The point where I have to jump off is when at 16, the young adult has just finished the drama practical exam, always jubilant and smiling, always deeply satisfied and proud. Listen to some testimony, not as an exercise in ego but rather to hear the 'honour' to which Ono is perhaps alluding to. Both student and teacher are honouring the craft that has allowed them, 'to become what one is'. For the students the public life of school and their private selves become indistinguishable. They have been encouraged to step out of the 'corner of their room, one spot near the window, one narrow strip on which they keep walking back and forth'[15] to discover something bigger than themselves. Previous certainties have been undone. Their reflections suggest the 'walk toward' will continue as they move to the next the stage of their young lives,

- 'You taught me discipline. You taught me dignity. Much more than drama, which you were supposedly teaching me, you taught me that I could achieve more than what I or other people thought I was capable of. Thank you for being genuine. Thank you for seeing me as a partner in learning and sharing. Thank you for being you' (Student)
- 'The journey that I have been on for the past five years has not only made me question the world but it has been the reason that I have taught myself never to diminish what I have and can do. I will forever hold it in my heart' (Student)
- 'A perfect example why the profession needs to respect more, those that keep teaching at the heart of their role for so many years. Where you've got those kids to, from where they were, says it all about your career and craft' (Teacher)
- 'When you know the students, it is impossible not to be moved by the progress and development of each student. I don't mean that in an educational sense, I mean that they have grown as human beings and will leave this school much more 'well-rounded' people than they would have without you. I was reminded of my priorities on Friday. But it was also inspiring - you reminded me what can be achieved when you have ferociously high expectations of students' (Teacher)

The process of transformation being reflected upon here in which both student and I have become 'someone else that you were not in the beginning'[16] happens when a series of requisites are in play. Pause for a moment; it's important to understand what one might mean by a requisite. Then a deep dive into each of the requisites in the context of both our private and public lives will require the reader to constantly 'play away' to find new contexts for further exploration once the book has been read. Hopefully it will bring its reward. From my extensive practice as a teacher of drama, wellbeing, oracy and project-based learning, there are many ideas that can be put into practice in both private and public spheres. Each chapter is based on a pedagogy that includes academics from the world of education, theatre, film, psychology, sociology and philosophy. Our search introduces the reader to these thinkers, and to others encountered in the 'never-ending' dialogue 'to be more fully human'.[17] Some may be familiar, some unfamiliar. You may feel overwhelmed by the extensive range of references, but it's all designed to provoke curiosity, taking the reader to new places. It's exactly this process over the last 33 years that has informed the art of my teaching. If it's leaving you feeling somewhat uncertain, scratching your head, but you still haven't thrown down the book, salute, your 'walk toward' finding new ways of thinking and seeing has begun.

1-McGough, R. 2003: *The Lesson from Collected Poems*: Penguin Books

2-Mali, T.2014: *What Teachers Make*: TED Bowery Poetry Club: https://www.ted.com/talks/taylor_mali_what_teachers_make

3-Mate, G. 2009: *In the Realm of Hungry Ghosts*: Vintage Canada

4-Vonnegut, K. 2006: *A Man Without a Country* : Bloomsbury

5-Houellebecq, M. Translated by Stein, L. 2015: *Submission:* Farrar, Straus & Giroux

6-Ibid

7-Maclean, D. 2017: *Anthony Bourdain condemns restaurant industry's meathead culture after Harvey Weinstein sex assault scandal*: The Independent

8-Bourdain, A. 2016: *'So long, and thanks for all the fish'*: Anthony Bourdain's final meal: The Guardian

9-Bourdain committed suicide at the age of 61, alone in a French hotel room while working on his CNN series, *'Parts Unknown'*. As the title of the TV show suggests, we will never fully know what caused him to take his life.

10-Gordinier, J. 2013: *"Sushi's New Vanguard"*: New York Times

11-*Jiro Dreams of Sushi*: 2011, directed by Gelb, D., Magnolia Pictures

12-Brook quoted in Roose-Evans, J. 1970: *Experimental Theatre-from Stanislavsky to Peter Brooke*: Routledge

13-Kierkegaard, S. 1992 [1846]: *Concluding Unscientific Postscript to Philosophical Fragments, Vol. 1*: Princeton: Princeton University Press

14-Freire, P.1985: *Reading the World and Reading the Word: An Interview with Paulo Freire*: Language Arts, Vol. 62, No. 1, Making Meaning, Learning Language: Published by: National Council of Teachers of English

15-Rilke, R. 2011: *Letters to a Young Poet*: Penguin Classics

16-Foucault, M. 1982: *Truth, Power, Self: An Interview with Michel Foucault - October 25th, 1982*. From: Martin, L.H. et al 1988: *Technologies of the Self: A Seminar with Michel Foucault*: London: Tavistock

17-Freire, P.1970: *Pedagogy of the Oppressed*: Continuum

CHAPTER 1: THE REQUISITES

Play away; techniques; strategies; concepts in this chapter that can be used in different contexts:

Requisites

Play away

Authenticity

Steadiness

A while back, the educationalist Guy Claxton talked to a small group of teachers in a fascinating, free-flowing, 90-minute conversation. He stressed the intentionality of the designed classroom. He's written extensively about this: 'It is about creating a culture in classrooms – and in the school more widely – that systematically cultivates habits and attitudes that enable young people to become better learners; face difficulty and uncertainty calmly, confidently and creatively.'[1] The capacity to 'walk toward' uncertainty, we can agree on. However, I may be doing Claxton a disservice, but when asked how one 'systematically cultivates habits and attitudes', he was reluctant to be tied down to any unchanging fundamentals. This troubled me. I've often been asked, 'How do you do it?' and have been similarly evasive, as I'd never been able to articulate a satisfying answer. I hadn't learnt my craft. However, watch Ono's film to see how he cultivates his own children and apprentices – all men, I'm afraid, for which not only Ono and particularly his son have been criticised, but for which the whole sushi industry is now rightly under scrutiny.[2] In the film, the Japanese food writer Masuhiro Yamamoto tried to capture how Ono does it. He came up with the notion of attributes,

'A great chef has the following 5 attributes: First, they take their work very seriously and consistently perform on the highest level. Second, they aspire to improve their skills. Third is cleanliness. If the restaurant doesn't feel clean, the food isn't going to taste good. The fourth attribute is impatience. They are not prone to collaboration. They're stubborn and insist on having things their own way. What ties these attributes together is passion. That's what makes a great chef.'

Instead of attributes, I'd like to call them requisites. By articulating what I do, I offer a series of requisites that, if nurtured over time, will make for those deeply satisfying experiences we strive for in our private and public lives.

The Requisites

1. **The four circles:**

   o **One-to-one conversations:** *Creating meaningful one-to one conversations using a common language*
   o **The wider school culture:** *Building a broader culture that champions and enacts its virtues and values*
   o **The wraparound services of pastoral care:** *Establishing a framework that envelops and nurtures the school culture*
   o **The inquiring classroom:** *Creating an environment in which the craft of teaching and learning can flourish*

2. **The process of resilience:** *Creating social contexts in which the attributes that make someone resilient can show up*
3. **Knowing oneself; knowing the child:** *Using unexpected tools to explore, know, and accept ourselves and others*
4. **Building community:** *Making community a sustainable place for transformation to occur*
5. **Expertise and empowerment:** *Merging craft and curiosity*
6. **Creating experiences:** *Creating experiences together that add up to more than a sum of their parts*

These requisites are not new; they're present in our everyday interactions. We are being invited to look at them with fresh eyes. Read what Rashid, a 16-year-old who grew up above his family's curry house in London's East End and went to Oxford[3], has to say about creativity. How many of the requisites mined over 5 years can you hear echoed in his writing?

'Well, the "correct" definition for this term is "involving the use of the imagination or original ideas in order to create something" (Oxford Dictionary). However, for me the definition for creativity is infinite. As a drama student, creativity is more than imagination; it's a frame of mind and a way of thinking. It's more than just merely adjusting something with imagination; it's creating and solving problems which never existed; it's adding your own touch to the world through your own means, whether it be art, or music or sports; it's taking a challenge, dissecting it, and putting it back in a way that has never even been thought of. With the fear of sounding like a cliché, creativity is thinking outside the box, and what is to stop one from changing the box into an oval or triangle?

Being creative is not just making something new, it can also be taking an old idea and simply bringing it back to life. Creativity is one of life's themes and undercurrents prevalent from the womb to old age. We all are creative in our own ways, from creative work to fashion sense to humour. Although, in my mind, it has strong connotations with art, but artistic creativity is not bound down to art studios or in the flick of a paintbrush. For example, the creativity present in our drama class is nearly as strong as the testosterone and it embodies every single member of our class. Those who may be shy or lack in confidence, their creativity throws them forward and forces them to contribute. However, the greatest advantage of creativity for me is it provides a change to the daily, monotonous life and literally blows fresh air into this materialistic world. Without it, life would be the same day in, day out. We as a society can also appreciate creativity from The Gherkin, to The London Eye, to knives and forks. Creativity is embedded into life and work and play. It's also very prevalent in religion, as God must have been creative when creating the world and all in it. To conclude, creativity, its uses, and presence in life is undeniable. It's the seed of all intellect and imagination. It both entertains and amuses us. It's a device used by all, and the only requirement to use it is a little imagination.'

No drafting went into this. Off the bat, he was asked to describe what creativity meant to him. But a response such as this arises out of a rich process that lies in the intersection where the private and public meet. It's what gives his writing edge. He has begun the 'walk toward' ideas, feelings, and experiences which can offer life, both private and public, meaning beyond the superficial.

Like Rashid, the Italian psychologist Loris Malaguzzi, founder of the education philosophy 'Reggio Emilia Approach', understands the need to avoid limiting ourselves but rather to give 'value to the potentials, the resources, and many intelligences of all children'.[4] His has been a lifelong search to liberate what he beautifully calls, 'the hundred languages of children':

> The child
> is made of one hundred.
> The child has
> a hundred languages
> a hundred hands
> a hundred thoughts
> a hundred ways of thinking
> of playing, of speaking.
> A hundred always a hundred
> ways of listening
> of marvelling, of loving
> a hundred joys
> for singing and understanding
> a hundred worlds
> to discover
> a hundred worlds
> to invent
> a hundred worlds.[5]

Malaguzzi has created schools based on requisites that serve to empower children's 'surprising and extraordinary strengths and capabilities linked with an inexhaustible need for expression and realisation'.[6] If anyone, child and adult, is willing to engage in this kind of dialogue, Malaguzzi believes it has 'infinite potential for transformation'.[7] It's transformation this book wants to explore. It will become clear that these requisites, which have such transformative power, exist in all meaningful relationships, in high functioning families, organisations, dressing rooms, as well as in the alive classroom. As we look closely, we find them. Or to turn it on its head, see what you find, for example, where the search for

Malaguzzi's 'Hundred languages of children' doesn't exist. It's highly likely you'll discover fear, anger, shame, shielding, lethargy, fragility, failure, resignation, and dysfunction.

But to be able to do this, it's worth considering a phrase used by Claxton in our conversation that stuck with me. He talked about 'playing away' in relation to transference and connections. We 'play away' all the time. It's part of the human psyche, what Freud called 'a universal phenomenon of the human mind' that 'in fact dominates the whole of each person's relations to his human environment'.[8]

> So, play away for a moment; what might we call a search that transcends both the private and the public? A search for what? In learning their craft, what is it teachers are searching for? What are students in search of? If you happen not to be a teacher, what is it you are in search of?

A friend suggested 'wisdom': 'To me, wisdom always implies a life lived and reflected upon – it's experiential and implies self analysis and discovery and some notion of timeless truths.' Play away and follow her trail, it takes us close. Read this description of wisdom; it could be straight out of a school handbook. You'd want to send your child there: 'Being wise is about knowing what's important; having sufficient insight into how we and others tick; having a handle on negative moods and emotions instead of being controlled by them; having an attitude of curiosity and a love of learning; understanding we're all in the same boat and therefore being compassionate towards ourselves and others.'[9]

However, it's not only educationalists who talk of such things. Psychologists also discuss what Freire alludes to when discussing life as a 'walk toward' certainty: 'An integration of knowledge, experience, and deep understanding that incorporates tolerance

6

for the uncertainties of life as well as its ups and downs. There's an awareness of how things play out over time, and it confers a sense of balance.' However, psychologists also warn us, 'It can be acquired only through experience, but by itself, experience does not automatically confer wisdom.'[10] So, who am I to talk about 'wisdom'? Perhaps, like Socrates, we should avoid the word, leaving true wisdom to the gods. While I'm not quite prepared to go all the way with Plato's Socrates, 'I know only one thing – that I know nothing', I have more sympathy with the declaration he made at his trial, 'The unexamined life is not worth living.'[11] However, 'wisdom' comes from the Greek for the love of wisdom, pulling us into the realm of philosophy. Let's not go there. So, if not wisdom, then how about a search for 'authenticity'?

Play away once more; ignore what I just said about philosophical discourse, read this passage about existence and then place it in a context. Who is talking? To whom? Where? Have you ever felt like this? Do you know anyone who has felt like this?

'The fundamental question, therefore, is not what is but that I am. 'My life has been brought to an impasse, I loathe existence, it is without savor, lacking salt and sense. ... One sticks one's finger into the soil to tell by the smell in what land one is: I stick my finger into existence – it smells of nothing. Where am I? Who am I? How came I here? What is this thing called the world? What does this world mean? Who is it that has lured me into the thing, and now leaves me there? Who am I? How did I come into the world? Why was I not consulted, why not made acquainted with its manners and customs? How did I obtain an interest in this big enterprise they call reality? Why should I have an interest in it? Is it not a voluntary concern? And if I am to be compelled to take part in it, where is the director? I should like to make a remark to him."[12]

In the pub with the slightly drunk, frustrated, work colleague in crisis? In a room with an angry, confused adolescent? It was, in fact, the writing of the Danish intellectual Kierkegaard, whose answer to sticking one's finger into existence finding it smells of nothing, is to create an 'authentic' relationship with something outside oneself that, for him, was God. That won't do for me. Then there's Heidegger and his word, *'eigentlichkeit'* – a neologism for 'authenticity'. It translates as 'being one's own'. Heidegger links it closely to *'verstehen'* which means 'understanding'. The etymological root, 'taking a stand', is a key concept in this book as we search for new stories about ourselves. Indeed, his concept of *'dasein'* centres on who one is in the moment and what one can be in the future. It's clear that Heidegger believed life is a search, a 'happening' or 'movement'. Our being is at stake, we're always 'in question' with ourselves in a process of 'storyization'. So far so good; but Heidegger joined the Nazi Party, refusing to repudiate the Holocaust, and allowed publication of his *Black Notebooks* which have too many anti-Semitic references to ignore. We won't debate whether his Nazism negates his philosophy. However, if you insist, then by all means play away; there are numerous articles on the subject; my refugee parents played Wagner endlessly.

So, if not Heidegger, then there are plenty of others to turn to. The French philosopher, Foucault, believed life was a search: 'To become someone else that you were not in the beginning.' In a rhetorical flourish, he asks why couldn't 'everyone's life become a work of art? Why should the lamp or the house be an art object, but not our life?'[13]. I wish I had shown this to Rashid, his life as a work of art. He would have liked it. But an 'authenticity' that focuses on preoccupation with the inner may fall foul of what Lasch defines as 'Narcissistic Personality Disorder'.[14] Bloom goes further and blames this self-absorption on neglect of the public and political self.[15] Indeed, in his aptly titled, *Jargon of Authenticity*,[16] one of Adorno's main objections to Heidegger is he sees it all as merely a 'grinding of teeth which says nothing but I, I, I' (time to get rid of the irritating 'it's all about you', this will pierce the most thick-skinned friend or colleague; try it, I have).

In his book, *Truth and Truthfulness: An Essay in Genealogy*,[17] the philosopher Bernard Williams is having none of it: 'The search for an authentic life is always questionable, and it is not a secret that it can lead to ethical and social disaster.' It's worth considering his ideas on 'steadiness' instead. In what can feel like a senseless world, in both the private and public lives we live, full of 'episodic feelings and thoughts', it then becomes a search 'of stabilising the self into a form'. In doing so, we can 'create a life that presents itself to a reflective individual as worth living'. After all, 'If I am around in the world at all, then I am in it as a human being.'

> Play away; read that again. Is education about stabilising the self into a form in order to help students and teachers create a life that's worth living? Is it essentially to bring us all to an understanding of what it means to be human? Go beyond teaching into how we live our lives. Are we all in search of this kind of steadiness?

In search of steadiness, it has been that for sure. It has been all of these things and more. The best I can come up with is, 'In Search…' because no singular word covers it. It's the search that's thrown up a series of requisites for authenticity, steadiness, wisdom, realness, whatever you prefer to call it. However, it's a search resting on the premise that these requisites can be applied and nurtured over time, both inside and outside the school environment, to make for more deeply satisfying experiences and connections in our public and private lives. It's a search that has created longevity.

1-Claxton, G. 2002: *Building Learning Power: Helping Young People Become Better Learners*: TLO

2-Fifield, A. 2016: *Roll over male sushi chefs. In Japan women challenge tradition*: Washington Post

3-Akram Khan, the wonderful dancer, in his film, *The Curry House Kid* (Channel 4, first shown 29.4.19), explores the kind of environment Rashid grew up in

4-Malaguzzi, L. As quoted on the website *Reggio Children*: http://www. reggiochildren.it/identita/loris-malaguzzi/?lang=en

5-Malaguzzi, L. Translated by Gandini, L. from the poem, *The Hundred Languages of Children:* as quoted on the website: https://reggioemilia 2015.weebly.com/the-100-languages.html

6-Edward, C. 2012: *The Hundred Languages of Children: The Reggio Emilia Experience in Transformation*: Praeger

7-Malaguzzi, L. 1998: *History, Ideas and Basic Philosophy*, in Edwards, C., Gandini, L. & G.E. Forman, G. (Eds) *The Hundred Languages of Children: the Reggio Emilia approach, advanced reflections*: 2nd edn. Greenwich, CT: Ablex

8-Freud, S. 2010: *An Autobiographical Study*: Martino Publishing

9-Baggini, J and Macaro, A. 2014: *What is wisdom?* : Financial Times

10-Psychology Today:*Wisdom*, https://www.psychologytoday.com/us/ basics/wisdom

11-Plato. 2015: *Apology*: Xist Publishing

12-Kierkegaard, S. 1941: *Repetition*: Princeton

13-Foucault, M. 2000: *Ethics: Subjectivity and Truth, Volume 1*: Penguin

14-Lasch, C. 1979: *The Culture of Narcissism: American Life in an Age of Diminishing Expectations*, New York: Norton

15-Bloom, A. 1987: *The Closing of the American Mind*: New York, Simon and Schuster

16-Adorno, T. 1973: *The Jargon of Authenticity*: London, Routledge and Kegan Paul

17-Williams, B. 2002: *Truth and Truthfulness: An Essay in Genealogy*: Princetown University Press

CHAPTER 2: THE FOUR CIRCLES

Play away; techniques; strategies; concepts in this chapter that can be used in different contexts:

The four circles:

- o *One-to-one conversations*
- o *The wider school culture*
- o *The wraparound services of pastoral care*
- o *The inquiring classroom*

Habitual leanings

Many of us work in isolation. We plough our narrow field without imagining how our work can be placed in a richer, broader landscape. It doesn't stop us from succeeding, but it's a limitation. 'We don't have to do all of it alone. We were never meant to.'[1] Once we see this, and what might be getting in our way, we begin to create infinite contexts where anything is possible. Peter Hyman, one of the founders of School21 – a school situated in the East End of London – uses the metaphor of the jigsaw to demonstrate school design is an organic structure which grows as the school evolves. I like the concept of a jigsaw very much. It's limitless; it can be moved around, pieces added and taken away. It encourages threads and connections which aren't obvious; what you do on a micro level is framed by the bigger picture. As you immerse yourself in the pieces, you create possibilities.

I believe the jigsaw contains four circles. The idea of circles comes from the American system where they're familiar with the idea of distinct academic, sporting, and arts circles that rarely cross over.[2] In our model, the circles richly impact each other, with wider significance beyond an educational setting.

- o **One-to-one conversations:** *Creating meaningful one-to one conversations using a common language*
- o **The wider school culture:** *Building a broader culture that champions and enacts its virtues and values*
- o **The wraparound services of pastoral care:** *Establishing a framework that envelops and nurtures the school culture*
- o **The inquiring classroom:** *Creating an environment in which the craft of teaching and learning can flourish*

In my setting, with my students, these circles were developed and woven into a common thread, giving students a coherence into which they could lean; 'habitual leanings,' a colleague called it (much more of him later). It's a sophisticated process, as we shall see. But first, take a moment to play away: how might these four circles play out elsewhere?

I'm a proud Crystal Palace supporter, taken to my first game as far back as 1968. Indulge me a little. I'm not exaggerating when I say I have 'measured out my life' in Crystal Palace fixtures. Ask my loved ones. Indeed, I'd claim 'any event of any significance has a footballing shadow'. Sadly, it's also becoming true that 'as I get older, the tyranny that football exerts over my life, and therefore over the lives of people around me, is less reasonable and less attractive'. I can hear you snigger but it doesn't bother me. You see, I know all the jokes. I'm resigned. The natural state for a Crystal Palace fan is one of 'bitter disappointment, no matter what the score'.[3] I'll prove it to you. One of the most painful periods, and there have been many, was the short time the famous former Dutch international Frank De Boer spent at the club. 77 days, played 5, no goals, no points; a Premier League record for being totally hopeless. I was in the perfect position to explain why, except no-one was listening. I tried calling into the radio, but to no avail.

Hattie likes to describe the act of teaching as gently closing 'the classroom door' and performing 'the teaching act'.[4] If Hattie was a Palace fan, which I doubt (he's from New Zealand), he might have said De Boer finally resorted to slamming the door and rudely performed whatever it was he thought he was doing. 'It has not helped De Boer's standing in the dressing room that he suggested the Palace players lacked courage following the Swansea defeat which he had said, pre-match, was a "must-win" game'.[5] De Boer failed because none of the four circles were in place. He was unable to talk to the players. 'Difficult to get along with,' said one Crystal Palace source. 'A bit of a weirdo,' said another. A tad harsh, perhaps. How well can you know someone in 77 days? Nevertheless, his personality – or lack of it – is said to have played a role in his sacking'.[6] As the players' wellbeing fell away, they were obviously working in an environment with no 'security and clarity of expectations'.[7] The 'habitual leanings' had disappeared. The players lost any inquisitiveness for the growth mindset needed to learn a new way of playing, the so-called 'Dutch Way'. I'm sure there are other well-documented stories of failed organisations that suffered in the same way. Thankfully, we now play 'The

Purley Way' under Roy Hodgson, the son of a Croydon bus driver. If this was a sports book – luckily for some of you, it's not – it would be interesting to show how Hodgson established the four circles with the same group of players, resulting in an upturn in club fortunes and Premier League survival.

Before we move on, we ought to mention Gareth Southgate, the England manager and former Crystal Palace player (of course he was) and his experiences at the World Cup in 2018. After years of trauma and failure, he knew change wasn't enough. Perhaps he didn't see things in the same way my colleague Jeffrey (as I said, more of him later) expressed it on his Twitter feed: 'Time to consider the tricky relationship with post-Empire nationalism and failure-trauma that I was born into as the son of colonial immigrants. It's a miracle I made it 36 years without developing a twitch. #football'[8] However, Southgate knew it had to be about transformation. To help him, a psychologist, Dr Pippa Grange, was employed to transform the culture in this male-driven world. She was asking something huge of these men: to reimagine their own masculinity. As a woman, this wasn't an easy task for her either. As Grange explains, when talking about her experiences with the New Zealand rugby team,

> 'Being a woman in a professional male team sports environment is a constant navigation, for everyone. I have no interest in being one of the lads and I don't quite fit in the 'nurturing mother figure' category in terms of the leadership work I do. I would be professionally ineffective if I remained in the background, psychologically safe with minimal voice, and I am not here to be the centre of attention as some form of entertainment. I don't want to be completely separate because that would make me inaccessible and probably be a lonely place to operate from. I don't want to fit in completely because frankly hanging out with a squad of 35 blokes has its limits. However, there are very few women role-models who I can look to as examples when it comes to getting this "fitting in" balance right.'[9]

Grange set out establishing the four circles by creating an environment in which Freire's 'walk toward' could begin. Like Freire, Grange is interested in uncertainty: 'I notice that the players are initially a little less certain, less relaxed, and more aware of themselves and their behaviours. They approach with caution until a relationship has well and truly been built, and they still apologise after swearing almost two years on. It is simply less comfortable, because no-one is quite sure "how to be".'[10]

As we examine each circle in detail, we'll see that these requisites nurture a vulnerability in which people can drop their shields and start to show up. In this context, these young men begin to create new conversations with themselves and with each other. 'This has reportedly included getting the players to sit down together in small groups to share their life experiences and anxieties, and to reveal intimate truths about their character and what drives them.'[11] Of course, England lost, standard, but Grange had established a set of values in a secure environment with a clear and different set of expectations. Winning and losing was now placed in the context of a growth mindset: 'Every day in our general lives and our sporting lives we will win some and lose some; it's just part of the way life should be. It could be missing out on a promotion, being pipped at the line in a running race, or bombing out in an exam – it doesn't matter – the important lesson is to learn from our failures, reassess, rethink, move forward (sometimes in a different direction), and keep those dreams and goals alive.'[12] Listening to Southgate explain his methodology, it's striking how it meets many of the requisites this book is exploring.

> Play away; in what environment outside of sport would you welcome someone talking in these terms? Have you ever spoken like this? What was the context?
>
> - 'We've spoken to the players about writing their own stories.'[13]

- 'We always have to believe in what is possible in life.'[14]
- 'I think if the players have some ownership of what's going on then that's going to help them make better decisions on the field and also buy into the way that we are trying to progress.'[15]
- 'As a coach, you always have to be there to support the person – improving them as a player becomes secondary to a degree.'[16]

Where the four circles exist, transformation is possible. In 2008, Iceland's three main banks imploded, leaving behind $85 billion worth of debt. Icelanders were among the heaviest drinkers in Europe and had no national football team to speak of. Today, Iceland is very different. Women make up 38.6% of the governing body; at the time of writing their prime minister, Katrín Jakobsdóttir, is from the Left Green movement; for the ninth time in 2016, Iceland was ranked the most gender equal country in the world by the World Economic Forum; in 2018 it became the first country in the world to make it illegal to pay men more than women; the *Economist* has named it the world's best place for working women[17]; what's more, their national football team has now risen 100 places in Fifa's world ranking, if you care about such things. Something has happened.

Back in 1980, Iceland elected the world's first democratically-elected female head of state, Vigdís Finnbogadottir – a single mother and breast cancer survivor, who spoke openly about her mastectomy. When one of the male contenders said she couldn't become president because she was only half a woman, Finnbogadóttir put him firmly back into his box: 'Well, I'm actually not going to breastfeed the Icelandic nation; I'm going to lead it.'[18] For a drama teacher, it's poignant this leader was a theatre director in her previous life. In all I've read, she was committed to the kind of conversations she used when practising

16

her art. The 'never-ending' search 'to become what one is' is beautifully articulated in an interview she gave, in which she threads together an argument that brings her to the very essence of who she 'be':

'Women tend to have a greater understanding of the human being. I think being a theatre director was very good preparation, that and having studied the humanities and being a literary person. From morning when the rehearsals start, until night when the curtain falls, theatre involves analysing humanity – the human being versus society, society versus the human being, love and jealousy, how people manage to live together – all the aspects of life. This leads me to the question: What is a presidency about? ...It's about human beings. It's about understanding and being sensitive to how people think and feel.'[19]

She understands a wider culture wanting to create a country, not a school, that 'functions, day in, day out, as an effective incubator of its chosen virtues'[20]; to design a country, not a school, where 'the espoused values do gradually become enacted values'.[21] She knew to build a broader culture 'takes thought, solidarity and determination'.[22] Read another answer she gave in the same interview. It's imbued with the Freirean 'spirit' in which 'we are certain by not being certain of our certainties'. It's the question she almost asks herself at the end which suggests she isn't quite sure:

'I understand my people – I understand the Icelanders, their way of thinking... The Icelandic way of thinking is very linked to nature. Icelanders have to get the hay into the barn before it starts to rain. They have to catch the cod before it swims past the coast. So they have to get things done and they are impatient and they are stubborn and stick very stubbornly to what they think is the truth. Icelanders are not trained in the art of discussion because they don't have philosophy in their heritage. The Nordics – except for the Danes who have Kierkegaard – don't have philosophers.

Say you're with six French friends and nobody agrees – the arguments are very intellectual: 'Remember what Pascal said,' someone will say. 'No, you can't say that because Schopenhauer...' another will say. They can always refer to ideas. We don't refer to ideas, and so our discourse can become very harsh. Do you think there is truth in that?'

Finnbogadottir laughs. She realises a lack of inquiry is a limitation; the infinite contexts are not there. Transformation is needed. 'This is a shortcoming that can harm us as an entity – because we are so few it is extremely important that we stand together and that we do not have feuds in our society.' So, she set about making the country inquisitive, asking them to consider what's important: 'I would always encourage the nation to concentrate on what is worth safeguarding in this country: identity, language – memories that are stored in the language – and not least, nature. I think that we have to take great care of the real treasure that is our nature. Safeguarding Icelandic nature is a huge responsibility.' However, the actor/theatre director in her, allowed her to realise herself, 'to become what one is', but carried out with a spirit of 'playfulness, inquisitiveness and self-reliance'.[23] You can hear it in her answer: 'I think those were good years for the Icelanders. I promoted the country. I was the first president to adopt that role because I became so well known after being elected. It was extraordinary. I was invited all over the world because – I would joke about it– the world wanted to see what kind of phenomenon this was: a woman president. It was so alien. I was like an alien.' Like Claxton and Lucas, Finnbogadóttir was aware the 'walk toward' needs to be set in a culture of 'security and clarity of expectations'. She leaves Michael Moore in no doubt of this: 'If the world can be saved, it will be women that do that. And they do not do it with war, they do it with words.'[24] In Moore's film, *Where to Invade Next*, there's a memorable moment in which the women tell Moore how they structure themselves with 'we', not 'me': 'We are like a big group and we try to take care of each other within that group.' As Moore flounders, they tell him, 'It's women, it's in our DNA.' It's the four circles. They're there when Brynhildur Heiðar, executive manager of the Icelandic Women's Rights Association, states: 'There is absolutely no doubt that there is an equivalency between more gender-balanced political representation and better policies for women. Parental leave, day care, the gender pay gap – none of these were seen as major issues before women ran for parliament.'[25]

Try and find the four circles in Trump's presidency. Topping reports depressingly, after the 2016 election, the US dropped from 52nd to 104th in the world for women's political representation. However, liberal female legislators co-sponsored an average of 10.6 bills related to women's health – an average of 5.3 more than their liberal male colleagues. A Stanford University study also showed female Congress members simply get more done, passing on average twice as many bills as male legislators in one analysed session of Congress. Finish the book and you'll see why that is. The requisites for transformation are certainly there.[26]

1-Brown, B. 2015: *Rising Strong:* Vermilion

2-Read Michael Sokolove's riveting book, *Drama High* (2013: Riverhead books) about Lou Volpe's four decades of teaching drama in an American blue-collar town. Volpe manages to break into the three circles; the sporting 'jocks' became some of his most successful performers. Apart from the extraordinary relationship Volpe forms with Cameron Mackintosh and the success of his former students, it's a wonderful chronicle of a great teacher who transformed lives. In wanting so much more for his students, the requisites shine through.

3-Hornby, N. 1992: *Fever Pitch:* Victor Gollancz Ltd

4-Hattie, J. 2003: *Teachers make a difference: What is the research evidence?:* Research conference of the Australian Council for Educational Research – *Building teacher quality: What does the research tell us?* Melbourne: Australian Council for Educational Research

5-Burt, J. 2017: *Crystal Palace players already questioning Frank De Boer's management:* The Daily Telegraph

6-Mokbel, S. 2017: *The players were baffled… and called him a weirdo: The inside story on Frank de Boer's calamitous 77-day reign as Crystal Palace manager*: The Daily Mail

7- Claxton. G. And Lucas. B. 2013: *What Kind of Teaching For What Kind Of Learning*: SSAT

8- Jeffrey Boakye @unseenflirt Jul 7/ Twitter

9-Grange, P. 2013: *Women in sport – fitting in:* Bluestone Edge: http://bluestoneedge.com/2013/11/03/women-in-sport-fitting-in/

10- Ibid

11-Saner, E. 2018: *How the psychology of the England football team could change your life*: The Guardian

12-Ibid

13-Ibid

14-Ibid

15-The Boot Room: *Southgate: "If a player feels you respect them, they are more likely to follow you"*: The FA: http://www.thefa.com/get-involved/coach/the-boot-room/issue-26/gareth-southgate-coaching-approach-060617

16-Ibid

17-Topping, A. 2017: *There's proof: electing women radically improves life for mothers and families*: The Guardian

18- Koon, N. 2012: *One woman's take on 'the high bridge'*: The Rocket: https://www.therocket.com.my/en/one-womans-take-on-the-high-bridge/

19-Andersen, A.2014: *Madam President, Vigdís Finnbogadóttir on fashion and the times*: The Reykjavik Grapevine: https://grapevine.is/mag/feature/2014/03/24/madam-president/

20- Claxton. G. And Lucas. B. 2013: *What Kind of Teaching For What Kind Of Learning*: SSAT

21-Ibid

22-Ibid

23-Ibid

24-Moore, M. 2015: *Where to Invade Next*: IMG Films

25-Topping, A. 2017: *There's proof: electing women radically improves life for mothers and families*: The Guardian

26-The fight back has begun. In the 2018 American congressional elections, women from an array of diverse backgrounds now make up nearly a quarter of its voting membership, the highest percentage in U.S. history. I recommend the Netflix film, *Knock Down The House*, which follows four women's attempts to break the male monopoly of power in their fight to be elected. Analyse Alexandria Ocasio-Cortez's personal and public transformation through the lens I'm proposing, and see where it takes you.

CHAPTER 3: ONE-TO-ONE CONVERSATIONS

Play away; techniques; strategies; concepts in this chapter that can be used in different contexts:

Distinctions:

- *Transformation (we don't know what we don't know) v Change (we know what we know; we know what we don't know)*
- *Fact v Opinion*
- *Respond v React*
- *Showing up v Shielding*

The Universal Human Paradigm – 'should/should not/ it is what it is'

The Winning Strategy

Already always listening

Infinite contexts

Vulnerability

Being Present

The Stand

A fundamental question is whether we are willing. My mentor once challenged me, 'When you can really get that, and I mean really get that, you will begin a new conversation, to discover what you don't know you don't know.' Most of the time we know what we know; we know what we do not know. For example, though we don't know what will happen tonight or tomorrow morning, we kind of do. However, the moment when we discover 'what you don't know what you don't know', is transformative. Run with it; you'll get it, I promise. For now, just note our first distinction, 'Change versus Transformation'.

In her book, *The Last Word on Power*, Tracy Goss defines this distinction: 'Change provides an improvement in the existing way of doing... Transformation provides the creation of that which does not yet exist...a new realm of possibility.'[1] We can use these distinctions in creating a common language that empowers two people in meaningful conversation. This isn't exclusive to a school context. Tracy Goss works in the realm of business. It can operate on a deeply personal level, too. It will be clearer if I share a meaningful conversation that extended over five years. As you can imagine, it's a long conversation, but hopefully will offer insight into what one means when we talk about a meaningful conversation informed by a common language.

Looking back over my professional career, my own conversation has been largely around how it 'should/should not be', refusing to accept 'it is what it is', unable to see the distinction. I was in Goss's Universal Human Paradigm, 'the water in which all human beings swim'. Try listening out for it during the day. You hear it everywhere. People telling those they think are listening how it should and should not be. As they pull people in, a head of self-righteous steam of 'should/should not' is created. It's normal and often satisfying. We all do it. However, this is about survival, 'being right, dominating and avoiding domination'. In her book, Goss defines the Universal Human Paradigm: 'There is a way things should be, and when they are that way, things are right, and when they are not that way, there's something wrong with me, them (other people), or it (anything in the world or the whole world in general).' I challenged; I resisted; at times I submitted, but didn't hear this was in fact Goss's Winning Strategy. 'The Winning Strategy' is 'a lifelong, unconscious formula for achievement and success' which, unknown to me, has designed 'me as a human being':

'It is the source of your success and at the same time the source of your limitations... Your individual Winning Strategy is a conversation that consists of three elements: *listening for* – the filter through which you interpret; *so as to act by* – your modus operandi; and *in order to* – your measure for knowing that life worked out.'

Some examples will help. It's important to note you can't recognise your own winning strategy without someone helping you to discover it. On the other hand, it isn't hard to hear someone else's winning strategy.

Play away; do you recognise these people Goss describes?

Person A:
Listening for: What's underneath? What's hidden?
So as to act by: Providing what's needed and wanted
In order to: be valued and avoid being left out

Person B:
Listens for: What's really going on here? What's the truth?
So as to act by: Doing what's appropriate; doing the right thing
In order to: Be certain and safe, avoid betrayal

Person C:
Listens for: Where's the fun?

> **So as to act by:** Provoking, moving, arranging and taking things lightly
> **In order to:** Be alive, feel everything and avoid being trapped
>
> Don't stop; play away with someone who knows you:
>
> Person D is you:
> What are you **listening for?**
> **So as to act by:**
> **In order to:**[2]

My mentor was already listening to my own 'already always listening'. She explained, 'The Already Always Listening is how you are being before you hear a word. It is how you are being when you enter a situation. It is who you are being in a relationship or when someone is speaking. The Already Always Listening is the filter in which we listen. The present is being determined by the past. Things do not always fit your picture. How you are about that can either get in the way or can support you to move towards your goals.'

> Play away; how many times do we know what someone is going to say before they say it? How many times do we know how a meeting will go before we even step into the room?

Our knowing is based on judgement, opinions, and points of view from our past. In other words, we're already always listening. It isn't new; The Talmud states: 'We do not see things as they are, we see them as we are, we do not hear things as they are, we hear them as we are.' My mentor continued, 'We are not our thoughts and feelings. If we are, then our thoughts and feelings have us.' We both knew full well I was (and often still am) my thoughts and feelings.

The conversation continued with participants in a training session as I proudly told them of my last frustrating conversation. In front of everyone (cringing as I write this), I ranted about a member of the management team for deliberately over-running his assembly. I knew he was going to be late before he was. I'd even gathered colleagues in a conspiratorial huddle earlier in the day, building up that righteous head of steam. I was already always listening, believing his actions were an exercise in power, blindly unaware how my thoughts and feelings held me by the throat. The fact my feedback was written verbatim on a whiteboard forced me to confront my own conversation. I was clearly gathering evidence for my righteousness, basing my present firmly in the past, like a hamster on a wheel. How many times had I ranted like this before? I shudder to think.

A new distinction was established: 'Fact V Opinion'. I insisted I was right even after all the opinion had been taken out of my statement leaving two mundane facts, 'The children arrived at 9.15. I started my lesson at 9.20.' That's what happened. The rest was my interpretation, the story I'd told myself over and over again until I believed it was true. The group was asked if anyone could see what I could see. No-one could. That was the moment I realised there was no box except of my own making, and understood the earlier distinction. I'd been firmly ensconced in the 'should/should not' rather than in 'it is what it is'. My mentor explained it to me like this, 'We are a meaning-making machine and it is infinite. New things show up depending on the context. It does not have to be that way, but often we say it is. It is defined; there is no room for infinite possibilities.' It struck home.

> Play away; re-read what my mentor said. How often have you, like me, limited yourself by telling yourself something over and over again until you believed it's true?

I started to feel what Einstein meant, 'The world we have made as a result of the level of thinking we have done thus far, creates problems we cannot solve at the same level of thinking at which we created them.'[3] I could see no point after so many exhausting years spent either resisting or submitting, a feeling I recognised too in some of my students.

My mentor clearly heard my 'there is no point' conversation continuing to push, not letting me off the hook. She wanted me to confront the meanings I'd created by repeating them as truth rather than as the opinions they were. Just as I've so often asked of students, I too had to learn how to be comfortable in the uncomfortable. A new distinction became clearer; Brene Brown's 'Shielding v Showing up'. I was being asked to drop my shields and to show up – a fundamental requisite if a conversation is to have any meaning.

Brown likes the word 'authentic': 'Authenticity is a collection of choices that we have to make every day. It's about the choice to show up and be real. The choice to be honest. The choice to let our true selves be seen.'[4] I was becoming vulnerable. Brown explains what that feels like: 'Vulnerability sounds like truth and feels like courage. Truth and courage aren't always comfortable, but they're never weakness.'[5] At the time, it felt incredibly uncomfortable staring at a list of possible meanings I may have made. I could now see those meanings I'd constructed and the conversation I was having with myself (deep breath):

- *I am scared*
- *I am without control*
- *I am not respected*
- *I can see no point*
- *I am selfish*
- *I am arrogant*
- *I am without confidence*
- *I am quiet*
- *I am without opinions*

My mentor asked how these meanings determined my actions. I replied (deep breath):

- *I do not trust people*
- *I shut down*
- *I cause conflict*
- *I write emails that I send/don't send*
- *I work as I have to be outstanding*
- *I seek others to confirm my righteousness*
- *I am full of opinions, judgements, and points of view*
- *I am in a reactive state*

The above was all in the realm of change; I knew what I knew, I knew what I did not know. Then my mentor mentioned the word 'save'. It arose when I attempted to coach another teacher. As we backslapped each other at the end of the conversation, feeling we'd really 'fixed' a problem, I was taken aback when the observers plainly told me I hadn't been the space in which he could fully embrace who he is. Previous jargon of micro/macro/me listening was now replaced by the concept of 'being present'. My mentor challenged me: 'Speaking does not give listening. If you are in the present, the other person will speak. Listening gives speaking.' The Soto Zen monk, Shunryu Suzuki, as you can imagine, spent much time developing his capacity to be present. He teaches us:

'When you listen to someone, you should give up all preconceived ideas and your subjective opinions; you should listen to him/her, just observe what his/her way is... Usually when you listen to some statement, you hear a kind of echo of yourself. You are actually listening to your own opinion. If it agrees with your opinion you may accept it, but if it does not, you will reject it or you may not even really hear it.'[6]

The anthropologist Gregory Bateson suggests if you're really present you might discover 'what you don't know you don't know': 'Sometimes if both people are willing to listen carefully, it is possible to do more than exchange greetings and good wishes. Even to do more than exchange information. The two people may even find out something which neither of them knew before.'[7] I discussed this with my daughters over Sunday lunch. Their response was immediate and unanimous: 'Dad, you've never been present.' It was a humbling moment. I could see my own 'save' conversation hadn't allowed the other person to be who he or she wished to be. I hadn't given people the space in which they could fully embrace who they are. I'd been in the way. Or as one of the observers put it, pulling no punches: 'The fact you want to save the other person and he wants to be saved, means that he won't be saved.' I was now in the realm of transformation; I didn't know what I didn't know. It's captured in a subsequent email from my mentor, an example of the one-to-one conversation that can only happen when a common language has been fully explored (the capitals are hers):

'The Purpose of the mind is survival: Survival of the BEING or whatever the BEING considers itself to BE. If the Being considers itself to BE "POINTLESS" that is what the mind will keep in survival! Life is meaningless and pointless. Once you can really get that and I mean really get that – Maybe you can stop looking for meaning outside of your life, and then BE willing to create a meaning or point for your life.

You are always RIGHT – Either being determined by your past, BEING an automatic point of view gathering evidence for your righteousness, or BEING a generated point of view determined by your commitment. You either have thoughts and feelings or thoughts and feeling have you.

No-one has ever saved you or can save you, as you don't need saving! You have everything you need if you are willing to fully embrace it and then you can stop trying to save others and be the space in which they can fully embrace who they are.'

Within her words lies the journey. The new insight of 'only I can be responsible for myself' led to the new distinction, 'React V Respond'. Like the hamster on the wheel, I re-enacted my past on a daily basis, my present firmly in my past as thoughts and feelings regularly grabbed me by the throat. My daily interactions were 'already always listening', full of judgement, opinion, and points of view from my past. It was clear I would need to reimagine myself. It would begin with taking responsibility.

> Play away; how would you define responsibility?

My mentor defined responsibility to me like this (compare it to your definition):

> 'Being responsible starts with the willingness to deal with the situation from and with the point of view, whether at the moment realised or not, that you are the source of:
>
> 1. Who you are – is who you say you are
> 2. What you do – actions are correlated to the conversations you are
> 3. What you have – is the result of your actions'

An ability to respond meant starting to create the present in the future. As part of this process of reimagining, I was encouraged to create a 'stand' – a requisite with which we fight the subconscious conversations that keep us stuck; there are always situations and people who pull us easily back into our past. Goss defines a stand:

> 'People often misunderstand what taking a stand means. It doesn't mean being resolute, stalwart, or grimly determined. It means committing yourself to continuously act consistent with the possibility you declared, from the moment the declaration is spoken, regardless of the circumstances.'[8]

Here's my stand. My declaration to myself:

'Who I be is who I choose to be. I am whole and complete, without flaw. Who am I is my word and I honour my word as who I am. I can now make a generated, conscious decision to be who I say I am. My actions can be purposefully determined. The consequence, what I have, will be the person who I want to be. It's the space in which I'm declaring I will generate my life from. However, I'm fully conscious I'm only empowered out of it as much as I say I'm empowered. Each day is a struggle not to return to the past, so each day I scratch my stand.'

I lapse regularly. My family, friends, and students often see me do this strange scratching movement close to my heart in moments of crisis when I have the choice to be who I say I be or to be something else. I have this choice now. A card from a colleague with whom I collaborated (more of that later) shows how meaningful conversations empower:

'My first big thanks come from the INSET. It gave me a new look at my life and affected me in a profound way. I don't know if I've found my stand or if I even know what a stand really is, but it has helped me to re-find myself...before working on this project I was seriously thinking of leaving the profession...it is so easy to allow yourself to be caught up in the business of life that you forget why you're there. Now I feel like I'm back and I know where I am (although not sure about where I'm going yet)...I owe this to you, there are so many times we can change another's life without ever knowing it.'

Teaching context

As I worked on myself in meaningful conversations with my mentor, I developed a method for similar conversations with some of my students. They, like me, needed to reimagine themselves.

Their inability to take responsibility had left them stuck, creating, on a daily basis, a present firmly in the past. The first question to ask the student is whether they're willing to have the conversation, which is why I created a contract:

One-to-one contract

Our aim is to create a context in which the future informs the present, not the past.

I agree to the following:

- ✓ *To be willing to take part in a one-to-one conversation*
- ✓ *To participate 100% (To show up)*
- ✓ *To commit to giving and keeping your word (Integrity)*
- ✓ *To meet 6 times on a weekly basis for 30 minutes (Resilience)*
- ✓ *To be on time (Relationships)*
- ✓ *The content of our conversations is to be kept strictly confidential unless an issue of child protection arises (This will be explained to you) (Trust)*
- ✓ *Any notes I take will be for reference only and may be accessed by you at any time*
- ✓ *A feedback sheet will be filled in by you and by me before the next session (Dialogue)*
- ✓ *Any additional work requested will be fully completed by the deadline set (Responsibility)*

I also created a pupil feedback sheet for students to fill in after the session:

Giving feedback

- • *What were the highlights for you today?*
- • *What insights have you had today?*
- • *What makes these insights important to you?*

32

- *What have you done today to allow you to come to the above answers?*
- *What has the teacher done today to allow you to come to the above answers?*
- *Was there any point when the teacher got in the way?*
- *Do you have any suggestions about what we should keep in our next session?*
- *Are there any takeaways, suggestions, advice you might ask yourself to think about before the next session?*
- *Are there any takeaways, suggestions, advice for the teacher to think about before running the next session?*
- *Identify 5 things you appreciate about yourself and the 5 things you appreciate about your teacher*

I also filled in a reflection sheet. The power of these one-to-one conversations was evident. I and the pupils recognised the ability to be present. Conversations were less successful where factors got in the way – my 'save' conversation; 'always already listening' with opinions, judgements, points of view; tiredness; distractions; a lack of time. I sometimes got in the way of that space in which a student can express who they wish to be. I also got burnt when one of my 'at risk' pupils was clearly not willing. I persisted (my save conversation), believing I could talk her round. It was upsetting for both of us. I subsequently wrote her an email which is worth sharing to hear the common language that was established, however flawed:

Hi,

Please consider the following:

–You have returned to school in Year 9 showing the same kinds of behaviour you have shown for the last 2 years and probably in primary school. This is the past.

–It would follow you are trapped in the past.

–It would seem you are unable to solve this by yourself/self-regulate. Whatever strategies you are using are not working.

–That means it is predictable you will continue to behave in this way.

–The school is asking you to base your present in the future.

–You need to be helped to create a new context/a new light in which to view your behaviour.

–You cannot do this by yourself. You need an adult/ally to help you do this.

–You choose to be who you wish to be. You are only responsible for yourself.

–In being unwilling to have a one-to-one conversation, you chose who you wished to be on Friday afternoon.

–You chose to be fixed.

–The school is asking you to adopt a growth mindset and to accept the offer to help move you from the past to basing your present in the future.

–To really understand what that means, you should consider having a meaningful conversation before rejecting it as 'rubbish'.

–The school has spent the last 2 years trying to support you. We will continue to do so. We believe you have all the answers. However, we believe you need help to discover what the answers are.

Subsequently, I pushed hard with my teacher hat on, forcing the issue as she continued to get into trouble. It climaxed in her being excluded internally. I spoke to her in the exclusion room, telling her

I was upset seeing her so angry. As her teacher, I wanted her to survive school and be able to choose to do whatever she wished to do at 16, complete and whole. She took GCSE Drama, so I taught her until the end of her school career. In spite of the setbacks, we had enough common language to create a context within which she could move forward to create her present in the future rather than the past. It was a meaningful conversation as she was willing to search, 'to become what one is'. She achieved an A in Drama and got an excellent set of results in her other subjects. On results day, as the tears rolled down her cheeks and those of her resilient, loving mother, we all knew the search had been worth it. From being in a perpetual reactive state, she now had the ability to respond (return to my mentor's definition of responsibility). She was moving forward, whole and complete, knowing the answers lay within her.

I have taken another of my 'at risk' students through the cycle, climaxing in the creation of his stand. Through this process, I have created a 10-step approach to creating a stand which staff have been trained to use with their own students.

> Play away; try these steps in a different context (although heed my family's warning, 'Don't you try and do that coaching stuff on us!' Expletives omitted.)

1. *The mentee is told in advance to consider what he/she wishes to talk about ('are you willing?'). The mentee then starts the session talking about whatever he/she wishes to talk about. The mentor takes notes, reflects back the conversation to check accuracy, and asks whether the mentee wants to add anything.*
2. *The mentor asks whether there's anything that has been said he/she wishes to create a new context for; to shine a new light on; to begin to create a new conversation. Once a moment has been chosen, the mentee is asked to think of an actual moment/experience to discuss.*

3. *The mentor writes up the chosen moment verbatim on the white board until the mentee is satisfied this is what happened. It's important the mentee can see what's been said.*

4. *The mentee is asked what meanings he/she has made and how meanings determined their actions. This is also written on the whiteboard.*

5. *The mentor and mentee look at the moment again and take out all of the opinion. Only the facts remain; this is actually what happened, not the story they've been telling themselves over and over again until opinion has become fact (The Past).*

6. *The mentee is asked again what meanings he/she now makes about what happened.*

7. *The mentee is now asked what he/she wants (The Future).*

8. *The mentee turns these wants into one goal.*

9. *The mentee and the coach discuss possible options; what could be done to achieve the goal. The mentee commits to a course of action to achieve the goal.*

10. *The mentee creates his/her stand.*

With my 'at risk' student, I felt it was important not to rush to goals until he'd said all he wanted to say about 'what happened'. With a far more grounded student, frustrated by the 'what happened' phase, we moved more quickly to the future. However, my 'at risk' student wanted to talk about two issues in his life: freezing and trust. Here was a child who'd spent the last two years unable to say what happened even when caught bang to rights. He was clearly frustrated by his inability to express himself. He'd been placed in my group 'to be saved', as he was under the threat of expulsion. However, because I was truly present, the one-to-one session created a space in which he could express who he wished to be. His stand was written with no support or guidance. A common language had been established by running alongside his one-to-one, a scheme of learning based on an edited version of the text, *Chewing Gum Dreams* (nothing like the TV adaptation, recommend)[9], which we explored in tutor time. The mining of the text allowed for distinctions to be unpacked in a different context and through an engagement with the characters in the play. Hear within his stand how the whole process had empowered the reimagination of the self:

My stand

I am a wheel rolling towards my future

I am a bottle overflowing without rage but control

I am a ball of light that bursts open to reality

I am a key that holds the power of my life

I am a safe that holds my future with a tight firm grip

I am who I choose to be and no-one can change the way that
I think of myself unless I am choosing to be someone different

It might surprise that he had a reading age of an eight-year-old and experienced all the subsequent access issues. The eloquence and power of his stand is testimony to the empowerment the transform model offers. Both of us entered the realm of what 'we did not know we did not know'. He still found himself in trouble re-enacting his past, shutting down, getting angry, not admitting to what happened. But I was able to tell him to scratch his stand; he knew exactly what I meant. It reached a crisis point when he stole a credit card in a gym outside of school. The experiential now combined with the cognitive in the most real sense. In a truly meaningful conversation, it was clear he now understood, 'he chooses who he be'. In that locker room, he'd been reactive rather than making a conscious decision to be responsible. He now felt the full force of my mentor's definition; it's worth returning to it once more,

'Being responsible starts with the willingness to deal with the situation from and with the point of view, whether at the moment realised or not that you are the source of:

1. Who you are – is who you say you are
2. What you do – actions are correlated to the conversations you are
3. What you have – is the result of your actions'

He was finally asked to leave the school; he stayed in touch for a while. My hope is he has given himself a 'stand' from which, if he so wishes, he can base his present in his future. One thing I'm sure of is that he understands the full force of what I mean when I say this.

1-Goss, T. 1995: *The Last Word on Power*: Rosetta Books

2- Adapted from Goss's book

3-Quote attributed to Einstein, but no source given

4-Brown, B. 2010: *The Gifts of Imperfection: Let Go of Who You Think You're Supposed to Be and Embrace Who You Are*: Hazelden Publishing

5-Brown, B. 2012: *Daring Greatly: How the Courage to Be Vulnerable Transforms the Way We Live, Love, Parent, and Lead*: Avery

6-Suzuki, S. 2006: *Zen Mind, Beginner's Mind*: Shambhala Publications, Inc

7-Bateson, G. 1972: *Steps to an Ecology of Mind*: The University of Chicago Press

8- Goss, T. 1995: *The Last Word on Power*: Rosetta Books

9-Coel, M. 2013: *Chewing Gum Dreams*: Oberon Books

CHAPTER 4: THE WIDER SCHOOL CULTURE

Play away; techniques; strategies; concepts in this chapter that can be used in different contexts:

Oracy curriculum

Wellbeing curriculum

The strong circle

The energy circle

The intersection

The four strands: the cognitive; the physical; the emotional; the linguistic

Talk protocols

'I bet you're thinking'

Talk detectives

Character strengths

Collective writing

Ghost reading

Flow

The introvert

In a large secondary school in Whitechapel in the East End of London, I had the privilege to be part of a year team run by an inspiring Year Head. Andy grew up in Middlesbrough and, like many working-class boys, left school to join the Marines. It wasn't for him, so he decided to put himself through night school to gain enough qualifications to be the first person in his family to go to university. I've always found people who have had the motivation to self-educate, to reimagine themselves, to be significant influences on my life. It seems to be a running theme. There was my father, a refugee, who had no choice but to make his way. There was my best friend at university who, like Andy, left school early but found factory life not to his liking. Instead, he studied politics and went on to create Volcano – a physical theatre company with a worldwide reputation. There's Rayne, who went travelling at 16, got married, had kids, emigrated, learnt a new language, and decided to return to education. Today, she's a high-powered IT expert working for a global company. There are my two friends who spent their early life living in squats until they realised it was going to end badly. They now work high up in local authority.

What makes these people so inspiring? Maybe Oscar Wilde also felt what I felt, 'if you meet at dinner' a person 'who has spent his life in educating himself – a rare type in our time... you rise from the table richer, and conscious that a high ideal has for a moment touched and sanctified your days'.[1] I was touched by Andy because he was 'passionately curious'[2]. But I would be failing if I didn't quote Chomsky, one of Andy's heroes. Chomsky is onto something when he declares, 'In order to speak about social reality, you must have the proper credentials.'[3] Andy certainly had the credentials.

There are two anecdotes worth sharing. Every teacher will know what it's like taking their pupils on school trips. In these days of risk assessment, it might never have been quite like the chaotic trip described in Willy Russell's (another person who left school at 15) *Our Day Out*. Nonetheless, there's still much that resonates. Mr Briggs stands at the front of the coach bellowing, 'Most of you don't know how to enjoy yourselves, so I'll tell you.'[4] It never works. Bags and pockets bursting with sweets and drinks, headphones in, phones at the ready, the young people tend to adhere to the first part of Mrs Kay's rule for the day out, 'That's the only rule we have today: think of yourselves' but tend to forget the second part, 'But think of others as well'. However, headed towards Alton Towers, I watched Andy make his way up and down the coach. He sat with groups of students, talking to them about subjects ranging from Chomsky (always), to photography, to climbing mountains, to art, to the Spanish Civil War; 'rapping' he called it. But that word doesn't do justice to what was going on there. He passionately committed to his year group over five years and beyond, by bringing all 'that I have experienced in my life so as to make what I am doing a witness for what I have felt and what I have understood'.[5] It was about living with his whole heart; something we will return to.

This leads to the second memory of Andy. I remember it because (with apologies to Einstein) 'education is what remains after one has forgotten' all the assemblies in which I've sat through. Andy delivered an assembly based on a famous speech in which Neil Kinnock, the once great orator, asked the country:

'Why am I the first Kinnock in a thousand generations to be able to get to university? Why is Glenys the first woman in her family in a thousand generations to be able to get to university? Was it because our predecessors were thick? Does anybody really think that they didn't get what we had because they didn't have the talent or the strength or the endurance or the commitment? Of course not. It was because there was no platform upon which they could stand.'[6]

Like Kinnock, Andy (he remains a Year Head in a different East London school after all these years) wants to create a platform for his students that's broad and wide. Every child, every teacher, was in the moment with Andy because many of the requisites were present. The one which was missing in this school was a wider school culture that, 'day in, day out', incubated those virtues

Andy lived. Nevertheless, that culture cultivated with 'thought, solidarity and determination' certainly existed within his team. His 'espoused values' gradually became 'enacted values'.[7] It was no accident my Drama GCSE group from his cohort created a stunning production of *Macbeth* set in Bangladesh, which headlined the Shakespeare School's Festival publicity that year. Some of their faces appear on the front cover of this book, as they did on the lead poster in every school in the country, both state and private. It was no accident the group achieved 100% A-C, over half obtaining an A/A*. It consisted of 40 pupils of mixed abilities, mixed backgrounds and gender, living in one of the poorest boroughs in the country. Their spirit of inquiry, bravery, and desire to push the boundaries, was absolutely in part to do with the culture Andy had created.

Move on several years and I had the chance to become a founding teacher of a new school in East London. It's interesting to compare similar anecdotes about a trip and an assembly to see if anything shows up about the impact a wider school culture can have on child and adult alike. Five years into the school, I took the founding cohort, now 16, to The Young Vic. As I sat on the tube, I had the privilege of witnessing this group of young adults discuss the forthcoming American elections and the Brexit vote. There wasn't a headphone or mobile in sight. They self-regulated a highly articulate debate, allowing each person to have the space to present fairly informed opinion, to challenge, to build, to move it on when it needed to. Impressive enough, but what shone through was what John Holt identifies: 'Children are born passionately eager to make as much sense as they can of things around them.'[8] As we walked to the theatre, a woman sidled up to me, moved by what she'd seen in the tube carriage. Like me, she knew she'd witnessed a meaningful conversation. She was taken aback when I told her we were going to watch a production of Joe Penhall's *Blue Orange*, as she'd presumed we were off to see the more populist TIE production, also showing in the theatre. As we entered the theatre, I started to worry I'd chosen the wrong show.

I began to think I would soon see a few of them asleep or sat back with their headphones plugged in. In one of those lucky coincidences, the pupils had spotted the actor and rapper, Kano, in the bar who, thankfully, was also going to see *Blue Orange*. I exhaled and could breathe again. I shouldn't have worried. *Blue Orange* turned out to be one of their favourite productions. Much of the play is essentially a cognitive debate and they revelled in it, the vibrant jousting of ideas filled with politics.

However, what happened on the trip wasn't an accident. I heard the impact of an overt oracy curriculum these pupils had experienced over the past five years. It provided not only the tools, but an inquisitive spirit which had been fostered in the numerous Philosophy for Children inquiries, Socratic seminars, and Harkness discussions they'd engaged in. It was present in the school's commitment to project-based learning that had seen them go out into the real world once a week for a term-and-a-half in Year 10, tasked with solving genuine problems for real organisations. They met high up in Canary Wharf to present the whole process to mentors, family, and teachers. The wellbeing curriculum we'd created from scratch had given these students a voice to articulate who they are and what they stand for, to live with their whole heart; that phrase again. It was the reason why we'd exposed them to an array of interesting people. There were the two entrepreneurial women who told them about their parents' struggle to make it in America as Japanese and Indian immigrants, as well as enthralling them as they explained how they had come to create their ethical business. David Blunkett and Lord Adonis told their remarkable stories of resilience. Inspiring volunteers from City Year shared their personal testimonies and dedication for bringing about social change. All the students created their own personal testimonies they carried within them, revisited and refined as they matured. They would be encouraged to share them with visitors or during interviews, powerful testimony of who they be. It was an intentionally designed whole school culture that had been missing for Andy's pupils. A broad and wide platform had been created with purpose and vision.

Teaching context

So, what kind of assemblies did these pupils experience? Certainly, those of us old enough to remember Billy Casper in *Kes*, hauled out of assembly by the scruff of the neck for daydreaming, might testify their school assemblies were very much like this. If they didn't end with the swishing of Mr Gryce's cane, for most of us they were ten minutes or so of herding and marshalling until all were kind of settled in the school hall. Then someone in authority would stand at the front and talk, usually from a faded acetate on an overhead projector (what's that?), to a sea of passive, restless, disinterested rows of tired students. The teachers never seemed to be listening either. The more lairy ones didn't have phones in those days (hard to imagine), so side-chatted to a mate stood next to them. The 'last minute' or stressed ones (no laptops back then) frantically scribbled chaotic lesson plans in a ring-bound planner which, like them, was slowly falling to bits. Then more time spent exiting the sterile, barren, and forgettable wasteland that was the school assembly.

We might now nervously scoff at the washed-up Mr Gryce with a, 'there but for the grace of God go I', and a smirk or frown as he wonders with exasperation why things haven't changed: 'The school's no better now than it was on the day that it opened. I can't understand it. I can't understand it at all.' However, assemblies seem to be no better today, but still we keep on doing them in the same old way. Gryce knows what actually we all know to be true but dare not admit: 'It's a waste of time standing here talking to you boys, because you won't take a blind bit of notice what I'm saying. I know what you're thinking now, you're thinking, Why doesn't he get on with it and let us go, instead of standing there babbling on? That's what you're thinking, isn't it?'[9] (A great example of 'already always listening', if ever you need one). Indeed, it is Mr Gryce; it's exactly what we think as we listen to the babble at nine o'clock on a Monday morning. Perhaps a little harsh on those of us who spend Sunday nights planning the next morning's thought for the day, but you get my point.

When visiting other schools, my head teacher always asked to watch a school assembly, because he felt you can tell everything about a school's ethos from what happens in those 20 or so minutes. Just read the memorable passage about the assembly Billy has to endure in *Kes* and you can tell everything about the kind of school Mr Gryce ran. It's why Mr Sugden's brutal PE lesson comes as no surprise (if you've never seen Brian Glover's performance as the tracksuited, egotistical, sadistic, overweight Sugden, then watch the wonderful 1969 film of the book; you're in for a treat). In this new school, with our blank piece of paper, we wanted to reimagine assemblies as a creative, vibrant space where important things happen. Our first decision was to create the ritual of a 'strong circle'. As the American psychologist, Birute Regine, reminds us, 'circle is not anything new'.

Play away; the next time you select a circle as your chosen space or you are asked to join a circle, pay homage to the culture Regine captures for us,

'Circle is an ancient process of consultation and communion, a place for slowing down, respectfully listening and being heard, a place to change the conversation and a way of being together that taps into the deep well of wisdom and creative thinking that is so needed in this time and place in history. Being in Circle is a matter of remembering our original way of being in community.'[10]

Susan Lucci is a circle facilitator where the circle can 'become a vehicle for women who want to participate and be agents of change'.[11] She, too, powerfully describes the power of the circle as 'one of deep connection, mutual respect and creative collaboration'. We wanted assemblies to imbue these values, a space that 'energizes, inspires and supports each of us to see and be seen, to hear and be heard, to become a better version of ourselves'.[12] We wanted to deliberately change 'the conversation in the safe container of a circle', and in doing so we would be 'modelling the new, emerging culture' that would be 'beautiful to behold'.[13]

Theatre has always understood this beauty; none more so than Peter Brook. Just replace the word 'theatre' in Brook's writing in his seminal work, *The Empty Space*[14] with 'assembly'. You will be starting to reimagine the empty space, turning it from something with little purpose to something that is 'necessary'. Imagine if we say:

> ➤ 'Today as at all times, we need to stage true rituals, but for rituals that can make (theatre-going) **assemblies** and experience that feeds our lives, true forms are needed.'

Imagine if we changed the story we tell ourselves and declare:

> ➤ 'The purpose of (theatre) **assembly** is... making an event in which a group of fragments are suddenly brought together... in a community which, by the natural laws that make every community, gradually breaks up... At certain moments this fragmented world comes together and for a certain time it can rediscover the marvel of organic life... The marvel of being one.'

Imagine if we plainly state:

> ➤ '(A stage space) **an assembly** has two rules: (1) Anything can happen and (2) Something must happen.'

Imagine if we make no excuses about our circumstances because:

> ➤ 'A beautiful place may never bring about explosion of life, while a haphazard hall may be a tremendous meeting place; this is the mystery of the **assembly** (theatre).'

Imagine if we, as adults, promise:

> ➤ 'There will be no trickery, nothing hidden. We must open our empty hands and show that really there is nothing up our sleeves. Only then can we begin.'

Imagine if we understand:

> ➤ '(Drama) **the assembly** is exposure; it is confrontation; it is contradiction and it leads to analysis, construction, recognition and eventually to an awakening of understanding.'

If we did all of this and more, remembering, 'Fun can be forgotten, but powerful emotion also disappears and good arguments lose their thread', then our 'walk toward' something new and vibrant may well bring us closer to Brook's understanding about the power of a collective event. Put this in your school handbook, filed under 'collective daily worship', and show Ofsted the next time they come knocking:

'When emotion and argument are harnessed to a wish from the audience to see more clearly into itself – then something in the mind burns. The event scorches on to the memory an outline, a taste, a trace, a smell – a picture. It is the (play's) **assembly's** central image that remains, its silhouette, and if the elements are highly blended this silhouette will be its meaning, this shape will be the essence of what it has to say.'

Set Andy's assembly about aspiration in this limitless context, then the meanings created become richer and deeper by belonging to a wider school culture. In school-speak, the assembly hits the 'sweet spot' when the cognitive and the experiential combine. My head teacher likes to call it, 'the intersection', where, when two contrasting elements combine, it takes things closer to the edge. It's in this space where interesting things happen. It becomes a space of curiosity and inquiry for both teacher and pupil. It's a safe space where student and adult can experiment and take risk. It's a space where sometimes 'the event scorches', 'the mind burns'.

This all might start to sound rather woolly by now; goodness knows what Gryce would've said. However, over five years, I created, led, participated in, and witnessed hundreds of these assemblies, along with those empowered students who went to the theatre with me. There was the one where the head teacher used a 'thunk'. The thunk website defines a 'thunk' as, 'A beguilingly simple-looking question about everyday things that stops you in your tracks and helps you start to look at the world in a whole new light.'[15] The 'thunk' he used when the group was in Year 7 was, 'What colour would a zebra be if it lost all its stripes?' I was sceptical it would last beyond 15 minutes if he was lucky. How wrong was I! I was in danger of being guilty of what Holt identifies, 'We destroy the disinterested (I do not mean uninterested) love of learning in children, which is so strong when they are small... We kill, not only their curiosity, but their feeling that it is a good and admirable thing to be curious, so that by the age of ten most of them will not ask questions, and will show a good deal of scorn for the few who do.'[16] These streetwise, inner city children, some with the shortest of attention spans, used a range of talking protocols from their oracy lessons to hold a deep inquiry over not one but two 50-minute assemblies. You can't imagine the areas the original premise allowed them to wander into. There was another assembly where the same teacher, leading from the front, was asked to demonstrate Bloom's Taxonomy by teachers who had never tried it, utilising the assembly as a space for professional development (the assembly as a professional development opportunity, think about that for a moment). He brilliantly used the death of Margaret Thatcher, unknown to many of the students, by giving each pupil a picture from her life, asking the ensemble to explore the inquiry question, 'Was Margaret Thatcher a great leader?' He facilitated the discussion, again employing the talk protocols, skilfully demonstrating how Bloom's enables higher order thinking. The scales started to lift, I got it. It deepened my practice significantly, as I'll show later when holding the door ajar to my classroom. For those dying to know the students' verdict, Thatcher, as a great leader, was sunk by her order to destroy the Argentine cruiser, the *General Belgrano*, resulting in the killing of 323 people on board.

But it's time to tell you about Colin Chaos. I decided to create a disorganised character struggling to cope with school and life in general. He was an open page, made up of multiple archetypal identities that the pupils could recognise. He grew up with the pupils, struggling to cope early in Year 7 with the transition from primary to secondary school, to being viciously bullied by his peer group in Year 8, to exploring issues around his sexuality in Year 10, to finally facing the pressures of Year 11 exams and an uncertain future. The students turned him into a fully-rounded, complex character who represented 'what it means to be human'.[17] Colin became the extra member of their year group. If we examine one assembly involving Colin, we might see how it meets Claxton and Lucas's challenge about the wider school culture.

It's early in Year 7 when pupils are struggling with the transition from primary to secondary school. The Year 7 pupils are sat in a 'strong circle'. It's 8.30 in the morning, and as leader of the assembly, I am acutely aware of Laevers' *Leuven Scales* of emotional wellbeing and involvement.[18] In the circle of both adult and child, including myself, there will be the full range of wellbeing levels, from extremely low, to low, to moderate, to high, to extremely high. I like to use this energy circle:[19]

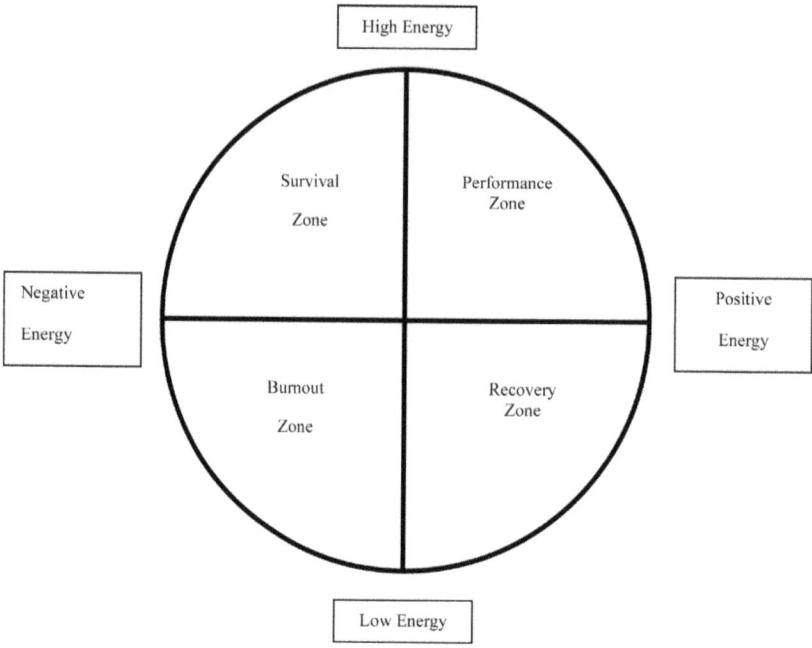

So often we arrive at work hanging on in 'survival' mode for complex reasons that might be home or work-related. Some of us have moved from survival and arrive absolutely 'burnt out'. You'll meet Hashim, a student, later in the book who, like Billy and Mr Gryce in *Kes*, arrived 'burnt out' on most days. The challenge is to move the entire ensemble to the right-hand side of the circle into 'performing' by fully participating in the 'exposure'; the 'confrontation'; the 'analysis'; the 'construction'; the 'recognition'. No mean feat with students like Hashim or with certain members of staff (young teachers and their phones, discuss). However, if we succeed, it will lead them into 'recovery' so that both adult and child leave the circle for their first lesson or first meeting of the day with a sense of calm and ease after experiencing Brook's 'awakening of understanding.'

Play away; use the energy circle in any environment, be it with family, friends or colleagues. The challenge is to find ways of moving people from the left-hand side to the right-hand side of the circle. How might you do this? Are you equipped to do this? Where might you find the training to be able to do this?

I ask a student to sound like a teacher, look like a teacher, and be the teacher, as she reads aloud the inquiry question for the assembly: 'What does good learning look like?' Another student will be called upon to read out the subsidiary question: 'What do we mean by "The Zone"?' These students may have been chosen beforehand for various reasons, such as poor participation or that they're just bubbling up, needing that nudge to gain the extra piece of confidence. The whole assembly are invited to sound like a teacher, look like a teacher, and be the teacher. Before that happens, I model the physical strand. We use four strands to develop the whole person and share this explicitly:

- **The Physical:** *How we use our voice (tone; pitch; pace; timbre); our face; our gestures; our body/movement*
- **The Emotional:** *How we make an impact on our audience (one-to-one; small groups; large groups; big audiences); our control*
- **The Cognitive:** *How we build our arguments; our logic; our ability to analyse*
- **The Linguistic:** *How we express ourselves; our 'beautiful' language; the formal and the informal*

Play away; a small digression, but it's worth emphasising what a breakthrough these four strands are. They can be used when observing a colleague in any setting, for example in an interview or when teaching a lesson.

Sometimes it can be all jazz hands – an over-reliance on the physical but lacking in any cognitive content. Conversely, top-heavy delivery of the cognitive might lose your audience. It can be used to analyse literature. Examine Lady Macbeth persuading Macbeth to kill the King through the lens of the four strands; they're all there, which is why he finally agrees to do the deed. Be brave and reflect on your marriage, you might find there's too much talk, or a particular kind of language is eroding the relationship, or you're not making yourself clear enough, or there may be problems with the physical side. Visitors, who the students met, came under close scrutiny. The students were able to use the four strands to articulate why a speaker was successful or not. The ones I mentioned passed with flying colours because they had the balance of the four strands exactly right.

On one memorable occasion, we were delighted to have a very famous broadcaster speak about World War 1 as he'd written a book about it (Google it). However, the students were soon bored and more importantly were able to tell me why. They said his physicality was wooden, his arguments were dry, and his language was overly academic. He'd misjudged his Year 8 audience and so made the wrong emotional impact. His delivery was more appropriate for a far older audience. He'd failed to modify a lecture he'd probably given many times.

We have only being going for a few minutes, but the four strands are already in action. I model a range of vocal patterns and movement that demonstrate a sense of inquiry (The Physical Strand). Both the student volunteers and I have made the right emotional impact at this time in the morning, attempting to provoke interest and engagement (The Emotional Strand). We've started to ask a cognitive question that over the course of three assemblies we, as an ensemble, will try to answer (The Cognitive Strand). During these assemblies, we will use four kinds of language: the language of the school; the language of the self; the language of the home; the language of the 'road' (the language they use with their friends) (The Linguistic Strand).[20]

I now move to the hook, adopting the role of a storyteller. Again, the four strands are clearly in evidence. I move around the circle delivering these lines – not the greatest verse ever written, but it's aimed at emotionally engaging and starting to shift the students towards the right-hand side of the energy circle.

> *'There is a boy, a lad*
> *Who some thought was bad*
> *And others labelled him sad*
> *And a few stated he was odd, somewhat mad,*
> *He went by the tag,*
> *Scribbled proudly with Tipp-Ex in the middle of his*
> *schoolbag,*
> *His name, his claim to fame,*
> *'Colin Chaos'.*

The ensemble feels ready to enter Colin's home. I've primed a student to be Colin's mother. Using spontaneous improvisation and teacher in role as Colin, I create several encounters between mother and child on a Monday evening from teatime until it's time to go to sleep. It's entertaining and a context is created. But it's more than that; there's an edge, as no-one is quite sure what's going to happen, especially if you've chosen one of the more volatile members of the year group to play Colin's mother (I once chose the at-risk student you met in the previous chapter. You can imagine the feisty encounter we had!). It fulfils Brook's requirements: (1) Anything can happen; (2) Something must happen. The student caused one of those special ripples when you know the ensemble is hooked, 'yaaaaaaaaa', that intake of breath, when she threw at me, in her reactive state, 'No wonder your father doesn't want to see you.' A new and important distinction has shown up: 'react' and 'respond' – we'll unpack this fully in a later assembly. The mother and Colin are their thoughts and feelings. They're full of points of view and judgement, blaming each other, the world, telling themselves how it 'should' and 'should not' be; Goss's Universal Human Paradigm. It's automatic and predictable; they've had this conversation so many times; because they're 'already always listening', they know what the other will say even before they say it; they know what the outcome will be. In other words, they've already chosen who they be, continually basing their present in the past. Sounds familiar? However we want Colin, his mother, and indeed both staff and pupils, to learn to have the ability to respond. That conscious decision where you add a level of thinking – a delay, if you like – to fully understand who you are is who you chose to be. You can only be responsible for yourself. This is the process of reimagination I experienced; it will be equally transformative for Hashim, as we will discover in the next chapter.

It's time to call out for students to be two of Colin's so-called friends, Noisy Nisha and Rudy Rude. With a lot of pupils now in the performing zone of the energy circle, there's no shortage of volunteers. As Colin, I ring them up in the middle of the night, interrupting their nocturnal computer gaming, again provoking a knowing ripple around the circle. Hashim certainly knows all about this. I ask them to send me their answers for the maths homework. Sometimes they will; more often they won't. Children can be very cruel. Next morning, another encounter occurs with the mother as Colin tries to leave the home late and can't find anything he needs. Finally, he leaves for school, but bumps into his friends – an opportunity for lots of banter. Importantly, it establishes the pecking order in the friendship, with Colin finding himself invariably stuck firmly at the bottom. I told you, children are innately cruel. When they meet the teacher at the school gate, Colin is always given a detention. Adults can be cruel, too.

I ask a teacher to play this part for lots of reasons. The teacher, like some of the pupils, might have poor participation (on their phone!) or needs a gentle nudge to build confidence in front of a larger audience. I never underestimate how stressful this can be for a teacher, finding myself offering lots of reassurance beforehand. But in this kind of experience, the teachers aren't passive onlookers; we're in fact team-teaching. I have 6 teachers on hand, which is a valuable resource to be fully realised.

I now ask each tutor group a question: 'What have been Colin's top three mistakes?' This is an opportunity to develop a key element in the school's jigsaw, the oracy curriculum. When starting out with this kind of work, an insight is to always scaffold endlessly until it's part of them and it becomes second nature, as I witnessed on that memorable tube journey to the theatre. It started here for those students. Another important insight isn't to allow any formal talk – be it with colleagues in a meeting or with students in a classroom – unless a talk protocol has been chosen. No more lazy or unthinking, 'talk to the person next to you'. Making people aware of the metacognition creates a higher quality of talk. Today, I want them to develop the talk protocol of a chaired discussion. A scaffold is provided not only for the pupils, but for the teachers who represent an array of different subjects. This is professional development; the same protocol can now be used in Science or Maths or History across the school, or in a departmental meeting or in a working group. The pupils are often asked by visitors how the oracy curriculum helps them outside of school. One pupil cheerfully replied, 'We often have a chaired discussion; it stops us arguing.'

The group take a moment with their teacher, who has observed their discussion, to reflect on the quality of their talk from a strength position; what are the qualities they will definitely keep, and what is the takeaway they will use to make the next chaired discussion even stronger? The tutor will also make notes on each child's contribution, so the oral development becomes a whole school responsibility. This is supported by a differentiated programme of oracy training for every teacher over the course of the year. A wider school culture is being created.[21]

I invite each group to write Colin's top mistake onto a Post-It note, and stick it on the appropriate part of my body. For example, if he's far too emotional and reactive, then they stick it on my heart; if he's lazy, then they stick it on my hand; a lot want to stick it on my bald, shiny head, for some reason. The Post-It notes tend to fall off. So, there I am, with Post-It notes stuck all over my body and lots lying around me on the floor. It's a strong visual image of not only Colin's chaotic life, but the kind of life many in the ensemble experience on a daily basis.

I continue with the cognitive strand, building an argument with a probing question: 'What character strengths might Colin need to lead a happier life, to go from Colin Chaos to Colin Calm and Collected?' Allow me another small digression. There are certain seminal books that have been transformative, moving me into the transformative paradigm I've mentioned, 'I did not know what I did not know'. Martin Seligman is one such influence. He has been described as 'the inventor of positive psychology and a major figure in the wellbeing movement. This makes him a significant figure in world culture'.[22]   In his review of Seligman's book, *Flourish*, Richard Layard – another proponent of the psychology of happiness – makes a staunch defence of an academy that has come under attack:

> 'A happier society requires us to attend much more to the quality of our inner life, and to proven methods for improving it. That is what positive psychology is about – it goes beyond the treatment of depression and anxiety to ways in which we could all live more rewarding lives. The exercises it offers include the systematic practice of kindness, gratitude to others, counting your blessings, and exploiting your strengths rather than attacking your weaknesses. It also teaches resilience and optimism. These two characteristics are apparently better predictors of a

person's educational achievement than their IQ. And they can reduce your annual chance of dying by 20%. So this is important.'[23]

I agree; it's important. I read Seligman's *Flourish*, and it opened up a new way to talk about the world with my students. Behind the question I'm asking the 11-year-olds in front of me is Seligman's emphasis of 'deriving happiness by using your signature strengths every day in the main realms of living'.[24] Seligman's fundamental belief about raising children is, 'Identifying and amplifying their strengths and virtues, and helping them find the niche where they can live these positive traits to the fullest.'[25] This is the cognitive argument I'm making to the Year 7s and it's what I'm asking the children to imagine, to grow Colin so that he can flourish. For Seligman, this is his 'gold standard': 'I now think that the topic of positive psychology is well-being, that the gold standard for measuring well-being is flourishing.'[26]

They're given another opportunity to develop their strengths because, as Seligman tells us again, flourishing isn't some abstract notion that exists only inside our head. Rather it's, 'A combination of feeling good as well as actually having meaning, good relationships and accomplishment.'[27] So, as a collective, they have another chaired discussion trying to agree on the top three character strengths Colin might need to flourish, to go from chaos to calm.

An opportunity is now created for the more introverted. In another influential book, *Quiet: The Power of Introverts in a World That Can't Stop Talking*,[28] Susan Cain makes a timely reminder:

'Consider that the simplest social interactions between two people requires performing an astonishing array of tasks: interpreting what the other person is saying; reading body language and facial expressions; smoothly taking turns talking and listening; responding to what the other person said; assessing whether you're being understood; determining whether you're well received, and, if not, figuring out how to improve or remove yourself from the situation. Think of what it takes to juggle all this at once! And that's just a one-to-one conversation. Now imagine the multitasking required in a group setting like a dinner party.'

The introvert knows well, as does Cain, 'there's zero correlation between being the best talker and having the best ideas'. Cain warns us that we underestimate the introvert at our peril.

> Play away: is this your experience of being an introvert or of the introverts you know?
>
> 'They listen more than they talk, think before they speak, and often feel as if they express themselves better in writing than in conversation. They tend to dislike conflict. Many have a horror of small talk, but enjoy deep discussions.'

Taking on board what Cain tells us about the need to find a way of ensuring 'ideas can be shared quietly', we created a protocol of talk, called, 'I bet you're thinking'. Again, it's heavily scaffolded, but it allows for the kind of empathic conversation Cain and Seligman believe we need to develop because, and here's the point, it 'takes more trouble about the wellbeing of others'.[29] They sit in threes showing 'proof of listening', which means positive, attentive body language; track the speaker by looking at him/her. Try it at the workplace, at home, in the coffee shop. It works. Using a sheet of new ideas and drawing on the chaired discussions, I ask a probing question: 'Have you heard, read, thought about anything that might now help Colin to lead a happier life, to flourish?' Here's the protocol we created and used to allow the students to explore the question:

'I bet you're thinking'

Step 1: What's the question? *To clarify*

Pupil A repeats the question that needs to be discussed.

Step 2: Guess what I am thinking. *To speculate*

Pupil B says to Pupil C, 'I bet you are thinking...'

Pupil C replies, 'Yes, I was thinking this, but I was also thinking...' or 'No, I wasn't thinking this, I was actually thinking...'

Pupil C can repeat this with Pupil A.

Step 3: Tell me what's important. *To build*

Pupil B now might say, 'I've listened intently to our discussion, but I'm dying to tell you both...'

This can be passed around the circle with pupils using stems like,

'The most important thing is...'

'I would like to stress...'

'I feel it's crucial...'

Step 4: What do we agree on? *To decide – 3 things the group can agree on*

'We both think that...'

'We disagree that...'

Step 5: Any final questions? *To reflect*

Pupils are given the chance to clarify anything they didn't understand, missed, or would like to be made clearer, to check in with each person to ensure everyone is on the same page.

'I don't understand...'

'It's weird that...'

'Why did...'

'I'm not sure about...'

'Have we checked...'

Step 6: What actions am I now prepared to take? *To act – how will we feed back to the others? What am I prepared to do in this feedback?*

Perhaps it's less easy to follow on paper but, trust me, the protocol really does free up the introverted speakers, as well as students who are beginning to learn English, and the special needs students struggling with the four strands – the cognitive; physical; emotional; and linguistic demands of this kind of activity.

Play away; what do you feel at a training event when placed in a group? Do you shut down or gabble nervously? What do you feel if your group is asked to feed back? The same? What do you feel if there's a dominant person in the group (probably a man) who likes the sound of his own voice? Submit or resist? I have used this protocol with business leaders. You only have to see the fear and anxiety spreading across their wealthy faces and into their bodies when they enter my drama studio to know this is a protocol that will help these highly powerful people express themselves during small group discussions. Cain gets this: 'We don't need giant personalities to transform companies. We need leaders who build not their own egos but the institutions they run.'[30]

In Step 6 of the protocol, the trios are able to choose how to feed back, including writing or drawing their responses. The dynamic of feedback is often avoidance or survival driven by fear. In designing the protocol, we were aware of what Cain describes in her book: 'The purpose of school should be to prepare kids for the rest of their lives, but too often what kids need to be prepared for is surviving the school day itself.' But rather we believed our design created a supportive and empowering culture, honouring the diverse personalities in any group of people: 'Introverts need to trust their gut and share their ideas as powerfully as they can. This does not mean aping extroverts; ideas can be shared quietly, they can be communicated in writing, they can be packaged into highly produced lectures, they can be advanced by allies. The trick for introverts is to honour their own styles instead of allowing themselves to be swept up by prevailing norms.'[31]

The ensemble is now given an opportunity to test some of their ideas. Pupils can choose to be anyone in Colin's life, such as his father, his sister, a cousin, or a teacher. Selecting an idea formulated in their discussions which they feel will help Colin, they're invited to test it by spontaneously improvising with the teacher in role who remains as Colin. I make it very hard, as there are no quick fixes. They can keep returning to their tutor group for new advice. By now, there's usually urgent, purposeful talk. The 'confrontation' has become real and 'necessary' for the circle. A protocol is needed so the students don't excitedly talk over each other or the dominant pupils fail to 'share the air'. It might be 'pass and go', where each person has a chance to speak, taking turns. It could be a 'shared/democratic discussion' where again all students have a chance to speak, taking turns. In the true spirit of demos, the last speaker decides the next speaker. To avoid the pitfalls of 'me listening', in both protocols the aim isn't to repeat or make your point regardless, but to build on the previous contribution – a hard thing for all of us to do at any age. It's clear the majority of the ensemble, including the teachers, is firmly in the performing zone of the energy circle. The teachers or students might play 'talk detectives' to develop higher quality talk. Their role is to be observers trying to look for specific aspects of developed talk, such as pupils who build on ideas, or ask questions rather than continually making bold statements. 'The talk detectives' then present their findings, once more using a strength approach that identifies what they should keep the next time they are involved in this kind of talk, as well as what they might develop to make the quality of talk even more effective.

> Play away; think how this strategy might be used in other settings. Who might benefit from adopting the role of 'talk detectives'? The reluctant speaker? The aggressive, overpowering speaker? Someone who is never really listened to? Someone who might need to see an aspect of talk in action to really get it? Keep adding to the list; there are plenty more.

To finish, a collective letter becomes an inclusive, reflective strategy. The whole ensemble is invited to write a letter to Colin, offering him advice about how he should now proceed with his life. The rules are: anyone can speak; whatever is said is written down verbatim (any editing can happen afterwards); the air is shared so that no-one dominates; they should 'play away', utilising their English skills to stretch for language such as metaphor, simile, alliteration, imagery, synonyms. After the letter is written, the ensemble 'ghost read' it, which is where the pupils decide how much they wish to read aloud, handing the 'ball' to another student whenever they wish, avoiding dominating or talking over each other. It's incredibly reaffirming as they hear their input read back to the ensemble, even if it has been minimal. It's always surprising who speaks. It can often be the introvert. Ciara literally cried when I asked her to speak during her first session with me in her tutor group on her first day in secondary school. Talking was that painful. A month later, she wanted to help with the Year 6 open evening where we recruit our new intake for the following year. We'd invited the parents to write a collective letter to the school, expressing their hopes, desires, and aspirations for their child's new school.

Play away; think about that offer for a second or two in the context of creating a culture, then get your organisation to ask your clients to do the same, or closer to home, ask your family to write such a letter. You may be surprised.

We asked the students to ghost read it. Ciara read a part. When I asked her about it a few days later, she replied that she just did it without thinking. The ghosts that had been whispering things like, 'they will laugh at me', 'I'll make a fool of myself', had vanished. The influence of a wider school culture was already making an impact.

The letter to Colin is put up in every Year 7 tutor group's classroom. It's a highly effective piece of testimony when one of the tutees inevitably behaves like Colin, often the next day! The tutor can point to the advice given, made even more powerful and immediate as it had been offered by the strong circle the student is a part of and in which the student may have made several significant contributions. For the student, it may well be 'an awakening of understanding'. In Claxton and Lucas's terms, 'the espoused values' are gradually becoming 'enacted values'.

The next assembly moves the argument on, asking what good learning might look like, exploring 'flow' or what we decided to call 'The Zone'. Colin is set an academic challenge, which the ensemble tries to work through to see if they can facilitate some kind of success. They learn that 'success requires persistence, the ability to not give up in the face of failure'.[32] It's an optimistic approach. The concept of 'flow' is introduced – something they'll explore right through school, as it's a vital component of the school culture. Seligman sees 'flow' in these terms: 'Engagement is about flow: being one with the music, time stopping, and the loss of self-consciousness during an absorbing activity, experiences which contribute to the 'engaged life'.'[33] For Cain, 'flow' is '...an optimal state in which you feel totally engaged in an activity... In a state of flow, you're neither bored nor anxious, and you don't question your own adequacy. Hours pass without your noticing.'[34] The psychologist, Mihaly Csikszentmihalyi, wrote a book called *Flow: The Psychology of Optimal Experience*. It's his belief, 'The best moments in our lives are not the passive, receptive, relaxing times... The best moments usually occur if a person's body or mind is stretched to its limits in a voluntary effort to accomplish something difficult and worthwhile.'[35] We will return to 'flow', but alas the bell has gone and it's time to move on.

1-Wilde, O. 2016: *The critic as artist from The Complete Works of Oscar Wilde: Novel, Short Stories, Poetry, Essays and Plays*: General Press

2-as quoted in Einstein's 1939 letter to President Franklin D. Roosevelt

3-Chomsky, N. 1977: *Language and Responsibility*: Pantheon

4- Russell, W. 2014: *Our Day Out*: Oxford Play scripts

5- An Indian actor speaking to Brook, quoted in Roose-Evans, J. 1970: *Experimental Theatre-from Stanislavsky to Peter Brooke*: Routledge

6- Kinnock, N. 1987: Speech at the Welsh Labour Party conference, Llandudno

7- Claxton. G. And Lucas. B. 2013: *What Kind of Teaching For What Kind Of Learning*: SSAT

8-Holt, J.1989: *Learning all the time*: Perseus Books

9-Hines, B. 1968: *A Kestrel for a Knave*: Michael Joseph, London

10-Birute, R. 2013: *The next evolutionary step: The power of circle*: The Huffington Post

11-Ibid

12-Ibid

13-Ibid

14-Brook, P. 2008: *The Empty Space*: Penguin Classics

15-www.thunks.co.uk

16-Holt, J. 1995: *How Children Fail*: De Capo Press: Perseus Books

17-Abbot, J. quoted in Robinson, K. 1999: *All Our Futures: Creativity, Culture and Education*: NACCCE report

18-There are numerous sites to access Laevers' scales. Here is just one: *Ferre Laevers emotional wellbeing and involvement scales: Early Learning HQ*

https://www.earlylearninghq.org.uk/earlylearninghq-blog/the-leuven-well-being-and-involvement-scales/

19-Adapted from: Morris, I. 2009: *Teaching Happiness and Well-Being in Schools*: Bloomsbury

20-The assemblies are able to become a place in which Alexander's repertoire of talk can be explored and developed: (1) Interactive settings (2) Everyday talk (3) Learning talk (4) Teaching talk (5) Questioning (6) Extending

Alexander, R. 2018: *Developing dialogic teaching: genesis, process, trial*: Routledge

21-The assemblies are also a place where students' oracy and wellbeing can be formally diagnosed and developed, with a clearly marked out line of progression. Here's how we tracked it at School21:

Character and Well-Being Progression	Diving	Surviving	Striving	Thriving
Identity *Who am I and what is my sense of purpose?* **Key components:** • Core values: Integrity and Humanity • Character strengths • Big goals • Purpose and motivation • Stand/ commitment • Passion	I do not know my strengths and feel I am not good at most things. I feel that I often fail at things. I lack pride in my culture and identity. I have no goals in life – getting through the day is hard enough. I don't know what my interests and passions are and feel I don't really have any.	I know my key strengths. I take pride in my background and culture. I can begin to set goals for myself, but I am not sure how to achieve them. I am willing to try out new experiences. I am aware of my values and those of the school.	I know my strengths and I can tell a positive story about myself and my background. I take the opportunities given to me. I have goals and I am focused on them. I know how to achieve them and look for help in doing so. I seek out new challenges and enjoy being stretched. My values are a strong part of who I am.	I know who I am, what my strengths are and where I am from. I am proud of who I am. I live my values every day and make decisions about my future based on those values. I am true to my word, *always*. I stand up for what I believe, even if it is unpopular. I have taken a stand, set ambitious goals, and have the plans and commitment to achieve them.

Character and Well-Being Progression	Diving	Surviving	Striving	Thriving
Belonging *What am I part of that's bigger than myself?* **Key components** • Giving • Kindness	I do not feel I belong part of any group. I am unhappy in my family or my peer group. I find it hard to engage with others and make friends. I struggle to empathise with others.	I have some friends and feel I belong in my family and peer group. If I work at it, I can make new friends. I know the value of kindness and I begin to understand the impact of unkind words and deeds.	I am at home at school. I contribute to my 'circles' so they are stronger and kinder. I have friends and I am happy to be myself with them. I show empathy when a friend or someone I know feels upset, and I know how to support them.	I have a sense of belonging to one or more groups when I feel 'at home'. I thrive in any setting, able to make friends, engage others, and think of others. I share and contribute to others, even if I don't know them. I have a passion for kindness and giving, both of which I do without being asked.
Control *Can I control my emotions and deal with stress?* **Key components** • Self control • Optimism • Humour • Mindfulness • Physical wellbeing	I find it hard to stay calm and frequently 'blow up'. I feel it's hard to look on the bright side of things. I do not take care of what I eat or what I look like, because I don't really care. I think about myself more than others.	I can control my emotions but only in response to certain adults and friends. I show optimism on occasion, but I don't know how to do it all the time. I think of others sometimes.	I play 'the right card' in most situations. I am aware of my 'emotional triggers' and have strategies to manage them. I keep calm, even in difficult situations. I listen to others as much as I listen to myself.	I control my emotions so I can respond but not react. I take responsibility for my decisions. I look on the bright side of situations and remain optimistic. I am an energiser, enthusing others to do better.

Progression in Oracy				
SKILLS	Apprentice	Developing	Confident	Expert
Physical	I am starting to project my voice so everyone can hear it. I am starting to vary the pitch, tone, and rhythm of my voice. I am beginning to use gestures and body movement to help convey the points I want to make.	I can develop my presence as a performer, controlling my voice and movement. I can use several different tones of voice and adapt my voice to the context. I can use subtle gestures and body language to indicate a range of different emotions.	I know how to vary my body language and tone of voice, adapting them to the situation and to what I am trying to say. I have a range of subtle changes in tone, pitch, and movement to suit different genres of talk.	I can control my voice and body with fluency and precision. I can teach others how to use their voice and body. I am always at home in the context.
Linguistic	I can use a limited vocabulary well. I am starting to choose my words more precisely. I can distinguish between informal and formal settings. I can identify different types of language: metaphor, tripling, emphasis.	I can use a range of descriptive words to suit different situations and use the 5 senses to ground my story. I can use full sentences with connectives and speak fluently without repetition for several sentences. I can speak formally, e.g. without using filler words (such as 'like'), and with dictionary words instead of street slang.	I can construct language effectively for a range of purposes, e.g. to persuade someone. I can use the subject specific language of different disciplines e.g. talk like a scientist, historian, mathematician, tour guide. I deploy excellent grammar when talking, using full sentences. I can select precise language and idiom to suit different audiences.	I can deploy language with great precision and nuance. I can use a wide range of vocabulary, idiom, and expressions to suit any audience. I can engage with ideas at a high level and express my ideas fluently in any setting. I can develop the linguistic tools of others.

Progression in Oracy				
SKILLS	Apprentice	Developing	Confident	Expert
Cognitive	I am beginning to identify what makes a good argument. I can use evidence to back up my point. I can order my talk into a beginning, middle, and end.	I can pursue a line of enquiry. I can spot flaws in other people's arguments. I can ask a range of questions, including probing questions. I can choose and organise the content of my speech to convey clear meaning.	I can take on different roles in discussion and can see both sides of an argument. I can use different thinking skills to engage with challenging material. I can summarise an argument and identify good and bad arguments. I can analyse arguments and select evidence to defend or rebut a position.	I can take into account the level of understanding of an audience and adapt my language. I can marshal sophisticated arguments and use language and different genres of speech. I can use and select metaphor, humour, irony, mimicry, and other rhetorical devices with flair and imagination to make my argument come alive.
Emotional social	I can find the confidence to speak in front of an audience. I show proof of listening. I can understand my character strengths and can build on them. I can support others in a discussion.	I can take turns in discussion, and listen to others and respond to their points. I can follow ground rules and make sense of them to others. I put my energy and whole-hearted commitment into discussions and speech to get the most out of any situation. I listen attentively to what others are saying and play back to them what they have said.	I can tell a story with no notes that engages an audience. I can read an audience and change my language, tone, and pitch to connect with it. I can respond to and build on the feelings and views of others. I can develop the wellbeing of others through coaching and other techniques.	I can take risks in the way I present to an audience in order to engage them: including using humour, surprise, etc. I can lead/chair a discussion in a range of contexts, making everyone feel involved.

22-Layard, R. 2011: *Flourish: A New Understanding of Happiness and Well-Being — and How to Achieve Them by Martin Seligman*: The Guardian

23-Ibid

24- Seligman, M. 2011: *Flourish: A Visionary New Understanding of Happiness and Well-Being*: Simon and Schuster

25-Ibid

26-Ibid

27-Ibid

28-Cain, S. 2012: *Quiet: The Power of Introverts in a World That Can't Stop Talking*: Crown Publishing Group/Random House, Inc

29- Seligman, M. 2011: *Flourish: A Visionary New Understanding of Happiness and Well-Being*: Simon and Schuster

30- Cain, S. 2012: *Quiet: The Power of Introverts in a World That Can't Stop Talking*: Crown Publishing Group/Random House, Inc

31-Ibid

32-Seligman, M. 2006: *Learned Optimism: How to Change Your Mind and Your Life*: Vintage

33- Seligman, M. 2011: *Flourish: A Visionary New Understanding of Happiness and Well-Being*: Simon and Schuster

34- Cain, S. 2012: *Quiet: The Power of Introverts in a World That Can't Stop Talking*: Crown Publishing Group/Random House, Inc

35- Csikszentmihalyi, M. 1996: *Creativity: Flow and the psychology of discovery and invention*: Harper Collins

CHAPTER 5: THE WRAPAROUND SERVICES OF PASTORAL CARE

Play away; techniques; strategies; concepts in this chapter that can be used in different contexts:

Fight or flight - the amygdala hijack

Maslow's expanded hierarchy of needs

Connection/addiction

In apology

Willpower

Distinction: Integrity v Sincerity

Cool cards

'What do you want?'

Living wants

Mind the gap

Guiding principals

Push and pull

Small move, big change

Feared/preferred future

The ally

The brain- the prefrontal cortex; the limbic system; dopamine

The power of paying attention; the delay; surf the urge; the wave

Mindful and meditation techniques

Pessimistic optimism

Let us move onto Year 11.

(Apologies to any poet reading this; you're free to give it a miss.)

> '*A lot has happened since then,*
> *You may be surprised to know Colin did in fact pick up a pen.*
> *He hasn't done too badly*
> *But, sadly, he hasn't done too great.*
> *Do you remember his mate, Rudi Rude?*
> *Well, he got asked to leave the school.*
> *This wasn't very cool,*
> *Got caught stealing a credit card*
> *And then trying to sell it in the school yard.*
> *As for Noisy Nisha, it's true to say, she turned the volume down,*
> *Stopped messing around, playing the clown,*
> *She knew it was time to get busy if she was to pass,*
> *She is now top of the class,*
> *Understands effort, effort, effort*
> *Combined with organisation.*
> *Short-term blood, sweat, and tears for long-term gratification.*
> *So, it's time to talk to our old friend*
> *Who used to drive us round the bend.*'

But instead of Colin, let's torch-beam onto Hashim. Hashim was Colin Chaos in real life. He lived in a small flat with two other siblings and a mother struggling to cope with all the demands made of her. Social services were supporting her but Hashim still came to school unkempt, with a filthy white collar, holes in his shoes, and a mop of unwashed hair. As you can imagine, he was soon isolated, often seen walking around the playground talking to himself. I'm sure, for him, it was very like Adrian Mitchell's terrifying playground:

> 'Dreamed I was in a school playground. I was about four feet high
> Yes dreamed I was in the playground, and standing about four feet high

The playground was three miles long and the playground
    was five miles wide
It was broken black tarmac with a high fence all around
Broken black dusty tarmac with a high fence all around
And it had a special name to it, they call it the killing ground.'[1]

We were increasingly worried about his mental wellbeing. He was
at the bottom of Laevers' scales of emotional wellbeing and
involvement. He wasn't engaging in lessons; he'd become
aggressive, getting himself into conflict with other pupils that
could become violent; he did little work in or outside school. He
was an addict – not a drug addiction, but a computer gaming
addiction. As soon as he got in from school, he would go onto his
PC and play computer games until four in the morning. I listened
to Johann Hari's compelling TED talk, *Everything You Think You
Know about Addiction is Wrong*, and his diagnosis seemed to
chime with what was happening to Hashim:

> 'What if addiction is an adaptation to your environment? ...
> Human beings have a natural and innate need to bond,
> when we are happy and healthy we'll bond and connect
> with each other but if you can't do that, if you are
> traumatised or isolated or beaten down by life you will
> bond with something that will give you some sense of
> relief... because that's our nature, that's what we want as
> human beings.'[2]

If one was to place Hashim on our energy circle, he arrived in
school, at best, in survival mode but more often, utterly burnt out.
Using Hari's diagnosis, it was because he was 'isolated' and
'beaten down by life'. He would do this every day, five days a
week. Neither his mother, the school, nor the school counsellors
were able to break into this addiction. Hari accurately describes
it as living in an 'isolated cage'. It's taken the World Health
Organisation 27 years to update their diagnostic manual, but
they've finally confirmed what anyone who works with young
people or who have children of their own have known for a long

time, classifying 'gaming disorder as an official mental health condition'.[3] So, it's official. Excessive gaming can seriously harm someone's mental health. Cambridge University carried out research, starkly reporting, '14-year-olds who spend an hour a day on screens during their leisure time score nine fewer points at GCSE when the sum of their grades is calculated – the equivalent of dropping two grades from a B to a D. Two extra hours results in 18 fewer points at GCSE.'[4] So, it's official. Habitual screen time can adversely affect academic achievement and, therefore, life chances.

It wasn't looking good for Hashim. He was at the halfway point in his GCSEs and was now part of a group of pupils whose stories we were unable to change. They were all creating a present in the past that was utterly predictable. The students, their families, and the teachers knew exactly how their day would go before it had even happened. We were all 'already always listening'. Hari talks candidly about the challenges of supporting an addict, 'It's hard to love an addict, you are angry a lot of the time... I wish someone would just stop you.' So, we called in the mother, we punished, we shamed, but for Hari this is the flaw in dealing with addiction. It puts up 'barriers between them reconnecting'.[5] I was tasked to carry out an intervention that might have an impact, in an attempt to help these pupils create a new story – a present based in the future rather than in their past. For the school believed, as does every teacher working with challenging pupils, it can never be 'defined by poverty'.[6] The fact that a school is filled with people means it will be 'filled with hope'.[7] A new context needed to be created for new things to show up, for these pupils to begin to hear a new conversation, to discover what they did not know they did not know. Easier said than done. It was at this point I became interested in experts who were trying to understand how the adolescent mind developed. I was no expert. I love how David Bowie describes feeling out of one's depth, as it captures how I was feeling with these students.

Play away; when have you felt like this, did you like the feeling? Was it a 'fight or flight' moment?

'If you feel safe in the area you're working in, you're not working in the right area. Always go a little further into the water than you feel you're capable of being in. Go a little bit out of your depth. And when you don't feel that your feet are quite touching the bottom, you're just about in the right place to do something exciting.'[8]

These experts really spoke to me, making explicit what I'd intuitively sensed but never fully understood. For me, it had always been how the American poet and essayist, Patricia Lockwood, describes what her Catholic faith had taught her. For her it's 'to live in mystery, even to love it', the idea that 'you accept facts about each other but there are deep wells of mystery'.[9] She embraced the uncertainty but, unlike her, I certainly didn't 'love it'. It wasn't good enough to throw our hands in the air, as one teacher did, frustrated by her attempts to get Hashim to engage, crying out in despair, 'He's just a mystery to me.'

Paul Randolph, an expert in the psychology of conflict, helped me out when he cites the neurological evidence showing the link between attacks on our self-esteem – what he calls 'social pain' – to actual physical pain: 'When we speak of "hurt" feelings, we acknowledge that any form of censure, from slight criticism to outright condemnation or rejection, affects our self-esteem and is felt as physical pain.'[10] Hashim was certainly in an almost permanent condition of pain, in and out of school. Randolph goes on to offer a cogent explanation about why Hashim was in 'flight' most of the time. Randolph first gives us the neurology of 'fight or flight' and the importance of the amygdala:

'The ability to monitor neural pathways helps us to see how our brain functions in conflict situations. For example, we now have a neurological explanation of our "fight or flight" instinct. This reflex is governed by the amygdala, two small structures in the brain that control our instinctive responses. Originally needed as a part of our evolutionary development, they enabled us to act swiftly and instinctively in the face of physical attacks in the wild.'[11]

Once I understood this, Randolph then offers the telling insight, the significant relationship of the amygdala with self-esteem, what he powerfully labels the 'amygdala hijack':

'Today the amygdala can be triggered by any attack on our self-esteem. When the brain perceives a threat, whether physical or on our self-image, the amygdala "takes control", diverting the signals away from the cortex, the "thinking" part of the brain. This "amygdala hijack" prevents us from engaging in logical or analytical thought, instead creating instant defensive reactions.'[12]

It was starting to make sense, particularly in relation to these hard-to-reach students. They were being regularly hijacked.

Of course, it led me to Maslow. Many of us are familiar with Maslow's 'hierarchy of needs' which he developed in the 1940s and 50s. However, late on in his life, Maslow developed his 'expanded hierarchy of needs' which is useful when looking at the wrap-around pastoral support Hashim received.

1. **Physiological needs: His home environment:**
    Hashim's basic needs were clearly not being met. Due to the long hours he spent gaming, his body was chemically unbalanced. Maslow explains it leads to the person unable to trust his environment, leading to high levels of anxiety. Hashim was very anxious most of the time.

2. **Safety needs:**
   Because Hashim's physiological needs weren't being met, the need for a predictable orderly environment where feelings of control and autonomy exist, was just not there for him. Maslow warns without this it leads to feelings of doubt and shame.

3. **Belonging needs:**
   Hashim loved his mother and his siblings, but such was his dysfunction he was unable to create an emotionally-based relationship with his family. At school, nearly all his relationships were socially negative. For Hari, Hashim's compulsive addiction to gaming is a replacement for the absence of connection in his life. His central thesis is caught in a needle-sharp soundbite we should add to our growing list, 'The opposite of addiction is not sobriety. The opposite of addiction is connection.[13]

4. **Self-esteem needs:**
   Human connection is fundamental to what it means to be human. Much of our appreciation of self is through our sense of contribution, of being valued for who we are. Hashim had none of this. Hence, he had little self-worth. One of the saddest glimpses into his inner world was when he was chosen to deliver his speech about 'passion' in front of his whole year group, to parents as well as to his teachers. The entire community was there. Of the four strands, Hashim has a compelling physicality and, surprisingly, actually enjoys performing. He really 'goes for it'. He did on that day. To his utter surprise, he received tumultuous applause and cheering. When I asked him the next day what the moment had felt like, he replied, 'I couldn't believe it, they liked me. I thought everyone hated me.'

My colleague, Jeffrey, has talked to me about teaching in 'apology'. He defines it as, 'Teaching with a sharp focus on some kind of interpersonal deficit. It is an acknowledgement that the student has not been recognised in the past. It's the equivalent of realising you haven't really been listening to someone, then turning off the TV, facing them, and listening intently to every word before responding, very carefully.' Although I had taught Hashim since he joined the school as an 11-year-old, I hadn't been listening in a way that had enabled him to speak to understand who he was being. This whole intervention was 'teaching in apology'.

> Play away; think how often in life we function 'in apology' or perhaps need to.

Maslow's four deficit needs were the diagnosis and the starting point for my intervention. Sarah-Jayne Blakemore, Professor of Cognitive Neuroscience at University College London, spends her life studying the way the mind of someone like Hashim might be working, in an attempt to explain and understand why the person might be behaving in a particular way. Like her, the school believed intervention was necessary and, crucially, it wasn't too late. Blakemore explains:

'Adolescence might give us a window of opportunity, not just for things like education and learning, but for intervention. There's a dogma in social policy and educational policy that the first three years of life are the critical window where you have to get in and intervene. What this research on the brain is suggesting is that the brain continues to develop; it is plastic, but in a heightened way, right throughout the teenage years, so it's not too late during the teenage years to intervene in the cases where people might need some extra help.'[14]

Hari supports this view that intervention can work, holding up the extraordinary success Portugal has had in reducing drug addiction. It's built on neuro-scientific evidence concerning the impact the reintroduction of care and support can have 'in creating the neural structure of emotional-resilience in early life'.[15] Portugal reduced addiction in half by introducing programmes whose specific purpose is to 're-create connection between the addict and their community'.[16] But importantly for me, when designing the intervention, I also needed to take on board the guidance offered by Gabor Mate, the controversial physician who has carried out seminal work with inner-city addicts in America. He too speaks from personal experience; someone who has lived with ADHD as well as depression. There was much I could learn. Mate makes it clear Hashim and his peers would undoubtedly need to 'finally face and feel the pain they have been trying to avoid'.[17] Crucially for Mate, this is 'ultimately an inner journey that must be taken by the individual'.[18] However, Mate cautions, 'You have to be with that pain, but you have to have support'.[19] The challenge Mate set me was to help the students find a way of being with their pain so they could actually 'know what it's really all about'.[20]

I'll play away for a moment and take you to Folsom Prison in America. It's the setting for the documentary, *The Work*,[21] where over four days, both the prisoners and the outsiders who come to help go through a therapeutic process based on the pedagogy developed by The Inside Circle Foundation. I was very aligned to their mission statement, as I too needed to create a similar environment for my hard-to-reach students: 'The goal of the ICF is to create environments in which prisoners can work and explore the issues in their lives that have prevented them from living up to their full potential as human beings.'[22] They too believed in the collective power of the circle but for these reasons: 'It is believed that since before recorded history began, men have been gathering in circles around campfires to discuss the day's events and the important issues in each other's lives. It is also believed by some that since men, for the most part, have lost access to these circles, they have consequently lost access to a shared collective wisdom that has left them isolated and out of touch.'[23] What really showed me just how far I would need to go with an intervention that had the potential to bring about long-lasting transformation, was their commitment to dive deep down into the well, arriving at the very bottom where the source of the pain lay. Like Mate, there's a shared belief that urges the person to stay with pain. We see this happen in the film. It's not an easy watch. But the healing we witness is in the insight I needed to hang onto: 'Right down next to where we hurt the most is our medicine.'[24] However, none of this would or should happen unless we were able to build 'containers of trust where they feel safe enough to explore together how they feel'.[25]

Teaching context

But enough of the theory. It's time to gently open the classroom door and shine a light on the 'extra help' I offered Hashim. As we shall see, it's an intervention made more powerful and effective by being set in a context of a wider wrap-around pastoral care that had established a culture of 'security and clarity of expectations'.[26] An inquiry question was asked that attempted to get to the heart of the matter, made more urgent when I asked Hashim and his peers how long they had left at school. The small group of our most disaffected students had no idea at all; indeed, most believed they had endless time ahead. They were momentarily surprised when they heard it was only two-and-a-half terms to go. They knew, as you do by now, I like a quote. So as not to disappoint, I placed before them Martin Luther King's urgent call to action:

> 'We are now faced with the fact that tomorrow is today. We are confronted with the fierce urgency of now. In this unfolding conundrum of life and history, there "is" such a thing as being too late. This is no time for apathy or complacency. This is a time for vigorous and positive action.'[27]

There was little response, as I was probably making them scared or reinforcing the powerful conversation they were having with themselves, 'I can see no point'. In Kierkegaard's terms, they had stuck their fingers into existence and found it smelt of nothing. Probably it was more like, 'he's going on again'. However, over time, a common language would be felt deeply. 'The urgency of now'; 'there is such a thing as being too late'; 'this is the time for vigorous and positive action' would become almost like mantras that would resonant with relevance and force. When I pointed to a poster I often liked to stand under, there was a collective groan, but over the next weeks they would actually feel it in the choices they were making on a daily basis. They would agree it wasn't making them happy, 'Doing what you have always done will get you what you have always got.'[28] It was time to put the inquiry question to them:

How can you create a meaningful conversation with yourself and with each other so you can create a space in which you can make a response to what is happening in your school life and beyond?

A further, urgent question followed on from this:

How can we change the story we are telling ourselves and create a future where we can get what we say we really want?

A set of premises were put to the students as a hook:

- *We have two important parts to our brains, the impulsive brain and the cautious brain, which would be worth finding out more about to help us understand why we behave in the way that we do.*
- *It's very complex being us, as we have multiple identities: identities of the past; present; future; immediate, that we adopt with an array of different people such as our family; our peers; people in authority.*
- *Your thoughts are going to happen. However, we can choose what to believe and what to act on.*
- *Willpower might be something we may find interesting and useful to explore.*

- *Temptation, stress, and self-criticism are the biggest enemies of willpower. This is from a book that has influenced me and might influence you. It's called, 'The Willpower Instinct: How Self-Control Works, Why It Matters, and What You Can Do to Get More of It' by Kelly McGonigal.[29] In her book, McGonigal also tells us self-awareness, self-care, knowing and remembering what's important, are the foundations of self-control. It might be interesting to explore what she means by this.*

Another of the four strands Hashim had a developed sense of, was not only the physical but also an engagement with the cognitive, if you were able to pull him into it. This was my hope with the hook, as it tried to address the fifth of Maslow's hierarchy of needs which belongs to what he called 'growth needs'.

5. Cognitive needs:

Humans have an innate need to explore and discover the world in which they find themselves. They find themselves in a state of confusion and a lack of control. If offered the right environment, they will be open to experience. That was my hope for Hashim.

However, it was hard to tell at this point if Hashim and the other students were being 'present', but at least no-one had yawned loudly or started to side-chat. Nevertheless, this was never going to be a comfortable experience. Hashim was going to be asked if he was willing to examine his behaviour, 'to know what it is really about'. Honouring their word was a central issue for Hashim and these students. A contract was placed before them, simply as a way of seeing how they might show up when they met or didn't meet the conditions.

- ✓ I agree I will be kind in the lesson
- ✓ I agree to participate 100% in all parts of the lesson
- ✓ I agree to speak from 'I'
- ✓ I agree I will talk honestly

✓ I agree not to talk about what is said outside of this lesson if someone asks for confidentiality
✓ I agree to carry out any task I am asked to do outside the lesson

As Maslow and Hari have already told us, for Hashim it was important that he could feel a part of an ensemble, a place of safety and trust. I started with a striking poem, *Our Greatest Fear*.[30] Hashim enjoyed the physical exploration we carried out as a group, as well as the cognitive and linguistic challenge in the poem:

'It is our light not our darkness that most frightens us
Our deepest fear is not that we are inadequate.
Our deepest fear is that we are powerful beyond measure.
It is our light not our darkness that most frightens us.
We ask ourselves, who am I to be brilliant, gorgeous,
Talented and fabulous?
Actually, who are you not to be?
You are a child of God.
Your playing small does not serve the world.
There's nothing enlightened about shrinking so that other
People won't feel insecure around you.
We were born to make manifest the glory of
God that is within us.
It's not just in some of us; it's in everyone.
And as we let our own light shine,
We unconsciously give other people
Permission to do the same.
As we are liberated from our own fear,
Our presence automatically liberates others.'

It was clear from the students' reactions that the poem had made an emotional impact. The poem talks about liberating ourselves from 'our own fear', so we stood in a circle to play 'cool cards'. I asked each person to tell the rest of us what cards they might want to throw away, cards that keep cropping up, cards they predict will keep cropping up, cards they need to fight, cards that are getting in their way. There was honesty in their response, a self-awareness that was meaningful. We had started to slow down and notice. We were being mindful of ourselves and of each other.

It seemed the right time to ask the fundamental question that's lifelong, as relevant to the newborn baby as it is to the dementia patient: 'What do you want?' It's the process of exploring this question that can offer insight. I started by asking them what they wanted, dividing it into categories such as, what they wanted at school; in their relationships with friends and family; for themselves; for the future. Here's what one of the students said he wanted:

- I want to be changed, and not be a statistic of the people that are predicted to not getting their qualifications
- I want to be more responsible
- I want to be trustworthy
- I want to be able to move on instead of lagging in the past
- I want to be more expressive at home with family – mum, sister
- I want to get to know my siblings who don't live with me and have a stronger bond with them
- I want to talk to my mother more and connect with her
- I want the same with my dad, but that's harder as he doesn't live with me
- I want to be more understood by teachers
- I want to be able to put things in a new perspective and do things in a new way
- I want a family, and make sure they all get along and know each other more than I know my siblings now

It's powerful testimony to how open and complex a question it is.

> Play away; what do you want? Group your wants under these headings or headings of your choice: work; relationships with friends and family; for yourself; for the future. Try writing your own list and see where it takes you.

The students' wants were then grouped under three headings:

- The personal
- The academic
- The future

They were asked to choose their top three 'wants', deciding whether they were short-term or long-term 'wants'. After this, they were offered a scale from one to ten, as part of something called 'mind the gap', which is when they were asked to place each 'want' onto the scale. If they were very close to achieving their 'want', they were to place it high up the scale; if they were far off from achieving it, they were to place it low down the scale.

> Play away; now do the same

The concept of something we decided to call 'living wants' came into existence from my dialogue with Jeffrey. These are the things we want every day, where nothing stands in our way from getting them: 'I want to see my friends'; 'I want to be on my phone'; 'I want to watch Netflix'; 'I want to go to the chicken shop after school.' For these students, and probably for us as adults, we are absolutely true to our word in these areas in a way we are not elsewhere in our life. Nothing ever gets in our way from using our phone every day, all week, every month, all year. The students enjoyed sharing their living wants and had no problem writing them down. However, when they were asked to place a living want against each of their top three 'wants', they were able to discover something. They were asked,

- Do your living wants help you get what you say you really want, or do they stop you getting what you say you really want?
- Are you making a great deal with yourself? Is it a fair trade-off?
- Would you make this kind of deal in any other area of your life?

The students were taken aback, as they could see their living wants were working against what they had declared they really wanted. They were making a bad deal with themselves. McGonigal doesn't use the term 'living wants', but rather, 'the false rewards that keep us distracted and addicted'.[31]

> Play away; make a list of your 'living wants', placing them against your top 3 'wants'. Then answer the questions I asked the students. How does it make you feel?

I wanted to push them further, to see if what they said they really wanted was indeed true. I knew they had explored values several times over the years in different settings. I needed a new way in. At the time I was exploring Tony Robbins' *Awake the Giant Within* with my Year 10 tutor group, because it was the moment in their life Martin Luther King identifies as the 'urgency of now'. Unless they awoke the giant within, they would discover, to their cost, that 'there "is" such a thing as being too late'. Everyone was telling them, 'This is no time for apathy or complacency. This is a time for vigorous and positive action.' For these challenging students, they were merely the fine words of a famous preacher and civil rights activist from the past in a far-off land, but nothing more. They were running for cover. I wanted to discover a new lens, a new language through which we could explore their current thinking, avoiding the stale, the over-familiar and the clichéd. I liked very much what Robbins had to say about resetting one's values:

> 'I began to think about what would happen if, instead of just teaching people what their values were and clarifying them, I actually got people to consciously select or redirect the order and content of their values hierarchy system… By doing this, you literally change the way a person thinks, feels, and behaves, in virtually every area of their life. I couldn't imagine a more profound shift that a human being could make.'[32]

By looking at the values the students felt existed at home, at school, within their friendship groups, for several within their religion, they went through a process Robbins describes here:

'At first I thought, "My values are great! I love my values. After all, this is who I am." But I had to keep reminding myself that we are not our values. We are much more than our values. These values were not the result of intelligent choices and a master plan. What I had merely accomplished until now was discovering what priorities were conditioned into my life, and I had consciously chosen to live within the system of pain and pleasure that had been programmed into me. But if I were to really design my own life, if I were to create a set of values that would shape the ultimate destiny I desired, what would they need to be?'[33]

Out of this process, Hashim now had a set of, what I decided to call, 'guiding principles' rather than values, that he felt were important to him. He then placed them next to his wants and living wants to see if they matched these principles. (Go on, play away, try it. You know you want to.) Another worthy quote from Robbins' book was put in front of them: 'The only way for us to have long-term happiness is to live by our highest ideals, to consistently act in accordance with what we believe our life is truly about.'[34] Hashim and his fellow students were now asked to choose one 'want', which we called a goal, that matched their new set of guiding principles. They seemed happy. It seemed a bit like when you make a New Year resolution which you break inside a week. It was all getting far too comfortable. It was clear the gap between achieving their wants was enormous and out of reach.

Things started to get rough when one of the students said he wanted to be a footballer. He was the best footballer in the school and in the team he played for on the weekend; a big fish in a small pond. I had learnt from my mentor the coaching technique of knowing when to gently 'pull' and when to forcefully 'push' with a strength that gets close to confrontation. (Watch *The Work* to see 'push' and 'pull' in action; it's very powerful.) Both are designed 'to empty the glass', for the coachee to drop the shielding and say what is actually happening. I had seen my mentor 'push' a university student who kept saying he wanted to be a musician but was unable to keep to any kind of deadline or follow through on any of his promises. She kept telling him what we could all see but he couldn't, that it was highly unlikely. It was time to push. So, I pushed my footballer to tell us about his lifestyle. It consisted of getting up late for school, spending another stressful day of avoidance where he was present only in body, and then returning home to fall asleep on the sofa. Homework – forget it. Study a training manual – forget it. Make some healthy food – forget it. More worryingly in terms of his goal, he rarely trained. 'I want to,' he sheepishly told us, 'but I just fall asleep, I can't help it.'

Hashim told the group he wanted to achieve a great set of GCSE results to make his mother proud. I pushed him to also tell us about his life as a computer gamer addict, suggesting it was as unlikely, as things stand, as the other student becoming a footballer. The sleeping and the gaming had their roots in what McGonigal calls 'bad stress': 'When we're stressed, our brains persistently mis-predict what will make us happy.'[35] Mate puts it another way when describing what he would like his epitaph to be: 'It's going to say, this life is a lot more work than I anticipated. Because it takes a lot of work to wake up as a human being, and it's a lot easier to stay asleep than to wake up.'[36]

There was now a rising anger in the room; they thought I was disrespecting them. It wasn't the time to back down. It was time to wake up. So, we read Mark Manson's hard-hitting essay, *The Most Important Question of your Life*, which continued to push. The students considered his premise:

'If I ask you, "What do you want out of life?" and you say something like, "I want to be happy and have a great family and a job I like", it's so ubiquitous that it doesn't even mean anything.

A more interesting question, a question that perhaps you've never considered before, is what pain do you want in your life? What are you willing to struggle for? Because that seems to be a greater determinant of how our lives turn out.'[37]

I asked my resisting students the question Manson asks: 'How do you choose to suffer?'

> Play away; how do you choose to suffer? For what? What are you willing to struggle for?

You may be feeling like Manson's respondents and my students, who tilted 'their heads' looking 'at me like I have twelve noses'. I tried to tell them what Manson told his audience, reading his prose aloud with the passion of a preacher:

'I ask because that tells me far more about you than your desires and fantasies. Because you have to choose something. You can't have a pain-free life. It can't all be roses and unicorns. And ultimately that's the hard question that matters. Pleasure is an easy question. And pretty much all of us have similar answers. The more interesting question is the pain. What is the pain that you want to sustain?'

Building up a head of steam, we continued,

'That answer will actually get you somewhere. It's the question that can change your life. It's what makes me me and you you. It's what defines us and separates us and ultimately brings us together.'

I reached a crescendo with Manson's final declaration,

> 'Who you are is defined by the values you are willing to struggle for... This is the most simple and basic component of life: our struggles determine our successes.'

Boom! Game, set and match!

Sadly not. At this point, I had battered them into submission. (Are you still hanging in there? No-one said it was going to be easy.) They looked blank. However, unbeknown to me and Hashim, at this moment another mantra would create a feeling within Hashim which he would later learn to embrace: 'Who you are, is defined by the values you are willing to struggle for.'[38] But we were far away from embracing anything other than the footballer telling me, 'I'll prove you wrong, you just wait and see.' McGonigal points out, who we mix with is catching: 'Both bad habits and positive change can spread from person to person like germs, and nobody is completely immune.'[39]

Play away; check who you mix with; if you have children or a partner or a sibling check who they mix with; see if you agree.

I was beginning to feel it probably hadn't been such a good idea to put all these students together in one room. Hashim joined in, 'You'll see, sir.' Really? Try this then. I shared with them Caroline Arnold's *Small Move, Big Change*.[40] She suggests you commit to changing something small in your life. It mustn't be difficult or unrealistic. It's not something you need to discuss with yourself to avoid 'decision fatigue'. It's useful to test drive it to see if it's manageable. It will be awkward at first until it goes into autopilot; it's in you. The theory goes if you do something for 21 days, then you are likely to do it forever. 'A micro resolution is a compact and powerful commitment designed to nail a precise behavioural target exactly and deliver benefits immediately.'[41] I pointed at the disgusting looking salad in my lunch box that reappeared on my desk four days a week. It always brought cries of total revulsion from the students (try washing it up). My weakness is bread. I could eat different kinds of bread every day of the week, four times a day or more, if I'm being truly honest. But once you turn 50, you really have to look after that waistline if you are to ever wear a Fred Perry polo shirt again with any credibility. I still like a Fred Perry; it's my age. Again, if I am being totally honest, being surrounded by all these toned, young teachers who spend their time running and going to the gym, there was also a little ego involved. So, I decided to cut out bread once a week, then twice a week, until I made a settlement with myself that I could go bread-crazy on the weekend, which luckily for us Jews starts on a Friday. The 21-day theory held and now, as the Nike advert says, I 'just do it'. Then I told them about my friend who said she would walk to work every day. She didn't manage it, as every day was too ambitious. Just as when Hashim used to say at the start of every term, 'I'm going to work hard in all my subjects', it's not realistic; it's a false promise. Then she told me she would walk to work once a week but wouldn't commit to which day. I told her this would fail, as she needed to name the day, sticking to it for 21 days, rain or shine. I tried to tell her that routine is everything, going somewhat over the top by misquoting Auden: 'Routine, in an intelligent (man) person, is a sign of ambition.'[42] I probably should have stopped there, but I gave her my example of swimming every Sunday morning at 8am for the last 25 years (I know, don't go there). Her reply was fully deserved, 'You are becoming a sanctimonious, self-help pain in the arse.' I was, but that's the price you pay when you dive into this world of psych- speak. However, these willpower gurus are right and, of course, she now drives to work every day. We still talk but about other things.

One of these gurus is Roy Baumeister, who argues willpower, like a muscle, can be exercised and made stronger.[43] So, I challenged the students to do some exercise. They would need to honour their word and carry out a 'Small Move Big Change' exercise. I asked them to record it on their iPads, using the app, *Book Creator*.[44] I shouldn't worry too much about iPads and apps, if I were you, because none of them carried out the task; of course they didn't.

> Play away; your turn to make a 'Small Move Big Change'. What would you choose to do? How likely are you to succeed? Who might you suggest to have a go at this? How might you support them? Good luck!

At the same time, another gift – if you can call it that – arrived in my inbox. The footballer had been out on work experience. He'd been given a tremendous opportunity at a London Premier League Football Club in an attempt to hook him into some kind of positive engagement. I'll leave it to the poor club official to tell you what happened (feel his pain):

> 'On several occasions I had to ask the boys to take their hoods down while "working". When asked, the boys tried to argue the point and get away with not removing it. However, as soon as our backs were turned, they put them back. As you can imagine, this was extremely frustrating for us, and although it was cold the reasons behind this were to make them look professional and to fit in with the club's staff who didn't have their hoods up, etc.'

There's more (ouch):

> 'Also, on a separate note, at numerous times during the night, I had to intervene and stop the boys from rugby tackling/wrestling each other on the floor mid-tournament. As you can imagine, this was highly embarrassing to have four boys rolling round on the floor during a primary school tournament with about 20 local schools in attendance. It got to the stage where, after a number of times of speaking to them, during the tidy-up time, I sent them inside and told

them to take no further part in the night, as they clearly were not interested in helping.'

Finally (are you feeling his pain?):

'To top it off, it was extremely disappointing to see this from the boys last night, as it seemed that none of them had any real interest in running/working on the tournament that they worked so hard to prepare, which is a shame. It even got to the stage where our coaches and partner schools were commenting on their attitude/behaviour throughout the night.'

This car crash was compelling evidence, but sadly only for me. The students shrugged or laughed it off. The distinction of 'Change v Transformation' is useful here. To paraphrase Goss, we were all in the realm of change, the altering of what you are doing to improve something that's already possible in your reality (More, better, different). Their present was based in the past, as predictably these students were just re-enacting known patterns of behaviour. They knew what they knew, and they knew what they did not know. However, as we have seen, Goss defines transformation as a function of altering who you are being to create something that's currently not possible in your reality. The future then determines the present. This is the conscious ability to respond, and in doing so infinite possibilities are created: 'You can accept total responsibility for your choices and actions. You are free to play full-out in creating and implementing an extraordinary future for yourself.'[45] In other words, it's the process of reimagination. The email from the football coach had made it clear we were far removed from any notion of an extraordinary future. Neither the students nor I were in the transformative realm where we 'don't know what we don't know'. However, this did happen, for both Hashim and me. Sadly, the footballer faded away, becoming an erratic attendee. He's not breaking into the Premier League any time soon.

The breakthrough moment for Hashim was when we explored 'our feared futures/our preferred futures'. McGonigal explains, 'Brain-imaging studies show that we even use different regions of the brain to think about our present selves and our future selves.'[46] With this in mind, I wanted to explore the notion of our 'feared/preferred futures'. I had stirred the class with the idea they could have the day off school, but there were a couple of restrictions. They would only have £10 to spend, and all of their friends would be in school. In other words, it would be a normal day. What would you do? Their answers were predictable as they re-enacted their past, what they always did. Most slept in; went on social media; watched morning TV while they were on social media; bought cheap, unhealthy food; went on social media while they ate their junk food; hung around while on social media, waiting to meet their friends when school had finished; hung around some more while on social media; stayed up late on social media. What did Hashim decide to do? He just played computer games (of course he did) from the time he got up until way into the night when most of the world is or should be asleep.

At first, they relished the idea, but then had to pause when I asked them what they would feel if this kind of 'feared future' was to be their daily reality after leaving school in a few months' time. We talked about the impact this kind of 'Groundhog Day' life might have on their physical and emotional wellbeing. They felt how Mate describes it; it doesn't make for comfortable reading: 'Boredom, rooted in a fundamental discomfort with the self, is one of the least tolerable mental states... Even our 24/7 self exposure to noise, e-mails, cell phones, TV, Internet chats, media outlets, music downloads, videogames, and nonstop internal and external chatter cannot succeed in drowning out the fearful voices within.'[47]

I then turned to their 'preferred future'. They were asked to write down what a normal day would be like a year from now, if they were to get into college. All described a productive day full of orderly routine in which most of Maslow's expanded hierarchy of needs were being met. Hashim subsequently told me months later, when he was starting to achieve, that this was the transformative moment when he began to discover what he did not know what he did not know. Robbins maybe describes what Hashim went through:

'All personal breakthroughs begin with a change in beliefs. So how do we change? The most effective way is to get your brain to associate massive pain to the old belief. You must feel deep in your gut that not only has this belief cost you pain in the past, but it's costing you in the present and, ultimately, can only bring you pain in the future. Then you must associate tremendous pleasure to the idea of adopting a new, empowering belief.'[48]

The school had been asking his mother for months to unplug his computer after teatime, with little success. Hashim told me he and his mother had now joined forces. Jeffrey's insight here is worth considering for a moment. He suggested everyone, however isolated or troubled the person is, always has someone who will help them.

Play away; reflect for a moment. Do you agree?

The importance of an ally cannot be underestimated. Hashim and his mother turned off the access to the computer games because he could now see what a bad deal he was making with himself. He was beginning to comprehend actually it wasn't what he really wanted. If he did lapse, his brain now associated 'massive pain to the old belief'. He felt deeply this had cost him 'pain in the past'; it was costing him 'in the present'; and, ultimately, would only bring him 'pain in the future'. McGonigal captures it perfectly: 'When we free ourselves from the false promise of reward, we often find that the thing we were seeking happiness from was the main source of our misery.'[49] His feared future loomed large. Mate's 'fearful voices within' were as loud as ever. However, it was more complex than just turning off a switch.

The last piece of the intervention helped him enormously to achieve his goal. For most of my life I've been utterly uninterested in anything scientific; I just didn't get it. I blame my teachers. So, it was a surprise, when learning some neuroscience, I became fascinated with what I discovered about the human brain. I recommend Sarah-Jayne Blakemore's TED talk, *The Mysterious Workings of the Adolescent Brain*.[50] As the title suggests, it's very entertaining. Have a listen:

> 'So there's a famous quote by Shakespeare from *The Winter's Tale*, where he describes adolescence as follows: "I would there were no age between ten and three-and-twenty, or that youth would sleep out the rest; for there is nothing in the between but getting wenches with child, wronging the ancientry, stealing, fighting." (Laughter) He then goes on to say, "Having said that, would any but these boiled brains of nineteen and two-and-twenty hunt in this weather?" (Laughter) So almost 400 years ago, Shakespeare was portraying adolescents in a very similar light to the light that we portray them in today, but today we try to understand their behaviour in terms of the underlying changes that are going on in their brain.'

Blakemore is very good at explaining about the different parts of the brain in the context of adolescence. Firstly, there's the prefrontal cortex. Have another listen:

> 'So adolescence is defined as the period of life that starts with the biological, hormonal, physical changes of puberty and ends at the age at which an individual attains a stable, independent role in society. (Laughter) It can go on a long time. (Laughter) One of the brain regions that changes most dramatically during adolescence is called prefrontal cortex. So this is a model of the human brain, and this is prefrontal

cortex, right at the front. Prefrontal cortex is an interesting brain area. It's proportionally much bigger in humans than in any other species, and it's involved in a whole range of high level cognitive functions, things like decision-making, planning, planning what you're going to do tomorrow or next week or next year, inhibiting inappropriate behaviour, so stopping yourself saying something really rude or doing something really stupid. It's also involved in social interaction, understanding other people, and self-awareness.'

Blakemore then drops the bomb. Hold onto your seats. For Hashim and his peers: 'Activity in this medial prefrontal cortex area decreases during the period of adolescence.'

> Play away; if you are in any way involved with teenagers, then silently scream.

It gets scarier when she describes the area of the brain Hashim and his peers live in most of the time – the limbic system. Listen closely and shudder:

'But now we try to understand that in terms of the development of a part of their brain called the limbic system, so I'm going to show you the limbic system in red in the slide behind me, and also on this brain. So the limbic system is right deep inside the brain, and it's involved in things like emotion processing and reward processing. It gives you the rewarding feeling out of doing fun things, including taking risks. It gives you the kick out of taking risks. And this region, the regions within the limbic system, have been found to be hypersensitive to the rewarding feeling of risk-taking in adolescents compared with adults, and at the very same time, the prefrontal cortex, which you can see in blue in the slide here, which stops us taking excessive risks, is still very much in development in adolescents.'

I did try my very best to share in her optimistic conclusion, but I have to say, at that moment in time, I was finding it hard,

> 'And yet, this is a period of life where the brain is particularly adaptable and malleable. It's a fantastic opportunity for learning and creativity. So what's sometimes seen as the problem with adolescents — heightened risk-taking, poor impulse control, self-consciousness — shouldn't be stigmatized. It actually reflects changes in the brain that provide an excellent opportunity for education and social development.'

Yes, but how about what the psychiatrist and toxicologist, Dr Gallimberti, who has treated addiction for over 30 years, has to say about the brain and addiction? He seems to be contradicting Blakemore: 'By taking advantage of the brain's marvellous plasticity, addiction remoulds neural circuits to assign supreme value to cocaine or heroin or gin, at the expense of other interests such as health, work, family, or life itself.'[51] Because, make no mistake, these adolescents were addicted to their living wants (can you hear the rising panic in my voice?). I turned to McGonigal for help. As I read what she had to say about how our brains work, a part of me felt like the comedian, Ben Rosenfeld, who just lists quotes from McGonigal's book, 'I consider this a comedy book'[52], which makes us laugh because there's a huge amount of self-recognition. But as I said earlier, McGonigal helped explain a lot of things about my own behaviour, which offered me a much needed self-awareness, one of the requisites for self-control I knew I was lacking: 'Self-awareness: the ability to realize what we are doing as we do it, and understand why we are doing it.' I could never understand why I would always get into arguments with my head teacher, who often liked to come into my room early in the morning before school had started, or why I felt slightly out of control with a level of unexplained anxiety until around break time. The answer was dopamine.

Wolfram Schultz, a neuroscientist, calls the cells that make dopamine, 'the little devils in our brain'.[53] I commuted from

Brighton into London every day for 25 years on Southern Fail or worse, on Thamesink(ing fast!); don't go there. A lack of sleep, a lack of breakfast, let loose 'the little devils' creating a dopamine rush that coursed through my brain. Perhaps my head teacher may have thought twice before talking to me at this time in the morning if he'd known the psychopathic state I was actually in (on several occasions, if I recall, he did think better of it; maybe he knew), 'The volunteers displaying high levels of psychopathic traits released almost four times as much dopamine in response to the stimulant as did their non-psychopathic counterparts.'[54] I made so many promises to myself about how I would deal with this situation that was doing my career untold damage. Much to my partner's growing dismay, I would never keep to them.

McGonigal was finally able to explain it to me; so here you have it: 'Low blood sugar levels turn out to predict a wide range of willpower failures.'[55] Rita Z. Goldstein, a professor of psychiatry and neuroscience in America, is testing whether 'neurofeedback, which allows people to observe their brains in action, can help addicts take more control over compulsive habits'.[56] This kind of feedback revealed to one of her clients the habitual bad deal I was attempting to show my students they were making with themselves on a daily basis: 'I keep thinking, I can't believe I've wasted all that damn money on the drug... It never balances out, what you gain versus what you lose.'[57] I was now able to explain to Hashim and his peers about much of their behaviour. I was able to demonstrate to Hashim what happens to him every day when he gets home. The extremity of McGonigal's explanation shocked both of us; it may well shock you if you happen to have a child or someone close to you who likes to play video games.

'A study found that playing a video game led to dopamine increases equivalent to amphetamine use – and it's this dopamine rush that makes both so addictive. The unpredictability of scoring or advancing keeps your dopamine neurons firing, and you glued to your seat.'[58]

The reason he couldn't stop was put to him in these stark terms:

'The worse a person felt about how much they drank the night before, the more they drank that night and the next.'[59]

It was then explained to him again, but in neuroscientific terms:

'Neuroscientists have shown that the brain is constantly processing the forbidden content just outside of conscious awareness. The result: You become primed to think, feel, or do whatever you are trying to avoid.'[60]

For McGonigal and all of these willpower experts, it was about moving from the limbic to the prefrontal cortex parts of the brain. Just look at what McGonigal tells us the prefrontal cortex can make us do; it is very persuasive:

'Robert Sapolsky, a neurobiologist at Stanford University, has argued that the main job of the modern prefrontal cortex is to bias the brain — and therefore, you — toward doing "the harder thing". When it's easier to stay on the couch, your prefrontal cortex makes you want to get up and exercise. When it's easier to say yes to dessert, your prefrontal cortex remembers the reasons for ordering tea instead. And when it's easier to put that project off until tomorrow, it's your prefrontal cortex that helps you open the file and make progress anyway.'[61]

But if Blakemore was saying the prefrontal cortex isn't fully developed in the adolescent, then how on earth was this to be done in a way that might bring long lasting change? It seemed as difficult as weaning a crack addict off heroin. I'm not being facetious here, for the source of the addicts' cravings lie in the limbic system and the coursing of dopamine through their bodies. Don't take my word for it; listen to what the experts have to say about this. When the clinical neuroscientist, Anna Rose Childress, a professor at the University of Pennsylvania, studied the brain scans of recovering cocaine addicts, it showed 'how subliminal drug cues excite the brain's reward system and contribute to relapse. When she showed images such as the one of cocaine on the left screen to patients for 33 milliseconds, their reward circuitry was stimulated.'[62] The conclusion could be devastating if one is in the business of trying to change these adolescents' stories. Antonello Bonci, a neurologist at the National Institute on Drug Abuse in America, wants me to take on the alarming idea: 'In a sense, addiction is a pathological form of learning.'[63] But lest we scare ourselves into a state of complete paralysis, losing all sense of possessing any willpower whatsoever, it might be better to run with McGonigal's comforting cheesecake metaphor: 'First, your brain is temporarily taken over by the promise of reward. At the sight of that strawberry cheesecake, your brain launches a neurotransmitter called dopamine from the middle of your brain into areas of the brain that control your attention, motivation, and action. Those little dopamine messengers tell your brain, "Must get cheesecake NOW, or suffer a fate worse than death."[64] But, and it's a big but, here's the kicker: Your body was born to resist cheesecake.' This is why I love Kelly!

I had to offer the students some hope. Let them eat cake! But I knew I had to offer them something more than hope. However, having read extensively, I was coming to the same conclusion, 'Science has been more successful in charting what goes awry in the addicted brain than in devising ways to fix it.'[65] I needed to dig deep. I was determined not to be 'humbled by my feelings of feebleness'.[66] So, I offered them a toolkit of what they might do when 'part of you wants one thing, and another part of you wants something else. Or your present self wants one thing, but your future self would be better off if you did something else. When these two selves disagree, one version of us has to override the other.'[67] Call it self-control, call it self-awareness. I rather like this: 'The science points to one thing: the power of paying attention.'[68] Mate defines self-awareness similarly, as 'attending with compassionate curiosity to what is happening within'.[69]

His word for this 'disciplined practice' or what he calls 'mental hygiene', is what the Buddhists call 'bare attention':

'Nietzsche called Buddha "that profound physiologist" and his teachings less a religion than a "kind of hygiene"... Many of our automatic brain processes have to do with either wanting something or not wanting something else – very much the way a small child's mental life functions. We are forever desiring or longing, or judging and rejecting. Mental hygiene consists of noticing the ebb and flow of all those automatic grasping or rejecting impulses without being hooked by them. Bare attention is directed not only toward what's happening on the outside, but also to what's taking place on the inside.'[70]

'The power of paying attention'; 'mental hygiene'; 'bare attention'; take your pick. Ultimately, it's all about the delay. Mate describes it in terms of freedom: 'It's a subtle thing, freedom. It takes effort; it takes attention and focus to not act something like an automaton.'[71] In other words, those students have about 30 seconds before they make the decision whether to leave my room, turn right and go to study club (the preferred future), or turn left to hang out with their friends who are waiting outside my door (the feared future). Those of us on a diet will recognise the moment of crisis when staring at the menu. Do I go for the greasy burger (the feared future) or do I go for the healthy salad (the preferred future)? Apparently, when McDonalds introduced lots of healthy salads onto their menus, the consumption of Big Macs increased because people's 'automatic brain mechanisms' were running in overdrive, diminishing the 'capacity for free decision-making'.[72]

Sarah Bowen, a research scientist in the Addictive Behaviours Research Centre at the University of Washington, and Dr. G. Alan Marlatt, the founder and director of the Addictive Behaviours Research Centre at the University of Washington – these are serious people – developed something called 'surfing the urge'.

'Surfing the urge' is 'how to cope with triggers and high-risk situations, how to manage urges and cravings. It also helps people get a better sense of their own personal journeys and the forks in the road that lead either to recovery or to falling off the wagon.'[73] The fork in the road is an image the students were familiar with; we even called a module we'd previously designed for the whole cohort, The Fork in the Road, as they were coming to the end of Key Stage 3. It's a powerful metaphor in this new context. As part of the process of reimagining themselves, I needed my students, like me, to practise this kind of 'mental hygiene'; to develop 'the ability to stand back, observe what is happening', and think about what they 'are doing rather than being on automatic pilot'.[74] It refers back to the distinction between reacting and responding we'd established when they were those young 11-year-olds in the Colin Chaos assembly in Chapter 4. I wanted to recommend to my students more than ever, 'Approaches that will help people see their feelings and then develop more of a sense of choice. It's when they're in the habit-stimulus response that most people get into drug use and its consequences.'[75] Viktor Frankl, a neurologist and Holocaust survivor, who more than most of us understands the fundamental need to create a life-giving space in which we can choose a response, defines the importance of the moment of crisis exactly: 'Between stimulus and response there is a space. In that space is our power to choose our response. In our response lies our growth and our freedom.'[76]

The first thing I needed the students to understand about 'surfing the urge' was that you can't rid yourself of your 'urges and cravings'; 'they are going to happen'.[77] If that's the case, then there's another equally powerful metaphor, The Wave: 'An urge is like an ocean wave that grows bigger and bigger as it approaches the shore. As it grows, there's the desire to just give in, but if you do, you'll reinforce the power of the addiction. Instead, you can ride the "wave".'[78] Marlatt cleverly points out, 'The word "dictator" has the same root as the word "addiction"; both are telling us to do something.' But I wanted to tell my students what the smoker-cum-surfer told Marlatt: 'You can at least ride the wave without getting wiped out.' My students knew they were rubbish at riding the wave, as they were always getting wiped out. But just like the surfers who chill outside their VWs, revelling in the telling of the tale, so too the students enjoyed telling each other about The Wave, the moment when Schultz's 'little devils', riding on the dopamine wave, surge through our body. It was an important step in the deep process of knowing oneself. They were 'attending with compassionate curiosity to what is happening within'.[79]

> Play away; when was the last time you paid this kind of internal compassionate attention on yourself? Is it time to? Do you know someone who would benefit from this kind of attention?

Here are the moments of crisis the students identified as their 'little devils' which caused a failure in willpower:

> Play away once more; how many of these do you recognise? They are extremely common and deep-rooted emotions within all of us. Feel free to add to the list.

- **'What the hell'**: *I've blown it; I'm no good; I'm so far behind, so there is no point*
- **False future**: *I can always do it tomorrow/later*
- **Denial/suppression**: *I won't think about it*
- **False promise**: *An all-or-nothing approach – I'm going to revise all my subjects this weekend*
- **The Pig**: *Immediate gratification; I will be happy; it's fun; if that's what I need, I will have it*
- **Rewarding**: *I'm owed a reward; I worked really hard in Maths; I'm going to take it easy in my next lesson*
- **I am**: *I'm tired; hungry; angry; sad*

- The 'double dukka' ('Dukka' in Buddhism is suffering): *I'm suffering but I tell myself, 'there I go again', which makes me feel even worse*

Once they recognised the physical sensations that occur when The Wave hits them (the power of paying attention), I offered them a whole range of techniques 'to surf the wave' (the power to create a space in which they can choose a response). Mate's experiences with addicts support this approach: 'Methods for gaining self-knowledge and self-mastery through conscious awareness strengthen the mind's capacity to act as its own impartial observer.'[80]

Here are a few choices I offered them so they could become this 'impartial observer'. Some are familiar mindful exercises, but in this context of relapse prevention, we are shining a new light on them. Certainly, for people in crisis, as these students undoubtedly were, the familiar exercises took on an urgency that lies in King's call to action – 'the fierce urgency of now'. A more Zen way of putting it might be to quote what Yip Man explains to the young Bruce Lee: 'We all have inner demons to fight, we call these demons, fear and hatred and anger. If you do not conquer them then a life of one hundred years is a tragedy. If you do, then a life of a single day can be a triumph.'[81]

> Play away; try out a few of these exercises; see how they might benefit you in the private as well as the public lives we lead? What might get in your way from experimenting with these techniques? What might you do to remove some of the barriers? Who could help you?

- **Stand centred; see dark** – this is from my tai chi practice, where we're taught to control the flow of our thoughts. First, put our big toes together. Have our hands hanging loose by our sides; pretend we have string on the end of our nose, holding our head upright. Then focus on two things: to keep still, and to see the dark of our eyelids. The more we sway, the more we are our thoughts and feelings. They have us. The effort of keeping still and seeing dark will help put in the delay. We can ride The Wave, moving from the limbic area to the prefrontal cortex. It can give us a chance to make a good deal. My tai chi teacher used to do this on a crowded, hot, polluted Bangkok bus. It can be done in the shower or just before walking into an exam room. I often do it just when I'm about to send an angry email (those psychopathic tendencies). The delay takes me to my stand and gives me the choice to choose who I be.

- **Body scan** – this is often carried out lying down, but can be done sat at a desk or standing up. The aim is to work on the inter-relationship of the mind/body body/mind. You flex every muscle in your body, starting with your toes, to your calves, to your thighs, to your buttocks, to your stomach, to your neck muscles, to your eyebrows, to the top of your head. Wherever there's ache or soreness, that's where the tension is. To alleviate it, you flex several times. Again, it allows for the delay stopping the dopamine flow.

- **Finger tracing** – take your left hand and spread your fingers. With your right hand, trace each finger in time with your breathing. On the in breath, trace up the finger; on the out breath, trace down. Don't force your breathing; the aim is to attune yourself to your natural breath. This has helped some of the students and me to sleep. When all of those 'little devils in our brain' start talking to us in the middle of the night, it helps to switch off the dopamine before we 'chase the dragon' becoming our thoughts and feelings. I've seen students use this technique in the middle of their GCSE exams, at the moment of crisis when it's becoming all too much and they're about to check out. I've seen pupils do it just before mediation with a teacher they don't get on with. It allows us to move from a reactive to responsive state.

- **Meditation walk** – the aim is to move from the limbic area to the precortex by noticing how we walk. You slowly raise your heel, place it down, and then raise yourself onto your toes. 'Heel/foot/toes' is the mantra you keep saying in your head. For the more spiritual, you might enjoy this beautiful mantra, 'Walk as if you are kissing the Earth with your feet.'[82] For an autistic student, this was extremely beneficial. He told me how coming to school was incredibly stressful, because he felt other people were talking about him. He was able to avoid turning around and staying at home by practising a meditative walk. A colleague used it as she approached the door to a difficult meeting that she didn't want to attend.

- **Meditation eating** – this is a well-known mindful technique. However, shine a new light on it, place it in a new context, and it can be used to help students and adults with difficult home relationships. As The Wave surges over them and they're about to repeat a conflict they've experienced so many times before, they turn their attention to an item of food, employing their senses. They raise the food slowly towards their mouth, looking at the texture from every angle; they smell it; place it in their mouth but mustn't bite down on it, noticing the sensations now occurring in their mouth; listen to the sound as they crunch into the food. A highly reactive student, who constantly fought with her mother around teatime, said it helped her to just keep her mouth shut and avoid answering back which always made things worse. She was practising that 'bare attention' which took her away from the 'should/should not' but rather placed her into a mindful state where, 'one can choose to be aware of the ebb and flow of emotions and thought patterns instead of brooding on their content. Not "he did this to me therefore I'm suffering" but "I notice that feelings of resentment and a desire for vengeance keep flooding my mind".'[83]

> Play away: next time you're about to kick off, which can often be around the dinner table, give meditative eating a try. You might look a little strange, but it works.

- **Inhale/exhale on a count** – students enjoy making this a challenge. It's very simple and can be done anywhere, in any situation. You breathe in on a count of, say 5, and then breathe out on a count of 5. You can then extend this to any number. Playing this game will move you to the prefrontal cortex area of the brain, helping you to surf the urge. Someone had alerted me to a report of a horrific attack on a tourist in Whitechapel where I used to teach. In the photograph, I could see one of the assailants was an ex-student of mine. He was lagging behind the main protagonists. However, I can only presume he just reacts, joining in the brutal attack for which he was rightly sent to prison. But just imagine what might have happened to the boy's life if he'd employed this strategy. It may have given him enough delay to go to his stand or to consider the consequences. It might have moved him to the more cautious part of his brain. We shall never know.

> Play away; this is life and death: 'In a moment, everything can change and in a moment, you can change everything.'(84)

- **Hold your breath** – set yourself a target. It's the same as the previous exercise. It's simple, and can be done anywhere in any situation.
- **A Sit In** – stare at something for 30 seconds; the aim is to honour your word you will just stare at an inanimate

object for 30 seconds. When any thoughts enter your head, you will rid yourself of them. Yoshi Oida, an actor, challenges us, 'You must train your concentration, just as an athlete trains the body.'[85] If one takes Oida's advice to train, then you can create a 'sit in' that can last 5 minutes in which those 'little devils' don't make an appearance. The students tend to enjoy the challenge of this, many of them able to remain in the moment for 5 minutes or longer.

> Play away; go practise

- **Sounds** – Listen to as many sounds as you can with your eyes shut; another simple exercise that will give us a chance of not being 'wiped out by the wave'.
- **Torch-beam** on a relative/friend who's not here. Shut your eyes, engaging your senses to imagine what they're doing; see them doing something; hear what they're saying; use your muscular memory to touch something they're touching; taste something they're eating; recall a particular smell you associate with this person. The exercise of paying attention will bring about a degree of self-control that is needed at the moment of crisis. It creates the vital, life-giving space which Frankl talks about in which we can then choose our response.
- **Emotional memory** – close your eyes and torch-beam on the last happy event you attended, using the senses in the same way. See it; recall some of the sounds, tastes, smells; touch something. It's not as easy as it sounds. Your mind will wander. But with practice at torch-beaming, you will increase your capacity to control the destructive urges. The importance of this is underlined by McGonigal: 'Self-control is a better predictor of academic success than intelligence (take that, SATs), a stronger determinant of effective leadership than charisma (sorry, Tony Robbins),

and more important for marital bliss than empathy (yes, the secret to lasting marriage may be learning how to keep your mouth shut).'[86]

- **Recite your mantra** – I asked the students to create a mantra that meant something to their future. In her inspirational TED talk, *Every Kid Needs a Champion,*[87] Rita Pierson describes how she gave a mantra to one of her tough inner-city classes, which was 'so low, so academically deficient'. Her fundamental core belief is if 'you say it long enough, it starts to be a part of you'. Here's the mantra she offered her disaffected students: 'I am somebody. I was somebody when I came. I'll be a better somebody when I leave. I am powerful, and I am strong. I deserve the education that I get here. I have things to do, people to impress, and places to go.' Apparently, after she had made this declaration, her kids spontaneously cried out, 'Yeah!' I too cried out, 'Yeah!'

Inspired by this wonderful testimony about the belief in humanity in the face of the toughest odds, I shared my own mantra with the students. I've said it so many times it's now in me:

'Breathe and believe
I am capable
I am whole
I will do what it takes
There is no evidence that if I do, then I will fail
Keep the faith'

I offered up other mantras:

'May I be safe
May I be peaceful
May I be gentle
May I be compassionate
May I allow myself to be who I am'

Or

'I will decide who I can be,
I will sculpt myself
I won't tolerate anything less
It is in my hands'

As The Wave takes hold, you recite your mantra as quietly or as loudly as you wish, in an attempt to move you to your goal, your 'preferred future', to what you really want.

Play away; if this sounds like 'hippy' talk and your first reaction is that it would never work in your environment, then read about how Bob Roth, the Executive Director of the David Lynch Foundation, uses Transcendental Meditation. Like Rita Pierson, he certainly doesn't practise it on the beaches of Goa: 'To date, we have provided scholarships for over 300,000 at-risk students in underserved schools in 35 countries to learn to meditate; we are working with the Veterans Administration, the Department of Defence, and the Wounded Warrior Project to bring Transcendental Meditation to tens of thousands of veterans and their families who suffer from post-traumatic stress disorder; and we are partnering with the Family Justice Centres and other similar organizations nationwide to teach Transcendental Meditation to women and children who have been victims of domestic violence.'[88] He identifies a need and an acceptance for this kind of fundamental work: 'I feel the tipping point has tipped with regard to the public's understanding and appreciation for the value of meditation, in general, and Transcendental Meditation, specifically. There is openness and a receptivity that I have not seen in the past 40 years of teaching.' The mantra is essential. In his practice, the participant learns how to 'think' it silently. You don't need a yoga mat to do it. So, what would your mantra be? Give yourself some time to write it, as it takes several drafts to capture what will work for you.

Several students said they used the techniques in the actual exam room to keep themselves on track. We ran several assemblies prior to the exam season in the actual exam hall, with the students sat in front of their exam desk. We used many of these techniques to allow them to take control of their emotions at the many crisis points when they were at their most vulnerable: the night before; prior to entering the space; the agonising wait before turning the paper over; the moment when you're faced with the paper; dealing with thoughts and feelings during the exam; coping with possible negative feelings afterward. We had them standing on the desks declaring their mantras as well as their stands. Like Roth, we found an absolute 'openness and receptivity'. During the actual exam period, we steadied the whole cohort with meditative sessions using these techniques, after which we took them down into the hall. We were giving some of them a chance. I witnessed many students in the exam hall 'finger tracing'; 'holding their breath'; 'inhaling/exhaling'.

There are a lot of studies being carried out about the impact of mindfulness and meditation, much of it very compelling. 'Researchers at the University of Washington showed that a program based on mindfulness was more effective in preventing drug-addiction relapse than 12-step programs... Meditation quiets the posterior cingulate cortex, the neural space involved in the kind of rumination that can lead to a loop of obsession.'[89] It's essential to empower whoever you are working with so that when they're on their own 'the little devils', the fearful voices within, don't overwhelm. I taught my students several meditations so they could carry out this 'mental hygiene' at home, to attend with compassion what was happening within when no-one was around.

One that worked for some of them was called **'The Rainbow'**. There are many versions of this guided meditation. My version goes like this:

'Sit in a fairly formal posture or lie down if you prefer. Shut your eyes. Start with breathing in and out, regulating yourself by using the "inhale/exhale on a count" exercise you're experts in. Now breathe into the pit of your stomach, hold the breath there for a moment, notice the pause, then as you breathe out through your tummy button, give the air a colour from the rainbow. Now breathe into your heart, hold the breath, notice the pause, then breathe out through your heart, giving the air another colour. Now breathe into your throat, hold the breath, notice the pause, then breathe out through your throat, giving the air another colour. Now breathe in through your mouth, hold the breath, notice the pause, then breathe out through your mouth, giving the air another colour. The throat and mouth are good areas to clear out all those things you've wanted to say that are getting in your way. Now breathe in through your nose, hold the breath, notice the pause, then breathe out through your nose, giving the air another colour. Now breathe in through your eyebrows, hold the breath, notice the pause, then breathe out through your eyebrows, giving the air another colour. Now breathe in through the top of your head, hold the breath, notice the pause, then breathe out through the top of your head, giving the air another colour. Now, when you're composed, repeat the sequence. At the end, just let the colours course through your body.'

I can testify from my own experience that if I've worked hard enough to let everything go and am present, the sensation of all the colours coursing through my body is like a natural high. A lot of the time I become distracted, so it fails, which is important to share. It doesn't always work. Don't beat yourself up.

Another useful guided meditation that spoke to some of the students was a 'Gratitude Meditation'. Again, there are numerous versions of this. Here's mine:

'Sit in a fairly formal posture, or lie down if you prefer. Shut your eyes. Start with inhaling and exhaling, regulating your breathing by using the "finger tracing" exercise you're experts in. Now chose someone you'd like to thank but have never thanked. Notice how your body reacts when you chose this person, as you let them come into your mind. Notice what's happening to your breathing, to your heartbeat. See this person in your mind somewhere in a place where you'd like to say thank you. Concentrate on the place, the colours, the light, the sounds, the smells, what things might feel like if you were to touch or taste them. Notice what's happening to your breathing, to your heartbeat, to the sensations in your toes, in your feet, in your stomach, in your chest, along your arms and into your hands, in your throat, in your mouth, in your face, on top of your head. Now, turn your attention to the person. Start at their feet: imagine they are barefoot, notice their toes, their feet, work your way up their body, what they're wearing, focus on their arms, their hands, their fingers. Now see their neck, their face, their lips, their cheeks, their eyes, their eyebrows, their forehead, their hair. Now place yourself where you would like to make your thanks of gratitude. See yourself working your way from your feet up your body, what you're wearing, focus on your arms, your hands, your fingers. Now see your neck, your face, your lips, your cheeks, your eyes, your eyebrows, your forehead, your hair. Now start to see yourself offer up your thanks. Mouth silently the words you want to say. Notice what this feeling of gratitude brings to your body. Notice where there's energy; a sensation. Give into it, let it in. Now notice the effect your gratitude is having on the person you chose to offer it to. Body scan this person, looking for signs your gratitude is being received. Start at their feet, imagine they are barefoot, notice their toes, their feet, work your way up their body, their legs, their hips, focus on their arms, their hands, their fingers. Now see their neck, their face, their lips, their cheeks, their eyes, their eyebrows, their forehead, their hair. To finish, feel the connection between both of you, and smile. See yourself smile; see your eyes, your lips, your cheekbones, your forehead. Do the same for the other person. Notice what's happening in your body as you do, where the energy lies, where the physical sensations are. Slowly open your eyes.'

It's easy to dismiss this as woolly, light, clichéd, but when Hashim is choosing his mother on whom he has inflicted so much pain, it's nothing of the sort. It's painful but also healing. It's astonishing over the years how many adolescent boys want to apologise to their mothers and offer up thanks. By committing to the meditation, they're also making a good deal with themselves, creating a new context where new things can show up, creating a new conversation that doesn't involve 'the little devils'.

We looked at a lot of other strategies that might help them be more cautious and have more control over their behaviour. We explored concepts of 'strategic optimists and defensive pessimists' in an article by Adam Grant, *The Positive Power of Negative Thinking*, concluding 'pessimistic optimism' might be a useful strategy to combat The Wave. Grant had explained to them: 'Ultimately, both styles are deadly at their extremes. Pessimism becomes fatalistic, and optimism becomes toxic. The key is to find the sweet spot, the more moderate ranges that combine the benefits of both approaches. In the words of Richard Pine, "The best chief executives — and that includes presidents — know that too much optimism is a dangerous thing, that wise and productive leadership means striking a balance between optimists' blue sky view of the world and pessimists' more clear-eyed assessment of any given situation."'[90] McGonigal confirmed this was the right strategy. She advised the way forward was to predict possible obstacles, predict moments when 'willpower failure' might occur, and have a specific plan to overcome what might well get in the way: 'You can ensure your future success by imagining your future failure. Anticipate what your setbacks might be, and when temptation might strike. Have action plans for those moments. The same researchers (Koehler, D.J., & Poon, C.S.K.) have shown that strengthening your intention doesn't increase the chance of success. Only strengthening your action plan helps – getting very specific about what you need to do and how you are going to do it.'[91]

> Play away; think how you might bring 'pessimistic optimism' into your public and private life. As you stare at the ceiling in the middle of the night, might it be better to work out an action plan rather than giving into those fearful 'little devils' who will overwhelm you with all sorts of crazy thoughts.

Finally, I asked each student to reflect on the intervention in the form of a poem. Why a poem? Simply because 'an addict just wants to be a human being'.[92] Here's Hashim's poem; it's worth taking some time to read it:

'The wisest person in the world said to me he who wastes time on frivolous things should be its thrall

I replied I decide what I do with my time

The wisest person in the world explained to me you are weak-minded until properly trained in the art of willpower

I then tried to explain I am weak-minded but not an idiot

The wisest person in the world pointed out to me thou shall hurt his loved ones if thou does not do what is right

I felt vulnerable

The wisest person in the world asked me do you know what is right and what is wrong?

So I asked, do you even know me at all?

The wisest person in the world challenged me, thou shall neglect the wasters and focus on loved ones

And I felt lost

The wisest person in the world challenged me, think straight, don't give into temptation

I thought, I know what I am doing

The wisest person in the world whispered to me, see the goal, stare at it and grab it

What I heard was secure your future

The wisest person in the world said about me, you are a strong boy but not determined enough

I then spoke about me, I know who I am, I can achieve in life

The wisest person in the world asked me what my goal is

I told the wisest person in the world my goal is to plough through things

And if I was to see the wisest person in the world when I am 17

I will say, look at me now, I knew I could do it,

I just need to put effort into my life'

The first thing to note is he handed it in on the deadline; small steps. It's useful analysing the poem using the four strands. Linguistically, it's eloquent using some of the language of will power. He was asked to share it with his tutor group. As I said, Hashim enjoys the physicality of performing and delivered his writing with passion. He certainly made an emotional impact, as many who were present including his tutor, spoke to me about it afterwards. It had been memorable. The key for Hashim was whether cognitively the argument he was making to himself lay in the domain of sincerity or integrity; in the domain of change or transformation. What showed up in the distinctions is whether he would fall back into his predictable behavior, or whether a new context had indeed been created in which he had begun to create a space for new things to show up; to begin to hear a new conversation; to discover what he did not know he did not know. Was it another false promise, or was he now beginning to understand who he is being? Was this the start of the reimagining of the self?

Let's return to the focus of this section, the wraparound services of pastoral care. My apologies for such a circuitous route but, as we noted at the outset, 'ordinary life is pretty complex stuff'. His poem is testimony to 'the encouragement of playfulness' and 'inquisitiveness'[93] which Claxton and Lucas see as one of the requisites for pastoral care. The school had developed a spirit of inquiry since he was 11 years old. So here he was, now 16 years old, in an assembly that was trying to entice him into grappling with Alinsky's *Rules for Radicals*, no less. Alinsky has things to say that take on a resonance in this context. He lays down the challenge Hashim had alluded to in his poem, when talking about the need 'to plough through things':

> 'Knowing that the mountain has no top, that it is a perpetual quest from plateau to plateau, the question arises, "Why the struggle, the conflict, the heartbreak, the danger, the sacrifice. Why the constant climb?" Our answer is the same as that which a real mountain climber gives when he is asked why he does what he does. "Because it's there." Because life is there ahead of you, and either one tests oneself in its challenges or huddles in the valleys of a dreamless day-to-day existence.'[94]

I was intrigued, as was Hashim. There were signs he was starting to heed Mate's call to wake up, to make his way out of the valley of his 'dreamless day-to-day existence'. Hashim was beginning to acquire the curiosity that needed to go hand-in-hand with Alinsky's call to action, so he could start 'to see what it is all about'. I can't be sure, but perhaps when he met a guest speaker who talked to the whole cohort about the importance of her mother in her life, her ally, Hashim could also see his mother as an ally in the same way. The visitor had gone to prison earlier in her life, but her mother had never abandoned her. She's now a successful senior probation officer. Whatever it was, something had created the circumstances for Hashim to work with his mother to unplug those computer games. The school was meeting Maslow's growth needs.

He was beginning to apply himself, understanding the aesthetics of what it would take to create truly beautiful work of depth. A milestone was when he achieved a distinction in his Drama V Cert several months before the exam season started. He was part of a small group of students who obtained the first qualifications in their cohort. The achievement was made even more satisfying because an IT error had disastrously wiped all of their portfolios which they'd poured blood, sweat, and tears over. The students had no choice but to re-do their portfolios. He didn't throw his hands in the air submitting to the 'should/should not' paradigm, giving lots of reasons why he now couldn't be bothered. He embraced the notion 'it is what it is'. It wasn't going to get in his way. We celebrated their achievement. Suddenly, Hashim was someone to look up to. The other students, including the increasingly apprehensive high achievers, had it all to do. Because Maslow's esteem needs for both oneself and the desire for respect from others were being met, Hashim was becoming far more present and receptive. He now wanted more. There was a dignity in his conversations, rather than the desperate dishonesty of his excuses and justifications. He was discovering purpose, and therefore he was discovering Hari's 'bonds and relationships with wider society'. The environment was providing a culture of 'security and clarity of expectations', which was, in turn, promoting self-reliance. He was, in Maslow's terms, actualising the self; there was a desire 'to become everything one is capable of becoming'.[95] It had been a search to 'become what one is'.

I met him on results day. He'd got himself a decent set of GCSEs. Had he reached the top of Maslow's needs – self-transcendence? This might be pushing it. But I looked at Hashim, his mother, his siblings in tow, and they were smiling and laughing. It was an image of integrity, a platform on which to build the next phase of his life. But here might be the place to add a word of caution. The inequality gap for working class students like Hashim is still as wide as ever. In her book, *Miseducation: Inequality, Education and the Working Classes*, Diane Reay makes the case:

'Those on free school meals and receiving pupil premium 27% are less likely to achieve five or more GCSEs at grades A*-C including English and maths. Four-fifths of children from working-class minority ethnic families are taught in schools with high concentrations of other immigrant or disadvantaged students – the highest proportion in the developed world, according to a report by the Organisation for Economic Cooperation and Development. Half of all free school meal children are educated in just a fifth of all schools.'[96]

It doesn't stop there. Even if Hashim was to get a good job after college, the gap is still as wide:

'UK professionals from working-class backgrounds are paid £6,800 less on average each year than those from more affluent families, a study has found. The class pay gap was highest in finance at £13,713, the research by the Social Mobility Commission concluded. The medical profession saw the next highest gap at £10,218, followed by information technology at £4,736. Commission chairman Alan Milburn said the 17% average pay gap showed the UK remained a "deeply elitist" society. The research, carried out by academics from the London School of Economics and University College London, analysed data from the UK labour force survey – a snapshot of employment in the UK with more than 90,000 respondents. The researchers examined the average earnings of people in professional jobs from different backgrounds, and found those who had come from a poorer family lost out by about £6,800 a year.'[97]

Would college meet Hashim's hierarchy of needs? Les Ebdon, director of Fair Access to Higher Education, doesn't think so. In response to a rise in the dropout rate in higher education of students from the most disadvantaged areas, Ebdon shares his concerns: 'The non-continuation rates for young people from the most disadvantaged backgrounds have risen faster than for other groups. People from disadvantaged backgrounds often overcome huge challenges to get into higher education. But access is truly meaningful only if students also complete their course. So it is crucial that universities and colleges are working across the whole student lifecycle to support all students, throughout their studies.'[98]

We could also place wraparound services of pastoral care in the context of knife crime. These hard-to-reach students I'd been working with were extremely vulnerable, as they were at the optimum age for grooming by the drug gangs. They were also at risk of being excluded, which meant they are '200 times more likely to receive a knife-carrying offence'.[99] When asked what might be done, the police and the Somalian mothers living on an estate in North London, whose children are in the frontline of the killings, talked about the solution requiring 'ambition'.[100] The school had shown ambition. The rigorous and relentless search to find meaningful wraparound pastoral care meant Hashim had received the support to 'know what it's really all about', and therefore he'd begun to value himself. It had given him connection, which in turn, had given him the emotional resilience to hopefully continue his 'walk toward' some kind of certainty in his life.

1-Mitchell, A. 1982: *Back in the playground blues from: For Beauty Douglas*: Allison &Busby, London

2- Hari, J. 2015: *Everything you think you know about addiction is wrong*: TEDGlobalLondon https://www.ted.com/talks/johann_hari_everything_you_think_you_know_about_addiction_is_wrong

3- Barr, S. 2017: *WHO classifying video game addiction as a mental disorder enrages social media*: The Independent

4-Weale, S. 2015: *Teenagers who watch screens in free time do worse in GCSEs*: The Guardian

5- Hari, J. 2015: *Everything you think you know about addiction is wrong*: TEDGlobalLondon

6- Adams, T. 2017: *Meet the neighbours: Alice Neel's Harlem portraits*: The Observer

7-Ibid

8- Jones, J. 2017: *David Bowie Offers Advice for Aspiring Artists: "Go a Little Out of Your Depth," "Never Fulfil Other People's Expectations"*: Open Culture

http://www.openculture.com/2017/01/david-bowie-offers-advice-for-aspiring-artists.html

9-Kellaway, K. 2017: *Patricia Lockwood: 'I am a show-off, a clown*: The Observer

10-Randolph, P. 2016: *Why being wrong really hurts*: The Guardian

11- Ibid

12-Ibid

13- Hari, J. 2015: *Everything you think you know about addiction is wrong:* TEDGlobalLondon

14-Blakemore, S. 2014: *Sarah-Jayne Blakemore: The Teenager's Sense of Social Self: Edge*

https://www.edge.org/conversation/sarah_jayne_blakemore-sarah-jayne-blakemore-the-teenagers-sense-of-social-self

I would recommend her latest book, *Inventing Ourselves: The Secret Life of the Teenage Brain*: Penguin (2018)

15- Hari, J. 2015: *Everything You Think You Know about Addiction is Wrong*: TEDGlobalLondon

16-Ibid

17-Mate, G. 2014: *What is addiction?*: https://www.youtube.com/watch?v=T5sOh4gKPIg

18-Ibid

19-Ibid

20-Ibid

21-Mcleary, J and Aldous, G: *The Work*: Dogwoof

22-http://insidecircle.org/

23-Ibid

24-Mcleary, J and Aldous, G: *The Work*: Dogwoof

25-http://insidecircle.org/

26-Claxton. G. And Lucas. B. 2013: *What Kind of Teaching For What Kind Of Learning*: SSAT

27-King, M. 1967: *Beyond Vietnam: A Time to Break Silence*

28- Non-attributable

29-McGonigal, K. 2011: *The Willpower Instinct: How Self-Control Works, Why It Matters, and What You Can Do to Get More of It*: Avery

30-Williamson, M. 1996: *A Return to Love*: HarperOne

31-McGonigal, K. 2011: *The Willpower Instinct: How Self-Control Works, Why It Matters, and What You Can Do to Get More of It* : Avery

32-Robbins, T. 2007: *Awake the Giant Within*: Simon and Schuster

33-Ibid

34-Ibid

35-McGonigal, K. 2011: *The Willpower Instinct: How Self-Control Works, Why It Matters, and What You Can Do to Get More of It*: Avery

36-Mate. G., quoted in Moorhead, J. 2018: *How dealing with past trauma maybe the key to breaking addiction*: The Guardian

37-Manson, M. 2016: *The Subtle Art of Not Giving a F*ck: A Counterintuitive Guide to Living A Good Life* : Harper

38-Ibid

39-McGonigal, K. 2011: *The Willpower Instinct: How Self-Control Works, Why It Matters, and What You Can Do to Get More of It*: Avery

40- Arnold, C. 2014: *Small Move, Big Change: Using Microresolutions to Transform Your Life Permanently*: Viking

41-Ibid

42-Auden, W. 1958: as quoted in *Oxford Dictionary of Quotations by Subject*: OUP Oxford 2010

43-Baumeister, R. 2012: *Willpower: Rediscovering Our Greatest Strength* : Penguin

44-https://bookcreator.com/ipad/

45-Goss, T. 1995: *The Last Word on Power*: Rosetta Books

46-McGonigal, K. 2011: *The Willpower Instinct: How Self-Control Works, Why It Matters, and What You Can Do to Get More of It*: Avery

47-Mate, G. 2009: *In the Realm of Hungry Ghosts*: Vintage Canada

48-Robbins, T. 2007: *Awake the Giant Within*: Simon and Schuster

49-McGonigal, K. 2011: *The Willpower Instinct: How Self-Control Works, Why It Matters, and What You Can Do to Get More of It*: Avery

50-Blakemore, S. 2005: *The mysterious workings of the adolescent brain*: TEDGlobal

51-Smith, F. 2017: *How science is unlocking the secrets of drug addiction*: National Geographic magazine

52- Rosenfeld, B, 2012: *The Willpower Instinct*: Quotes: bigben comedy blog http://www.bigbencomedy.com/blog/archives/the-willpower-instinct-quotes/

53- Schultz, W. 2012: *Dopamine reward prediction error coding: Dialogues in Clinical Neuroscience*

https://www.ncbi.nlm.nih.gov/pmc/articles/PMC4826767/

54-Dutton, K. 2013: *The Wisdom of Psychopaths*: Random House

55- McGonigal, K. 2011: *The Willpower Instinct: How Self-Control Works, Why It Matters, and What You Can Do to Get More of It*: Avery

56-Smith, F. 2017: *How science is unlocking the secrets of drug addiction*: National Geographic magazine

57-Ibid

58-McGonigal, K. 2011: *The Willpower Instinct: How Self-Control Works, Why It Matters, and What You Can Do to Get More of It*: Avery

59-Ibid

60-Ibid

61-Ibid

62- Smith, F. 2017: *How science is unlocking the secrets of drug addiction*: National Geographic magazine

63-Ibid

64- McGonagall, K. 2011: *The Willpower Instinct: How Self-Control Works, Why It Matters, and What You Can Do to Get More of It*: Avery

65- Smith, F. 2017: *How science is unlocking the secrets of drug addiction*: National Geographic magazine

66- Mate, G. 2009: *In the Realm of Hungry Ghosts*: Vintage Canada

67- McGonagall, K. 2011: *The Willpower Instinct: How Self-Control Works, Why It Matters, and What You Can Do to Get More of It*: Avery

68- Ibid

69- Mate, G. 2009: *In the Realm of Hungry Ghosts*: Vintage Canada

70-Ibid

71-Ibid

72-Ibid

73-Griffin, K. 2010: Interview with G. Alan Marlatt: *Surfing the Urge*: From Online Exclusives for the Spring 2010 issue of *Inquiring Mind* (Vol. 26, No. 2), Inquiring Mind

https://www.inquiringmind.com/article/2602_w_marlatt-interview-with-g-alan-marlatt-surfing-the-urge/

74-Ibid

75-Ibid

76-Frankl, V.: Widely quoted but source unknown

77- Griffin, K. 2010: Interview with G. Alan Marlatt: *Surfing the Urge*: From Online Exclusives for the Spring 2010 issue of *Inquiring Mind* (Vol. 26, No. 2), Inquiring Mind

78-Ibid

79- Mate, G. 2009: *In the Realm of Hungry Ghosts*: Vintage Canada

80-Ibid

81-From the film, *Dragon: The Bruce Lee Story* (1993)

82-Thich Nhat Hanh, 1995: *Peace Is Every Step: The Path of Mindfulness in Everyday Life*: Penguin (If you are interested to find out more about Thich Nhat Hanh's work, there is a documentary, *Walk With Me*, narrated by Benedict Cumberbatch)

83- Mate, G. 2009: *In the Realm of Hungry Ghosts*: Vintage Canada

84-Wallace, D. 2014: *Kings and Queens of Roam*: Simon and Schuster

85-Oida, Y. 1992: *An actor adrift*: Methuen Drama

86- McGonigal, K. 2011: *The Willpower Instinct: How Self-Control Works, Why It Matters, and What You Can Do to Get More of It*: Avery

87-Pierson, R. 2013: *Every Kid Needs a Champion*: TED talks education

88-Roth, B. 2013: *Bob Roth: The tipping point has tipped: Transcendental Meditation*

https://tmhome.com/experiences/bob-roth-the-tipping-point-has-tipped/

89-Smith, F. 2017: *How science is unlocking the secrets of drug addiction*: National Geographic magazine

90-Grant, A. 2013: *The Positive Power of Negative Thinking*: Linked In

https://www.linkedin.com/pulse/20131015140307-69244073-the-positive-power-of-negative-thinking

91-McGonigal, K. 2009: *The Virtue of Pessimism*: Psychology Today

ttps://www.psychologytoday.com/blog/the-science-willpower/201008/how-pessimism-can-make-you-rich

92- Mate. G quoted in Moorhead, J. 2018: *How dealing with past trauma maybe the key to breaking addiction*: The Guardian

93-Claxton. G. And Lucas. B. 2013: *What Kind of Teaching for What Kind Of Learning*: SSAT

94- Alinsky, S. 1989: *Rules for Radicals: A Pragmatic Primer for Realistic Radicals*: Vintage

95-Maslow, A.H. 1987: *Motivation and Personality. (3rd ed.)*: New York, NY: Harper & Row

96-Ferguson, D.2017: *Working-class children get less of everything in education – including respect*: The Guardian

97- Sellgren, K. 2017: *Social mobility: Class pay gap found in UK professions*: Family and Education, BBC News

98-Baker, S. 2017: *Dropout rates for young UK students rises again*: Times Higher Education

99-Townsend. M. 2018: *County lines gangs: how drug-running is fuelling knife crime*: The Guardian

100- Ibid

CHAPTER 6: THE INQUIRING CLASSROOM

Play away; techniques; strategies; concepts in this chapter that can be used in different contexts:

Body sculpting

The inner v the outer

Culture and identity

Parenthood

Personal map

Archetypes

Emotional memory

The realised self/the imaginary self

The movement of tai chi

In one of her first speeches as Ofsted's Chief Inspector, Amanda Spielman caused quite a stir when she asked an inquiry question, not dissimilar to the one Vigdís Finnbogadottir had asked about the meaning of her presidency: 'What do we understand to be the real substance of education? When we think about what the core purpose of education is, what comes first to our minds?' In her conclusion, she laid down a challenge: 'School leaders need to recognise how easy it is to focus on the performance of the school and lose sight of the pupil. I acknowledge that inspection may well have helped to tip this balance in the past.'[1] Thank goodness for that acknowledgement.

Ken Robinson's seminal report, *All Our Futures*, all those years ago, stated categorically the 'core business of schools is cultural education'.[2] The report places a central question at the very heart of what schools should be about: 'What does it mean to be human?' Perhaps much of what was being asked is captured by Pooja in her drama diary; she was only 13 at the time:

> 'There was a person within me waiting to come out and discover more but it was not easy. Year 7 was the beginning, as I moved onto year 8 I could feel a change in myself. In the Sita project I started to develop an interest in different cultures and aspects of the project. During that time I wanted to share my opinions with others, it was like letting part of my world go. It was then, when the Bollywood project came along, there was something to share with others. Everyone looked up to me. The platform on which I stand is now broad and wide. I wish to develop this platform even further.'

I've kept in contact with Pooja, and I can say with certainty that she still stands on that 'broad and wide' platform, an educator, arts manager, published author, curator, and artist. In her speech, Spielman rightly harks back to: 'a time (long ago) when teachers were taught the theory that underpins curriculum planning'.

But Robinson urges us to go beyond the theory, 'to forms of practice and provision'. So, in that spirit, let's explore some of this 'practice and provision', by opening the door, leaving it ajar for a moment. What did students like Pooja experience when the classroom door closed and the act of teaching was performed?

We always like to begin with a question, often a challenging and provocative question.

Play away; what might your relationship be to these two complex statements?

- 'My identity and my history are defined only by myself – beyond politics, beyond nationality, beyond religion and beyond skin.'[3]
- 'Knowledge of the self is the mother of all knowledge. So it is incumbent on me to know myself, to know it completely, to know its minutiae, its characteristics, its subtleties, and its very atoms.'[4]

Who am I; Who are We: Roots/Routes – a scheme of learning for 15-year-olds – is an inquiry into what Sawhney and Gibran are alluding to. Implicit in the homophone is a sense of journey and self-discovery. I was in search of a collective experience that would set us all on 'the walk toward' creating a dialogue with the self and with each other. By looking at an experience removed from the pupils' experiences, the first part of the inquiry offers a metaphor through which pupils can make connections that are personal, local, and global. Bolton states: 'Paradoxically, when drama experienced is distanced from the actual, the more "real" it will feel to the participants – more real and, of course, more significant... the problem of the teacher is to find a way of helping the child to tap his store of past feelings and to use physical resources as symbols.'[5]

Taking up Bolton's challenge, the unit begins with a chair and an old Jamaican woman. The chair is an easily transferable symbol on which the teacher can place any culture he wishes to explore, to offer the distance Bolton is recommending. For instance, when I taught in Thailand, I placed a Chinese woman, as China has played such an important part in Thai culture and history, something I knew many of the pupils were unaware of but had strong connections to. Another practitioner in a different context placed an old miner from the North of England on his chair.

Play away; who would you invite to sit on your chair in the centre of the room?

Part 1 – Grace

Pieces of colourful cloth are laid out on the floor. Pupils are asked to discuss what memories are triggered by the cloth. Having done a unit of work on Stanislavsky in Year 9, they understand an emotional memory can 'vibrate through the whole body'[6] but 'the problem is to recapture the emotion that once flashed by like a meteor'.[7] Responses range from past events – some funny, some sad – to memories of people such as grandparents and siblings, to memories of places, to sensory memories of smells and sounds. Ben Okri writes, 'stories are the secret reservoir of values',[8]; it's a key theme in the work.

A picture of an elderly Jamaican woman, Grace, is analysed.[9] A piece of narration is introduced:

'Grandma was sitting at her favourite spot, the big soft chair in front of the picture window.'[10]

A pupil sits on the chair with a patchwork quilt and a memory box. The pupils are asked to speculate by body sculpting. Pupils move parts of the student's body, justifying how it reveals an aspect of the woman's inner life. Maria, the student who'd been body sculpted, begins to speculate, nothing is certain:

> 'Amin suggested to me, "You should place Grace's hands under the patchwork quilt as it symbolises her reaching for her secret desires." As I moved my hands, this revealed a new perspective for me to reflect on, extending my views on Grace, as now I could picture her to be reserved. However, the experience allowed me to reflect that perhaps she wasn't reaching for a "secret desire" but instead seeking her trapped memories of her 'roots/routes'. I withdrew this, as Grace was looking ahead, symbolising a cloak blinding her from the sight of what she was searching for, suggesting that she was far from the reach of her roots. The proxemics between the box and myself as Grace's figure resembled the distance between Grace and her origin, which built up from the fact that the box was closed.'

In order to build, a further piece of narration is layered in:

> *Tanya, where is she? Grandma flexed her fingers to keep them from stiffening. She sucked in some air and said, "My mother made me that quilt but sometimes the old ways are forgotten."'*

Pupils are asked to record an initial response on a stick-it note and present it dramatically to the class, using the chair, the quilt, and the memory box as the central focus. The open response can range from poetry, to an inner monologue, to a drawing. Their responses are stored in the memory box along with a number of artifacts such as jewelry, old photographs, a passport. The emphasis is on deconstructing the outer signs to discover her inner life. 'Everything presented to the spectator within the theatrical frame is a sign.'[11] Listen to another student's early inquiry, to get a flavor of the kind of engagement the pupils were experiencing; he's clearly in a dialogue:

'When I first saw the image of Grace, I received a strong impression of loneliness. Her distant gaze and body turned against her quilt brought out that she was solemnly remembering another, perhaps better, time in her life. I wanted to convey these initial feelings of isolation in my solo sequence of haikus: *"The patchwork woman/ She is tearing at the seams."* Using a length of cloth as a prop, I forcefully wrapped it around my arm, using an angular, tense body to bring out Grace's internal pain, showing her restlessness in being bound to her memories, her old age. Conversely, I said the first section of the line with a soft tone, a slow pace to convey Grace's outward calm facade which hid her chaotic inner. After this, I sharply pulled on the coiled cloth, unwinding it in an aggressive manner by crouching at a low level, thrusting my right arm high above me to represent Grace unravelling her memories, perhaps yearning to return to better times. The speech that accompanied this was elongated, said with a slow pace but high intensity and pained tone to show Grace's solemn mood in returning to moments of the past which were no longer with her. This idea was challenged by peers, who labelled the cloth, a 'tacky fabric', claiming the quilt did nothing to console Grace by appearing to be hostile to the cloth, even abandoning it completely in their explorations, showing how they prioritised the present day over the struggles and pleasures of the past. At this point, despite being at an early stage in the exploration, I felt that Grace's routes – the memories she has, the things she has done – very strongly made up her roots, her background.'

New layers are added, a picture of a market and third piece of narration:

'We used to go to market once a week.'

A whole class sound collage of the market is created; pupils leading a blindfolded partner on a sensory 'tour' of the market;

these are activities that build to improvisations of memories Grace recalls as she sits alone on her chair. Then she remembers the huge storm that hit Jamaica in the 1950s:

> *'Grace's eyes grew dark and distant. She turned away and gazed out of the window absentmindedly rubbing the pieces of material through her fingers. She remembered when they called for her mother the day after the storm to come quickly. Her mother left straightaway. It was morning of market but the familiar sounds, the familiar crowds were not there. When she reached the square she would never forget what she saw. Things were never the same after this.'*

The class physically turn the studio into the unforgettable picture Grace has of that terrible moment when she entered the market square. The teacher in role, as the young Grace, now enters the created landscape and begins the search for her mother. It's often a powerful, collective experience. Afterwards it's important to give the students space in small groups to explore further and deepen the ideas, feelings and themes that had arisen. Here's what Shazna experienced; her 'walk toward' is allowing her to make connections, to start to see things through a new lens:

> 'Following the decision of her being separated from her mother in the storm, our initial idea was to have a sound collage consisting of what she heard in the situation. However Nahid's idea of using mirrors developed my understanding because we were in the moment ourselves. His idea deepened the understanding of Grace's character as now I related to her being a child, forced to grow up because of the situations she was placed in. The pain that Grace must have felt shaped my feelings, leading me to think about the transient aspect of the things we treasure the most. Using this newfound interpretation, I decided to treat the whole class sequence as an opportunity to present parts of my haikus, *"Wanting to turn away/ Needing to move forward."* Playing a hesitant Grace when I went out helped

me physicalise her confusion. I decided to reach out then immediately retracted as if the idea of facing the truth caused Grace immense pain which forced me to think of the times where she would've been forced to face the reality of where her 'roots' lay, even though she wished "to move forward". Her past was looming over her which I showed by repeatedly looking back hinting at the existence in Grace's mind of an unseen force that she ran from. Grace would have never ended up in Britain without the disaster in Jamaica, and if the conflict within her had led her to go down another path, another route, present day Grace would have been a lot different. It took me to thinking about my parents' 'roots/routes' and to my own understanding of this.'

In the reflection that follows, historical information from Dodgson's *Motherland*[12] is given about the 'push' and 'pull' factors at this time in the Caribbean. *Motherland* is made up of testimony from women who'd lived through these times in the 1950s. An extract from the BBC's *Windrush* series is also watched. The consequence of this was Camilla now needed to 'research my grandmother coming to England because she was one of the first to leave Dominica'. Camilla's desire to research had begun her 'walk toward'.

It's worth pausing for a moment. I've offered this experience many times to several generations of young people. Therefore, over time, I thought I'd gained a fairly extensive understanding about this period of history. However, like so many of us, I'd no idea about what one politician called 'a national disgrace': 'My parents were from Guyana. Their ancestors were enslaved and colonised like millions of others in the Caribbean, and when they were invited to come to rebuild Britain and our public services after World War II, they were invited as citizens. The way in which the Windrush children are being treated is a national disgrace. This is not a glitch in the system – this is the system.'[13] There may well have been students in my drama studio experiencing what Nadine has had to endure. Born in Birmingham, growing up in London along with her mother and two sisters, she has been unable to obtain a British passport:

'My mum applied for passports for her and my two younger sisters and that's how it came out that, because she wasn't born here, she wasn't a British citizen, so therefore we weren't either. Because of that they confiscated my passport. We've been told that we have to do a citizenship test in order to get passports and ever since then it's been a battle as to whether we're going to get them or not.

We wouldn't be able to afford the cost of applying for citizenship. I was only 13 when this happened and my mum didn't tell me any of it until I got a bit older. We tried to get passports again but every route brought a dead end. I just put it to the back of my mind until recently when this Windrush situation came up. Not being able to travel has had a big impact on our lives. There are places I'd like to go and see that I can't because I don't have a passport. I'm stuck here. It even affects me work-wise because there are jobs I've applied for in the past that I've been turned down for as a result.'[14]

I know my students would have engaged in Nadine's search for her identity:

'I still feel British in the sense that I was born here but I don't feel British because I can't get a British passport. I do everything that a British person does. I work, I pay taxes, I pay my bills, I pay rent, I live here every day. It's my home, but at the same time I can't get a passport. It feels like I'm here but I don't belong here. My mum was born in St Lucia, so some people would argue that she's St Lucian, but she hasn't been there since she was 8. I don't feel St Lucian because I've only been there once. I've never lived there so I don't know it, whereas I know Britain. Britain is more my home than St Lucia.'[15]

People have spoken out. Natalie Barnes was one of the first: 'I'm so glad we spoke out and I'm so glad it meant so many other people came forward with their stories.'[16] Her mother, Paulette Wilson, is 61 years old, a former House of Commons canteen worker (you really couldn't make it up) and has lived in Britain for 50 years. Despite this, she was shamefully held in Yarl's Wood detention centre, having been wrongly classified as an illegal immigrant, sent to Heathrow and threatened with deportation to Jamaica, a country she hasn't visited since she was 10. She did finally receive an apology from the immigration minister at the despatch box in the House of Commons.

> Play away; notice what reading this makes you feel.

All our certainties have been challenged once again. We have to begin, once more, the 'walk toward' if we are to make sense of what we now know. What I'm certain of is there are several generations of students who've grown up. Because of what they experienced in the drama studio, it's my belief they will be prepared to carry on with their 'walk toward' understanding the dialogue is indeed 'never-ending'.

Part 2 – Leaving and Arriving

A context is now set. Work is done on the dockside as the young Grace leaves for England. A picture from Dodgson's *Motherland* of Victoria station with newly-arrived immigrants from the Caribbean is also explored. A shocking piece of film from the BBC's *Windrush* series is watched, in which pupils hear testimony about what life was like for the new immigrants living in England in the 1950s. They're rocked back to hear the slogan, 'KBW-Keep Britain White', and appalled by the undercover black reporter trying to unsuccessfully find accommodation. Some empathetic role play, in which pupils play both a pregnant Grace and the landlord, allows them to understand Steven Lawrence's father,

Neville, plea for the importance, 'to be able to see what it might be like to be in someone else's situation... we can only change ourselves, perhaps it's a tiny grain of sand but sooner or later all those grains together mount up to something very powerful'.[17]

It all leads to an extensive piece of work entitled 'Leaving and Arriving'. Pupils are given the space to make a response but are also invited to have a conversation with someone who experienced this kind of leaving and arriving. They are asked to bring in an object that can be used in the drama. It isn't as easy as it sounds, for many students have never had this conversation. Clint Dyer, the director of the outstanding production, *The Big Life*, explains: 'My parents never really spoke to me about the journey or the first 10 or 15 years over here. I talked to them when I was finessing the script... it was one of the most beautiful times of my life with my parents... when I asked before they said, 'some of it was really bad and I don't want to go into it'... but now they enjoyed talking about it. They also loved it that I was impressed. Doing this has really helped me realise who my parents are.'[18]

Similarly astonishing things happen with the students. Syed's elderly father reached under the bed and brought out a suitcase containing the clothes he'd worn on arrival in England. Fozia's mother climbed up and brought down a box with possessions she'd hastily gathered as she left her village in Bangladesh at the age of 14. Neither child had ever seen these things, let alone talked about them. Syed's use of the sweat-stained, red handkerchief; Fozia's use of the Bengali cardboard snakes and ladders; Rahim's use of the key he'd never seen before, which his mother had used to open her first door in England – all framed within the context of Grace's experiences – allowed the pupils to get inside Rilke's assertion:

'We are born, so to speak, provisionally, it does not matter where. It is only gradually that we compose within ourselves our true place of origin so that we may be born there retrospectively and each day more definitely.'[19]

> Play away; unpick the complex layers within Rilke's writing to discover what it means to you. What would it mean to Nadine and the children of the Windrush generation?

It certainly challenges the racist provocation of Tebbit's 'cricket test': 'If all the time somebody is looking back over their shoulder to the country from which their family came instead of to the country where they live and are making their home, you scratch your head if you are an integrationist and ask: are they really integrated or are they just living here?'[20] For Gayatri, the drama allowed her to phone her grandfather who, in telling her the origin of her name for the first time, explained to her what life was like under British rule. It was something she was feeling keenly, as her family was facing deportation back to India at the time. (It was happening then; mercifully she was allowed to stay, achieving 10 A/A* GCSEs.) Zainab, who was having difficulties in her relationship with her mother, was able to write in her coursework:

'Talking to my mum has really inspired me. I have used the feelings that my mum felt when she thought it was her against the whole world. It has also helped my mum as I was the first child to ask about her journey to Britain. It helped her to open up and build more trust in me. It made my mum very happy and proud as I was taking an interest in the land where my roots go down to. It also made me feel very good about myself, it has brought me and my mum closer together.'

For Adil, who'd just returned from Pakistan due to the death of his grandmother, the use of her gold watch was part of his grieving:

'This is the only reason
This is the only reason I am living
She passed away, it was clarified

139

This clock is now what I remember her by
Then I thought of what she said,
She wouldn't last long.'

Part 3 - Generations

In this phase, the complexities of the generations are explored. In her challenging book, *Why I am No Longer Talking to White People about Race*, Reni Eddo-Lodge captures many of the issues and feelings swirling around the drama studio as the project returns to the present and Grace's relationship with her daughter, Georgia and granddaughter, Tanya. 'If you are an immigrant – even if you're second or third generation – this is personal. You are multiculturalism.'[21]

It's interesting that dual heritage is always raised by the students as they inevitably want to make the father of Grace's own child and grandchild from another ethnic group. There's clearly urgency amongst the students to explore what Eddo-Lodge describes here: '"My mum's white and my dad's black," says Jessica, "and really both my mum and my dad have brought me up in a kind of colour-blind way... When I see a white parent with a mixed-race kid, I think, 'Is that child going to get what they need?' Because I didn't get what I needed."'[22] Eddo-Lodge reflects, 'Jessica and her mother's relationship is nuanced.' She believes it shows 'a truth that is often left out in clunky media coverage' and probably left out in school classrooms. She puts forward a reason which is the thesis of her book, 'that it is not enacted by malicious monsters driven by ill will, but that it happens by way of whiteness'.[23]

> Play away; discuss. Be warned, it will spark a heated debate.

My inner London classroom, just like our sporting teams, is born of a contemporary Britain full of 'youth and vigour and diversity and modernity'.[24] However, Eddo-Lodge and others point out, while this is all for the good, we shouldn't kick back and become too comfortable: 'A diverse nation is a boon in the modern world. It is a fact of life. But it throws up challenges.'[25] Far from shying away from such challenges, the students are eager to explore these nuances. It's the 'depth of interplay'[26] between cultures which Brahmachari and Landon-Smith talk about. Some may ask, is multiculturalism nothing more than a variant on contemporary art practices? For it not to be, then it has to be about relationships and the conditions that will allow a meeting of cultural identities possible. This work allowed a group of young people 'with different past and different futures' to 'hear their stories, listen to their language, music and backgrounds, seeing the images and designs that move them... to understand other cultures from the inside'.[27] Peter Brook expresses it like this: 'Each human being carries within him\her all the continents, but each of us knows only one of them. So when a person with one known continent and a mass of dark continents meets someone else whose condition is the same, and they communicate, there is illumination for each.'[28]

To facilitate this exploration, an inclusive strategy is chosen which allows everyone to have a space to 'communicate'. The class writes a collective letter from Grace to the newly-born grandchild, Tanya, that she will give to her when she is old enough. It's safely stored in the memory box. The character of Tanya is a complex symbol of who the pupils are and wish to be. She's the child many of these students will bring up in later years. It's part of that conversation which keeps cropping up, to live with a whole heart. We've seen earlier in the book how the wider school culture has placed these pupils in this ongoing conversation. In their collective letter, these adolescent students passionately urge the child to 'think of me as an angel that will always be there for you. Always be proud, hold your head high, never give up, for it is you who carves out your destiny. May this memory box serve you as it has served me.'

A multiple hot-seat is carried out in which the pupils go around and ask questions of four different people who knew Grace and her daughter, Georgia, as she was growing up. Georgia is as close to the pupils' parents as we can get. The hot-seaters present speeches getting to the essence of the relationship that are intercut by flashbacks of the relationship presented by the rest of the class. Pupils make a presentation entitled, 'Georgia'. It involves them taking out and putting away a memory using the powerful artifact of the memory box, as they search for deeper ways of expressing their ideas and feelings about the relationship between a mother and her daughter.

The previous narration about Tanya is read and these lines added: '*Grandma turned her head towards the sunlight and closed her eyes.*' The class is told there's some kind of tension existing between Grace and her grandchild. Exploratory strategies such as freeze frames; improvisation; Forum theatre; teacher in role, can all be used to explore this. We watch an extract from the BBC's adaptation of *White Teeth*, entitled *The Trouble with Millet*. It's the moment when Irie Jones, the dual heritage teenager, has to painfully endure being the helpless observer of the unrequited love of her life, Millet – the charismatic Bengali leader of the Year 11 gang – flirt with the white girl at the school fence. We're now firmly in world the students have to navigate every day. The students are invited to create a response called 'Tanya', which offers them a space to explore this complex world; their lives and their relationships, 'the personal and the local'.

But it's my world, too. Here's an opportunity to introduce *On Children* by Kahil Gibran – a poem that has had a profound influence on my life. The poem has been, and still is, my guide over the last 28 years, in a determined attempt to avoid Larkin's self fulfilling prophesy:

> 'They fuck you up, your mum and dad
> They may not mean to, but they do.'[29] (the key line,
> I never meant to!)

142

As a flawed father of two daughters, I present the poem to my students, telling them here's how I tried to bring up my own children. For some of the students, it's a shock – two daughters given what they see as a great deal of freedom; some are not so certain anymore. I tell them, just wait until we explore *Equus* and what this will bring up about parents and their children. 'The walk toward' has only just begun.

> Play away; how were you brought up? As a parent or a parent-to-be, what's your relationship with Gibran's poem?

'Your children are not your children.
They are the sons and daughters of Life's longing for itself.
They come through you but not from you,
And though they are with you yet they belong not to you.

You may give them your love but not your thoughts,
For they have their own thoughts.
You may house their bodies but not their souls,
For their souls dwell in the house of tomorrow,
Which you cannot visit, not even in your dreams.
You may strive to be like them,
But seek not to make them like you.
For life goes not backward nor tarries with yesterday.

You are the bows from which your children
As living arrows are sent forth.
The archer sees the mark upon the path of the infinite,
And He bends you with His might
That His arrows may go swift and far.
Let your bending in the archer's hand be for gladness;
For even as He loves the arrow that flies,
So He loves also the bow that is stable.'[30]

I'm able to perch on top of Bloom's ladder, as I sit on the floor as a friend of the family who has known the three generations of this family. Through the safety of role, I create with the students what it might feel like to bring up dual heritage children. Likewise, through the safety of role, the students, as Grace or Georgia or Tanya, are able to run all the way up and down Bloom's higher order thinking taxonomy as they explain, clarify, justify, compare, and finally create what it feels like for them 'being human'.

Part 4 – Personal Map

At this point, we pull out of the drama context. The pupils are told they will spend some time working on themselves making connections with their inner life, as well as with each other and the drama they've created. One of the aims is to introduce them to the concept of archetypes. I've increasingly drawn on Jung's definition of Archetypes linking our 'stories'/schemes of learning to the cognitive development of the students. At the centre of Jungian thought is: 'All the most powerful ideas in history go back to archetypes.' These are not inborn ideas, but 'typical forms of behaviour which, once they become conscious, naturally present themselves as ideas and images'.[31] This is the stuff of the drama studio, as is Jung's fundamental belief the psyche operates by means of four functions: thinking, feeling, sensation, and intuition. Because we've understood about the importance of paying attention to our inner life, it's a core theme. Just like Jung, we know only the person who's willing to 'Consciously assent to the power of the inner voice becomes a personality'.[32]We also know by now, in doing so we are 'enabled to live life more completely'.[33]

These are the archetypes I offer the pupils, but of course there are many more:

THE MAGICIAN: *The ability to make/bring about change*
THE WANDERER: *When we are searching*
THE ALTRUIST: *When we help people*
THE ORPHAN: *When we feel lost*

THE INNOCENT: *When we become childlike; naive*
THE WARRIOR: *When we stand up for what we believe/ when we take risk*
THE FOOL/THE CLOWN: *When we mess about/draw attention to hide our true selves*
THE TRICKSTER: *When we play people/we are dishonest*
THE HERO/HEROINE: *When we commit acts that are 'heroic'*
MOTHER/FATHER: *When we play a paternal role*
SON/DAUGHTER
BROTHER/SISTER
KING/QUEEN: *When we feel so good about ourselves*
DEVIL: *When we commit acts that are very wrong*
THE CREATOR
THE DESTROYER: *Positive and negative*
THE RULER: *Positive and negative*
THE SAGE: *When we seek truths that will set us free*

We can identify these multiple archetypes in their thoughts, feelings, sensations, intuition, in a poem about the 7/7 bombing:

'There are some that say
"You thought you were untouchable
But it's England's time to pay
What goes around comes around
Another Iraqi massacre found
Not a word is said
For the thousands dead."
An old woman shakes her head
And quietly, without a shout
Points out
"The Koran says that if you kill a single person
You kill all humanity."
I am confused, I don't understand…
Everything's changed
Everything's different
But I know my fear

145

Has made me strong
For fire is my beat, my pulse, my song
At the moment I feel ripped apart
But I have fire in my heart
And nothing can extinguish it.'

(Part of a longer collective poem, written in 2005 by a drama ensemble two days after the bomb exploded at Aldgate, five minutes away from the school in Whitechapel, East London.)

Rukia will express her multiple identities in a poem she wrote to the National Theatre, in reply to their question, 'Who are you?'

'...I am lucky you see
There is more than one factor
Which defines me.
Sure I'm a Muslim but I am Bengali too
And I am a teenager, a woman
So yes I am confused
But not about my life
Or the person you think I'm forced to be
What you don't understand is
That I feel and I am so free
Never once in my life have I felt
Suppressed or constrained
By my religion or my identity...'

As will Naomi, in an extraordinary performance that explored her identity as a black woman growing up in a predominantly Bengali environment:

'I am no-one's victim
I will not wear scarves you have spun for me
Nor the sorrow you have composed for me
I am a King, I dare you to tell me otherwise
My skin is as dark as midnight
As black as charcoal...'

146

I will use the archetypal model to modify Jahid's behavior, telling him he was a Trickster the other day giving into peer pressure because he's hiding feelings of being an Orphan, unable to break free of the negative influences of his friends. We talked, and in doing so both us became Wanderers. Unfortunately, Jahid never made the vital step to becoming the Warrior he needed to be if he was to break free. In despair, his parents fled with him to Kent. Turn back to Chapter 5 and identify all the multiple archetypes swirling around in Hashim's poem.

> Play away; take a typical day this week. Identify the multiple archetypes you adopted. How were they expressed on your outer? What does it tell you about your inner life? Then, if you feel so inclined, keep a diary noting the archetypes you continue to adopt; which ones keep cropping up? Which are the archetypes you rarely take on? As you pay heed to your inner voice, what insight might this offer you about who you are and who you wish to be? It's all part of a reimagining of self.

But I'm jumping ahead. The pupils briefly return to Stanislavsky's question: 'Can you picture to yourself what our emotion memory is really like?'[34] Stanislavsky goes on to offer the metaphor of the emotional memory as a huge house. Within it lie numerous rooms, in which stands a huge desk. If you open the drawers of any of the desks, you'll find a tiny bead. Each bead is a specific memory. Pupils are reminded it's entirely their choice which beads they wish to handle, but whatever ones they choose, they must be sure they can handle them. In other words, they're being asked to edit. No-one is asking them to recall painful moments in their life. I've carried out the exercise in numerous settings with pupils and adults. So far, no-one has ever run out of the room or broken down. However, that's not to underestimate in any way what Pearson describes: 'Archetypes provide the deep structure for

147

human motivation and meaning. When we encounter them in art, literature, sacred texts, advertising – or in individuals or groups – they evoke deep feeling within us.'[35] So, just as Stanislavsky asked 'an actor to work on himself', the pupils are given the tools to do this – an A3 sheet of paper and a set of coloured pens. They're told no-one will see the paper; it's theirs; it's confidential. They find their place, their 'nest', in the room where they will lose the outer and work with the inner. It's also worth noting these are pupils I've known for at least a year in a GCSE ensemble, but many of the pupils I've taught over several years. It's not something I would attempt unless there was this level of trust.

> Play away; join in, have a go at your own personal map and see what you discover about yourself.

Stage 1

They are asked to record on the sheet the basic facts of their life. 'I was born; I went to primary school; my sister got married.' They're asked to think of their life as a shape. If they believe it has been a straight line with few issues, then they record the facts in this shape. If they feel it has been rather messy and random, then they place the facts in a shape to reflect this feeling.

Stage 2

In a different colour, they're asked to attach a memory they associate with each fact. The example I offer is, 'I went to primary school and it was raining.'

Stage 3

In a different colour again, they're asked to attach an object they associate with each fact and memory. My example continues, 'I remember the shiny black shoes my mum made me wear.'

Stage 4

In another colour, they attach to the memory the emotions they recall feeling. 'I remember I felt excited and scared.'

Stage 5

My list of archetypes is offered. They're asked to attach to each memory, in large capital letters, the archetypal role or roles they felt they adopted. I tell them on my first day at Primary School I played several roles: 'I was the Orphan because I was scared, the Wanderer because I wanted to know what school was going to be like, but I played the Clown to hide my mixed emotions.' This is a powerful moment, because by now the page is always very full. It shows them no life is ordinary. We all live unique and full lives. It also shows them the type of roles they've been adopting, which tells them something profound about who they are and might become. If Warrior appears a lot, then they've had the capacity to stand up for what they believe. If the Altruist has appeared many times, they've been selfless and caring.

Stage 6

They now write a heading, 'The Realised Self', under which they list all the things they believe they are today, here and now: 'I'm good at football; I love my parents; I'm hard working.' Then they write a heading, 'The Imaginary Self, Positive', under which they're invited to list all the positive things they could become: 'I could work in another country; I could have children.' Then they're asked to reverse this and under the title, 'The Imaginary Self, Negative', they're invited to write all the things they imagine they couldn't possibly become: 'I won't let money influence my choice of job; I'll never intentionally hurt someone.' The sheet now tells them a huge amount about who they are and who they wish to become. They can clearly see the personal map is something everyone carries with them throughout their life. It's part of the 'never-ending' dialogue. They're encouraged to reflect on the issues they've successfully resolved, on the issues they would like to address before they leave school, and on the issues they know they will need to return to at a later date.

Stage 7

They're asked to write 3 Haikus about their life to capture the 'deep feeling within'. They're told they may be asked to share their Haikus, so they have to decide whether to be overt,

> 'One day he was late
> One day he couldn't make it
> One day he had gone' (GCSE student)

Or abstract, so no-one needs to know what exactly the poem is about,

> 'I step after step
> Towards the white unlocked door
> I see them waiting' (GCSE student)

Haikus are an excellent form, as they're quick to write, don't require huge amounts of language, and cut to the essence. More challenged pupils don't have to become caught up in issues of meter. It might be worth sharing how Shubna was feeling at this moment. It may be similar to the concerns some may have at this point:

> 'I suddenly remembered the day my dad had a heart attack 7 years ago, he was only 35. At the time I was 8 years old. My stomach began to knot itself and I felt sick. When I was kneeling on the classroom floor, the image I remember is of me praying with my mum and begging God not to take my dad away.'

Not all students would be having such intense feelings. Some, like Marwan, would 'feel very comfortable to write all that has happened to me. I never thought my life looked that way until I wrote it down.' However, all would be feeling what Anish Kapoor beautifully expresses, 'If there is anything I deeply believe in, it is that one has to somehow learn to live with not quite knowing what's going on. That is the process out of which this thing we call art arises.'[36] Kapoor is aligned to Freire's 'spirit in which we are certain by not being certain of our certainties'. Look at what the 'the walk toward' had led the students to feel.

By the end of the work, Shubna was now able to say this: 'For me, this was one of the most challenging lessons this term, nonetheless I felt a real sense of achievement as I felt members of my group had faced many of their demons. I had let someone else invade my space and this has been a great accomplishment for me. I feel I have developed a lot.' For Marwan: 'To me, life is very sacred. I think life goes by so quickly that you don't have time to despair, I just think life has many ups and downs which makes me the person I am today, very comfortable and confident with myself.' Deepa concludes: 'I am dealing with my past. I am proud I was able to let it out. I learnt that I am a strong person full of emotions, even though there are things going on in my life.' Zakiya described the activity as 'one of the most important days of my life, as this has opened my eyes'. The next section will show how the inquiring classroom allowed these pupils to arrive at such affirming experiences.

Part 5 – Connections

Pupils are given a new body of movement through which they'll express themselves. They're taught a sequence of tai chi and yoga moves, because that's what I practise.[37] Pictures are put on the floor. Pupils label the archetypes they feel are portrayed in the images. Quick freeze frames are made of some of the archetypes using the new body of movement. The striking originality of their images is due to the newly-acquired language. Contrasting paired words are offered such as 'courage/fear; compassion/cruelty; independence/dependence'.

Pupils are asked to interpret the words by creating a motif, using the tai chi/yoga movement. They repeat this three times until they have a sequence of six words. They're then asked to return to their personal map to create a solo ceremony about themselves, based on six contrasting words. They can only use the new movement, their Haikus, and any personal object. Once created, pupils choose someone they trust to share their ceremonies with, emphasizing it's entirely up to the individual how much they wish to divulge. In pairs, they now create their own ceremonies called 'Connections'. Deep, complex conversations naturally occur about similarities and differences, using the language of archetypes. The sharing and the connections made is a key milestone for the group in their search 'to become someone else that you were not in the beginning'.[38] As one student put it, 'It was a chance to see the real Jalal.' It's all part of the process of the reimagining of the self.

Part 6 – A Final Response

The last stage is to offer a wide range of texts that explore the themes, ideas, and feelings which have arisen from the project. Texts range from film to literature to articles.[39] Pupils are given the space to explore with others whatever has interested them in a final response. They're empowered to search for content and form. Like Kapoor, they're learning 'to live with not quite knowing what's going on'. But you'll have to take my word for it; the 'walk toward' did produce 'this thing we call art'. It was created for no-one but ourselves, private, behind the door. It's the same process Mate captures when articulating his motivation to write, it's an inner need to express oneself 'so that others might hear me but so that I could hear myself'.[40]

This glimpse of what goes on behind the door of an inquiring classroom is hard to define by a single word. However, the students are always the greatest advocates of this kind of nurturing, empowering experience that straddles both our private and public selves. I'll leave it to Akbar to define what the 'never-ending' dialogue means to him; in doing so he's asking us to reimagine the world,

> 'As an art form, drama captures much more than a mere painting. Therefore, drama would strengthen the analytical skills of anyone who is curious about understanding things below the surface. Drama isn't about "acting things out". Drama is essential for a human being if he is to express his feelings and ideas in such a way that others will understand your point of view. In my opinion, if all the people in the world obtained these skills to express themselves exactly and to be able to understand the feelings beneath another fellow human being, the world would be much more peaceful, free, and understanding. Such is the power of drama.'

1-Spielman, A. 2017: *HMCI's commentary: recent primary and secondary curriculum research*: Gov.UK

2-Robinson, K. 1999: *All Our Futures: Creativity, Culture and Education*: NACCCE report

3-Sawhney, N. 1999: Album notes from, *Beyond Skin*: Outcaste Records

4-Gibran, K. 1918: *The Madman, His Parables and Poems*: Alfred A. Knopf

5-Bolton, G. and Heathcote, D. 1995: *Drama for Learning: Dorothy Heathcote's Mantle of the Expert Approach to Education*: Heinemann

6-Ribot, T. 2006: *The Psychology of the Emotions*: Kessinger Publishing

7-Stanislavsky, C. trans. Hapgood, E. 1986: *An Actor Prepares*: Methuen

8-Okri, B. 1996: *Birds of Heaven*: Phoenix

9-The picture is taken from a picture book: Flournoy, V. 1996: *The Patchwork Quilt*: Scholastic Printing

10-Ibid (all the narration is from the picture book)

11-Aston, E. and Savona, G. 1991: *Theatre as sign-system: a semiotics of text and Performance*: Routledge.

12-Dodgson, D. 1984: *Motherland*: Heinemann

Elyse Dodgson died in 2018. In her Obituary, I was very moved to read:

> 'At her funeral, her family showed an extract from *Motherland,* the verbatim play Elyse had created with her students from Vauxhall Manor girls' school in 1982. She had asked her students to interview their mothers who had come to England on the Windrush. In the extract, a Jamaican mother is afraid to say goodbye to her daughter so tries to leave without saying goodbye but the daughter catches her. Brilliant and heartbreaking.'

Angelis, A. 2018: *Elyse Dodgson remembered by April De Angelis*: The Guardian

13-Sanghani, R. 2018: *The forgotten women of the Windrush scandal*: The Stylist

14-Gil, N. 2018: *'"They Took My Passport": A 26-year-old On How The Windrush Scandal Has Impacted Her Family*: Refinery29: https://www.refinery29.uk/2018/04/197369/windrush-scandal

15-Ibid

16-Gentleman, A. 2018: *'"I'm glad we spoke out": Windrush victim who shone a light on the scandal*: The Guardian

17-Bennathan, J. 2001: Education resource materials: *My England*: ARC Theatre Ensemble and Carel Press

18-Ojumu, A. 2004: *Reach for the ska*: The Guardian

19-Rilke, R. Trans Hull, R. 1946: *Selected Letters of Rainer Maria Rilke: 1902-1926*: Macmillan

20-Buettner, E.2016: *Europe after Empire: Decolonization, Society, and Culture*: Cambridge University Press

21-Eddo-Lodge, R. 2017: *Why I'm No Longer Talking to White People About Race:* Bloomsbury

22-i Team. 2017: *Reni Eddo-Lodge interview: 'White people are absolutely terrified of being branded racist'*: i News

23-Eddo-Lodge, R. 2017: *Why I'm No Longer Talking to White People About Race:* Bloomsbury

24-Muir, H. 2018: *How England's World Cup progress gives us a shot at a hopeful future:* The Guardian

25-Ibid

26-Brahmachari, S.,Landon-Smith, K. 2001: *Time 2001-placing teachers' voices at the centre of intercultural debate:* Drama 8.2(Summer 2001)

27-Robinson, K. 1999: *All Our Futures: Creativity, Culture and Education:* NACCCE report

28-Brook quoted in Roose-Evans, J. 1970: *Experimental Theatre-from Stanislavsky to Peter Brooke:* Routledge

29-Larkin, P. 2001: *This be the verse from Collected Poems:* Farrar Straus and Giroux

30-Gibran, K. 2015: *On Children* from *The Prophet:* Wisehouse Classic Edition

31-Jung, C. Ed: Fordham, M. 1953: *Psychiatric Studies. The Collected Works of C. G. Jung Vol. 1:* Routledge

32-Ibid

33-Storr, A. 1983: *The essential Jung:* Princeton University Press

34-Stanislavsky, C. trans. Hapgood, E. 1986: *An Actor Prepares:* Methuen

35-Pearson, C. 1986: *The Hero Within: Six Archetypes We Live By:* Harper Collins

36-Kapoor, A. 2009: *Anish Kapoor shows how art can access the sublime:* Metro

37-A language of movement based on tai chi and yoga:

> Turn Carry the ball Defend Pause Lift Hang Punch Jump Hand circle Open the door Stepping Roll Push Bend Walk Kick Bow and Arrow Stretch Rock Glide Hover

38-Foucault, M. 2000: *Ethics: Subjectivity and Truth, Volume 1*: Penguin

39- Clips range from Spielberg's *Amistad*, Arc Theatre's *My England*, Winterbotttom's *In This World*, Broomfield's *Ghosts*, Prasad's *Brothers in Trouble*, Chadha's *Bhaji On The Beach*, The BBC's *Life Isn't All Ha Ha Hee Hee* and *Goodness Gracious Me,* as well as documentaries around subjects such as Steven Lawrence, the banning of the veil in France, extremism, The BNP, The London Bomb, The Bangladesh Community in Tower Hamlets. A booklet is read which includes extracts from Smith's *White Teeth*, Macpherson's definition of Institutionalised Racism, extracts from *Telling it Like It Is: Young Asian Women Talk* (Livewire) Kassam. N (Editor), Zephaniah's discussion about identity, *What Am I Going On About* (from his introduction to his *Too Black, Too Strong*), as well as his poem, *What Steven Lawrence has Taught us.* Other poetry includes Savriti Hensman's *Just Another Asian*, Claude McKay's *I Shall Return,* Bhatt's *Search for my Tongue*

40-Mate, G. 2009: *In the Realm of Hungry Ghosts*: Vintage Canada

CHAPTER 7: THE PROCESS OF RESILIENCE

Play away; techniques; strategies; concepts in this chapter that can be used in different contexts:

Resilience

Action theory model/creativity model

Multiple worlds

Story of learning

Growth/fixed mind set

Vulnerability

I always feel slightly inadequate switching radio channels when Melvin Bragg's *In Our Time* comes on and listen to Talk Sport instead. I've nothing against Melvin; I've tried hard to listen to several of the episodes. There was the one about 'Kant's Categorical Imperative'; then there was the one about 'The Paleocene-Eocene Thermal Maximum'; I think the one about 'Zeno's Paradoxes' did for me. I just don't understand what they're talking about. It's like all these very likeable, erudite intellectuals are talking a different language, so I drift off. Sorry, just being honest. However, a recent edition held my attention. I'll let Melvin introduce the episode:

> 'Hello, Frederick Douglass was born into slavery in Maryland in 1818 and, once he had escaped, became one of that century's most prominent abolitionists. He was such a good orator, his opponents doubted his story, but he told it in grim detail in 1845 in his book, *Narrative of the Life of Frederick Douglass, an American Slave*.'[1]

> Play away; if you're a regular listener of the programme, what senses are recalled when you hear Melvin's voice in this introduction? The *smell* of coffee? The *feeling* of those bubbles in the bath? The familiar *sight* of traffic jams on the M25? For me it's all the senses and my dog, Milly, who's sadly not with us anymore, but that's for another time.

It was the word 'orator' that encouraged me to listen on. When Black History Month comes around, Douglass is often held up as 'not a monument, but a mind-set'.[2] Even Trump gets in on the act; he praised Douglass at a Black History Month event (yep, he was there) in his unique, monosyllabic style, fingers pointing and jabbing (The Physical Strand – it would make a great lesson): 'Frederick Douglass is an example of somebody who's done an amazing job and is getting recognized more and more, I notice.'[3]

'Amazing job.' Trump's words; I'm not making it up. Got to also love the fact the White House misspelt Douglass' name in a press release as they announced Trump would be outing Douglass at the event. I should really out someone as well – my colleague, Jeffrey. He's in fact Jeffrey Boakye. As well as being a teacher, he's the author of two books which I can highly recommend – *Hold Tight: Black Masculinity, Millennials & the Meaning of Grime* and *Black, Listed*. He also writes a blog under the pseudonym, Unseen Flirtations. In a blog entitled, *Teaching to the converted, Black History Month*, he writes:

> 'With another Black History Month on the horizon, I'm thinking that I might have a responsibility to offer these kids deeper insights into Black British culture, not because I'm black, but because I appreciate the nuances of that culture. I can see the provenance of various urban genres and their wider socio-economic relevances. I can place myself in a socio-cultural historical context. I'd like to think that I can hold my own in a rave just as much as in a debate about UK race relations in the 21st century. And if we're serious about giving kids a cultural capital that means anything, perhaps we should offer them opportunities for similar understanding of their selves. Definitely something to think about.'[4]

Douglass' family reacted to Trump by reminding the world of what he stood for:, 'Like the President, we use the present tense when referencing Douglass' accomplishments because his spirit and legacy are still very much alive, not just during Black History Month, but every month.'[5]

The more I listened to Melvin and his guests unfold Douglass' life, the more it offered me 'definitely something to think about'. It was indeed nuanced. It was certainly not to place him on some dodgy 'Great Orators of the Past' module, 'read this passage carefully and answer the questions afterwards making sure you write clearly in the boxes provided' kind of approach, by jumping all over passages such as this:

Passage A):

An American observer recalled Douglass' presence as a speaker: 'He was more than six feet in height, and his majestic form, as he rose to speak, straight as an arrow, muscular, yet lithe and graceful, his flashing eye, and more than all, his voice, that rivalled Webster's in its richness, and in the depth and sonorousness of its cadences, made up such an ideal of an orator as the listeners never forgot.'

Passage B):

Individualist feminist Elizabeth Cady Stanton saw how, at a Boston antislavery meeting, 'with wit, satire, and indignation [Douglass] graphically described the bitterness of slavery and the humiliation of subjection to those who, in all human virtues and powers, were inferior to himself... Around him sat the great antislavery orators of the day, earnestly watching the effect of his eloquence on that immense audience, that laughed and wept by turns, completely carried away by the wondrous gifts of his pathos and humor... all the other speakers seemed tame after Frederick Douglass... [he] stood there like an African prince, majestic in his wrath.'[6]

Whatever one thinks of *In Our Time*, it's not fluff. If my memory serves me right, I don't remember Douglass being referred to as 'an African prince'. One of the guests, Celeste-Marie Bernier, Professor of Black Studies in the English Department at the University of Edinburgh, tells the story of when, in November 1826, Douglass was 'given' to Thomas Auld, who sent him to his brother, Hugh, in Baltimore. Hugh's wife, Sophia, began to teach Douglass to read. Douglass describes her husband's repugnant reaction when he finds out, 'if you learn him how to read, he'll want to know how to write; and this accomplished, he'll be running away with himself'.[7] However, the flame had been lit. Douglass now realised, in Bernier's words, 'literacy was the path to not only physical freedom but intellectual freedom'. Karen Salt, Assistant Professor in Transnational American Studies at the University of Nottingham, another of Bragg's guests, continues the story. She tells us when Frederick was 12, he heard his friends read from Caleb Bingham's *The Columbian Orator*, an anthology of speeches first published in 1797. Salt explains *The Columbian Orator* is indeed a 'very radical book': 'It's got Socrates in it, it's got Cicero, it's got actual parliament speeches in it, it's founded on liberty and freedom and equality (even though it was) supposed to teach you about elocution, teach you about oratory, about the power of speech.' Douglass would claim the book 'gave tongue' to his 'own soul'. Jim Powell, an expert in the history of liberty, intriguingly describes Douglass now being in 'rehearsal', (aren't we all?):

'With The Columbian Orator in his hand, with the words of great speakers coming from his mouth, he was rehearsing. He was readying the sounds – and meanings – of words of his own that he would one day write. He had the whole world before him. He was Cato before the Roman senate, Pitt before Parliament defending American liberty, Sheridan arguing for Catholic emancipation, Washington bidding his officers farewell. The book included a "Dialogue between Master and Slave", in which the slave tells the master he wants not kindness but liberty. There was also a short play, "Slave in Barbary" , where the ruler Hamet declares: "Let it be remembered, there is no luxury so exquisite as the exercise of humanity, and no post so honourable as his, who defends the rights of man."'[8]

For Douglass, this was a moment of transformation where he discovered 'what he did not know he did not know'. His 'walk toward' had begun; there would be no turning back. Read Douglass describing his feelings, it's a powerful piece of testimony capturing what personal transformation can feel like, when infinite possibilities have been created in someone who was living under such extreme oppression,

'The silver trump of freedom had roused my soul to eternal wakefulness,' Frederick recounted. 'Freedom now appeared, to disappear no more forever. It was heard in every sound, and seen in everything. It was ever present to torment me with a sense of my wretched condition. I saw nothing without seeing it, I heard nothing without hearing it, and felt nothing without feeling it. It looked from every star, it smiled in every calm, breathed in every wind, and moved in every storm.'[9]

For Salt, it was in the disconnect: 'That world is not mine, that does not seem fair or equal or even just especially if you live in a place founded on independence, being against tyranny.' It was this which gave Douglass 'an awareness of becoming a person'; there's that phrase again, 'to become what one is'. The more I listened, the more I couldn't stop playing away as Bernier spoke about Douglass and oratory. Listen for a moment to some of the things she articulated:

- 'Douglas and oratory is a lifelong song' *(Play away; it's the 'never-ending' dialogue)*
- 'Oratory as well as education in general was the route to emancipation' *(Play away; it's the raison d'être for an oracy curriculum)*
- 'For Douglass, oratory was the way to get past the dominant written word and communicate freedom' *(Play away; drama empowers in the same way as we'll explore further on in our search)*
- 'Before Douglass was an orator, he was a listener' *(Play away; the importance of really listening once again)*
- 'The enslaved in Maryland taught him how to debate, they taught him how to reason, they taught him how to theorise' *(Play away; remember my students on the tube?)*
- 'Language must have power and speak to those who die and suffer' *(Play away; Hashim and I never died, we were both suffering but we both managed to find a language that had meaning and force)*

162

- 'He is a witness... I come to you as a witness' *(I, too, come as a witness)*
- 'To understand the human rights struggle in every lens, in every perspective' *(Play away; the urgent need for expertise, which we'll also explore in a later chapter)*
- 'Can you integrate a sense of human rights and justice... use it to effect real social change' *(More of that later)*
- 'The relationship between activism, authorship and artistry... as a living human being' *(Much more of that later)*
- 'The struggle – The inner via the outer man' *(Play away; the relationship of the inner with the outer, a constant theme)*

I could have put Bernier's brilliant turn of phrase before a group of young adults, suggesting all of this is in fact what we're doing with our craft as well. I could have done the same with a bunch of teachers, for that matter. Here we have the private and the public so intertwined, impossible to separate. But let's not go there just yet. The programme hasn't ended. It was when Bragg weighed in with, 'The amazing thing is he never gives in. I am still dazzled by the way he got where he got to', that Bernier finds the words to eloquently sum up what Douglass meant to her: 'He says to his grandson – be strong, be cheerful, be brave. Later he writes, "I have never lost heart or hope." For Douglass, the lesson is keep going, never give up, never turn away, and he insistently maintained if there is no struggle there is no progress, that is life against death.'

Here's a good moment to turn off the radio. For me, like Bernier, what showed up after reflecting on Douglass' life, was that overworked word, 'resilience'. Politicians use it in terms of teaching something they like to call 'character'. The awkward title of an all-party report, *Character and Resilience Manifesto*, tells you where that's going – probably not somewhere we might want to follow – but they're right to challenge the horrible phrase that's lazily banded around, 'soft skills': 'Indeed, even talking about "soft skills" is something of a misnomer because these aren't fluffy or superficial skills we're talking about – this is about having the fundamental drive, tenacity and perseverance needed to make the most of opportunities and to succeed whatever obstacles life puts in your way.'[10] So, no more calling anything 'soft skills' ever again. If anyone wants to challenge this, then I'd invite them to try out some of the work, then we'll see who's 'soft'.

However, as we're quoting the politicians, some might say the emphasis on resilience in terms of the individual over the social conveniently frees them from essential state-sponsored help and support that's often lacking. Ok, a bit of a dig, but the idea of the individual and the social gives notions of resilience nuance. In their fascinating study, *Applied Theatre: Resettlement: Drama, Refugees and Resilience*, the writers go far deeper, placing resilience in a complex process:

> 'Our understanding of resilience shifted from us seeing it as a personal trait, a quality or set of abilities that can be developed in individuals over time, to a more holistic understanding of resilience as a process, that is context bound, complex and for some, fragile. An individual or indeed a community's resilience is to great extent determined by the specific social context within which they are operating at any given moment.'[11]

They later ask us to consider the findings of a study of refugees during their first three years in Melbourne, Australia, which concluded that the capacity for optimism and resilience was 'powerfully shaped by the prevailing social climate and structures that are openly inclusive or exclude'. Importantly, they also point out with humility, 'Some of the individuals we worked with may have already been far more resilient than others already living in the community and hence our initial desire to develop their resilience may have been somewhat misplaced.'

Pause for a moment; hold all of this in your head. Now, take a look at the stamps you buy next. You may find the picture of

Sophia Duleep Singh to commemorate the centenary of the 1918 Representation of the People Act, which gave the vote to all women over 30 and all men over 21. BBC broadcaster, Anita Anand, was inspired to write her biography, *Sophia: Princess, Suffragette, Revolutionary*, because in her words, 'We are terrible at writing women's history, but we are catastrophically bad at writing about women of colour... And here is one who has been at the forefront of the suffragette movement, is the reason I can vote today, is the reason I am a political journalist, and I didn't know anything about her.'[12]. Me, too; I'd never heard of Sophia Duleep Singh. I blame my teachers once again. However, I was drawn in by the link to oracy: 'the way to get past the dominant written word and communicate freedom'; 'the route to emancipation'. In survey after survey, people say their biggest fear is not death but public speaking. There's the old Seinfeld joke (Go, Jerry): 'That means to the average person, if you have to go to a funeral, you're better off in the casket than doing the eulogy.'[13]. Boom, Boom! But this fear was real enough for Singh. The accounts show she wasn't comfortable speaking formally in any public arena: 'In 1911 she was reluctant to make speeches in public or at Women's Social and Political Union meetings. She refused to chair meetings, telling her WSPU colleagues she was "quite useless for that sort of thing" and would only say "five words if nobody else would support the forthcoming resolution".'[14] So what changed her into the fiery orator, 'a rock star of defiance'[15] taking up Douglass' challenge to 'integrate a sense of human rights and justice' into her being in order to 'effect social change'?

Singh was the daughter of an exiled Punjabi Maharajah, 'a 19th century "IT" girl' who debuted with her two sisters at Buckingham Palace in 1894. 'She becomes this butterfly in the court,' says Anand. 'She is at every party, she is everywhere that it matters to be seen. She is a fashion icon. She scandalises with her antics and she knows how to play the media. She is one of the first women in Britain to ride a bicycle in public. Everybody adores her.'[16] But then her 'walk toward' begins when, in 1903 on a trip to India, she witnesses the poverty and racism British rule had brought about. Like Douglass, her lens had been transformed. Her lifelong search for human rights had begun, for now she too 'saw nothing without seeing it... heard nothing without hearing it, and felt nothing without feeling it. It looked from every star, it smiled in every calm, breathed in every wind, and moved in every storm.'[17]

Anand marks this transformation, from her politicisation in India that had given her 'a thirst for cause', to her return to England when she found her calling in the suffragettes' struggle: 'It changed her from being somebody I think I would hate to be stuck in a lift with – quite boring and vacuous – into this amazing, courageous, will risk it all and sacrifice everything suffragette.'[18] She was with an inclusive group of women who all had common purpose in the most challenging of contexts. She didn't learn resilience. The specific social context she was in revealed an existing resilience. So, she went from feeling 'useless for that sort of thing' to 'a fully-fledged militant suffragette'. But as Balfour et al. had observed when working with refugees in Australia, it was already in her.

> Play away; how many people do we know who start out saying they're useless and can't do it, end up experiencing infinite possibilities within the contexts they're now living in? Can you separate the private and the public in this process of reimagination?

There was no stopping Singh now: 'She was used as a propaganda tool by Emmeline Pankhurst and "deployed like a weapon". She was a major donor. She fundraised. She sold *The Suffragette* newspaper outside her Hampton Court Palace home, a residence bestowed to her by Queen Victoria.'[19] When she joined the Women's Tax Resistance League, refusing to pay her taxes, all of her possessions were taken and sold at auction. Such was their resilience, the suffragettes would send people to go buy them back. There's a memorable story of what happened to Singh on the notorious Black Friday March on 18th November, 1910, when, on the instructions of Churchill to 'tire' them out, the police employed the most terrible brutality. Anand tells it better than me, bringing it into the world we live in today:

> 'Sophia is kettled. She sees one police officer picking up a woman she doesn't know, throwing her and slamming her onto the pavement repeatedly. She sees a gap in the kettle, she dashes out – she's a tiny 5.1ft woman – and slams herself in between the police officer and the woman, screaming at him to let her go.
>
> He drops the woman and then tries to melt into the crowd because, as far as he is concerned, it's like Kim Kardashian has just popped up in the middle of a riot. But Sophia, not content with just saving this woman, follows him into the riot screaming at him, "Tell me your number!" She sees it – V700 – and commits it to memory.'[20]

It could be a familiar tale of our times of police brutality. It's also a tale of how you can take on the establishment and win. Sophia didn't have the access the internet gives people these days, putting up petitions to force debates in Parliament. No 38 degrees or Change.org for her. Instead, she carried out a highly effective letter campaign, insisting V700 be taken off duty. Our very own Winston Churchill, who was prepared to take on the Third Reich and win, had had enough of this singular woman: 'Because she is so important this complaint escalates through the Metropolitan Police to the Home Office until you have a signature from Churchill himself saying: "send no more replies to her".'[21]. It didn't stop with the PM; it went right to the top. Apparently, King George V was furious, asking in exasperation, 'Have we no hold on her?'[22]

But it's interesting to note that once the suffragette movement is over, Singh loses her context and therefore her purpose. She's no longer optimistic, and becomes lost. She's no longer resilient, falling into depression. It demonstrates clearly the relationship of the private and the public. It exposes the complexity and fragility of resilience as a process Barbour et al. also noted. For Anand, 'She's too brown to marry a white man, too white to marry a brown man. Incredibly maternal, but never able to exercise that. She has a very romantic personality, but never has love.'[23] However, she's lifted out of her depression and her resilience returns because a new, more personal context is found. During the Second World War, she became godmother to her housekeeper Bosie's daughter. She relocated with them to Buckinghamshire, where she also took in three evacuee children. According to Annad, this is where 'she is the happiest in her life'. I'll let her finish this remarkable story:

> 'It is just quite the most extraordinary little household. Her sister Catherine comes back from Germany and they have houses across the road from each other. In the day she is with the children or waiting for the children to come back from school, or she sends the Rolls Royce to go and pick them up. These children become her life, and they loved her. They stayed in her care for six years and remained in contact with her until her death in 1948.'[24]

Teaching context

In a study of Australian single women, it emphasises: 'The everydayness of the women's achievement of resilience... the everyday is not simply a vessel in which lives are lived, rather it is the milieu in which the social processes of resilience are enacted daily.'[25] Now change some of the words: 'The everydayness of the students' achievement of resilience in the classroom, the everyday classroom experience is not simply a vessel in which lives are lived, rather it is the milieu in which the social processes of resilience are enacted daily.' This moves resilience into a social process and into the classroom.

Just as for Douglass and Singh, so in the classroom there has to be struggle if there's to be progress. It's in the process of struggle the students will experience what both Douglass and Singh experienced, 'an awareness of becoming a person'; 'to become what one is'. It's the difference between a classroom that's alive and a classroom that's dead. Just as it was for Douglass and Singh, it's a place where they learn to listen, to debate, to reason, to theorise, to bear witness as human beings weaving that relationship between activism, authorship, and artistry. It was the lifelong song of both Douglass and Singh; it's the lifelong song of a meaningful classroom.

Devising a 30-minute piece of drama over the course of ten weeks, in a group of five or six people from different backgrounds, of different abilities and different genders, with nothing more than a given theme, is an incredibly rigorous process, both academically and socially. There's nothing 'soft' about it. It's as mighty a challenge for adults taking a Community Drama GCSE in Norfolk as it is for 16-year-olds taking a Drama GCSE in East London. I know; I was there. It's nothing short of somehow turning the natural order of things on its head by 'making an event in which a group of fragments are suddenly brought together... in a community which, by the natural laws that make every community, gradually breaks up'.[26]

The metaphor I use before we embark is one of a journey. Like every journey, it will be long (as is this sentence, hold on tight, don't let go), at times exciting, at times tedious, at times exhilaratingly speedy, at times tortuously slow, at times you'll forget everything else as the journey will consume your every thought, at times you'll want to get off the bus and never want to get back on, there might be people who never finish the journey, there will be bumps in the road, there will be twists and turns, we might even crash, recover and move on, but a journey (as well as this sentence) cannot go on forever so you do have to know where you're heading. I end by telling them I have experienced these journeys many times over the last 33 years; they're one of the most exciting things I can do in my life, so long as it's carried out with integrity. But 'a journey of a thousand miles begins with a single step'[27]. A creativity model is put before them:

Preparation - becoming immersed in problematic issues that are interesting and arouses curiosity. Ideas, feelings, thoughts are shared; preliminary research carried out; early connections made. Some experimentation is occurring. A lot is discarded. Nuggets are seized upon. There's a sense of being disorientated and a searching for paths to follow. It feels like a dark forest with a few chinks of light one needs to head towards, but unsure which ones to choose.

Incubation – ideas churn around below the threshold of consciousness. Lots of the material, discussions, experimentations are being internalised. Thoughts and ideas crop up at strange times; in the shower; in bed waiting for the alarm to ping; watching *Master Chef*.

Insight – the 'Aha!' moments when the idea is formulated clearly. It feels right. These moments happen continuously through the process.

Evaluation – deciding if the insights are valuable and worth pursuing. If they are, then these moments are kept. They're experimented with, explored, built upon. They are key milestones on the journey.

Elaboration – translating the insights into final work. This is when all of the material generated is crafted in what's now a rich, exciting, empowered drafting process. It takes hour upon hour. But this is never a problem, as now there's real ownership because the process has had integrity. It's highly satisfying; a depth is discovered. There's a real sense of joy as the students and adults revel in a journey that has momentum and feels exhilarating.

In academia, this creativity model is called an 'action theory model'. 'Action theorists point out that in real life, creative ideas often happen while you are working with your materials. Once you start executing an idea, you often realise it is not working out how you expected, and you have to change what you had in mind. Sometimes the final product that results is nothing like your beginning idea... Creativity takes place over time, and most of the creativity occurs whilst doing the work.'[28] Sawyer's conclusions are interesting, very much chiming with my own experiences working within a creativity model (I kind of prefer this term to an 'action theory model'. What do you think?):

- Creativity isn't a special mental process, but involves everyday cognitive processes.
- Creativity isn't a distinct personality trait; rather, it results from a complex combination of more basic mental capabilities.
- Creativity doesn't happen in a series of magical moments of insight; rather creative products result from long periods of hard work that involve many small insights, and these mini insights are organised and combined by the conscious mind of the creator.
- Creativity is always specific to a domain. No-one can be creative until they internalise the symbols, conventions, and language of a creative domain.

Interestingly, Sawyer has worked closely with Mihaly Csikszentmihalyi, who we've spoken about before. Might they both say a requisite for a process of any complexity would involve the following attributes?

- Effort – to do what it takes.
- The ability to find new solutions, strategies; to be agile, adaptable; to bounce back; talking about a journey rather than mistakes or failure.
- To play with ideas – to try out possibilities.
- Common purpose leads to positive relationships.
- Independence – problem-solving.
- Drafting/critiquing – a strength approach; never personal; the desire to create 'beautiful work'.
- Vulnerability – to show up; to take risk.

- Reliability – to turn up; meet deadlines; issues outside the classroom cannot get in the way.
- Inspired by others, not threatened.
- Dealing with emotions – frustration; fatigue; hyperactivity.
- Transference – able to make connections academically and personally, in Claxton's phrase, 'playing away'.

These attributes aren't taught. They show up in the complex, fragile social processes of resilience that's 'enacted daily'. They exist in a 'prevailing social climate and structures that are openly inclusive'. They belong in the intersection of the public and private self. I'm a witness to hundreds of young people who have demonstrated this kind of resilience, much of it sadly on VHS (what's that?). Their art is the struggle of 'the inner via the outer', as they mine their sense of self in the multiple worlds they live in:

- Their inner world
- Their family world
- Their school world
- Their area world
- Their London world
- Their England world
- Their Great Britain world
- The world where their roots lie
- BBC world – the events swirling around them
- Not forgetting, of course, their social media world

However, that final act of bringing their art to realisation, Brook's special time, special place, is nothing short of a rite of passage. The last words they speak will be, for most of them, the last drama they'll ever do in their life. The exam is always just before the GCSEs begin; so school, as they know it, is coming to an end. My five-year relationship with them is closing. They have moved through many identities, from Orphan to Trickster to Altruist to Sage to Creator, but at this moment they're all Warriors, declaring the person they have become, to 'become what one is'. If the point of school is to create beautiful work then they are the beautiful work. For many, it's nothing short of the reimagination of the self. Those of us who've ever been on a long journey with a group of people that Martha Graham rightly described as 'remorseless'[29], then at its fruition, you'll have experienced what Brook describes as 'the marvel of being one'(dwell on this phrase just for a moment):

> 'The purpose of theatre is… making an event in which a group of fragments are suddenly brought together… in a community which, by the natural laws that make every community, gradually breaks up… At certain moments this fragmented world comes together and for a certain time it can rediscover the marvel of organic life. The marvel of being one.'[30]

Let's torch-beam on two students who experienced the journey. Alisha arrived in Year 7 as a resilient child, very able, very popular. She moved smoothly through the gears, arriving five years later in Year 11 displaying the attributes that had given her so much success. Goss's 'Winning strategy' had clearly worked. I set up a 'story of learning' with my students from a very early age. It's an ongoing conversation that can take many forms, from making models to capture their reflections, to creating a presentation for their family. A lot of the time it's explored with me in a one-to-one conversation that continues for five years. At its core, it's about the physical and emotional growth of the child. Alisha really did get Dweck's growth mindset. Let's tick it off – she 'enacted daily':

- ✓ 'The passion for stretching yourself and sticking to it, even (or especially) when it's not going well'[31] meant Alisha was never in danger of falling off the bus.
- ✓ 'The best thing they can do is to teach their children to love challenges, be intrigued by mistakes, enjoy effort, and keep on learning.'[32] Alisha was passionate about Drama. As an empowered student, she was able to experiment and explore with a sense of playfulness and inquiry.

✓ 'As growth-minded leaders, they start with a belief in human potential and development – both their own and other people's.'[33] She was 'kinder than necessary',[34] an important mantra we often used across the school. She was generous and giving, nothing was too much trouble. Because of this, her group developed a resilience they carried with them right to the end of the journey.

✓ 'You have to work hardest for the things you love most.'[35] I have learnt over the years that there comes a point where the first four phases of the action theory model need to end, as time is always finite. I appoint a writer in every group with the ability to pick up all that had been discovered and created. I set the writer the challenge to craft it into a 'beautiful' script. For this to be achieved, it would need to be drafted as many times as it takes 'to get the job done'.[36] Alisha got the job; she got the job done.

She was highly experienced, taking part in several productions such as a *Macbeth* set in the context of child soldiers (much more of that later), to a version of *The Caucasian Chalk Circle* that toured around local primary schools. She had experienced a rich and rigorous five-year drama curriculum as well as watching numerous live productions, lucky to have the world of London theatre on her doorstep. However, there was always a sense she played it safe. She was brilliant at empowering others but held back when it came to herself. There was a lack of risk in her work, exposing a fear of vulnerability that, over the years, she had become highly adept at hiding from others.

> Play away; who do you know who adopts this kind of winning strategy?

At the start of her final journey in Year 11, I put before her what Brene Brown has to say about what it might mean to 'show up' (she calls it authenticity, but we're not using this word). For Brown it's: 'A collection of choices that we have to make every day. It's about the choice to show up and be real. The choice to be honest. The choice to let our true selves be seen.'[37] We'd talked about this openly and honestly several times in the context of her 'story of learning'. Here was her last chance on her drama journey to discover the resilience to make herself vulnerable, a requisite for her if she was to truly understand that: 'Drama is exposure; it is confrontation; it is contradiction and it leads to analysis, construction, recognition and eventually to an awakening of understanding.'[38]

It's uncanny how, year after year, the majority of students who have this kind of resilience, without fail play themselves through the safety of role. Sometimes it's a conscious choice but mostly it's subconscious. I can hear their story as I'm on the outside. I'm not encouraging them to be autobiographical, but the process will invariably take them there. Freud compares the conscious mind 'to a fountain playing in the sun and falling back into the great subterranean pool of subconscious from which it rises'.[39] For Stanislavski, too: 'The main factor in any form of creativeness is the life of a human spirit, that of the actor and his part, their joint feelings and subconscious creation.'[40] Make no mistake; all of this is about resilience as much as anything else. One of my theatrical heroes, Mike Leigh, makes the connection: 'My work requires acting at its most committed – it demands actors of enormous resilience, but also intelligence and wit.'[41] But Alisha has the intelligence and the wit to know all of this. She has explored Stanislavsky and Mike Leigh in Year 9. It was now about whether she would 'dare greatly'. It would be nothing short of heroic. For the child\actor\creator, 'to create (her) own material... to be (her) own matrix and, at the same time, shape the results into objective signs' was indeed 'an heroic task'.[42]

I was fascinated about her choice of character. Listen to how she introduces herself to the audience:

'There was once a girl - a ladki, Sundar ladki (Hindi for 'beautiful girl')

She came from a land that, like her, had been riven and split asunder

A beautiful girl,

Her golden brown skin,

Her shiny brown hair,

Her bright clothes,

Struggle to be seen, struggle to be heard, struggle to achieve

Struggle to show the world what you can do, struggle to breathe and to believe

She felt as different on her outside as she felt within.'

This is Alisha. Her parents are from India. Her father is Muslim and her mother is Hindi. They had met during the time of partition. Alisha had talked to me about the complex and difficult process of how she'd decided to become a practising Muslim and what this had meant to both her parents. However, to her peers she was the beautiful, clever girl with the 'golden brown skin, the shiny brown hair and the bright clothes'. Early on, her character displayed meanness. In this scene, she picks on an old woman because she can sense the old lady can see through her mask:

'They both met one day in the market.

'A': I saw her from a distance because she wasn't from my world. She didn't belong here, her demeanour made that evident.

Old Lady: I saw her from a distance, strong and powerful that only the arrogance of youth has. It felt like being in a foreign land, a different place, a different language.

'A': *I walked up to her like a dog sniffing out the dangers.*

(She growls and behaves like a menacing dog)

I was intrigued by her; her silence spoke a thousand words,

(The growling goes quiet)

But no one understood them.

(She suddenly barks loudly to scare the old lady)

She seemed to shield herself from my advance.

(Bark)

Old Lady: Scared

(Bark)

Old Lady: Frightened

(Bark)

Old Lady: Petrified, afraid to recall feelings of the past
(Rita, who played the old lady, would draw on her own mother's experience growing up in apartheid South Africa as a black woman who had witnessed, amongst many things, a 'necklacing' – the chosen method to set fire to a collaborator.)

'A': *I've never seen you around here,*

Do you belong here? Who are you?

Both: She looked to the right. There was no reply.

I'm talking to you, old lady, not air.

Both: She looked to the left. There was no reply.

Can you not speak? Another one in this town who doesn't have the capacity to talk?

Old Lady: Another one?

'A': *Oh, so you do have words, use them next time someone asks you a question. Don't believe yourself to be too noble for our town, because at the end of the day you're the outcast, you don't belong. You're the one who is different, not me; never me.'*

Alisha could be cruel at times in school. But it was, as she suggests at the end of the scene, a way 'to repair' her 'self-esteem... by assigning blame or making excuses'.[43] She knew it and wanted to go there. In the climax of the play, the mask is ripped away. Only those who really know Alisha will experience the emotional nakedness of this moment when the words of another,[44] 'with a great rush of air', invade her 'every pore':[45]

'Don't be fooled by me.

Don't be fooled by the face I wear

For I wear a mask, a thousand masks,

Masks that I'm afraid to take off,

And none of them is me.

Pretending is an art that's second nature with me,

But don't be fooled,

For God's sake, don't be fooled.

I give you the impression that I'm secure,

That all is sunny and unruffled with me, within as well as without,

That confidence is my name and coolness my game,

That the water's calm and I'm in command

And that I need no-one,

But don't believe me.

My surface may seem smooth but my surface is my mask,

Ever-varying and ever-concealing.

Beneath lies no complacence.

Beneath lies confusion and fear and loneliness.

But I hide this. I don't want anybody to know it.

I panic at the thought of my weakness exposed.

That's why I frantically create a mask to hide behind,

A nonchalant sophisticated facade,

To help me pretend,

To shield me from the glance that knows.'

She also paid tribute to her mother and father. She wanted to go there, too. The specific social context she was working in offered her the resilience to have the most difficult but affirming conversations with her parents about what it was like for them marrying across a religious and caste divide at a time of acute danger. 'I am born from such bravery,' she writes. Read this section in the play, marvel at the fusion of the different patterns of language, but imagine what it would take for Alisha to perform this. A complex and sophisticated process of resilience was required for her to 'show up' in this way:

(To help you visualise, this moment was performed with two handheld masks of different shades. Much of it had the quality of dance.)

Time after time

These old memories

Come crawling back.

The struggle takes over,

We thought we had survived.

You see Death has passed my way,

Death has claimed my Father, and half my life,

Death had claimed my friend and the other half of my life.

Thoughts of the future haunt me.

My mother was born into a caste, society had told her:

In the eye of the constitution,

In the eye of the law,

"You are the lowest of the low."

Her life has already been written in fine print.

A lower caste woman is like

A piece of sheep fat in the sun.

Everything will come and feed on that fat.

My father, a handsome young man,

Lived life written on his own terms

For he belonged to the caste of

Warriors and soldiers,

This gave him immense power.

Caste is not a physical object like a wall of bricks

Or a line of barbed wire which prevents,

Caste is a notion; it is a state of the mind.

Therefore, it is to be pulled down.

These two weren't meant to meet,

Two households, both alike in dignity,

A pair of star-cross'd lovers,

"Come, gentle night; come, loving, black-browed night;

O, she doth teach the torches to burn bright!

Give me my warrior; and, when I shall die,

Take him and cut him out in little stars,

Did my heart love till now? Forswear it, sight,

For I ne'er saw true beauty till this night."

Warriors didn't run,

Soldiers didn't run

So he didn't run.

But she did.

So they left. They wanted their life to be theirs.

My father,

Imposing in build and height,

A gentle giant, not one to fight

Unless the cause was just and right.

My father cried out,

"Until all who walk the earth

Hate evil, hate untruth, hate oppression,

And, hating them, to strive to overthrow them, merciful God."

I am born from such bravery,

A story that does not exist in the past of those who knew them, of those that loved them,

A story that only exists in the future.'

On completion of the five-year journey, Alisha wrote this, testimony to where 'the walk toward' had taken her: 'The journey that I have been on for the past five years has not only made me question the world, but it has been the reason that I have taught myself never to diminish what I have and can do. I will forever hold it in my heart.' It captures the coming together of the private and public self. Hers is no longer a story that exists in the past, hers is now a story 'that only exists in the future'. (A footnote: Now at university, Alisha is campaigning vigorously and openly against Modi's alarming new citizenship law. She will not be diminished. The reimagining of the self has created a never-ending dialogue that is absolutely in the intersection where the private and public meet.)

Chantelle was another student, almost the complete opposite to Alisha. She arrived in Year 7 angry and confrontational, with a strategy of shutting down if things didn't go her way or she didn't want to do something. Over time, the fleeing from her vulnerability in the form of this perpetual emotional shut-down, created a void that she experienced 'as alienation, as profound as ennui, as the sense of deficient emptiness'.[46] She met Dweck's descriptions of someone who had a 'fixed mindset'. Let's tick it off; she 'enacted daily':

- ✓ 'The minute they hit a snag, their confidence goes out the window and their motivation hits rock bottom. If success means they're smart, then failure means they're dumb. That's the fixed mindset.'[47] Chantelle thought she was 'dumb' – she used this word sometimes – which is why she would shut down or avoid doing the work. Over time, her setbacks had labelled her.
- ✓ 'As soon as children become able to evaluate themselves, some of them become afraid of challenges.'[48] I was surprised at the end of Year 9 when she said she wanted to carry on, opting to take GCSE Drama. She found the idea of any physicality utterly exposing, even in a small group. We'd also clashed over the years, creating some memorable bust-ups which usually resulted in her storming out of the room. The choice to carry on was made by an existing resilience. She was, in fact, prepared to take a risk.
- ✓ 'What's more, it's not as though the fixed mindset wants to leave gracefully. If the fixed mindset has been

182

controlling your internal monologue, it can say some
pretty strong things to you.'[49] Her inner monologue was
so strong, she was making little progress across the
curriculum. It was telling her, 'You have permanent traits
and I'm judging them.' It was incredibly hard for her to
believe, 'You are a developing person and I am interested
in your development.'[50]

✓ 'A no-effort relationship is a doomed relationship, not a
great relationship. It takes work to communicate
accurately and it takes work to expose and resolve
conflicting hopes and beliefs.'[51] She fell out with almost
every girl in her cohort, sometimes spectacularly, with fist
fights at break-time or in lessons.

It was no different at home. She came from a duel heritage
background. Her parents had split. She'd tried living with her
father, but for the same reasons as we were all floundering with
her, he couldn't cope either. Instead of choosing 'fight', he chose
'flight', lacking the resilience needed to hang in there (who am I to
judge?). She'd returned to live with her mother, but her mother
struggled to create boundaries, finding her daughter's behaviour
too challenging.

While it wasn't plain sailing in her GCSE, the highly complex and
fragile social process of resilience had slowly been nurturing those
attributes that had made Alisha so successful. Often Chantelle's
best work was achieved with the sensitive, very able boys who
offered her inclusivity. She was inspired by them rather than
threatened, which meant she was able to deal with those
destructive emotions that often got in her way. She started to take
ownership of the work. It inspired her to bring in her own
planning, which she enjoyed experimenting with. It was all bound
by a common purpose, 'to get the job done'. These boys would do
whatever it takes and so would she. It was evident she was now
feeling what it was like 'to love challenges, be intrigued by
mistakes, enjoy effort, and keep on learning'.[52] The reimagining
of herself had started. However, with everything that was swirling

around her outside the drama studio, creating a piece of art over ten weeks in a 'remorseless' process was going to be a challenge for not only her but for those who were 'on the bus' with her. I joined her up with the boys who had begun to bring out her resilience. At first, she retreated, becoming lost. She couldn't keep up. She was overwhelmed. I called her in for a one-to-one. She wanted to talk about the loss of her one true ally, her Nan. Her Nan had been a constant during the turbulent years growing up. Chantelle had been in the assembly Hashim had been in when they met the probation officer who had talked about the power of her ally, her mother. We'll talk later about the power of building shared experiences, but here was a live example in its rawest sense. Her Nan had just died. She wanted to go there. It was evident her drama was now going to be a rite of passage, honouring her Nan. This wasn't something subconscious. We both said aloud the journey she was about to embark on would be part of the 'never-ending' dialogue she would have with her Nan. Clearly inspired, she went away, writing pages and pages, pouring out her emotions. She was emptying her glass. We sat together editing, selecting what she would like to craft into art. We found Agard's *Half Caste*, which spoke to her because she'd been racially bullied; her Nan had helped her through it. Getting her to perform this monologue was a long process. She pretended she hadn't learnt it, when she had. She said she wasn't being supported by her group, when she was. (Those sensitive boys would support Crystal Palace if they could!) She failed to show up for rehearsals. I was beginning to think she was becoming so fixed she would never move. I was starting to have a little more sympathy for her dad. Then just before her exam, there was a crucial run-through of her entire play. Her group would be utterly disadvantaged if she didn't show, as it was a finely tuned ensemble piece with everyone in the space for 30 minutes. She was integral, her group had honourably kept her on the bus. She never turned up. My thoughts and feelings grabbed me by the throat. I picked up the phone, giving her poor mother two barrels of angry frustration. Chantelle lived over an hour away from the school, a journey involving a tube and a bus ride. It certainly wasn't easy for her. Just coming to school was an act of resilience. Unbeknown to her mother and me, she'd had a huge argument with a group of girls in her last lesson so had run off. Of course, she did. Her group left school that evening understandably stressed. They didn't deserve this. It was now six o'clock. All the students had gone home, but I was still unloading onto a member of SLT who was edging towards the door (those psychopathic tendencies once again) when Chantelle suddenly entered the room. She'd come all the way back from her home. She was unable to articulate why, but for me, it showed she was in a process of resilience. She'd made the transference, asking herself what it would mean if she let down her Nan.

Like Alisha, you would have to know Chantelle to feel the courage she showed in the actual performance to show up and be seen in honour of her Nan. She had found the 'steadiness' we'd all been searching for through those tumultuous years, which in turn had allowed her to finally release her inner self. The social process of creating a piece of art had stabilised 'the self into a form'. In doing so, Chantelle had created a life that was now perhaps 'worth living'. Read a section from her performance, it's clear she's in the world 'as a human being':

'It wasn't my mother, it was my Nan, she was my very best friend.

Her kitchen wall played host to a round, brown plastic clock,

One side of the table was pushed up tight against the wall,

Brown and white envelopes and shopping receipts sat on last year's calendar,

Two cushioned wooden chairs sat at either end of Nan's table,

Crumbs from homemade macaroni cheese sought refuge between the stitching.

To walk into this room and see you smile,

I walked over and hugged you all the time.

You were so strong,

The day when they teased me

And you showed me they were wrong.

(After many months of blocking, it was here, in the actual performance, that she captured her Nan's spirit in Agard's words.)

"The next time they make you

Stand on one leg and make you say,

"I'm half-caste"

Explain to them

What do you mean

When you say half-caste?

Explain yourself

What do you mean?

I'm sure you'll understand

Why I offer you half-a-hand

But you come back tomorrow

With the whole of your eye

And the whole of your ear

And the whole of your mind

And I will tell you

The other half

Of my story."

Nan, you showed us that life can't be all that bad,

"There's always a light at the end of a tunnel"

Scared,

Since the day she wasn't well,

It can't cripple love

It can't shatter hope

It can't corrode hope

Scared

I sense something is wrong

Scared

I know something isn't right

It can't invade the soul

It can't silence courage

It can't, it can't, it can't

It can

Cancer

There was this moment; one of those moments we know right there and then that shifts the course of our life. It was a Thursday afternoon, funny how you remember such things, when she tried to get out of the chair she always sat in to watch her favourite TV programme but she gasped and just sat back down again. She caught my eye and because she could see a tear silently fall, she found the energy to sit up. I should have said something but I didn't.

Try to picture when I walked over to her side

My chest getting tight

Try to picture her eyes

Those were just for me

Letting me know you love me

Try to picture on the way home my granddad saying, 'everything will be fine',

Tears running down his face

Try to picture, just try to see

Not knowing if my Nan would die today.'

In her final scene, in an act of such courageous resilience, 'with a great rush of air' invading her 'every pore', ask yourself who she spoke these words to:

'Picture this all of you,

I told God I was angry

I told the Lord I hate Him

I told Him that I hurt.

You have the power

And could have stopped

But You chose not!

You kill and You make alive; You wound and You heal

I'd lost all hope,

I could see no future

But I realised, hiding among the bushes is the affair of cowards,

Let the Sun shine on your face, let everyone see you!'

1-In Our Time: *Frederick Douglass*: BBC iPlayer Radio (Feb. 2018)

2-Moore, R. 2017: *Douglass*: *'Not a monument, but a mind-set'*: Newscentre, University of Rochester

http://www.rochester.edu/newcenter/douglass-not-a-monument-but-a-mindset-215212/

3-Wootson Jr. C, 2017: *Trump implied Frederick Douglass was alive. The abolitionist's family offered a history lesson*: The Washington Post

4-Boakye, J. 2015: *Teaching to the converted: Black History Month*: Blog, Unseen Flirtations

https://unseenflirtspoetry.wordpress.com/2015/09/27/teaching-to-the-converted-black-history-month/

5-Wootson Jr. C, 2017: *Trump implied Frederick Douglass was alive. The abolitionist's family offered a history lesson*: The Washington Post

6-Powell, J. 1997: *Frederick Douglass: Heroic Orator for Liberty*: Foundation for Economic Education

https://fee.org/articles/frederick-douglass-heroic-orator-for-liberty/

7-Ibid

8-Ibid

9-Ibid

10-Paterson, C; Tyler, C; Lexmond, J. 2014: *Character and Resilience Manifesto*: The all-party parliamentary group on Social Mobility

http://www.educationengland.org.uk/documents/pdfs/2014-appg-social-mobility.pdf

11-Balfour, M; Bundy, P; Burton, B; Dunn, J; Woodrow, N: 2015: *Applied Theatre: Resettlement: Drama, Refugees and Resilience*: Methuen Drama

12-Saul, H. 2018: *Sophia Duleep Singh: The Indian princess and 'rockstar' suffragette forgotten by history*: i News

13-Seinfeld, J. 1998: *I'm Telling You for the Last Time - Live on Broadway*: HBO

14-Ahmed, R; Mukherjee, S. 2011: *South Asian Resistances in Britain, 1858-1947*: A & C Black

15-Saul, H. 2018: *Sophia Duleep Singh: The Indian princess and 'rockstar' suffragette forgotten by history*: i News

16-Ibid

17-Powell, J. 1997: *Frederick Douglass: Heroic Orator for Liberty*: Foundation for Economic Education

18-Saul, H. 2018: *Sophia Duleep Singh: The Indian princess and 'rockstar' suffragette forgotten by history*: i News

19-Ibid

20-Ibid

21-Ibid

22-Anand, A. 2015: *Sophia, the suffragette*: The Hindu

23-Saul, H. 2018: *Sophia Duleep Singh: The Indian princess and 'rockstar' suffragette forgotten by history*: i News

24-Ibid

25-Balfour, M; Bundy, P; Burton, B; Dunn, J; Woodrow, N: 2015: *Applied Theatre: Resettlement: Drama, Refugees and Resilience*: Methuen Drama

26-Smith, A. 1972: *Orghast at Persepolis: An Account of the Experiment in Theatre Directed by Peter Brook and Written by Ted Hughes*: London: Eyre Methuen

27-Lao Tzu, Trans: Minford, J. 2018: *Tao Te Ching*: Penguin Random House

28-Sawyer, K. 2012 (second edition): *Explaining Creativity: The Science of Human Innovation*: Oxford University Press

29-Graham quoted in Roose-Evans, J. 1970: *Experimental Theatre-from Stanislavsky to Peter Brooke*: Routledge

30-Smith, A. 1972: *Orghast at Persepolis: An Account of the Experiment in Theatre Directed by Peter Brook and Written by Ted Hughes*: London: Eyre Methuen

31-Dweck, C. 2006: *Mindset: The New Psychology Of Success*: Random House

32-Ibid

33-Dweck, C. 2017: *Mindset: How You Can Fulfill Your Potential*: Little, Brown Book Group

34-Palacio, R. 2012: *Wonder*: Knopf

35- Dweck, C. 2006: *Mindset: The New Psychology Of Success*: Random House

36-Dweck, C. 2017: *Mindset: How You Can Fulfill Your Potential*: Little, Brown Book Group

37- Brown, B. 2010: *The Gifts of Imperfection: Let Go of Who You Think You're Supposed to Be and Embrace Who You Are*: Hazelden Publishing

38-Brook, P. 2008: *The Empty Space*: Penguin Classics

39-Freud quoted in Thiessen, D. 2012: *Bittersweet Destiny: The Stormy Evolution of Human Behaviour*: Transaction Publishers

40-Hapgood, E. 1989: *Building a Character by Constantin Stanislavski*: Taylor and Francis

41-Sawyer, M: 2011: *Mike Leigh: Creativity is a life-blood for people*: The Guardian

42-Roose-Evans, J. 1970: *Experimental Theatre-from Stanislavsky to Peter Brook*: Routledge

43-Dweck, C. 2006: *Mindset: The New Psychology Of Success*: Random House

44-Finn, C. 1966: *Please Hear What I Am Not Saying-The Mask*:

https://poetrybycharlescfinn.com/pages/please-hear-what-im-not-saying

(You can read a collection of stories about the poem's impact in *Please Hear What I'm Not Saying: a Poem's Reach around the World* : 2011: AuthorHouse)

45-Brook, P. 2017: *The Shifting Point*: Bloomsbury

46-Mate, G. 2009: *In the Realm of Hungry Ghosts*: Vintage Canada

47-Dweck, C. 2006: *Mindset: The New Psychology Of Success:* Random House

48-Ibid

49-Ibid

50-Ibid

51-Ibid

52-Ibid

CHAPTER 8: KNOWING ONESELF; KNOWING THE CHILD

Play away; techniques; strategies; concepts in this chapter that can be used in different contexts:

'Third Culture Kids'

Glocal

The mind/body/body/mind

The Ramayana

Rabindranath Tagore

Salman Rushdie's 'Haroun and the Sea of Stories'

Community, art, and ritual

Encounter

The triangular relationship between text, child, and adult

To create a meaningful conversation with Alisha and Chantelle, it's a requisite to know them. I'd known them for five years. Before their group began their GCSE course, I knew this about the students:

- Two students experienced panic attacks
- Several students were in counselling
- One student never finished anything
- One student had a history of dishonesty
- One student never really spoke at primary school
- One student was autistic, suffering from selective mutism
- Several students had anger management issues
- One student had ADHD
- One student was bright but stayed in her comfort zone
- Several students had attendance/punctuality issues
- Several students found making relationships challenging
- Several students had academic and social issues across the school

None of this surprised me; it's likely to be typical of most classrooms around the country and beyond.

> Play away; a whole range of needs are probably there in any organisation you care to mention. You don't need to go that far; they're there in your family.

However, I believed none of this would ultimately get in the way of their achievement. It's believing the Hindu philosophy: 'We are responsible for what we are, and whatever we wish ourselves to be, we have the power to make ourselves.'[1] In this chapter, let's fly away from the East End of London and land in Thailand, to further explore this requisite of knowing.

When my children were young, I was on the all-too-familiar treadmill of modern life; they were asleep when I left for work and they were asleep when I got back from work. No telling of stories at bathtime for me. On the weekends, I was usually asleep on the sofa when they wanted to play. Dolly Parton, not someone I normally associate with, kind of sums up what I was starting to feel at the time: 'Never get so busy making a living that you forget to make a life.'[2] Quite so. I was in danger of forgetting, and in doing so, I was in danger of not knowing my own children. Quoting Dr Seuss, 'Oh, the places you'll go!'[3] I persuaded my partner to give up her life, which she was enjoying very much, to go live in Thailand. This was back in 1999 when only the intrepid traveller went East. We certainly hadn't ventured out of European campsites. We ended up travelling to 12 countries in three years, from Cambodia, to Bali, to Vietnam, to Nepal, to China – all well trodden these days by young people before they hit their early twenties (Where on earth will they go when they are 40? Probably Devon). But in those days, we felt like we were entering the last frontiers. (To show off, we sent postcards – pre-Facebook days; hard to imagine, I know.) We spent lots of time in family rooms, in camper vans, in tents, in high-end hotels, thrown together out of necessity. We got to know each other in new and beautiful ways that living abroad can bring. Melville's words spoke true: 'It is not down in any map; true places never are.'[4] When we finally returned from our South East Asia adventures, we went straight back to our rainy French campsite, persuading ourselves we had missed it. The kids stared out of the car on a washed-out day and asked, 'Why?' Things were never the same. I think our next holiday was Mexico.

We taught in a large International School in Thailand, situated on the outskirts of Bangkok. The school body was made up of 55 different nationalities. It incorporated the full range of academic, emotional, and language needs. The school required the students to speak English, although this wasn't the first language for many students. The majority of the students might be defined as 'Third Culture Kids'. I'd never come across students with this kind of background before. If my relationships were to be meaningful, then I needed to start 'the walk toward' afresh.

I discovered 'Third Culture Kids' refers to: 'Someone who has spent a significant period of time in one or more culture(s) other than his or her own, thus integrating elements of those cultures and their own birth culture, into a third culture.'[5] Many of the students had lived in several countries, facing the real prospect of moving again at short notice. One of the effects of this is the submergence of self, as a strategy to survive whereby, 'TCKs cope rather than adjust becoming both a 'part of' and 'apart from' whatever situation they are in. Brought up in another culture or several cultures, they feel ownership in none.'[6] For my own children, it took some getting used to turning up to school only to find a friend had vanished without any warning. They got over it. But for TCKs, the loss of home and friends are talked of in terms of grief: 'Most TCKs go through more grief experiences by the time they are 20 than monocultural individuals do in a life time.'[7] This is further complicated by the fact many of the pupils are from culturally mixed families. A typical child might have an American father; a Thai mother; Chinese grandparents, but will call him\herself English because that's where he\she was born. However, the submergence of self is also due to the values of the institution and how it operates. The impact on the child can be severe. The therapist, Edith Sullwold, articulates what can happen:

'Within these particulars are rules; values and systems to which the child begins to adapt, becoming shaped by them. This shaping often happens to such an extent that the child is no longer connected to those aspects of his being which do not fit within the structure of these outer forms and expectations. For some, adaptation means that those gifts which do not fit within the structure or are not valued are submerged and consequently lost, not only to the individual but to the culture as well.'[8]

A friend of mine, who lives abroad and sends her child to an International school, challenged me. She felt the Third Culture Kids' narrative is so negative, contradicting the positivity of the multicultural and intercultural lives of the students in the UK.

> Play away; consider her assertion, 'I think that especially in the late capitalist times we're living through, most children are living in a different culture to that of their parents, regardless of whether they are expats, immigrants, or living in the same place as their ancestors.' Is this another moment when our certainties have been challenged once again? Is she asking us to begin once more the 'walk toward' if we are to make sense of identity in the ever-changing world we live in today?

However, what I was discovering was these were students with complex needs I needed to get to know, finding contexts in which a meaningful conversation could take place. Framing all of this was a personal journey. A requisite of knowing the child is also to carry out Socrates' call to 'know thyself',[9] 'You are an expatriate, see? You hang around cafes.'[10] Well, a lot of expats do that, for sure. For me, it felt more like Brook's actors sent out to work in different parts of the world to absorb other influences and ideas. Brook was conscious: 'Everything feeds the work and everything surrounding it is part of a bigger test of awareness.'[11] I was starting a new dialogue by immersing myself in all that was around us, often with my family, sometimes with a colleague, sometimes on my own. I worked with a Buto specialist; a Chinese dragon troupe; 'Hun Lak Hon Lek' puppets at the Joe Louis Theatre down by the Chao Phraya River. I visited a Sikh temple to hear some of our children sing ragas; I wandered down Silom during the vegetarian festival; I heard a Carnatic singer from Bangalore. We went to the wonderful Patrawadi Theatre on a number of occasions; we watched an incredible collaborative performance of *The Ramayana* by artists from seven SE Asian countries. I studied masks in Bali; Khatakali in Kerala. I was inspired by a wonderful presentation of Kathak dance, as well as watching some Peking Opera in Beijing. We saw some of the 'Politicos' of the region unmasked; watched from afar earthquakes, two peaceful revolutions, a violent revolt. I also had the opportunity to work with Simon, who had developed a world theatre practice, having spent most of his teaching career in South East Asia. I had the privilege to get to know him on both a personal and professional level. But as Gladwell points out, it's not only about being given the opportunities but having 'the strength and presence of mind to seize them'.[12] I seized it with both hands.

But what was I to do with all of this? I fundamentally disagreed with Brook's view that it was, 'something mythical and remote, from another culture nothing to do with my life'.[13] It had made a deep connection on many levels, but particularly with my craft as an arts practitioner. It was more how, when William Faulkner was accused of plagiarism, he replied, 'When I am in the throes of my genius, I take whatever I need from wherever I can find it.'[14] Genius? Ok, I can hear you sniggering, so let me put it another way. In my search, I knew I was going to take whatever it was I needed in an act of creative fusion. It's been there in my practice ever since – sometimes great overt, chunks of it; sometimes hints and traces. My dialogue had gone 'glocal', which meant the 'glocalisation' of my practice; the global had been fused with the local. I like the word, you might not. I shall try to explain it anyway. As I travelled around the region, an influential book at the time that started to make more and more sense was Barba's and Savarese's A Dictionary of Theatre Anthropology.[15] It's an incredible piece of visual research in which each chapter is devoted to a different part of the body. They show how the East has mined every part of the body, connecting it to holistic philosophies about the harmonious integration of the mind and body as one, while Western tradition – both religious and secular – has often been reluctant to encourage this kind of relationship between the physical and mental.

Barba's and Savarese's work set me on a 'walk toward' a new context for the work I had brought over to Thailand from Inner London. This non-dualist approach created fascinating points of intersection. A simple example is the common breathing exercises we carry out. But here the idea of flow between mind and body takes one to the interrelationship between breath, mood, emotion, and ultimately the kind of action you might take. There's an intricate relationship between the private and public self. Hence in a stock Key Stage 3 scheme of learning about a woman who suddenly arrives in a feudal village, she's re named 'Sita'. So, when the students invariably move the drama to witchcraft and the burning of women, I was able to place *The Ramayana* into this context. There's an invisible veil that exists where we place the great Western texts in front of students who are often both of the West and the East (those Roots/Routes once again). But we fail to immerse them in two of the great texts of the East – *The Ramayana* and *The Mahābhārata*. They span across the whole of Asia. Wherever I went, I saw Rama highways, Hanuman shopping bags, cartoons and comics featuring Bima and Draupadi. I'd promised my partner I would never travel on a motorbike with the children. But there we were, 4s up, no helmets, me, the kids and a Khathakali actor from Cochin heading up a sandy dirt track for a performance of a tale from *The Mahābhārata*. Then one day on a trek deep in the Himalayas, we passed through a small, traditional village. In a window I saw the image of Sita in flames. After finally rescuing his loved one from the clutches of Ravana, the demon King, instead of embracing her in his arms, Rama asks Sita to walk through fire. If she burns to death, then the Gods have shown she has been unfaithful. When I ask my students what she should've done, they always speak as one when they say she should've told Rama to go do one. Of course, for the women in the Nepalese village it wasn't as simple. The burning of women from Medieval England stretching across continents led me to Deepa Mehta's film, *Fire*,[16], set in modern-day India. The students are shocked, enraged, that making a film which challenges societal norms allowing for the subjugation of women, had led to death threats to Mehta's life and the banning of the film in many Indian cities. Avoiding the sexual content in the film, I show the students in London some of the extraordinary imagery that clearly references *The Ramayana*. We deconstruct the last, emotive scene in which the young cousin, Sita, finally meets up with her married cousin, Radhi. In the previous scene, her husband has violently pushed Radhi away, her sari catching alight. The image is exactly the one I'd seen in the window in the Nepalese village. However, Radhi survives her 'Agni-Pareeksha' – a test by fire. The meeting is set against an ancient ruin; the music of A.R. Rahman has the beats of both the ancient East as well as the modern West; the rain has arrived; they're dressed in the vibrant colours of their traditional clothes. It all creates a rich intersection of values and contexts my multicultural ensemble of students are well able to deconstruct. It's also an invitation to reimagine themselves by considering they are of both the West and the East; of values grown from tradition as well as from the modern world they're trying to navigate. It's in their music, in their clothes, in their food, in their language as they switch code, moving with ease from English to home language and back again all day long. Now they were being invited to put it into their art, as they explored theatrical and dance forms from both the East and the West. In the dialogue this 'glocalisation' had created, it placed the students' art within a new context where the possibilities had now become infinite.

A Bengali teacher in London had introduced me to the Bengali poet, playwright, novelist, philosopher, and artist, Rabindranath Tagore via a picture book, an adaptation of a Tagore play, *Amal and the Letter from the King*.[17] The allegory lent itself to an exploration of mask. But it was also an opportunity to introduce Tagore to my students, many of whom were Bengali, but none of whom had heard of him. The invisible veil, once again. Tagore is the Eastern Shakespeare, winning the Nobel Prize for Literature in 1913. He was a friend of Ghandi and wrote the *Amar Shonar Bangla* and the *Jana Gana Mana* – the national anthems of Bangladesh and India.

On arriving in Thailand, Simon had sent me on a mask course in Bali. Yep, Bali (apologies if your last training request just got turned down). It was there, standing in the temple at three in the morning, I would start to comprehend what happens when community, art, and religion join (that intersection once again). Arundhati Roy, whose writings explore this triangulation, powerfully marks the moment in her wonderful turn of phrase: 'Little events, ordinary things, smashed and reconstituted. Imbued with new meaning. Suddenly they become the bleached bones of a story.'[18] I returned to London 'reconstituted', not only with a bag of amazing Topeng masks carved by the local mask-maker, but also with a new lens through which to reimagine my practice. For here in my Inner London drama studio was the coming together of community, art, and ritual. It wasn't only me. Tagore, in an epic encounter of Eastern and Western minds, was to teach this to Einstein:

'Matter is composed of protons and electrons, with gaps between them; but matter may seem to be solid. Similarly humanity is composed of individuals, yet they have their interconnection of human relationship, which gives living unity to man's world. The entire universe is linked up with us in a similar manner, it is a human universe. I have pursued this thought through art, literature and the religious consciousness of man.'[19]

But I'm jumping ahead. Back in Bangkok, we now had a pressing concern. We were tasked with putting on the yearly school production – a big event in the calendar of an International School. Showtime! Simon and I decided to search for a text that could offer what Grotowski calls an 'encounter'. If the 'encounter' is to be meaningful, then there has to be a three-way relationship between text, student, and adult. Within this triangulation or intersection, the student will show up so we know them and they will know themselves. The search for texts is never-ending. It's highly political. Look up the storm of controversy, some of it wilfully vicious, provoked when Lola Olufemi, women's officer for the Cambridge University student union, wrote an open letter to the English Faculty, accusing the teaching of English at Cambridge of encouraging 'a "traditional" and "canonical" approach that elevates white male authors at the expense of all others. 'Whilst some have argued this approach has its merits and there have been welcome attempts to address the absence of women writers, there is more that can be done. What we can no longer ignore, however, is the fact that the curriculum, taken as a whole, risks perpetuating institutional racism.'[20] She goes on to highlight the failure of acknowledging Edward Said's insight, 'our histories are interconnected and intertwined'. Many writers came to her defence. While acknowledging first the complexities of 'an English literature syllabus in Britain to entirely or at least radically "decolonise" itself', Arundhati Roy goes on to support Olufemi: 'But an argument for there to be greater diversity in the canon of what is considered "great literature" is surely unimpeachable. If there are still institutions of learning that want their students to remain innocent of the myriad new ways of looking at old histories, at our fascinating present and our uncertain future, God help those young people.'[21] Similarly for Hanif Kureishi, it's impossible to ignore the political: 'If literature is to have any point for young people, it must be to examine and dismantle the structures that maintain white power. The literary is also the political. If we open the "canon", we also open our minds.'[22] The poet, Daljit Nagra, widens the debate, arguing: 'A global tradition exists of black and Asian poets who have written in English over recent centuries. I could suggest many outstanding poets of colour but will name a few who would enrich the "canon" with their aesthetic excellence and help to complicate it with their fresh ways of using English, a new cast of characters and different themes.'[23] Turn to the theatre and hear what Jatinder Verma, co-founder of Tara Arts, was writing as far back as 1990 in a programme note, when he suggested the aim of his theatre was 'to give a voice to what is being done by the act of living in Britain'.[24]

However, it goes back much further than this. I was once asked to review Colin Chambers' meticulously researched book, *Black and Asian Theatre in Britain: A History*.[25] Chambers argues it's a history that's been 'downgraded, ignored or suppressed'. As his research demonstrates, it's a long and complex history of 'struggle for self-definition, of a struggle in an often-hostile culture to create spaces for self assertion and self expression'. The book starts its exploration in the 1550s, focusing on individuals. It then moves beyond the achievements of the individual in the last decades of the twentieth century when: 'The black and Asian presence in British theatre, however disputed, fraught and fragile, acquired a level of organisation, dynamism, and reach that made it recognizable as a distinct and autonomous phenomenon.' In Chambers' view, this resulted in the reimagining of what British Theatre could be, which led to the creation of infinite possibilities: 'New performance aesthetics shaped by diasporic customs reinvigorated the traditional repertoire and introduced countervailing images and new verbal and visual vocabularies that challenged British preconceptions.' In the same way, schools too need to rethink what Theatre is. Chambers quotes Kedar Nath Das Gupta, born in Chittagong, Bangladesh in 1878, whose motto was 'a nation is known by its stage'. I think a school, too, is 'known' by the kind of text it's prepared to put on 'its stage'.

> Play away; consider the kind of productions your school or your child's school performs; consider the productions the big theatres put on. What does it say about these institutions?

Part of my motivation in agreeing to review the book was the 'never-ending' dialogue around the search for texts that would allow whatever student body I was working with, be it in Bangkok or elsewhere, to have an 'encounter', in order to give, in Verma's memorable soundbite, 'a voice to what is being done by the act of living'. I recommend Chambers' book, as there's a wealth of texts that may offer the 'encounter' you're searching for.

We searched and searched and searched, until finally we stumbled on Salman Rushdie's *Haroun and the Sea of Stories*. There was no-one more political than Rushdie – he of *The Satanic Verses* and the fatwa that forced him into exile. We certainly didn't tell the head teacher about the murder of Professor Hitoshi Igarashi, the Japanese translator of *The Satanic Verses*, or how the Norwegian publisher of the book was shot three times in the back (he survived), or how the Italian translator of the book was stabbed (he, too, survived). *Haroun and the Sea of Stories* was the first book Rushdie wrote after *The Satanic Verses*. At one level, it's a private experience between Rushdie and his son, Zafar; the coming together of a father and son through the telling of stories. Unlike me, the busy commuter, Rushdie created time to know his son by telling the six-year-old Zafar nightly bathtime stories. Entertained by these short vignettes, Zafar asked his father to turn them into a much longer story. His wish wasn't fulfilled for another five years. Fair enough, forced into hiding, a lot had been going on! When reflecting on what motivated him to finally meet his son's wishes, Rushdie talks about writing the story for him 'at two ages'.[26] There's the 11-year-old who would get 'an 11-year-old's pleasure' from what Rushdie called his book – 'a hymn to the imaginative life': 'I wanted Zafar to see how the world of the imagination worked, how its power is potentially greater than ordinary power.'[27] But Zafar is now grown up and he wanted to write for him, too, to see what happens when the imaginative life becomes poisoned. Continually in dialogue with himself, Rushdie wanted to return to an adult story he'd written sometime before, based on the travels of the Arabic Marco Polo, Ibn Battuta. He'd found a new context for it: 'There was a war between chatterers and silence which is quite similar to the conflict in Haroun. Years later I fished it out. It had found its context. It was important to show language in conflict with silence, an open against a closed society.'[28] For the adult reader, Rushdie explained he was attempting to 'talk about the battle between speech and those who would strangle it, those who would gag it, silence it, and that very much came out of the experience that I had just gone through, and which now as you say, sadly, many people are going through, have gone through'.[29]

It's a text that works on multiple levels. It poses big questions for students and adults alike. A central question at the heart of the book is: 'Why do stories matter if they aren't even true?' To explore such a question is to begin a search. For Rushdie, the search for certainty is rooted in our need to tell stories: 'Well, in many ways the book is an attempt to answer that question. It's really trying to say that we are all, human beings, we are story telling creatures, you know. We're the only species on the planet that does this very weird thing of telling itself stories in order to understand what kind of a creature it is.'[30] Like Said, he sees interconnectedness: 'Some of those stories are of course true stories, and some of them are like family stories, and some of them are national stories, and some of them are make-believe.'[31] It's through stories we come to know ourselves and each other: 'I think it's that mixture, the need to understand ourselves through story is very central to human beings. When a child is born, once the child feels safe and well-fed and warm, etc., very early on what it wants is a story. Tell me a story, children say. And so it's something very deep rooted in human beings the need for story.'[32]

But as another writer, James Fenton, points out, there's a spirit of uncertainty at the heart of the text, which is where, for me, its interest lies: 'Haroun is not a tract. Ideas are played with, but not forced into too tidy an order.'[33] For Rushdie, 'there had been enough preaching'. He wanted 'to talk about important things, but in a much lighter way'.[34] Fenton appreciates this desire; he's a poet very much concerned with language. He captures how Rushdie revels in the playfulness of language:

'The fantasy is charmingly conceived and related in a conversational style which, one feels, derives partly from the way the author talks to his son, and partly from the popular culture of which they are both fond. The prose is full of puns and jingles, three words (typically for Rushdie) are gleefully pressed into service where one would have done, and any vernacular is liable to be ransacked. I was reminded of the way its author once demonstrated, over lunch, how the accents of India vary with the geographical regions. I feel sure that there is much here that is intended to be heard, and that not all the intended mimicry comes across on the page.

One would expect the book, in normal circumstances, to lead on to a film.'[35]

Perhaps the filmic quality Fenton finds in his encounter with the text is because Rushdie is exploring oral storytelling; Indian storytellers in particular, who still attract large crowds from across the whole spectrum of society. Their influence in his writing is here in Rushdie's admiration of their craft. It could be a description of the story he wrote and why we were so drawn to it:

'Story-tellers don't tell a tale from beginning to end. They start with something out of mythology, but the myth becomes overlaid with twirls, digressions, anecdotes, rude jokes about politicians and songs. What they are doing seems haphazard, but it can't be. Everything is geared to keeping the audience listening. The story-teller is a juggler: his display of pyrotechnics is as important as the story itself. In the written form, you have the same effect, the feeling of a juggling act, with more than one story at a time.'[36]

Teaching context

So, it was evident *Haroun* was a rich text: 'A magic land, the quality it possesses being something between a Persian miniature and an animated cartoon.'[37] We had found Nagraa's 'new cast of characters and different themes.' We believed such a text would offer our international ensemble living in Bangkok an 'encounter'. We were lucky The National Theatre had adapted the book for the theatre. Like Rushdie, who delighted in Tim Supple's production,[38] we too 'wanted a creative response, not just a play'.[39] We wanted to offer this British International School a 'walk toward' a new kind of theatre. Chambers defines exactly what we were searching for: 'New performance aesthetics shaped by diasporic customs' would reinvigorate 'the traditional repertoire' and would introduce 'countervailing images and new verbal and visual vocabularies' that would challenge 'British preconceptions.'[40] In the context in which we were working, it was a political as well as an artistic challenge.

Many of the early rehearsals were characterized by discussions with students about their own cultures and discovering ways in which their experience could be brought out in the performance. We knew the characters would have to take themselves, their community, and the audience on a journey which would end in a feeling of respect and understanding for the people they are – Brook's 'awakening of understanding'. It was a journey a Year 10 student, Rakesh, needed to go on. He'd been surviving in school by operating as 'the clown' to the point where his peers, as well as some of his teachers, weren't taking him seriously and had stopped listening to him. In Jungian terms, he was 'the Orphan' who needed to find out who he was. He was born of Sri Lankan parents but had been adopted, growing up in a white Australian family. In early discussions when asked who he was, he said he was Australian and wasn't at all interested in anything to do with Sri Lanka. Although he had classical Tamil features, he'd been told off on a field trip for using the words 'Paki spot'. His confusion was clear to us when he was adamant a way into the melodrama and comedy of his character wouldn't be through Bollywood, informing us it would remind him of the bad time he and his family had had when living in Bombay. We weren't convinced, but starting from where he was, we set about hot-seating and improvising off text. Rakesh was asked to explore a character that's an object of much ridicule because of his love for a woman. In an early piece of improvisation, in an attempt to find some humour, he and others had the idea of dropping his trousers at a certain point. However, over time a passionate character emerged, totally committed to his deep feelings of love, now utterly distraught the woman had been kidnapped.

The transition from the light and superficial to something more serious and substantial was exactly the journey we were hoping for Rakesh. Interestingly, it was starting to lead him towards Rama in *The Ramayana*, the ancient Hindu text, whose great love, Sita, had been captured by the demon King, Ravana, and taken to Sri Lanka. No accident. His would be a huge portrayal of a 'Warrior' – someone standing up, determined to fight for what he valued. In doing so, Rakesh revealed himself to the ensemble to be passionate; tender; attractive as well as committed; reliable; and able to take risks. This wasn't the Rakesh they knew. They were being asked to reimagine him. However, under huge pressure from his peers, he included the dropping of the trousers in the first performance. Before the second performance, he came up to me, asking whether he should keep it in, sensing it was now inappropriate and not part of him anymore. I told him I didn't think it was appropriate, but it was up to him. He kept it in the second performance but still wasn't happy. In the third performance, the trousers stayed up. He'd moved from 'Orphan' to 'Wanderer' through to 'Warrior'. Another extraordinary thing happened. We had left the scene where the characters were to be married. We knew a Year 7 pupil danced at Hindu weddings in Bangkok. Pushed for time, it turned out to be a piece of improvisation in which the student and two of her Thai friends performed a Hindu wedding dance in front of the reunited couple who were above them on a platform. Suddenly, without warning, the Year 7 student went to Rakesh and pulled him down, starting to dance with him as is the custom for grooms at Hindu weddings. The symbolism was clear. Rakesh was embarrassed but, with the cast clapping as one, he joined in. On the last night, when the trousers stayed up, this developed into a huge event. We watched the whole cast, including some resistant white students who'd complained the dance was too long, clapping in tune with the audience while Rakesh was out in the space, a free spirit, dancing at an Indian wedding. We were witnessing the recognition and validation of the cultural experience of an Indian community who'd previously remained hidden and unrecognized in the school. It was also a celebration of Rakesh. In Brook's phrase, here was 'an actual moment of truth'.[41] Theatre had offered this Sri Lankan boy, who'd grown up in a white Australian family and didn't want to be reminded of India, 'a special possibility, for a short time, of seeing life more clearly'.[42]

It can be heard in Rakesh's reflections, as he describes a process which now offered him a way of living that had infinite possibilities: 'It brought out a new part in me as an individual. I've had a negative attitude to this performance since it started, but now I look back with regret at my attitude and I'm proud that I didn't quit. There is a lot more to discover in this world. I'm hoping this experience leads others into discovering this world.' The 'encounter' with a text that had allowed for the triangular relationship between text, child, and adult to flourish; between community, art, and ritual; between Eastern and Western art forms; between the private and public self, had enabled this kind of knowing. For myself, for my family, for Rakesh, we'd all been on a search that had asked us to 'know what we are', which had, in turn, taken us to a place to know 'what we may be'.[43]

1-Vivekananda, S. 2017: *Complete Works of Swami Vivekananda*: Oregan Publishing

2-Audley, A. 2014: *From singer to animal saviour: the wit and wisdom of big-hearted Dolly*: The Telegraph

3-Dr Seuss 1990: *Oh, the Places You'll Go!*: Random House

4-Melville, H. 2003: *Moby Dick*: Penguin Classics

5-Branaman Eakin, K. 1998: *According to my passport, I'm coming home*: Family Liaison Office, Washington, DC

6-Ibid

7-Ibid

8-Sullwold, E, in Abrams, J, Ed. 1990: *Reclaiming the Inner Child*: Jeremy P. Tarcher, Inc. Los Angeles

9-Plato. 2015: *Alcibiades*: Aeterna Press

10-Hemmingway, E. 1957: *The Sun Always Rises*: Pan Books

11-Brook, P. quoted in Roose-Evans, J. 1970: *Experimental Theatre-from Stanislavsky to Peter Brook*, Routledge

12-Gladwell, M. 2008: *Outliers: The Story of Success:* Little, Brown and Company

13-Carriere, Jean-Claud, translated by Brook, P. 1985: *The Mahabharata:* Harper & Row, New York

14-Faulkner, W. as quoted in: Wertlieb, M.; Bodette, M. 2015: *Salman Rushdie On Fiction, Religion And Freedom Of Expression:* Vermont Reads

http://digital.vpr.net/post/vermont-reads-2015-haroun-and-sea-stories-salman-rushdie#stream/0

15-Barba, E; Savarese, N. 2011: *A Dictionary of Theatre Anthropology:* Taylor and Frances

16-Mehta, D. 1996: *Fire:* Zeitgeist Films

17-Gajadin, C. 1992: *Amal and The Letter from the King:* Magi Publications

18-Roy, A. 2005: *The God of Small Things:* Atlantic

19-Gosling, D. 2007: *Science and the Indian Tradition: When Einstein Met Tagore (India in the Modern World):* Routledge

20-2017: *Decolonising the English Faculty: An open letter:* Posted by cambridgefly

https://flygirlsofcambridge.com/2017/06/14/decolonising-the-english-faculty-an-open-letter/

21-2017: *'Open the doors and let these books in' – what would a truly diverse reading list look like?:* The Guardian

22-Ibid

23-Ibid

24-Verma, J. 1990: *Programme note to Tartuffe:* National Theatre quoted in Daboo, J. 2017: *Staging British South Asian Culture: Bollywood and Bhangra in British Theatre:* Routledge

25-Chambers, C. 2011: *Black and Asian Theatre In Britain: A History:* Routledge

26-Neill, H. 1998: *Saved by a sea of stories*: The Telegraph

27-Ibid

28-Ibid

29-Wertlieb, M.; Bodette, M. 2015: *Salman Rushdie On Fiction, Religion And Freedom Of Expression*: Vermont Reads

30-Ibid

31-Ibid

32-Ibid

33-Fenton, J. 1991: *Keeping Up with Salman Rushdie*: The New York Review of Books

34-Neill, H. 1998: *Saved by a sea of stories*: The Telegraph

35-Fenton, J. 1991: *Keeping Up with Salman Rushdie*: The New York Review of Books

36-Neill, H. 1998: *Saved by a sea of stories*: The Telegraph

37-Fenton, J. 1991: *Keeping Up with Salman Rushdie*: The New York Review of Books

38- Rushdie, S; adapted by Supple, T; Tushingham, D. 1998: *Haroun and the Sea of Stories*: Faber

39- Neill, H. 1998: *Saved by a sea of stories*: The Telegraph

40-Chambers, C. 2011: *Black and Asian Theatre In Britain: A History*: Routledge

41-Roose-Evans, J. 1970: *Experimental Theatre-from Stanislavsky to Peter Brook*: Routledge

42-Ibid

43-Shakespeare, W. *Othello Act 4 scene 5*

CHAPTER 9: BUILDING A COMMUNITY

Play away; techniques; strategies; concepts in this chapter that can be used in different contexts:

Habitus

Prochaska and DiClemente's 'Cycle of Change'

Cultural capital

Social capital

Virtuous cycle

Unconditional

Values

Common purpose

Vulnerability

To do what it takes

Positive relationships

Loyalty

'Respicio'

Let's now travel back to Brighton where I live. I like to swim every day if I can. Over the years a little community of outdoor swimmers has formed. We chat about not very much, but there's a lot of smiling and laughter bound by the fact we're all prepared to crack the ice, diving into freezing water in the depths of the English winter, whatever the weather. Recovering in the sauna after one of these invigorating dips (I recommend it), one of my comrades had been telling me about a table tennis club he worked for and that they needed drivers. I had some spare time and didn't really think much more deeply than I quite liked playing table tennis as a child. I had also read Howard Jacobson's hilarious novel, *The Mighty Walzer*, which asks us to consider the profound question (take your time): 'Why is it that, in 1950s Manchester, lots of Jewish boys played table tennis to competition standard?'[1] Why, indeed? Go read it to find out; it's very funny. I took up my compadre's kind offer, thinking nothing more about it other than I quite like driving minibuses filled with the buzz of expectant kids going off somewhere different. I even enjoy listening to their music.

But then I entered The Fitzherbert Centre, the home to Brighton Table Tennis Club. It was founded in 2007 by Tim Holtam and Harry McCarney, originally starting out in a youth centre with two broken tables – humble beginnings. In 2015, the Catholic Church decided to give the club sole use of a 12-table venue in what was a Catholic primary school. It's on prime land in a fashionable part of Brighton, Kemptown. The church could have made a fortune selling to a private developer or to a supermarket chain. Instead, it heeded the Pope's call, that what was needed in these troubled times was 'tangible demonstrations of help'.[2] It was a shout out for community. So, what had persuaded the church in Brighton to hand over the keys to Holtam and McCarney? The gravitas came in the form of a different kind of tract – *The Metaphysics of Ping Pong*. There really is such a thing. Don't be put off, consider this definition and tell me you're not intrigued to find out more:

'There exists a supranational tribe that numbers close to four hundred million and goes under the name of The United Colours of Table Tennis. Were it not for TT, where else would you interact, as I have, with anyone from Madagascar? Or Mongolia? Or Suriname? Or Kyrgyzstan? The language barrier is eliminated, as we all speak the lingua franca of TT. In fact, as in time I began to frequent clubs all around the country, every barrier is elongated; class, colour, race, creed and so on. The TT planet seems to be a parallel world, de facto more enlightened, fair and friendly than the one we normally live in.'[3]

If the *Metaphysics of Ping Pong* is a bit too way out for you, then meet Jon Kaufman, the founder of London Progress Table Tennis Club, Tim Holtam's guide, mentor, and source of inspiration. Kaufman's core belief is rooted in inclusion: 'Not out of some token piece of political correctness, but out of a belief in the infinite possibilities of all humans.'[4] It's those infinite possibilities once again. For Kaufman, common purpose is a requisite for building community: 'Nation, race, and religion fade in the face of a common human purpose, even though that common purpose is nothing more than a local table tennis club.' One of Kaufman's mottos he often likes to quote is: 'There are only two types of people in the world, talkers and doers.' More of Kaufman later; his is a riveting story. Without doubt Holtam and McCarney are doers. The club has grown into an inclusive and diverse community of over 1,000 players a week passing through their doors. It was awarded the first ever 'Club of Sanctuary' by Brighton & Hove Council as part of the City of Sanctuary programme – 'A network of local groups that includes boroughs, towns and cities across the UK and Ireland, all committed to building a culture of welcome across every sphere of society.'[5] In June 2016, Brighton Table Tennis Club won a national prize from Migration Work UK, an award for best practice in community integration and cohesion in the United Kingdom.

Play away; it's worth quoting the judges, when awarding the honour, to get some insight into the kind of community it is; is this a powerful definition of what community might look like?

> 'In the end the Brighton Table Tennis Club won because they do something simple and necessary with such flair and enthusiasm. The Brighton Table Tennis Club is an outward facing and open project, involving a broad range of communities in Brighton, collaborating with social services and schools as well as refugee and migrant communities. The broad remit contributes to migrants and non-migrants becoming actively engaged in a range of different things in Brighton. Working with young people is very positive, especially unaccompanied minors who can find themselves very isolated. Everyone involved can take their learning back into their communities. The community integration occurring daily at Brighton Table Tennis Club is very powerful. We are watching through sport, "sons and daughters" of Brighton forming incredible friendships with victims of trafficking from Vietnam and orphaned refugees from Mosul and Aleppo.'[6]

If that has you hooked, then I refer you to Holtam's TED talk in which he captures the spirit of this life-affirming community. Watch it and you can meet the community.[7] I've been going to the club. It's everything a community aspires to be. It's everything a classroom aspires to be.

An American teacher, Erin Gruwell, realised: 'If you can change a classroom, you can change a community, and if you change enough communities you can change the world.'[8] Gruwell's belief is a bold one, but given substance as it grew out of her experiences when faced with a group of 'unteachable' students. Listen to one of these students for a moment and you'll see what she was up against: 'We had only three things in common: we hated school, we hated our teacher, and we hated each other.'[9] They were living in the toughest of environments where survival was the only priority; it was seriously hard core. 'Many of the students who entered Erin Gruwell's freshman English class weren't thinking about how to make it to graduation, but how they could make it to sixteen years old. Racial and gang tension had peaked and a record 126 murders had occurred in Long Beach that year. With the external stresses of a divided city, the students of Room 203 were not concerned with the education system that had already failed them on multiple occasions.'[10] So, what was Gruwell, a rookie teacher just out of college, to do? She turned to another adolescent living in even more extreme conditions, where survival was her only priority. Gruwell picks up the story: 'It was just after the Rodney King riots and racial tensions had spilled over into the school. After one of my students said, "I feel like I live in an undeclared war", I decided to share Anne Frank's diary with my class. I desperately wanted my teenage students to learn how to pick up a pen, rather than a gun or their fists to fight injustice in their community.'[11] She did what Holtam and McCarney did. She did what I did in my drama studio. She built a community, an ensemble, 'a diverse family'. Her students named this community, 'The Freedom Writers', after the bravest of Civil Rights activists, The Freedom Riders. In the safe space that had been created, the students felt free to write in the form of anonymous journals about their lives. They not only wrote about the violence and abuse they experienced, but also about 'love, and everything else real teenagers dealt with on a daily basis'.[12] Together they turned these journals, full of 'rawness and honesty', into a book. They sent 50 copies to every single publication house in America, 'like a message in a bottle'.[13] All declined apart from one. Incredibly, the publishing house that published *The Diary of Anne Frank*, decided to take a chance on the book the students had now nicknamed, 'the little book that could'. *The Freedom Writers Diary*, an instant New York Times Best Seller, had been born out of community.

Gruwell bears witness in several TED talks that include footage of her students. In *Becoming a Catalyst for Change*,[14] she tells how her 'diverse family' of students raised enough money to follow the trail of the Freedom Riders, another community fighting for human rights. They achieved their goal, making it to Washington DC. There's some remarkable footage where the students recount how, all 150 of them, were holding hands in the hotel, wearing badges to remember those of their peers who had died. They left the hotel, still holding hands, walking as one, to the Washington Memorial, some distance away. They intentionally stopped the traffic because, as a student explains: 'The world just goes by and no-one stops to look at somebody in their face, to actually look at them for who they are and so we stopped traffic and you could feel the presence, this was something bigger than us.' A disgruntled driver unwound the window and shouted, 'What are you doing?' A student replied, 'We are changing the world.' It's clear these students had become a community that now had a common purpose, 'to rewrite their ending'. In the film, you can see what they've become. The limitations that had been getting in their way – for some, fatally so – had been replaced by the newly-created contexts, thereby the possibilities had become infinite. They'd been empowered to reimagine themselves, resulting in all 150 Freedom Writers graduating, with many going onto higher education and forge flourishing careers.

It doesn't end there. Gruwell's desire to bring about change, just like Holtam and McCarney, drives them all to create more communities. Their motivation is captured in the Warhol quote: 'The idea is not to live forever, it is to create something that will.'[15] Gruwell has a mission to create wider, global communities. She has created 'The Freedom Writers Foundation', 'to help other educators mirror Erin and the Freedom Writers' accomplishments and ensure a quality education for all students'.[16] Brighton Table Tennis Club is now in the position to make alliances with groups beyond table tennis. Holtam has visited Jordan's Za'atari refugee camp, home to over 80,000 Syrian refugees, where a project run by the International Table Tennis Federation, with UNHCR, the

UN Refugee Agency, has been training refugees to become coaches. It's part of his 'never-ending' dialogue, as he searches for new contexts in which to place his own community.

It never ceases to astonish me how the threads intertwine if one continues to search. Recently I've been with Holtam to visit Carney's Community – a boxing club working on the front line of inner-city London. It was founded by Mick Carney MBE. Carney, now sadly deceased, really was the embodiment of what Warhol was trying to express. To my surprise, Daniel Day Lewis, who has featured in many a lesson in my drama studio over the years, was one of Carney's participants at the legendary South London boxing club, Fitzroy Lodge. Day Lewis wrote an evocative obituary when Carney passed away in 2011. He beautifully captures what Holtam, in his talk, was trying to articulate about the requisites for creating a community – the passion and the endurance. Carney selflessly devoted himself to a community, 'rain or shine; frozen or thawed; week, month and year after year'.[17] I read Day Lewis and I hear new ways to describe the kind of resilience I know I clung onto, sometimes against the odds, as a requisite for creating a long-lasting community. Holtam does the same.

'All of this – every detail absorbed – passed through the calm, studious, occasionally exasperated eyes of Mick Carney. Eyes that had seen it all before but were willing to see it again and again and again.'[18]

Play away; does this describe you or a colleague or someone you admire? Is this a definition of what meaningful teaching is, the willingness to unconditionally 'see it again and again and again'?

Carney offered his passion always as 'himself', motivated by a selfless core belief, 'A whole, lived, lifetime of a being and mostly for the benefit of others.'[19] For Carney believed essentially he was developing the whole person by creating a community bound by a conviction he held onto, even when faced with the most challenging of circumstances: 'Most of our members will never be champions but "the Lodge" helps them to be the best they can be.'[20] Like others who've portrayed the world of pugilism, Day Lewis uses a religious metaphor to describe Fitzroy Lodge's diverse community back in the day as 'a ragtag congregation' full of 'cabbies (numerous), clerks, ex-marines, trainee coppers, local villains, local "faces", apprentice toolmakers, plumbers, electricians, city boys, layabouts, (even, God forbid, a couple of actors) fitness fanatics, fatsos (some of us fell into two or more of these categories), retired pros and future prospects, estate agents (vicious), chartered accountants (extremely vicious), a journalist (dunno who let him in), a photographer, and just about anyone who came through the door and had the stomach for it or couldn't think of an excuse quick enough'. You know within minutes when you've walked into a vibrant community, because there's always a soundtrack. I often talked to other teachers about the 'health' of a class. Having carried out numerous observations, I knew when a community of children had been created just by listening to the soundtrack of purposeful talk. I know I would've loved Carney's gym, because the soundtrack of his workplace was always jazz. Have a listen:

'Cool, classic jazz: Stan Getz, Charlie Parker, John Coltrane. Jazz and the dull, rhythmic, arrhythmic, contrapuntal percussion of leather-on-leather; of gloves on heavy bags and speed balls and bodies and heads: thwappety-thwap; babbedy, babbedy, babbedy; thunk-thunk-thunk; thunk-thunk; THUNK. And the whipping and whirring of ropes, thrashing and tip-tapping on the shiny hardwood floor; grunts, sh's and s's expelled through the whistling apertures of gumshields and the regular, shrill interruption of round-timers.'

His legacy is Carney's Community, the boxing club I visited with Holtam. We were 'playing away' to see if there was transference, to place Carney's work in a different context. The community was created and is still led by another inspirational person who has spent years developing his craft within a specific community. George Turner knows what he's talking about. He has a degree in Sociology and Criminology. He specialises in 'gang work, youth justice, child protection, young people in care, mediation, substance misuse, prevention of violent extremism, family breakdown, crime prevention, mental health, sexual exploitation, employment, education and training, youth participation, parenting and project development'.[21] Turner told us the majority of the participants at the club are 'at risk', mostly severely disadvantaged, excluded, involved in criminality and anti-social behaviour, usually gang-related, often driven by fear and despair. In our conversation he captured his core belief: 'The people that are the ones most often excluded from society are precisely the ones that need including.' But he understands it takes time; there's no quick fix. There's no quick turnover. Instead, they invest. He told us about one of their participants who has finally broken the cycle of offending and self-harm. It took 17 years. When we asked about his funding streams, he explained how he's often asked about the numbers of 'exits' the club has each year, the numbers of participants who successfully transform themselves, avoiding slipping back into their 'old ways'. George laughed: 'We don't 'exit' people, we are a community.' In that moment, you have Turner's requisite for building a meaningful community in the kind of environment he describes in his challenging TED talk – *Young and in Trouble, Walking in their Shoes*.[22]

The French sociologist, Pierre Bourdieu, used the word 'habitus' to describe the way in which the culture of a particular social group is internalised by the individual during childhood. Consider the relationship of the private and the public in Bourdieu's definition of habitus: 'Society written into the body, into the biological individual.'[23] Like Gruwell's students, the habitus many of Turner's young people grow up in is an environment of violence, rejection, loss, stress, despair, anger, offending, recidivism. It's a constant cycle of homelessness, offending, and prison. We got a glimpse into the habitus when, during our visit, Turner described how one of the participants had recently been murdered. The police had called upon his help to mediate between the deceased family and a teenager who they believed had committed the murder; they lived two streets away from each other. Turner is literally saving lives in his community.

The habitus creates what Bourdieu called, a set of 'durable dispositions' – ways of acting, seeing, and making sense of the world. In his talk, Turner tells us about John, who is now 22, and the impact the habitus has had on his life, the kind of 'society written' into John's body since he was a child. Turner has worked out how much it has cost the taxpayer for all the numerous agencies that have tried unsuccessfully to engage John; a staggering one million, twelve thousand, five hundred and ninety pounds. I'll just pause here while you take this in. Turner's analysis of why John has failed to engage with any of the agencies is because there's no consistency. They're not there when he needs them. The constant turnover of staff meant he would often be talking to someone new. In other words, there are no meaningful relationships. In his desire to create a community that would offer the kind of substantive, durable relationships these young people desperately need, Turner felt there are 4 requisites underpinning everything that happens in his club. They are:

1. **The Long term** – there are no short-term interventions with little after-care. It's not time limited; it's there when the participant needs it, which is often out of office hours. Previously, the only constant – the 'durable dispositions' – in the young person's life, available night and day, was the drug dealer or the gang leader.

2. **Being consistent** – a key intervention is based on Prochaska and DiClemente's *Cycle of Change*.[24] It provides a consistent framework within which the whole community work. It applies not only to the young people but can be used with some of Turner's team, several of whom started their life at the club as an 'at risk' participant. The basis for this model is a person at any given time is at a certain stage in the cycle. Its cyclical nature

means there's no end to the process of change. If relapse occurs, the cycle can repeat. The stages are:

- *Precontemplation*: Turner's participants often arrive feeling they have no need to change their behaviour; the person may be unaware a problem exists. Turner and his team work hard to move them to the next stage so they feel there may be a better version of themselves. Turner told us often they needed to do it 'almost by stealth so as not to scare the participants off'. It's more complex than this. Habitus isn't a set of consciously held beliefs or values. Rather, it operates subconsciously, 'without any deliberate pursuit of coherence',[25] enabling us to deal with a wide variety of situations in predictable ways, just as John had done. However, this implies habitus can be changed, as it's not fixed. Bourdieu argues, 'that when an individual encounters an unfamiliar field, habitus is transformed'.[26] Turner's community creates a transformational habitus that another French sociologist, Loïc Wacquant, also discovered in a boxing gym in a similarly deprived area of Chicago's South Side. Wacquant's ethnographic research consisted of a three-year observational study, during which he immersed himself among local fighters, amateur and professional. His aim was to understand 'the social logic' of a boxing gym. The habitus in both Turner's and Wacquant's gym is based on discipline, the control of emotions and a moral code of honour. These are the very things the young people have been resisting outside of the gym. However, 'the social logic' is explained by Bourdieu's belief that these practices which happen inside the gym only become natural if frequently practised in the same environment: 'It is through the dynamic mediation of habitus, an embodied internalised system of schemes, dispositions, perceptions and appreciation, that positions in the social space are translated into practices.'[27] Wacquant's work signifies the importance of the gym in nurturing and protecting its fighters: 'Above all, the gym protects one from the street and acts as buffer against the insecurity of the neighbour-hood and the pressures of everyday life.'[28] Carney's Community creates an alternative habitus of family, support, friendship, loyalty, trust, safety, positive role models. Because of this, it becomes a 'public theatre of expression where young men (and women) from working class backgrounds devote everything to'.[29] This public expression, the new habitus, impacts on the private self, bringing a participant to feel there's a different way to live. The habitus has created 'living conditions' that operate 'as a matrix'[30] whereby the participants can present themselves, discover and develop their identity; thus allowing for the reimagining of the self.

- *Contemplation*: The first phase of the cycle can take a long time. However, there comes a point when the person becomes aware there's a problem. It's close to the transformative moment when the person discovers 'what he/she did not know what he/she did not know'. It's starting to create a present in the future. It's often provoked by an event such as having a child, or a friend being murdered, or having served a prison sentence.

- *Preparation*: The person is now intent on taking action to create a different story for him/herself. This is a transitional stage that refers back to previous chapters where we have explored the distinction between sincerity and integrity. The participant may well relapse, still unable to move away from Goss's Universal Human Paradigm, 'the water in which all human beings swim',[31] where the person is saying it should be like this or it should not be like this, giving reasons, excuses, judgements to justify harmful behaviour. The present is being created in the past once more. If that's the case, then the cycle is started again without judgement, but rather with unconditional support.

- *Action*: The person is now putting into action an agreed plan. It's vital at this point that the participant is given support in order to facilitate the action plan. It's a holistic approach where any relevant agencies such as social services or a GP, for example, can be involved in supporting the participant. In this phase, the participant is now gaining in positive 'cultural capital'. For Bourdieu, cultural capital is what dictates your position in the social order. It's all the things you acquire from belonging to a particular social class, which in turn creates a collective identity. It's the way you speak and hold yourself, it's the tastes you have, it's your material belongings, it's the skills you have acquired. Previously, the participants' cultural capital had come from the streets. Critics of cultural capital point out that it feeds elitism where particular cultural knowledge is prioritised at the expense of others. It can fail to acknowledge skills young people learn on the street simply in order to survive, that can often translate into a creativity and confidence found nowhere else. Far from denying this, Carney's Community intentionally develop a cultural capital. Unpick Bourdieu's rather dense prose and you'll see what's at work here:

> 'An education system which puts into practice an implicit pedagogic action, requiring initial familiarity with the dominant culture, and which proceeds by imperceptible familiarisation, offers information and training which can be received and acquired only by subjects endowed with the system of predispositions that is the condition for the success of the transmission and of the inculcation of the culture.'[32]

By explicitly creating a particular kind of cultural capital, Turner and his team are developing what the political scientist, Robert Putnam, defines as social capital. For Putnam, social capital 'refers to connections among individuals – social networks and the norms of reciprocity and trustworthiness that arise from them'.[33] Putnam identifies three kinds of social capital: moral obligations and norms; social values; and social networks. The sense of belonging, the trust, the networks, the moral framework underpinning their values, were all previously created on the street. However, the participants' social standing, wellbeing and interests within the world of the gym have shifted. The aim is for their social capital to begin to change outside of the gym. Many talk about avoiding the 'silliness' they've previously been involved in. However, if they lapse, there are consequences. If Turner and his team hear they've been fighting in or out of school, then they may have to attend a session but aren't allowed to put on the gloves. They are never banned; the cycle just starts again.

- *Maintenance*: Sustained change occurs and new behaviours replace old ones. Carney's Community are committed to providing opportunities in education, training, and employment. They're fully conscious of the power of networking, 'the hidden job market'. Just look at these persuasive statistics; it really is who you know: 'A job seeker who is referred is conservatively three to four times more likely to be hired (some studies found that a job seeker who is referred is 14 times more likely to be hired) than someone who applies for a position without a referral.'[34] Carney's Community are fully aware of the advantages social capital can offer. So, they maximise all of their networks to find employment opportunities to give the participants every chance to sustain change. Several have started up their own businesses as well as their own social enterprises, including a clothing label (we bought the t-shirts), fitness and personal training projects. For some, if they've shown the maintenance of sustained positive change, they're offered opportunities within the club to become a staff member or a peer mentor or a boxing coach. There's no 'exit' from the community; they will always be part of the community, but their roles change. Turner described it to us as a 'virtuous cycle of support and positivity'.

> Play away; where in your life are you a part of or see this kind of 'virtuous cycle'? What does it make you feel to be part of such a 'virtuous cycle of support and positivity'?

3. **Empathy** – An essential requisite is there's no judgement. Listen to Turner's TED talk; hear how he arrived at this understanding by supporting a sex offender who originally disgusted him. However, once he'd really listened, it brought him to the fundamental belief we shouldn't judge people 'unless we have walked in their shoes'. He poignantly leaves us with the Brazilian novelist, Paulo Coelho's words: 'We can never judge the lives of others, because each person knows only their own pain and renunciation.'[35]

4. **Unconditional** – For Turner, the most important requisite is the unconditional support the community offers, 'what any good parent gives their child'.[36] It's a support that has clear boundaries and consequences, but it's unconditional. If you watch any of the documentaries about the club,[37] they all talk in terms of family who are there for each other whatever has happened, whenever, 'rain or shine; frozen or thawed; week, month and year after year'. The participants recognise Turner's selfless devotion, 'the calm, studious, occasionally exasperated eyes... eyes that had seen it all before' but crucially are unconditionally 'willing to see it again and again and again'. It's this that gives him credibility. It's why these hard-to-reach young people still come through the doors and engage in search of a different kind of connection. It's the reason why this community exists.

> Play away; as knife crime continues to take young people's lives without any end, should those who wield power have the courage to start a conversation with George Turner and begin the 'walk toward' interventions that may have a lasting impact? Is it time to reimagine the conversation?

Maybe all of this is a bit too hard-core, far removed from the lives of many of us. Gruwell also entered a very different world, Hollywood, who made a film about her life, *Freedom Writers*,[38] starring Hilary Swank, which may take us even further away from our daily grind. Tragically, it takes us right back into Carney's and Turner's world. Armand Jones, an actor in the film, played a character named Grant Rice. Rice was active in the church, an intern at NBC, and an up-and-coming rap artist who went by the tag of 'Young Prozpect'. The film captures the day he was walking out of a convenience store when a drive-by shooting occurred, killing a person close by. Rice survived, but the actor, Armand Jones, wasn't so fortunate. In 2006, he'd attended a celebration to mark the end of filming *Freedom Writers*. After the party, he and his friends had gone to Denny's Restaurant, where they were robbed at gunpoint. Jones decided to follow the gang members out into the car park where he was shot dead in cold blood. Too far away from the world of English table tennis? Buxton Williams was a co-founder, friend and mentor to Jon Kaufman when they set up the London Progress Club together. Buxton Williams was murdered in the club: 'Six bullets in the back of the head... while making a cup of tea.' Kaufman was devastated: 'Buxton was full of the life force and now he was gone.'[39] Kaufman talks powerfully about how Williams taught him what a meaningful community means: 'It was Buxton that first taught me that Progress should belong to anyone who wanted to make it their home. Don't be exclusive. Don't be cliquey. Don't exclude anyone.'

Teaching context

Gruwell, Holtham, Kaufman, Carney, Turner – they're all teachers, even if their settings aren't in the traditional classroom. For over 33 years, my setting was a drama studio. In an article I wrote, *Professional Conversations, How Do You Do It?*,[40] I tried to put forward elements I felt were requisites if one is to create a meaningful community or, in drama terms, an ensemble.

Play away; are these requisites present wherever genuine communities have been created? Are there other requisites you'd add to this list? How could you establish and nurture these requisites within a community you work/ live in?

1. *A set of values is established*: I make the values explicit from the moment they step into my drama studio. These are the values we live by. I'm not joking when I explain I spend more time in my drama studio than in my own home. One student actually believed I slept there. The notion of home is important. I'm not going to negotiate the values. This is my habitus. I'm not telling them they must be their values outside my studio. That's for them to work out, as we have seen earlier on with Hashim and his peers. However, I tell them if I was invited round, I'd certainly be respectful of the values of their home. When you walk into someone's home, you can tell a lot from just looking around. Many of the values are reflected in the artefacts on display. I want this feeling when anyone, child or adult, enters the drama studio. They're entering a community founded on a set of values. Before a word is spoken, a set of shared values are there to see. When I walked into Turner's gym, it was exactly like this. Everywhere I looked I could see the social and cultural capital of the habitus. As we've seen, Day Lewis likes to use religious imagery. He talks about the working space being 'sacred'. At the centre of the sacred space is the boxing ring, 'an altar of sorts'.[41] The film director, Martin Scorsese, whose deep sense of Catholicism seeps into all of his work, pays homage to the mythic ring in the opening of *Raging Bull*. He films De Niro's ascension into the gladiatorial space in a slow dance to the operatic soundtrack of the Intermezzo from *Cavalleria Rusticana*. It's religious ritual. But around Turner's 'altar' were photographic collages of the numerous participants, carefully presented behind framed display boards, validating who they are and their sense of belonging to something bigger than themselves. The history of the club was there to see, wherever you

glanced, from the big events when world champions such as the all-time great, Manny Pacquiao, came to visit, to the personal events such as a recent Halloween celebration. By one wall was a rack of gloves, looking almost like a pugilistic installation in some trendy Hoxton art gallery space. But above the entrance door you couldn't fail to read the core value behind the gloves, chalked up in bright colours:

> 'You can play Football
> You can play Rugby
> You can play Tennis
> But you can't play Boxing'

So, my studio is full of artifacts from my travels around the globe, giving a sense of a bigger, exciting, diverse world out there. Areas of wall space are carefully divided. There's method in what might seem a colourful mash-up of random images and sayings. Above my desk are my personal values. For example, I'll always have the *Daily Mail*'s front page when they outed the killers of Stephen Lawrence. I tell the students this will never come down until all of them have been brought to justice. It provokes inquiry. There's a wonderful poster made up of thousands of images of Obama's face that I bought from a vendor on Venice Beach in LA, weeks after he'd been elected. I tell the students how the black woman who sold it to me cried tears when I explained I'd be putting it up in my studio in London with the words 'Yes We Can' emblazened across it. I often bump into ex-students in the street, some of whom have left school years ago. They like to quote some of the sayings on these posters: 'Life's a journey not a destination, innit sir?' (I love the way I'm always called 'sir', even though they're all grown up and they know my name is Daniel.) There are other areas that are about creativity;[42] there's a space devoted to identity;[43] there's a lot about resilience;[44] there's a great deal about the growth and fixed mindset;[45] there are naturally many images and quotes from the world of theatre that connect to the whole being;[46] there are areas about the power of one's voice; about learn to learn; about passion, and everywhere there are photographs of the students achieving. Everything they take part in outside of the curriculum, such as productions, theatre trips, cross curricular projects, are put on the wall as a shared history. Embedded in the history is a set of lived values. The power of the shared, lived history is there when some of the students, just before they leave school, sneak into the studio to remember all they've experienced. There are tears, the emotional memory is powerful. Every time I've left a school to move on, I always spend a few solitary moments, sat in the middle of the studio, just looking around staring at all the images, remembering. I can hear the voices, I can hear the cries, I can hear the laughter. This is a house we built together, based on shared values.

The process of creating this kind of community always begins with a letter I give to my Year 7 students in their very first encounter with me, about who I am and what my values are:

> Play away; what's the relationship of the private and public self in this letter? What am I asking the young students new to secondary school to reimagine?

Hi,

I want to extend to you and your family my warmest welcome to our school. My name is Mr Shindler and I will be your drama teacher this year. I'm 55 years old and have been teaching for over 30 years. That makes me very experienced so I hope to share lots with you. Drama is my passion. I know how much this wonderful art form can help young people grow and develop. However, like you, I am still learning. I believe you never stop learning. I know you and your community will be able to teach me so much. We are about to go on an exciting journey together.

When I'm not in school, I live down in Brighton on the south coast next to the sea. I live with my wife. My two daughters have left home. Ellie is 27 and Rosa is 25. I will tell you lots more about them as we get to know each other. I hope to get to know lots about your family. I had a gorgeous dog called Milly, but sadly she recently died. One day I will get another dog, but not just yet. I love playing football every Sunday evening with my friends. I've supported a football team since I was 8 years old. I shall probably bore you to death talking about this team. I also swim outdoors every weekend, rain or shine, to keep fit. My other love is travelling. When my children were younger, we lived in Thailand for 3 years and travelled to over 12 different countries. It was quite an experience!

My philosophy for learning is that each child is unique, and each child learns in a different way. One of my jobs as a teacher is to help you discover your individuality and work alongside you to maximize it. Your classmates will help you, inspire you, and become your friends. So be kind. Be patient. Because the more patient you can be with people here, the more patient you will be with them out there in the world.

My voice is the best tool I have to help you through the school day. When you feel weak, my voice will be strong to support you. When you're tired, my voice will be energetic to help you off the floor. When you're discouraged, I will encourage you. All this I will do with my volume, my tone, and my words. I want you to hear just how much I will commit to you so that you can achieve whatever it is you want to achieve. I want your voice to fill this school. I want your voice to be one of the many threads that builds this community. Sometimes I will ask you not to talk. Not because I want to silence you. I want you to listen, to yourself: your breath, your heart, and your true thoughts. I want you to listen to other people. Enjoy this opportunity, don't waste it by chatting.

I know sometimes my jokes aren't funny. I try to make light of how hard school can be because we all know that it's hard. Every teacher you'll have, including me, has cried here, hurt here, wanted to leave here. So, we joke because we understand how hard this is. The fact we persevere is the one thing that connects us all. I want this experience to be at least a little bit fun. However, often the best kind of fun comes when you've been pushed very hard, when you've come out of your comfort zone, when you've taken risk and achieved things you never thought you and others could achieve. I will have the highest expectations and will push you hard at times. If you can meet the challenges set, then I'm sure you'll grow and develop, gaining huge amounts of personal satisfaction.

All the teachers at the school, including myself, will try to be consistent and fair. We'll treat you politely and will show, by example, how you should treat others. We'll try to listen to your point of view and realise you are an individual. We'll try to encourage you to learn from your mistakes. We'll try to teach you to become self-reliant and to trust in your own judgement. We'll try to praise you when you have done well. Above all, we'll try to help you realise how special you are by showing we value you.

I am here to help you every step of the way. So, let the journey begin!

Warm regards,
Mr Shindler

> Play away; try writing a letter about who you are and your core values to someone who's meeting you for the first time, but with whom you wish to create a long-term relationship. It'll take a few drafts.

2. *Vulnerability*: When meaningful communities and ensembles are created, then something very powerful happens. Brene Brown gets to the heart of it: 'I define connection as the energy that exists between people when they feel seen, heard, and valued; when they can give and receive without judgment; and when they derive sustenance and strength from the relationship.'[47] If an ensemble

attempts to live by the values set out in my letter, then what follows is vulnerability which allows people within a safe, inclusive community to 'show up' and take risk. Vulnerability is a requisite if 'we want to experience connection'.[48] It's through connection that we grow and develop. I share this explicitly with both student and adult alike, capturing it in a poster I return to again and again:

```
Commit -> (Leads to)

Being part of an ensemble -> (Leads to)

Building Trust -> (Leads to)

Taking a risk -> (Leads to)

Growing and developing -> (Leads to)

Success
```

Step outside the classroom for a moment. Holtam introduces us to Alex. Alex was: 'Born into a family of cattle-herders, semi-nomadic and pastoralists in South Kivu, The Democratic Republic of Congo. Growing up he survived extreme poverty, hardship and violence at a terrifying scale.'[49] For Holtam, his relationship with Alex gave new meaning to 'showing up': 'What Alex taught me was that people are born in places around the world where what matters is that you were born in the rainy season or the winter, or the summer or in places where local councils don't have records in filing cabinets. What matters is that you are born at all. As a human.'[50] Holtam recounts how, during his asylum process, Alex was asked for proof of his date of birth. Alex replied: 'Is me not standing here in front of you, proof to you that I am alive?'[51] Alex continued to show up, gaining an MA in Anthropology of Conflict, Violence and Conciliation at the University of Sussex, becoming an inspirational speaker. Alex owned his story. He's one of Maya Angelou's 'strong blackbirds of promise who defy the odds and gods and sing their songs'.[52] She knows all too well why the caged bird needs to sing: 'There is no greater agony than bearing an untold story inside you.'[53]

Holtam also understands the need for many of his participants to be able to tell their untold stories they carry within. He invited an artist, Becky Warnock, into his club, because he knows for some 'reality is too complex'. He hoped the healing power of telling stories would 'give it form'.[54] Both Holtam's and Warnock's agreed aim within the context of the Table Tennis Club was 'to explore stories, memories and the ideas that connect us'.[55] However, this would require vulnerability if the person was 'to show up'. It isn't an easy process, as Brown points out: 'Owning our story can be hard but not nearly as difficult as spending our lives running from it.'[56] Warnock's way in was to explore 'the objects we use to tell our stories, to consider how these change across different cultures, ages and backgrounds'.[57] Watch Warnock's remarkable film; interestingly you'll not see the young people. They 'show up' by the viewer just hearing their untold stories. I think it allows you to really hear the honesty in the telling of these intimate testimonies. The young people have been able to embrace their vulnerabilities because a meaningful community has been created. Listen to Wazir, an unaccompanied minor from Syria, telling his story:

'You start caring when you hear the whispering. ....I try to say I don't care, I am different but deep inside you do, you do know you want acceptance... people forget where you came from, "It is not too difficult anymore, cheer up." You are ignored now, happy? ...you don't know what's what, then you reach a stage of serious insecurity, then you start to feel other pressures... there needs to be something, the need to achieve, to earn, to accomplish after you learn. It chases you... then you reach the high place you always aspire to, the fulfilment of your personal potential because it made you being with people, probably loved ones but in the end you don't believe in love. ....whatever I write will certainly vanish. You after me will be dead. ...nothing, nothing is left except for fragmentations of unheard words coming from the mouths of humans who will obviously perish so now what's the point of all of it?'

If you meet Wazir, he's very driven, but then you hear his inner story and it places his ambition in a context. However, in spite of his internal struggle, Wazir lives by another requisite for any meaningful community – to do what it takes.

3. *To do what it takes*: It's having a shared understanding we will do whatever it takes. If it means coming in on Saturdays, after school, then so be it. If it means spending 5, 6 hours planning or drafting coursework, so be it. If it means getting up at 5 in the morning to go to a tournament, getting back at 2 in the morning, so be it. Simply put, 'Nothing in the world is worth having or worth doing unless it means effort, pain, difficulty.'[58] But the unaccompanied minors like Wazir, like Faisal, at the table tennis club, don't need reminding of this: 'Faisal turned out to be an exceptional character – eager, hungry and full of fight, passion, energy and enthusiasm; ready to work for and grasp opportunities that came his way. He has spoken recently of travelling across land in cars crammed with up to 40 people, sometimes 6 to a boot, of walking, getting lifts wherever possible, and of working together with others to walk halfway across the planet to escape misery and seek a better life.'[59] In a less extreme context, my challenging GCSE pupils also grew to understand what it meant when someone says, we'll do what it takes. They would think nothing of getting out of bed on a Saturday, no mean feat, and working through from 10am (It was meant to start at 9am, but hey, what can you do?) to 1pm without a break, not even to go to the toilet. Other staff never believed me. Ofsted did: 'Participation in the Saturday session in the week of the inspection was outstanding.'[60]

4. *Common purpose*: For any kind of genuine commitment, there has to be common purpose. I would always tell my students I'm

not here to teach them drama, nor is the teacher next door here to teach them Maths or Science. Slightly taken aback, this would eventually lead them to the essential question we would keep returning to: 'What kind of person do you want to be at 13 or at 16 or beyond?' In answering this over a long period of time, often five years, we might find a common purpose. For Gruwell and her students, it's partly about becoming citizens of change. For Holtam, it's about seeing the individual as a person, rather than as someone who has cancer or is a traveler or has ADHD or is a refugee. For Carney and Turner, it's about helping young people to be the best they can be. But all of us might answer that our common purpose is to empower young people to flourish once they leave us as creative, inspiring, skillful, confident, agile, articulate, brave, resilient, generous, reflective human beings, comfortable with each other and with themselves, prepared to stand up for what they believe.

5. *Positive relationships*: With common purpose, positive relationships are created. I liked to throw this one at my students: 'If you hang out with chickens, you're going to cluck, and if you hang out with eagles, you're going to fly.'[61] Some remarkable relationships are made at Holtam's and McCarney's club. (It may be why they won best sports club in Britain in the 2019 prestigious *Daily Mirror Pride of Sport Awards*, some achievement.) In his TED talk, Holtam described the relationship three-times UK-Chinese Champion and club coach, Wen Wei Xu, has with Harry Fairchild as, 'brothers, they identify as brothers'. Harry is the godfather to Holtam's daughter. Google Harry and you'll find him on YouTube; in *The Guardian*; in the local paper; on numerous table tennis sites; on Down's Syndrome sites; on the BBC Sport website, where you can even watch a film about him.[62] Harry is the world's first table tennis Level One Coach with Down's Syndrome. He's the National Down's Syndrome Champion and won a bronze medal in the World Trisome Games in Italy. He returned from the World Down's Syndrome Championships as a gold medal winner in the men's doubles.[63] Watch him appear on the stage with Holtam during his TED talk, and you'll see a

man – he's in his late twenties – who's creative, inspiring, skillful, confident, agile, articulate, brave, resilient, generous, reflective, comfortable with others and with himself, prepared to stand up for what he believes. But it's the relationships that are so special. For his mother, Linsey, it has opened up, 'a whole new world for Harry, both at home and abroad. It is a world which he is thoroughly happy to be living in'.[64] My aim was to also make my Drama studio a world in which students would be 'thoroughly happy to live in'. We saw this in an earlier chapter with Chantelle and the able boys. This was the only environment in her entire week, both in and out of school, where she found such positive, life-enhancing relationships. We saw it with Alisha and her group. During a weekly 'gratitude' tradition in assemblies, to offer a space for students to give praise to anyone who had helped them, one of Alisha's group was impelled to tell her entire year how much her group meant to her, not only in drama but giving her the strength to get through the week. She tearfully finished by declaring, 'I love my group.' Perhaps a little over the top, but she was prepared to make herself vulnerable, to 'show up' in front of her peers, to express her feelings about a complex process that had created such positive relationships bound by a common purpose.

6. *Loyalty*: All of these requisites inspire loyalty. I have many tales of the extremes which students will go to, against all the odds, to avoid letting down their group or me. But it also inspires a special loyalty in the adult. In 2010, I was caught in Thailand during the Icelandic volcanic ash episode, when all planes were grounded. It was weeks away from the Year 11 practical exam. I was in despair; nothing was moving. I even emailed the exam board, who said the show must go on; of course they did. Then a plane was leaving for Madrid. I rushed to the airport, but found only First Class was available. I paid an astronomical sum, way beyond the means of a drama teacher, to discover – when I got to Madrid – pandemonium. Looking lost and bereft, two Swedish women approached me, offering to drive all the way if I was prepared to pay all of the tolls. I accepted on the spot. I slept in the back seat, only waking to hand over some money. I made it home just as term was

starting. Naturally, I had to recount the story to my Year 11s often. While this entertained them, what really impacted was my loyalty to the common purpose and to our relationships. (The boys half joked about being alone with two women. So the story also became one of loyalty and commitment to one's partner and family. I've talked to numerous boys over the years about drawing a circle in the sand and stepping inside it. It's trying to begin a 'walk toward' a new understanding of what loyalty might mean to young men who often lack this kind of role model in their lives.)

Step outside the classroom for a moment and hear how Holtam helped Anh – the first unaccompanied minor to be brought to him by a social worker who felt the table tennis club could offer Anh a home. While the Home Office had accepted Anh was a 'Victim of Trafficking', he'd been refused asylum. Holtam called it a 'privilege' to accompany Anh to Heathrow Immigration Removal Centre – a detention centre for asylum seekers aged over 18, where there's also an asylum court. The Judge listened to both sides. The Home Office made their case: 'The barrister from the Home Office argued that Anh's story that he had given 18 months earlier when he first arrived in England was not credible or consistent and that he could be relocated back to another part of Vietnam and that he would be fine.'[65] According to Holtam, the solicitor and barrister provided by Brighton Housing Trust were both 'fantastic'. However, it took two weeks before a verdict came in. Holtam describes what it was like: 'Anh was waiting to hear about the future of his whole life. On a knife-edge.' Then the verdict arrived. Unable to understand the 20 page verdict from the judge he'd received through the post, Anh immediately rang up Holtam for help: 'I met him and read the letter with him, both totally unsure about the outcome. Amongst a huge amount of other factors that contributed to the Judge's decision, two sentences stood out to me: "He has settled into Brighton, has a good relationship with his foster carers. He is currently studying, working part-time and is an accomplished Table Tennis player that receives coaching... The appeal is granted on asylum grounds.".'[66] Anh was granted five years' leave, but when it expires he will have to apply for indefinite leave to remain in the UK. He's getting on with his life, attending college, and has become a Level 1 table tennis coach. However, his case remains uncertain, as it does for many of the unaccompanied minors who attend the club. The loyalty Holtam shows these young people creates a community of sanctuary.

Gruwell's students, Turner's boxers, Holtam's table tennis players, my drama students, all came to an understanding about what respect really means. The root of the word comes from the Latin, 'respicio'. Its meaning is nuanced. True respect, 'respicio', can mean to look back at; to gaze at; to consider; to respect; to care for; to provide for. Those of us who've built and have been a part of meaningful communities in which the possibilities are infinite know the importance of 'respicio', for a community involves all of these things. It's a complex process of reimagining what this might mean: 'Alone we can do so little; together we can do so much.'[67] It's a process in need of deconstruction, because many communities worth anything have been created with intention and purpose. They don't just happen. They are public spaces in which the private self can discover itself.

1-Jacobson, H. 2016: *The Mighty Waltzer*: Oberon Books

2-Kirchgaessner, S. 2015: *Vatican to take in two refugee families as Pope calls for 'every religion' to help*: The Guardian

3-Mina di Sospiro, G. 2013: *The Metaphysics of Ping-Pong*: Yellow Jersey Press, London

4-Kaufman, J. 2005: *The meaning of success, the rise and fall (and imminent demise?) of London Progress Table Tennis Club*: Nima Print and design services

5-www.cityofsanctuary.org

6-www.integrationawards.uk

7-Holtam, T. 2018: *How Table Tennis Can Change The World*: TEDxBrighton

8-McLellan, D. 2000: *On Road to Unity With Freedom Writers*: LA Times

9- Freedom Writers Foundation: http://www.freedomwritersfoundation. org/index.php/about-us/our-story

10-Ibid

11-Gruwell, E: *I was inspired all over again*: anne frank house

http://web.annefrank.org/en/Education/Teachers-portal/From-the-classroom/I-was-inspired-all-over-again/

12-Freedom Writers Foundation: http://www.freedomwritersfoundation. org/index.php/about-us/our-story

13-Mcleod, M. 2007: *Interview: Erin Gruwell, author of "The Freedom Writers Diary"*: Showbizmonkeys.com: http://www.showbizmonkeys. com/movies.php?id=30

14-Gruwell, E. 2012: *Becoming a Catalyst for Change*: TEDxChapmanU

https://www.youtube.com/watch?v=Thd8xw_poNo

15-Warhol, A.: source unknown

16-Freedom Writers Foundation: http://www.freedomwritersfoundation. org/index.php/about-us/our-story

17-Day Lewis, D. 2013: *The Fitzroy Lodge: Mick Carney*: Port Magazine

http://www.port-magazine.com/uncategorized/the-fitzroy-lodge-mick-carney/

18-Ibid

19-Ibid

20-Carney's Community: http://carneyscommunity.org/about-us/mick-carney/

21-Ibid

22-Turner, G. 2103: *Young and in trouble, walking in their shoes*: TEDx SquareMile

https://www.youtube.com/watch?v=FnfaapUl9JM

23-Bourdieu, P. 1990: *In Other Words*: Stanford University Press

24-Prochaska, J., DiClemente, C. 1982: *Transtheoretical therapy: Toward a more integrative model of change*: Psychotherapy: Theory, Research & Practice, Vol 19(3)

25-Bourdieu, P. 1984: *Distinction: A Social Critique of the Judgement of Taste*: London, Routledge

26-Bourdieu, P. 1999: *The Weight of the World: Social Suffering in Contemporary Society*: Stanford University Press

27-Bourdieu, P. 1984: *Distinction: A Social Critique of the Judgement of Taste*: London, Routledge

28-Wacquant, L. 2004: *Body & Soul: Notebooks of an Apprentice Boxer*: Oxford University Press

29-Wacquant, L. 1995: *The pugilistic point of view: How boxers think and feel about their trade* Theory and Society, Vol. 24(4), Springer

30-Bourdieu, P. 1991: *Sport and social class* in: Mukerji, C., Schudson, M. (Eds.). *Rethinking popular culture: Contemporary perspectives in cultural studies* Berkeley: University of California Press

31-Goss, T. 1995: *The Last Word on Power*: Rosetta Books

32-Bourdieu, P. 1984: *Distinction: A Social Critique of the Judgment of Taste*: Harvard University Press

33-Putnam, R. D. 2000: *Bowling Alone: The collapse and revival of American Community: New* York: Simon and Schuster

34-The CareerXRoads 2014: *Source of Hire Report* http://www.careerxroads.com/news/2014_SourceOfHire.pdf

The Harvard Business Review called it the UK's 'hidden job market'

Lees, J. 2011: *Crack the Hidden Job Market:* Harvard Business Review

Most British businesses are small (84%). The British Federation of Small Businesses reported that 47% of their members found jobs through word of mouth and 31% through existing employees

FSB report, 2009: *The Job Centre is not working*

https://www.fsb.org.uk/docs/default-source/fsb-org-uk/policy/assets/fsb-report---reform-the-job-centre.pdf?sfvrsn=1

35-Coelho, P. 2007: *The Witch of Portobello*: Harper Collins

36-Turner, G. 2103: *Young and in trouble, walking in their shoes*: TEDx SquareMile

https://www.youtube.com/watch?v=FnfaapUl9JM

37-A good place to start is, *Born a Believer - Full Length Documentary*

https://www.youtube.com/watch?time_continue=13&v=4QSfoHC8yN8

38-*Freedom Riders*: 2007, Paramount

39-Kaufman, J. 2005: *The meaning of success, the rise and fall (and imminent demise?) of London Progress Table Tennis Club*: Nima Print and design services

40-Shindler, D. 2018: *Professional Conversations, How Do You Do It?*: National Drama: Drama, Vol. 6.2

41-Carol Oates, J. 2006 (first published February 20th, 1987): *On Boxing:* Harper Perennial Modern Classics

42-Some quotes on my Drama Studio wall:

Creativity

- 'All children are artists. The problem is how to remain an artist once he grows up' Picasso (Quote attributed to Picasso in TIME, October 4, 1976: *Modern Living: Ozmosis in Central Park*)
- 'You can't use up creativity. The more you use, the more you have' Maya Angelou (Quoted in Ardito, M. 1982: *Creativity:*

It's the Thought that Counts: Bell Telephone Magazine, Volume 61, Number 1)

- 'After nourishment, shelter and companionship, stories are the thing we need most in the world' Philip Pulman (Widely quoted, source unknown)
- 'Nothing is finite. We have built a context to explore so now we can use our imaginations to dive into it further. This will become a personal journey of discovery through your choices and decisions' (Daniel Shindler)

43-Identity

- 'To be an immigrant, good or bad, is about straddling two homes, whilst knowing you don't belong to either. It is about both consuming versions of blackness, digging around in history until you get confirmation that you were there, whilst creating your own for the present and the future' Reni Eddo-Lodge (Shukla. N.2016: *The Good Immigrant*: Unbound)
- 'How much do we give up and how much do we retain of our cultural identity in order to be ourselves?' Stuart Hall (Adams, T. 2007: *Cultural hallmark*: The Guardian)
- 'Awareness of our situation must come before inner changes, which in turn come before changes in society. Nothing happens in the "real" world unless it first happens in the images in our heads' Gloria Anzaldua (Anzaldba, G. 1999: *Borderlands/La Frontera: The New Mestiza*: Aunt Lute Books, San Francisco)

44-Resilience

- 'If you always do what you've always done, you'll always get what you've always got' Anon
- 'Deferred gratification: Blood +Sweat + Tears = Long term gratification' (Daniel Shindler)
- 'There's really no such thing as the 'voiceless'. There are only the deliberately silenced or the preferably unheard' Arundhati Roy (Roy, A: The 2004 Sydney Peace Prize Lecture)

- 'Finally I was able to see that if I had a contribution I wanted to make, I must do it, despite what others said. That I was OK the way I was. That it was all right to be strong' Wangari Maathai (As quoted in the article Maathai, W.: *You Strike The Woman* by Sears, P. 1991 In Context #28)

45-The growth and fixed mindset

- 'In a growth mindset, challenges are exciting rather than threatening. So rather than thinking, oh, I'm going to reveal my weaknesses, you say, wow, here's a chance to grow' Carol Dweck (Dweck, C. 2006: *Mindset: The Psychology of Success*: Ballatine Books, New York)
- 'If you are prepared to stick your head out you will grow. No one is going to chop it off!' (Daniel Shindler)
- 'It's not that I'm so smart, it's just that I stay with problems longer' Albert Einstein (Widely quoted, source unknown)
- 'You don't have to be in a boxing ring to be a great fighter. As long as you are true to yourself, you will succeed in your fight for that in which you believe' Muhammad Ali (Widely quoted, source unknown)

46-The world of theatre/ the whole being

- 'I like it when the workplace is treated as a sacred space' Daniel Day Lewis (Wazir, B. 2002: *Age of experience*: The Guardian)
- 'I live my life because I dare. I dare to show up when everyone else might hide their faces and hide their bodies in shame' Gabourey Sidibe (Sidibe, G. 2014: In her speech at the Ms. Foundation for Women's Gloria Award and Gala)
- 'I had to concentrate on my mind and my partner's mind; these are my circles of attention' Year 9 pupil
- 'An actor must train the concentration, train the body, focus the body as well as the mind...learn to release it and travel freely' Yoshi Oida (Oida, Y. 1992: *An actor adrift*: Methuen Drama)

- **'You must make your invisible inner experience visible'** Konstantin Stanislavsky (Stanislavsky, C. Trans. Hapgood, E. 1936: *An Actor Prepares* New York: Routledge, 1936)
- **'Acting is not about being someone different. It's finding the similarity in what is apparently different, then finding myself in there'** Meryl Streep (Widely quoted, source unknown)

47-Brown, B. 2015: *Rising Strong:* Vermilion

48-Brown, B. 2010: *The Gifts of Imperfection: Let Go of Who You Think You're Supposed to Be and Embrace Who You Are:* Hazelden Publishing

49-Holtam, T. 2016: *A Club of Sanctuary:* Sporting Polemics: http://www.sportingpolemics.com/

50-Ibid

51-Ibid

52-Angelou, M. 1969: *I Know Why the Caged Bird Sings:* Random House

53-Ibid

54-Godard, L. - widely quoted, source unknown

55-Warnock, B. 2017: *Crossover Point:* HOUSE Biennial: https://housebiennial.art/exhibition/crossover-point/

56-Brown, B. 2010: *The Gifts of Imperfection: Let Go of Who You Think You're Supposed to Be and Embrace Who You Are:* Hazelden Publishing

57-Warnock, B. 2017: *Crossover Point:* HOUSE Biennial: https://housebiennial.art/exhibition/crossover-point/

58-Roosevelt, T.1897: *American Ideals: And Other Essays, Social and Political:* G.P. Putnams and Son, New York and London

59-Holtam, T. 2016: *A Club of Sanctuary:* Sporting Polemics: http://www.sportingpolemics.com/

60-Inspection of Swanlea School, Ofsted Reports, 2005: https://reports. ofsted.gov.uk/provider/files/800703/urn/100973.pdf

61-Maraboli, S. 2013: *Unapologetically You: Reflections on Life and the Human Experience*: Better Today

62-BBC Sport 2018: *World's first table tennis coach with Down's syndrome*: https://www.bbc.co.uk/sport/get-inspired/39271645

63-Caleb Yule made an award-winning short documentary, *Believe That*, which follows the journey of Team Santos, three players from Brighton Table Tennis Club including Harry, as they prepare to represent their country at the European Down's Syndrome Championships. I cooked the wood-fired pizzas off a truck for the premier at the Duke of York's Picturehouse, Brighton; true story (https://www.believethatfilm.com)

64-Down's Syndrome Association, 2016: *Brighton table tennis player wins bronze medal in first World Games for athletes with Down syndrome*: https://www.downs-syndrome.org.uk

65-Holtam, T. 2016: *A Club of Sanctuary*: Sporting Polemics: http://www.sportingpolemics.com/

66-Ibid

67-Lash, J. 1980: *Helen and Teacher: The Story of Helen Keller and Anne Sullivan Macy*: Merloyd Lawrence Book: Delacorte Press/Seymour Lawrence, New York

CHAPTER 10: EXPERTISE AND EMPOWERMENT

Play away; techniques; strategies; concepts in this chapter that can be used in different contexts:

Duality of motivation

T thinking

Erasure

The Matilda Effect

Nurture/Nature

Sexism/racism/anti Semitism

Passion

To live with your whole heart

Science

The race for the double helix/DNA

Project-based learning

Critical thinking/'ordinary thinking done well'

Content and inquiry

Authentic achievement

The inquiry question/The driving question

The necessary text

Grotowskian shocks

Variable extraction

Mantle of the expert/ 'the commission'

Critiquing

'Brilliant mistakes'

The creation of excellence/ 'beautiful work'

Drafting

Drafting an oral response

Modelling

Teacher as learner

Mentoring

Creating and delivering a lecture

Assessment for learning/ formative assessment

Pedagogy of 'engagement'/ pedagogy of 'contingency'

Cooperative learning

Questioning

Bloom's taxonomy

Substantive conversations

Negotiated scaffolding

Visible learning

Argumentation

Teacher in role

Enacting dialogue

Teacher artists

Accountable talk/accountability to language

Cumulation

Dialogic teaching

Pink's three drivers of motivation

Craft

Designing schemes of learning

Text as a happening

The Stand revisited

*A word of caution, this chapter is long. I also call up a lot of experts. Too long? Over-quoted? Perhaps, but we're talking about expertise and empowerment. It takes time. If you don't believe me, then hear it from the Spanish painter who also was – get ready, it's a very long list – a sculptor, printmaker, ceramicist, stage designer, poet, and playwright (10 points if you can say who it is): 'It took me a lifetime.'[1] It isn't something you can do on your own. Who are we to disagree with the Hindu proverb, 'If you would be an expert, keep company with experts.' So, big breath, here goes...

'Daniel, what do you feel about joining up with the science department to design a project about DNA?' asked my line manager one day. I shuddered. My experience of science at school hadn't been a good one. I had spent all my life feeling like Macbeth when he tells the doctor, who is looking after his wife, 'Throw physic to the dogs; I'll none of it.'[2] I took Cicero's advice and kept my mouth shut whenever anything scientific came up: 'No-one can speak well, unless he thoroughly understands his subject.'[3] I hadn't a clue about DNA. However, Csikszentmihalyi, one of those experts we've met before, identifies the duality of motivation in this context:

> 'Each of us is born with two contradictory sets of instructions: a conservative tendency, made up of instincts for self-preservation, self-aggrandizement, and saving energy, and an expansive tendency made up of instincts for exploring, for enjoying novelty and risk –the curiosity that leads to creativity belongs to this set. But whereas the first tendency requires little encouragement or support from outside to motivate behaviour, the second can wilt if not cultivated.'[4]

So, spurred on by survival, vanity, and the feeling of challenge, I set to work. I was doing a lot of T Thinking. We all know a little about a lot of things such as politics, food, sport, music, and so on. This lies across the top of the bar. For most of us, however, we know a great deal about one, if we are lucky, two or three areas we spend the majority of our waking hours practising. My deep dive down the 'T' is drama. That's all I really know. It's been my lifelong craft (I have started to learn a new craft, ethical cooking, as the burns on my arms can testify – long story).

Breadth of Knowledge

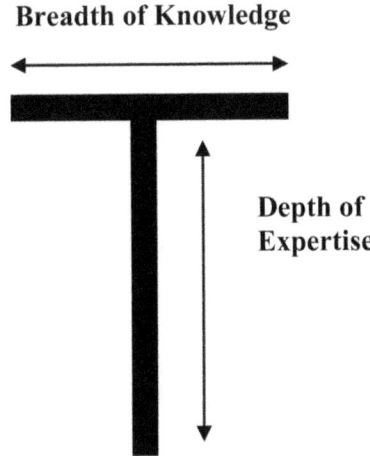

Depth of Expertise

Now I was tripping perilously across the top of the bar, finding out what everyone seemed to know apart from me; that Crick and Watson discovered the structure of DNA, 'the double helix', in 1953. Then, in my increasingly panicked search, I stumbled across a scientist called Rosalind Franklin, who I'd also never heard of. I blame my teachers once again. It was one of those breakthrough moments when, 'Never again will a single story be told as though it were the only one.'[5] It's hardly surprising, when you discover how many women scientists from the past have been erased from the textbooks. I started to learn about 'erasure' – 'a blunt word for a blunt process' that asks the fundamental question, 'Whose stories are taught and told?' 'Erasure' is an insidious process involving 'the practice of collective indifference that renders certain people and groups invisible. The word migrated out of the academy, where it alluded to the tendency of ideologies to dismiss inconvenient facts, and is increasingly used to describe how inconvenient people are dismissed, their history, pain and achievements blotted out.'[6] This led me to the pioneering work of Professor Margaret Rossiter, who called the erasure of women scientists and their work, 'The Matilda Effect'. Just like many women scientists working in the field today, Franklin suffered from 'The Matilda Effect'. The most recent example is that of Dame Jocelyn Bell Burnell who discovered radio pulsars, but it was her male collaborators who received the Nobel Prize for Physics in 1974, not her. As an acknowledgement for her lifetime achievement in science, she was awarded the 2018 Breakthrough prize, winning £2.3 million pounds. However, she has decided to donate it to the Institute of Physics to fund women, under-represented ethnic minority and refugee students to become physics researchers. She set up the Athena Swan programme to combat what Dame Athene Donald, fellow of the Royal Society and Professor of Experimental Physics at Cambridge University, calls out here: 'Many female scientists are either not there at all on Wikipedia or just [have] stubs... It's not just the historical characters, it's the current ones, and these very eminent women just somehow get overlooked.'[7] In an attempt to fight this systemic sexism, Dr Jessica Wade, a British physicist, writes 270 Wikipedia pages each year in order to record the achievements of women scientists. She has championed Angela Saini's award winning book, *Inferior: The True Power of Women and the Science that Shows It,* raising enough money for the book to be sent to every secondary school in the country. It counters an argument stretching back to Darwin, who promoted the belief that the lack of women's achievements was down to their intellectual inferiority. It's still a view held today by some. Google's technical workforce is made up of a mere 20% of women. James Damore, a Google software engineer, was sacked for writing a memo after attributing this to biological differences. As you can see, I was starting to dig around.

Then I discovered Rosalind Franklin wasn't only a woman and a scientist, but she was also Jewish. Here was my motivation. Rather than wilting in the face of something I knew nothing about, Csikszentmihalyi's 'expansive tendency' of inquiry was provoked. My curiosity pricked, I was away, sliding down the T bar in search of depth. I read Brenda Maddox's book, *Rosalind Franklin: The Dark Lady of DNA*[8] (a reference to a disparaging remark made by one of Franklin's colleagues, Maurice Wilkins, in a note to Frances Crick in 1953 – much more of these two later); I watched *PBS Nova documentary DNA: The Secret of Photo 51*; I went to Jewish sources; I looked at feminist opinion. The more I found out, the more empowered I was becoming. There were so many possibilities for my students and for me to explore in search of depth, rather than thinly skating across the top.

> Play away; see if any of what you're about to read provokes you to slide down the T bar with me and my students.

Franklin's Jewish background – Her great grandfather, Abraham, had immigrated to England in 1763. Rosalind was born into a wealthy Jewish family that might be described as 'Liberal Orthodox'. Her mother and father committed a lot of their time working with the German/Jewish Refugee Committee in Woburn Square. They even took in two Jewish children who had escaped Nazi Germany. For a time, Rosalind shared her room with a woman whose father had been sent to Buchenwald. Immediately I was making connections with the link between DNA and Hess's chilling definition of Nazism, 'applied Biology'. Eugenics was something young people needed to have some knowledge of.

Nurture/Nature – This was a chosen area the science teacher wanted the students to explore. All the accounts about Rosalind growing up could offer a particular context to dive deeper into this debate. As a privileged, liberal woman, her background should have had a huge pull in the direction of political, educational, and charitable forms of community service. However, from an early age her mother describes her nature as someone who 'could never accept a belief or statement for which no reason or proof could be produced'.[9] She had a natural fascination with physics and chemistry, nurtured by going to one of the few schools in the country at the time, St Paul's, which allowed girls to study the sciences. She continued to live in an environment that would continue to shape her. She studied natural sciences at Newnham College, Cambridge. Apparently, this was in spite of her father's disapproval of women receiving university education, initially refusing to pay for her tuition. It was only through her mother's and her aunt's resistance – the aunt offering to pay – that her father gave in. Not all women of the time were so fortunate to have such strong allies. My refugee grandfather didn't believe Oxford or Cambridge would give a 'foreigner' a scholarship, refusing to give one of his daughters the money to register her application – £5 at the time. My aunt always believed his motivation was because he wanted her to work for him in his business and probably help with the housework. She wound up studying commerce at Birmingham University and living at home. Ironically, soon after, she did actually get herself a job in Cambridge to be near her fiancé, so never ended up working for her father.

However, for Rosalind, it was because of these forces in her background that she had the opportunity to continue to live in such a formative environment. Her close friend was a French physicist who influenced her intellectually, giving her a love of France. She would spend the happiest years of her life working in Paris. She wrote to her mother, the strong sentiments perhaps rooted in her heritage: 'I have always preferred "foreigners" to the English.'[10] It's interesting there are no recorded reasons why she decided to leave a place in which she was thriving to seek a research post in London in 1950. Maddox hints at a love interest in the head of the Parisian laboratory, the crystallographer, Jacques Mering, who apparently was a philanderer.

This is 'the game of life' we get pupils to explore, looking at their 'road map' in order to examine the influences surrounding the decisions they make. They start to see the human being is, indeed 'a bundle of relations, a knot of roots, whose flower and fruitage is the world'.[11] By trying to untangle the knots of Franklin's life, the young people could start to slide down the T bar with me, beginning to engage with complex ideas inherent within statements such as this: 'In the real world there is no nature vs. nurture argument, only an infinitely complex and moment-by-moment interaction between genetic and environmental effects.'[12]

> Play away; debate, as we did, Mate's assertion, true or false?

Expertise – Franklin spent her short life becoming an expert. Her body of work is extraordinary in light of the obstacles she faced and her early death at the age of 37. She earned a PhD from Cambridge in 1945, publishing five influential papers still cited today. She continued to publish papers in coal research throughout her professional life. In Paris, she became an expert in X-ray diffraction techniques, a skill enabling her to gain a post to work with DNA fibres. Her talent, as an artist and a machinist, empowered her to build her own molecular models and equipment. This would lead her to carry out the most important work of her life – developing a new technique for studying DNA structure by using X-ray diffraction. Can you hear how interested I was now becoming? I was also getting excited. There's a brilliant moment that exemplifies Franklin's expertise when, in 1952, she travels up to Cambridge to view Watson and Crick's first attempt to build a model to represent the structure of DNA. Franklin took one look at it and got on the next train back to London. 'Brap!' as my students would say. Crick and Watson's humiliation was complete when Cambridge ordered them to stop all work on DNA. However, there was no stopping Franklin. Her expertise led to finally proving, in her now famous Photograph 51, that the structure of DNA was, in fact, a double helix. She was the first person to ever discover this – an extraordinary achievement: 'Her photographs are among the most beautiful X-ray photographs of any substance ever taken.'[13]

When she finally left King's in 1953, she went to Birkbeck College where she published 17 papers, no less, on Tobacco Mosaic Virus, breaking new ground in this highly specialised area. Even when battling with three kinds of cancer, she still managed to publish 13 papers and was part of a team developing a vaccine for Polio. There comes a stage when both students and adults become resistant 'to do the work'. Watson and Crick had certainly not done the work; hence they lacked all credibility in the eyes of Franklin. I call it 'pub talk'; Plato is more brutal: 'An empty vessel makes the loudest sound, so they that have the least wit are the greatest babblers.'[14] The challenge wasn't to babble on about DNA but to talk from a position of knowledge and expertise if the students, as well as I, would be taken seriously.

Sexism/racism – In the post-Weinstein era and the safe spaces debate in universities, Franklin's experiences have never been more relevant. Science was, and still is, a male dominated environment. I knew about the BBC's exposure into female pay, so wasn't surprised to learn that female scientists were paid less than their male counterparts. I wasn't too shocked to hear at King's there was a male common room that barred Franklin from mixing with her colleagues. But once again, my certainties were overthrown when I read a disturbing article, 'Why science breeds a culture of sexism'.[15] Batty and Davis expose the full extent of what it means to be a woman working in science today. Unlike me, Franklin probably wouldn't have been surprised to hear how,

> 'The hierarchy, working environment and male-dominated culture of science, not only in their university but in their specialism/discipline, makes tackling sexual misconduct more complex and challenging than in other academic fields and industries. Not only can harassment have a devastating impact on the victim's career and mental health, it often results in them leaving science altogether, depriving society of their contribution to solving important problems, from health to the environment and engineering.'

Franklin would have recognised much of what Dr Kate Clancy, an American anthropologist, describes,

'There's actual sabotage of people's work, there is alienation and exclusion... We heard from a number of women who were denied access to fossils or other types of materials that they needed to conduct their work, and others who if they did not have sex with the field site director were not allowed to come back to the site.' In other cases, she says, 'women were only allowed to clean archaeological finds, rather than work on the excavations'.

Another expert, Dr Karen Kelsky, sums up the environment Franklin faced, clearly still prevalent today, pointing to the way academic research is structured as being part of the problem. It's not only the long hours, isolation, and late-night research, but the strict hierarchy with the all-powerful male professor at the top, exactly as Franklin found it. Unlike Franklin, many women simply leave the 'leaky pipeline' that's only now starting to be exposed. The misogyny is there to be read in James Watson's book, *The Double Helix: A Personal Account of the Discovery of the Structure of DNA*.[16] Based on three short meetings with Franklin, he creates a picture of a physically unattractive woman with a difficult, aggressive personality, who was impossible to work with. Listen to his jaw-dropping description of Franklin, referring to her as 'Rosy' throughout the book,

'I suspect that in the beginning Maurice hoped that Rosy would calm down. Yet mere inspection suggested that she would not easily bend. By choice she did not emphasize her feminine qualities. Though her features were strong, she was not unattractive and might have been quite stunning had she taken even a mild interest in clothes. This she did not. There was never lipstick to contrast with her straight black hair, while at the age of thirty-one her dresses showed all the imagination of English blue-stocking adolescents. So it was quite easy to imagine her product of an unsatisfied mother who unduly stressed the desirability of professional careers that could save bright girls from marriages to dull men.'

Or when he describes a walk he took one cold winter night: 'Certainly a bad way to go out into the foulness of a heavy, foggy November night was to be told by a woman to refrain from venturing an opinion about a subject for which you were not trained.' Then there's his summary of the conflict between Franklin and Maurice Wilkins, a fellow researcher in the King's Research unit, who later gave Watson Photograph 51 without Rosalind's knowledge: 'Clearly Rosy had to go or be put in her place... unfortunately, Maurice could not see any decent way to give Rosy the boot.' The solution for a man like Watson was of course this, 'The best home for a feminist was in another person's lab.' In fact, Franklin decided to leave of her own accord. Wilkins rejoices in a letter to Crick, 'I think you will be interested to know that our dark lady leaves us next week... at last the decks are clear and we can put all hands to the pumps! It won't be long now. M.'

The phrase 'the dark lady' takes us beyond the undoubted pernicious misogyny to an anti-Semitism that existed at the time and still exists today. Slide down the T bar once more and research the phrase to see where it takes you. The search took me to places I'd never visited, leaving me breathless. It certainly motivated me to want to somehow share it with my students as something urgent and relevant in 'the walk toward' forming serious positions on gender and race. It first took me back to the Black Death persecutions and massacres across Europe in the mid-1300s when: 'Panic emerged again during the scourge of the Black Death in 1348, when widespread terror prompted a revival of the well poisoning charge. In areas where Jews appeared to die of the plague in fewer numbers than Christians, possibly because of better hygiene and greater isolation, lower mortality rates provided evidence of Jewish guilt.'[17] Sarah Liton calls her study of anti-Semitism in the Middle Ages, *Dark Mirror*, in which she concludes, 'Whenever we create images of a stranger, we should bear in mind that we are also creating an image of ourselves.'[18]

This distortion was never seen so clearly than in Nazi Germany. In *Mein Kampf,* Hitler describes 'the black haired Jewish youth' as someone who 'lies in wait for hours on end, satanically glaring at and spying on the unsuspicious girl whom he plans to seduce, adulterating her blood and removing her from the bosom of her own people. The Jew uses every possible means to undermine the racial foundations of a subjugated people.'[19] These deeply racist stereotypes are echoed in the then MP, now of the Brexit Party, Ann Widdecombe's description of Michael Howard – the leader of the Tory Party at the time – as having 'something of the night about him'. This prompted the prominent broadcaster, Jeremy Paxman on *Newsnight*, referencing the imagery of Dracula, to ask whether the Conservative Party was ready for a leader of 'Transylvanian heritage'. Howard's father had fled persecution in Romania. It was no coincidence Peter Mandelson, one of the architects of 'New Labour', was widely tagged as 'the prince of darkness' – a 'serpentine' Machiavellian figure scheming in the shadows. It might be useful to remind ourselves that Jews couldn't become MPs until 1858. If one is to exclude the baptised Disraeli, Jews didn't appear on the Tory benches until as late as the 1950s. When Thatcher in the 1980s had appointed several Jews to her cabinet, the ex-Prime Minister, Macmillan, quipped, 'The thing about Margaret's Cabinet is that it includes more Old Estonians than it does Old Etonian.'[20] (Eton used to require its students' fathers be British by birth, thus preventing Jews from attending.)

Then we have 'the alt-right' marching on Charlottesville, chanting, 'The Jews will not replace us.' This has led to a flurry of articles asking whether Jews are 'white'. I asked my black colleague, Jeffery, this question. His answer was simple. If the white supremacists say you're not, then you're not. Many writers agreed: 'After Charlottesville, it's clear we no longer have the luxury of debating the finer points of this question. For the time being, the racists have settled it for us.'[21] The startling notion that perhaps I'm not perceived as white led me to read, with further astonishment, an excellent article by Robert A. Slayton, the Henry Salvatori Professor of American Values and Traditions at Chapman University. I'd no idea, and probably you didn't either. I'm not sure who to blame for this.

> Play away; how do you think a group of inner-city students from a range of backgrounds would respond to this passage? What's your response to it?

'While today we recognize that impoverished Jews from Eastern Europe were frequently pale-skinned, a standard descriptive used to be the "swarthy Jew". Jacob Riis, the anti-slum crusader, told audiences that Jews and Italians (another "swarthy" group) were not as clean as black tenants, and a sociologist in Boston spoke of streets "where, while Jews are moving in, negro housewives are gathering up their skirts and seeking more spotless environment". Charles Woodruff, an army surgeon who authored 'The Effects of Tropical Light on White Men', argued that when it came to the great American definer, skin colour, "the Semitic type is the link between the Negro and the Aryan..." If a blond Aryan could be described as having a level-one pigmentation, with African-Americans ranked as ten, Jews were three or four. Tom Watson, the Populist reformer who became one of the country's fiercest bigots, wrote that "the black man's lust is not much fiercer than the lust of the licentious Jew for the gentile". Such sentiments had real implications, facilitating the lynching of Leo Frank in 1915. In Pine Bluff, Arkansas, in 1912, a recently-arrived Jewish immigrant was almost hung because locals thought he was a black man walking with a white woman.'[22]

I didn't know how they'd react, which made it even more exciting. But I knew I wanted them to respond to it. I wanted to also share with them how Noel Ignatiev, in his book, *How the Irish Became White*, described the status of the Jew as, 'an intermediate race located socially between black and white'.[23] Ignatiev places it in a context where colour lines for immigrants in an earlier period were far from distinct. What would my students feel about the Irish, for example, being referred to in the 19th century as 'niggers turned inside out' and blacks being labelled 'smoked Irish'? What connections with their own lives would they make when reflecting on Slayton's conclusion: 'What Goldstein referred to as "the Jew's troubling racial indeterminacy" created a dilemma for the country. If fellow citizens "were certain that the Jews were a distinct 'race' or were not sure if they were black or white".'

What was becoming apparent was a deep dive such as this would inform any discussion about race. It was important to make some of the connections with today's world. It still rages. Comicbook. com published a post by Matthew Mueller, provocatively entitled, *Wonder Woman: There IS A Person Of Color In The Lead Role*.[24] Mueller argued Israeli actress, Gal Gadot, was the first woman of colour to appear in the superhero genre because, according to Mueller, 'Gal Gadot is not actually Caucasian, but is in fact Israeli.' Mueller's argument was now turning my head towards the anti-Semitism engulfing the Labour Party.

> Play away; if you've struggled to follow the controversy, are the roots of it here?

'The ambiguity of Jewish ethnicity serves as a perverse weapon in hands hostile to Jewish identity. It leaves Jews historically vulnerable to anti-Semitism from extreme ideologies on both sides of the political spectrum; Jews are at once the ultimate insiders (white) or ultimate outsiders (other).'[25]

The look again, to re-search into what lies behind the phrase 'the dark lady', belongs to the 'never-ending' dialogue that asks complex questions about both the private; how I see myself and the public; how others perceive me. It was asking me to reimagine myself.

Other things show up the deeper you dive into the characters involved in Franklin's story. In the epilogue to *The Double Helix*, using her proper name, Watson seems to acknowledge Franklin's essential contribution and some of his own failings. But pause for a moment, for it could take you into the denial of many of the men who've been caught in the post-Weinstein fall-out. I was sceptical when I heard the tone in Watson's justification of the stealing of Franklin's work:

> 'Let's just start with the Pauling thing. There's a myth which is, you know, that Francis and I basically stole the structure from the people at King's. I was shown Rosalind Franklin's X-ray photograph and, Whooo! That was a helix, and a month later we had the structure, and Wilkins should never have shown me the thing. I didn't go into the drawer and steal it, it was shown to me, and I was told the dimensions, a repeat of 34 angstroms, so, you know, I knew roughly what it meant and, uh, but it was that the Franklin photograph was the key event. It was, psychologically, it mobilised us.'[26]

But then I read about Watson today, and was appalled. Watson has tried to apologise for remarks he made in an interview with *The Sunday Times* in 2007, saying he was 'not a racist in a conventional way'. That's ok then. But it's hard to read some of the abhorrent things he apparently said and not draw a different conclusion. The journalist, a former handpicked student of his at his Cold Spring Harbour Laboratory in New York, reported Watson was 'inherently gloomy about the prospects of Africa' because 'all our social policies are based on the fact that their intelligence is the same as ours – whereas all the testing says not really... people who have to deal with black employees find this not true'.[27] Yarden Katz, a fellow in the department of systems biology at Harvard Medical School and an affiliate of the Berkman Klein Center for Internet & Society at Harvard University – with credentials as long as this, undoubtedly an expert – speaks for many of us: 'It's time to take the "great" white men of science off their pedestals.'[28] Angered by the naming of a new state-of-the-art research institute in the centre of London, 'The Frances Crick Institute', he accuses Crick of also being a racist:

'In the early 1970s, Crick defended other prominent racist scientists who proposed a plan where individuals deemed unfit would be paid to undergo sterilisation. Crick wrote in one letter that "more than half of the difference between the average IQ of American whites and Negroes is due to genetic reasons", which "will not be eliminated by any foreseeable change in the environment". He urged that steps be taken to avoid the "serious" consequences. Crick also proposed that "irresponsible people" be sterilised "by bribery". In the brochure of the institute bearing his name, Crick is nonetheless presented as a scientific hero known for his "intelligence and openness to new ideas".'

In response to this, Jerry Coyne, an American biologist, currently a Professor Emeritus at the University of Chicago in the Department of Ecology and Evolution (so he has credentials), defends Crick. I'll leave it up to you and my students to decide.

'It is fatuous to suggest that we should demonise Crick and "revisit" his monuments because of a few remarks he made in private letters, remarks whose context isn't given. Even if Crick thought there might be a genetic IQ gap between blacks and whites, or suggested some form of voluntary sterilisation, those were never public remarks. If you want to argue that those private statements in letters are sufficiently bad that they outweigh the good that Crick did, well, you're welcome to, but you'll be on shaky ground, accusing him of Thought crime.'[29]

However, the core argument all of this raises, which was certainly worth putting in front of my students, is captured brilliantly by Adam Rutherford, a former geneticist, now science writer and broadcaster:

'"No-one really wants to admit I exist," says Watson. That's not it. It's more that no-one is interested in his racist, sexist views. Watson, alongside Crick, will always be the discoverer of the double helix, to my mind the scientific breakthrough of the 20th century. Here's our challenge: celebrate science when it is great and scientists when they deserve it. And when they turn out to be awful bigots, let's be honest about that too. It turns out that just like DNA, people are messy, complex and sometimes full of hideous errors.'[30]

Debate and discussion of Rutherford's proposition would require high-level thinking and a level of expertise. It would certainly be worth the time.

Passion – We often like to talk about passion and purpose. As we're talking about passion, maybe we should leave it to the experts – the poets – to express it on our behalf. Let's first turn to Jalal ad-Din Muhammad Rumi, poet, Aleppo-trained Imam, Sufi master, who would be chuffed to know that he's one of the biggest selling poets in Trump's America.[31] Writing over 800 years ago, Rumi spoke about passion and purpose: 'Let the beauty of what you love be what you do.'[32] If we really want to romanticise the people of passion, as many of us often do, then turn to the great Chilean poet, Pablo Neruda:

'As if you were on fire from within,
The moon lives in the lining of your skin.'[33]

Franklin's passion for science and what it can achieve is unquestioned. We can hear it in her letter to her father, after he suggested her scientific and secular view of the world had made her somewhat cold: 'In my view, all that is necessary for faith is the belief that by doing our best we shall come nearer to success and that success in our aims (the improvement of the lot of mankind, present and future) is worth attaining.'[34] Mandela would have approved of her grand purpose to improve the lot of humankind: 'There is no passion to be found playing small – in settling for a life that is less than the one you are capable of living.'[35] As would Camus, who might have held Franklin up to be the living embodiment of his definition of passion: 'There is scarcely any passion without struggle.'[36] For Sir Aaron Klug, the recipient of the Nobel Prize for Chemistry, who was Franklin's closest collaborator at Birkbeck, the main thing he says he learnt from her 'was to be single-minded'.[37]

But here's where it becomes complex. We can romanticise like Neruda and we can nod unthinkingly in agreement with Emerson's suggestion, 'It is not length of life, but depth of life.'[38] However, Franklin paid a heavy price for providing 'the ultimate answers to the chemical underpinnings of human existence'.[39] Dali went even further, calling the discovery of DNA, 'the real proof of the existence of God'.[40] Nevertheless, the reality was it meant hour after hour in the laboratory taking X- rays, which exposed her to high levels of radiation. On the one hand, that fixation changed the course of our understanding of humankind. On the other hand, the fixation was the highly probable cause of her death at the age of 37. Like many people, Franklin was a complicated mix of the fixed and growth mindset, as well as a combination of the introvert and the extrovert. One reviewer of Maddox's book describes these seemingly irreconcilable traits by claiming Franklin was afflicted by lasting dualities of character from an early age:

'Her social affability was at odds with a natural insularity, argumentativeness, and later sexual prudery. Quoting one of Franklin's long-time girlfriends, Maddox writes, "She did not talk about men as the rest of us did... and it seemed impossible to break down her reserve" (pp 84, 85). However romantically inhibited Franklin remained, she was at all times intellectually gifted, with an easy aptitude for science and math and a resolute standard of academic triumph. Yet her talent and drive were often destabilised by unfounded self-doubt. An 18-year-old Franklin was certain she bungled her chemistry acceptance examination to Cambridge. Despite her apprehension, she placed first.'[41]

Her younger sister, Jenifer Glynn, portrays her as a vivacious, outward-going woman with the sophisticated tastes of someone who had spent time living in Paris: 'The pile of family letters talk far more about her holidays, her friends, or living conditions in post-war Paris, than about her work. She would go off with friends cycling for weekends, or for longer trips to Italy or to the Alps. She had a love of grand scenery, and became a formidable climber.'[42] So, consider Maddox's claim that, unlike Crick and Watson, Franklin was unwilling 'to go beyond hard evidence' because she demanded irrefutable data. For Franklin, 'An outrageous leap of the imagination would have been as out of character as running up an overdraft or wearing a red strapless dress'.[43] Is this a fixed mind or a mind that grew as a result of this attitude? For Klug, her weakness was isolation: 'She needed a collaborator and she didn't have one – somebody to break the pattern of her thinking, to show what was right in front of her, to push her up and over.'[44] Some have argued that the real problem between Wilkins and Franklin was essentially Franklin was an extrovert, thriving on forceful, intellectual debate. Wilkins was an introvert who hated arguments; someone who needed Franklin to heed Shakespeare's advice, when in 'the whirlwind' of her passion to, 'acquire and beget a temperance that may give it smoothness'.[45]

I, too, am this mixture. My passion has been very single-minded as I dedicated myself to learning my craft over 33 years. It's not been easy, because it might surprise people who know me that like Georgia O'Keefe, 'I've been absolutely terrified every moment of my life'.[46] However, like her, 'I've never let it keep me from doing a single thing I wanted to do'. But there's been a price. I often ask myself whether I've lived a life 'with my whole heart'.

Play away; consider Brene Brown's ten guideposts to living wholeheartedly.[47] I know which ones I've struggled with:

- Cultivating *Authenticity* – Letting go of what people think

- Cultivating *Self-Compassion* – Letting go of perfectionism
- Cultivating *A Resilient Spirit* – Letting go of numbing and powerlessness
- Cultivating *Gratitude and Joy* – Letting go of scarcity and fear of the dark
- Cultivating *Intuition and Trusting Faith* – Letting go of the need for certainty
- Cultivating *Creativity* –Letting go of comparison
- Cultivating *Play and Rest*– Letting go of exhaustion as a status symbol and productivity as a self-worth
- Cultivating *Calm and Stillness* – Letting go of anxiety as a lifestyle
- Cultivating *Meaningful Work* – Letting go of self-doubt and 'supposed to'
- Cultivating *Laughter Song and Dance* – Letting go of being cool and 'always in control'

Franklin raises the fundamental question of how we might choose to live a life with our whole heart, as well as to live a life worth living. Is there always a price to pay?

The purpose of science – One of the reasons for the project was because the students were becoming disaffected in their science lessons. It was too hard. They were starting to see little point in applying themselves. But I was now fired up. I was becoming empowered because of what I was discovering. At one level, 'the race for the double helix' was an exciting story, full of intrigue and deceit, with a cast of villains, a single heroine, and a few secondary characters. The very meaning of life was up for grabs. When in 1962, Watson and Crick were awarded The Nobel Prize without any mention of Franklin, the credibility of the Nobel Prize, just like the Oscars today, was under scrutiny. Huge institutions, like St Paul's and Newnham College, have been compelled to make apologies and to rewrite the narrative. Newnham now has a Rosalind Franklin Building; St Paul's Girls' now has a Rosalind Franklin design technology engineering workshop; The National Portrait Gallery placed her photograph beside that of Wilkins and beneath those of Watson and Crick in its science room. But, like all good drama, none of it is clear. Maddox puts the defence for Wilkins: 'Maurice had a perfect right to that information. There was so much going on at King's before Rosalind came.'[48] It's this that makes it such fertile ground.

On another level, there's the legacy. After 277 attempts and many miscarriages on the way, Dolly the Sheep was finally cloned. This provoked such an outcry that scientists were accused of 'playing God'; the cloning of human beings was nearly upon us. I found myself reading one article entitled, *Playing God in Frankenstein's Footsteps: Synthetic Biology and the Meaning of Life*.[49] I ought to send it to Melvyn Bragg and the *In Our Time* team. It starts like this:

> 'The emergent new science of synthetic biology is challenging entrenched distinctions between, amongst others, life and non-life, the natural and the artificial, the evolved and the designed, and even the material and the informational. Whenever such culturally sanctioned boundaries are breached, researchers are inevitably accused of playing God or treading in Frankenstein's footsteps. Bioethicists, theologians and editors of scientific journals feel obliged to provide an authoritative answer to the ambiguous question of the "meaning" of life, both as a scientific definition and as an explication with wider existential connotations. This article...explores the relationship between the "playing God" theme and the Frankenstein motif and examines the doctrinal status of the "playing God" argument.'

Tempted to read more? Go ahead, just click on the link:

https://www.ncbi.nlm.nih.gov/pmc/articles/PMC2837218/

'Designer babies' is a short side-step away. I found myself reading an article entitled, *Deaf Lesbians, "Designer Disability", and the Future of Medicine*.[50] It starts like this:

> 'A deaf lesbian couple in the United States have deliberately created a deaf child. Sharon Duchesneau and Candy McCullough used their own sperm donor, a deaf friend with five generations of deafness in his family. Like others in the deaf community, Duchesneau and McCullough don't see deafness as a disability. They see being deaf as defining their cultural identity and see signing as a sophisticated, unique form of communication.'

Tempted to read more? Go ahead, just click on the link:

https://www.ncbi.nlm.nih.gov/pmc/articles/PMC1124279/

Then there's the exciting forensic work DNA has now opened up, with many murderers being caught and many innocent people being released. I could update the history behind the picture of Stephen Lawrence's killers hanging above my desk. Two of the killers, Dobson and Norris, were eventually convicted of his murder due to the discovery of fibres and human hairs found on their clothes. I was glad I could now engage with the science that had finally brought some kind of partial justice:

> 'The hair found on David Norris's jeans matched Stephen's DNA profile. The first sign of blood came when scientists used an instrument called a microspectrophotometer to detect the colour of one of the fibres on Dobson's jacket. They decided to go over the rest of the jacket with a microscope, magnifying it 40 times. A spot of blood 0.5mm x 0.25mm was found soaked into the collar – it also matched Stephen's DNA. In the past, DNA testing on such tiny samples of blood and hairs was not possible so forensic experts wouldn't normally have looked for them in the first place. But new forensic techniques developed since 2000

helped LGC bag the vital evidence and counter claims that the clothing could have been contaminated.'[51]

We can cross the Atlantic to the American courtroom drama of 'The DNA wars' that led to O.J. Simpson's wrongful verdict of innocence. Take your pick; there are so many crime sites that report on these emotive cases, making the case for and against the validity of DNA in solving crimes. What about the heart-warming stories with the happy endings you can find on YouTube when twins, who were separated at birth, find they're actually siblings through DNA testing? There are lots. Go read the story starting with, 'I found my identical twin on YouTube',[52] and tell me you don't want to find out more. If that doesn't do it for you, then watch the fascinating film, *Significant Strangers*,[53] which explores the lives of quadruplet brothers who were separated at birth and are reunited for the first time after 25 years. It's extraordinary how different they all are, raising fundamental questions 'whether we are defined in our lives primarily by our experiences or our genetics'. We can dive into a Terry Pratchett novel and engage in the big debate:

> '"Don't tell me from genetics. What've they got to do with it?" said Crowley. "Look at Satan. Created as an angel, grows up to be the Great Adversary. Hey, if you're going to go on about genetics, you might as well say the kid will grow up to be an angel. After all, his father was really big in Heaven in the old days. Saying he'll grow up to be a demon just because his dad became one is like saying a mouse with its tail cut off will give birth to tailless mice. No. Upbringing is everything. Take it from me."'[54]

We can wrestle with Simon Baron Cohen who, just like his brother, Sasha 'Ali G', 'Borat', Baron Cohen, provokes and challenges: 'What worries me is that the debate about gender differences still seems to polarize nature vs. nurture, with some in the social sciences and humanities wanting to assert that biology plays no role at all, apparently unaware of the scientific evidence to the contrary.'[55] But over all of this strides Rosalind Franklin, the scientist. She was a brilliant scientist. The bio-crystallographer, Desmond Bernal, who worked with her at Birkbeck College in London, stated: 'As a scientist, Miss Franklin was distinguished by extreme clarity and perfection in everything she undertook.'[56] In his acceptance speech for the Nobel Prize in 1982, Klug held up Franklin for setting 'the example of tackling large and difficult problems'.[57] For Franklin, science was about giving 'a partial explanation for life. In so far as it goes, it is based on fact, experience and experiment.'[58]

I'll stop here because I was confident there was more than enough to engage and challenge the students. However, I have a confession. Despite all of the searching, despite all of the things I've just made you wade through (I thank you for doing so), I still didn't understand Franklin, not a word of it, when she said, 'The results suggest a helical structure (which must be very closely packed) containing probably 2, 3 or 4 coaxial nucleic acid chains per helical unit and having the phosphate groups near the outside.'[59] I was feeling like the students. The science was just too hard.

Teaching context

The challenge for myself and the science teacher was set by Ron Berger: 'Unless students find reason and inspiration to care about learning and have hope that they can improve, excellence and high achievement will remain the domain of a select group.'[60]. Ron Berger spent 25 years being both a teacher and a carpenter in rural Massachusetts. He developed pedagogy to inspire 'quality and character in students, specifically through project-based learning, original scientific and historical research, service learning, and the infusion of arts'.[61] Berger is an expert, so we turned to him for help. In his definitive book, *An Ethic of Excellence*,[62] he outlines essential components of the project-based learning he advocates:

- Building literacy through the work
- Genuine research

- The power of the arts
- Models
- Multiple drafts
- Critique
- Making work public
- Using assessment to build stronger students

These requisites Berger believes make for deep learning, are based on the belief we very much shared:

'The project model where I teach is predicated on every child succeeding. Not just finishing, but producing work that represents excellence for that child... the classroom is the hub of creation, the project workshop. The overall quality of the work that emerges is a concern for every member in it... there is a sense of peer pressure to keep up with the standard. These projects are made public and every student knows it.'[63]

Inspired by Berger, we planned our project using his requisites as our framework, in an attempt to make the exploration of DNA a meaningful experience for both the students and ourselves. It was a collaborative process summed up by Hattie: 'Planning can be done in many ways, but the most powerful is when teachers work together to develop plans, develop common understandings of what is worth teaching, collaborate on understanding their beliefs of challenge and progress, and work together to evaluate the impact of their planning on student outcomes.'[64] However, the final public 'product' was problematic. It's much clearer when there's a definite, engaging, and complex problem to be solved. For example, one brilliant project at my school was when pupils designed mathematical models to prove how building new concrete factories on the edge of the Queen Elizabeth Olympic Park would damage the environment. The students made alliances with local groups, wrote academic papers, lobbied, and campaigned. They even managed to speak at the council's planning committee. Their work was viewed by the wider community as integral to the application finally being turned down. The local councillor, Terry Paul, acknowledged the difference they made: 'The concrete factory applications have been defeated by a brilliant local campaign, and I'm particularly proud of the students at School 21, who worked with residents to alert everyone to the dangers of air pollution.'[65] It's not hard to see how Berger's requisites were at play in this project. It met Newmann's and Wehlage's criteria for 'authentic achievement' (Ouch, how did that word sneak past?):

'(1) students construct meaning and produce knowledge, (2) students use disciplined inquiry to construct meaning, and (3) students aim their work toward production of discourse, products, and performances that have value or meaning beyond success in school.'[66]

I've also shown earlier on, when the Year 11 Drama students had a very clear 'product', a piece of drama lasting around 25 minutes to be shared in a public space, Berger's claims for project-based learning certainly happen: 'Anytime you make the work public, set the bar high, and are transparent about the steps to make a high-quality product, kids will deliver.'[67] Nevertheless, we didn't have anything as clear-cut. We toyed with several products, such as creating a campaign for 'Jeans for Genes' who support children affected by a genetic disorder. We considered the students creating a project for primary schools to help them explore different aspects of DNA. Another idea was to create a book to be sold at a Science Museum or at a Cambridge University bookshop. One thing we were certain of was the students would have to exhibit their learning at 'The Grand Exhibition' which happens in the school at the end of every term and is open to the general public. Every pupil in the school, from the age of five to 18, is involved; it's quite something to behold. For many of our pupils, 13 years old, 'The Grand Exhibition' was more than enough reason 'to do the work well, and it's not just because the teacher wants it that way'.[68] The first time we ran the project, the 'product' had three elements:

- A performance of extracts from *Rosalind* by Deborah Gearing.[69]
- A performance of the students' own verbatim plays exploring different aspects of DNA.
- Discussion circles, in which pupils shared their story of learning, engaging the general public in meaningful conversations around the subject of DNA.

The science teacher wanted to see if their scientific knowledge could be even deeper, so the second time we taught the project we decided the product would be groups of students giving academic lectures in the science labs to the general public. In both cases, we tried to ensure there was, importantly, 'latitude for personal choice and artistry'.[70]

Before choosing our product, we needed to discover our inquiry question. For Larmer and Mergendoller:

'A good driving question captures the heart of the project in clear, compelling language, which gives students a sense of purpose and challenge. The question should be provocative, open-ended, complex, and linked to the core of what you want students to learn. It could be abstract (When is war justified?); concrete (Is our water safe to drink?); or focused on solving a problem (How can we improve this website so that more young people will use it?).'[71]

We created an abstract question to drive the project: 'Is it ever right to play God?' We could see from the very start that the inquiry question was a hook, a provocation in itself, gauged by the animated discussions we structured in small groups. When we gave the students cardboard cut-outs of body parts – including different coloured eyes, hair, skin tone – asking them to design their own babies, they were away. We followed this up with an exploration of values, which led once more to engaged, structured discussions. Our aim at this point was for students to engage and commit. There was a lot of 'babble', 'pub talk', but we hoped this would prove a baseline. We would be able to see how far their depth of critical thinking had been developed at the end when they held different kinds of conversations at 'The Grand Exhibition'.

In his persuasive TED talk, *Inspiring Wonder through Learning and Thinking*, Garfield Gini-Newman asks schools to take up two challenges in the digital world we live in today: 'Wonder needs to be the driver for learning, to want to know more about but also we need to put thinking at the core of learning.'[72] However, he goes on to pose an essential question: 'How are we going to get there?' There was a tension in our project, arising from the science teacher's fearful agenda concerning, in her mind, the necessity for the students 'learning' a large body of content. Not her fault, by the way. She wasn't the only one worried about this. National Curriculum Science is so loaded with difficult content. The then Secretary of State for Education was warned about the implications of his actions by 98 academics no less, in a letter headed, *Gove will bury pupils in fact and rules*.[73] Gove flicked it off as the thinking of, what he and Dominic Cummings liked to call, 'the Blob'; academics who they believed were blocking change. Gove went on to infamously reject expertise in a single soundbite (which won't be added to our list): 'People in this country have had enough of experts.'[74] But for those of us at the chalk face, there was a growing awareness that the students in their science lessons were feeling 'buried' by the hugely difficult content. Gove might have been wiser to have listened to the educationalist, Richard Livingstone, who, way back in 1941, had advised:

'The test of successful education is not the amount of knowledge that a pupil takes away from school, but his appetite to know and his capacity to learn. If the school sends out children with the desire for knowledge and some idea how to acquire it, it will have done its work. Too many leave school with the appetite killed and the mind loaded with undigested lumps of information.'[75]

Livingstone concludes with another favourite soundbite (which will be added to our list): 'The good schoolmaster (teacher) is known by the number of valuable subjects which he declines to teach.' However, as with any soundbite, it's never so simple. Gini-Newhman argues the dichotomy between content and inquiry is a false one. He warns about the 'blinders' approach of 'exploring what I already know but nobody opened my eyes to the world beyond'. Believing one can't 'think in a vacuum, you don't think about nothing', he places an obligation on schools 'to make sure kids are learning the content, the concepts that they need to explore ideas to solve meaningful problems'.

Mergendoller has a clever soundbite calling this kind of critical thinking 'ordinary thinking done well'. He argues critical thinking is 'not a different type of thought, a handspring of the mind that vaults above ordinary thinking. Instead, it is ordinary thinking done well, that is, reflectively, with attention to criteria, and with the goal of making a defensible, reasoned judgment.'[76] For the science teacher, she didn't want the students to simply look something up. For her, 'ordinary thinking done well' in science would be defining 'terms, consider whether information and concepts vary according to context, weigh multiple explanations, evaluate evidence, and compare alternative actions based on their probability of success'.[77] Rosalind Franklin probably would heartily agree with this as a definition of what lies at the very heart of scientific exploration.

There were 75 kids in the group we were teaching. At times, we taught them as one ensemble; at other times, we split them in half – one half going to a science laboratory and the other half coming to the drama studio. In both spaces our aims were twofold: to build what Gini-Newhman calls 'the competences' they would need, but also to excite them. Berger explains the need for 'the competences': 'In the course of a thematic study there may be three or four significant projects, most of which require research, writing skills, drafting skills, and sometimes mathematical or science skills.' These skills or competences are then put to use 'in the service of an original project' but crucially with 'high student investment'.[78]

The hook was the easy part. The science teacher now had her body of content to teach. What was I to do in the drama studio? Gini-Newhman set me the challenge, no avoidance, he made it as clear as day: 'We need to invite kids into the space to explore meaningful, authentic problems and build their understanding for them to be able to engage in those problems.' My invitation would always be the same. I had to find a 'necessary' text: 'One which is an urgent presence in our lives, speaking to us in our wholeness.'[79] In my search, I read several plays written by scientists who felt theatre might be a means through which to explore their ideas. I hate to disagree with Tennessee Williams, as he was someone who turned my adolescent head towards the theatre all those years ago: 'I believe the way to write a good play is to convince yourself it is easy to do... It is never as bad as you think, it is never as good'[80]. No, sorry, these plays are simply awful. Go read some, just for the pleasure of seeing how really awful they are. But just as panic was starting to take hold, I found *Rosalind* by Deborah Gearing. Here was a text that would allow for the kind of Grotowskian 'encounter' we explored in Chapter 8. Grotowski is interesting in this context. Like the science teacher, he calls his workplace, a laboratory: 'In Grotowski's theatre, as in all true laboratories, the experiments are scientifically valid because the essential conditions are observed. In his theatre, there is absolute concentration by a small group and unlimited time.'[81] I certainly had time to establish a meaningful three-way relationship between text, student, and adult. In Grotowskian terms, we would create a series of shocks. My hope was that if the students could start to catch 'the vibratory qualities', then 'the song' would begin 'to sing to us'.[82] As in Grotowski's laboratory, so in the drama studio, students would have:

- The shock of confronting him/herself in the face of simple irrefutable challenges.
- The shock of catching sight of his/her own evasions, tricks, and clichés.

- The shock of sensing something of his/her own vast and untapped resources.
- The shock of being forced to question what the point of it all is.
- The shock of being compelled to recognise such questions do exist and the time has come when they must be faced, discovering that he/she wants to face them.
- The shock of what Artaud called being 'cruel to myself' by committing with a dedication they may not have shown up to now in their science lessons or even in their school life.

> Play away; read these series of 'shocks' again. How many shocks are you in need of? Who do you know is in need of some if not all of these shocks? What kind of transformative process would bring about these kinds of shocks? Are you even willing to be shocked?

High ambitions for 13-year-olds, you may say, but Brook's hopes for Grotowski's actors – 'And of course they were not all ecstatic about their experience. Some were bored' –were the same as the hopes I had for my students. Brook aptly quotes Arden:

'For the apple holds a seed will grow,
In live and lengthy joy
To raise a flourishing tree of fruit,
Forever and a day.'

In *Rosalind*, Gearing created two fictional characters, Esther and Joe, who are siblings. We became involved in their lives by hot-seating people who knew them but aren't featured in the play; they gathered quotes, placing them in either the nurture or nature column; we used forum theatre to explore possible moments in their past that may have had significance, which made some students change their interpretation, shifting their quotes to the other column. The competencies were being developed. The science teacher pointed out a transference of skills was occurring, the skill of variable extraction. She'd identified what Koedinger and Wiese had discovered:

'That the process of identifying a character's views is comparable to variable extraction in a science context, if we think of a "view" as a feature that differs one character from another. Variable extraction, moreover, is a skill of argumentation, because claims are often statements of relationships among variables. Thus, through science discussions, students may have learned a specific skill – variable extraction – that helped them in their English exams.'[83]

Alongside this, the students were asked to carry out interviews with their families, to begin to consider how much of their life had been down to nature and how much had been down to nurture. If they had siblings, they carried out further interviews to explore similarity and difference. At one level, they were wearing Heathcote's 'mantle of the expert', seeing themselves as researchers tasked with a commission. 'Mantle of the expert' is a sophisticated process: 'An active, urgent, purposeful view of learning, in which knowledge is to be operated on, not merely taken in.'[84] They were asked to record their interviews verbatim, gathering possible material to be 'operated on' later in the process. (Heathcote had a great interest in science, often using its language 'to get to the heart of things', she once told me at a coffee break during a conference we were both attending; a moment to treasure.) For many of the students, it was to be their first 'shock', to see some of the key events in their life and their important relationships through a nurture/ nature lens. New perspectives were being formed; 'the walk toward' had begun.

Rosalind Franklin enters the play as an abstract figure delivering a monologue that further complicated the students' interpretation of how much depends on nature and how much is environmental. Their discussions were gaining more depth as some of the students were playing away, making the transference from what they were learning in science and bringing it to bear in their discussions about Franklin's opening monologue. It started to provoke students to carry out their own independent research into questions they were now finding interesting such as, 'Are people born violent? Is there something inherent in men's genetic makeup that makes them more violent than women? Is this true? Are women different to men? Are some people naturally good at the sciences, at sport, at the arts? Are some people naturally hard-working? Are some people born shy? Would I have been a different person if my parents had not immigrated to England?' They were certainly starting to realise such questions exist, and now might be the right time to explore them in depth so they would be able to put forward a credible point of view. Some were starting to catch sight of their own evasions, tricks and clichés, how they'd been living. They were beginning to want something more for themselves. A new dialogue was beginning to be created with themselves and with others. In Berger's terms, students were starting 'to invest in their own growth'.[85]

When Rosalind talks to Esther about her Jewish heritage and the Holocaust, fundamental questions about science were raised:

> *'Rosalind: So much of science in the war had been about death. With the help of science it had become possible to kill thousands of people in a matter of seconds.*
>
> *It had become possible*
>
> *It had been done.*
>
> *Thousands of people had died in the blink of an eye, the split of an atom.*
>
> *We did not want that.*
>
> *We wanted our science to be - unequivocally good-to be of benefit, to be the science of life, not the science of death.'*[86]

The students were provoked by this passage. It was an opportunity to debate whether it's possible for science to be solely a force for good, inspiring further independent research. Students were in 'shock' when they examined some of the Nazi propaganda founded on a false view about the nature of the 'Aryan race' and the nature of 'the Jew'. They were even more shocked when we read Carole Cadwalladr's exposure of Google's use of algorithms. Cadwalladr was an inspiring role model to put in front of them, shifting their own role as researchers to investigative journalists. She discovered, to her and our horror: 'Still, anyone searching for information about the Holocaust – if it was real, if it happened, if it was a hoax, if it was fake – was being served up neo-Nazi propaganda as the top result.'[87] At the end of Cadwalladr's article, we discussed the explanation for Google's motivation, given by Danny Sullivan, a leading expert on search engines: 'Google has changed its algorithm to reward popular results over authoritative ones. For the reason that it makes Google more money.' It's interesting the origin and etymology of the word 'science' is the Latin 'scientia', which originally meant knowledge, a knowing, an expertise, as in Bacon's 'Ipsa scientia potestas est'; 'Knowledge itself is power.'[88] It was important for the science teacher to arm them with the evidence to prove the racist 'eugenic' theories to be false. As in all meaningful inquiries, new questions were generated about the students' own world, in which so much is written and spoken about in terms of gender, race, culture. The students were beginning to understand the requisite to acquire a gravitas that would empower them in a world full of 'fake news'. They could start to appreciate the imperative that 'ordinary thinking' had to be 'done well'.

In her play, Gearing makes the relationship between Wilkins and Franklin nuanced. The students didn't have any 'fixed' views about either character, as they were unaware of the history. They examined the relationship as it's portrayed in the play. They were asked to take away all the opinion expressed in the encounter, to see what facts were left. Sympathies were divided. It allowed them to look at themselves and how they viewed others, as well as how people viewed them. 'The shock' was to see how much of what they believed they were telling themselves about other people and about themselves, as fact, was really just opinion. They were able to see how 'fixed' such attitudes can be. The girls particularly wanted to discuss self-image, using this distinction between what's fact and what's opinion .They could identify with the anxiety they heard in Rosalind's repetitive worry: 'What do they think of me, what do they think of me, what do they think of me?'[89] However, they now understood this would require deliberative thought. Evidence needed to be found and evaluated. Arguments needed to be crafted. They could start to self-evaluate the quality of their own and their peers' reasoning. They could begin to tell the difference between 'thoughtful' and 'thoughtless', between 'thinking carefully and carelessly'.[90] In other words, they were learning to critique. We may eagerly sign up to Dylan Wiliam's assertion: 'Engaging in classroom discussion really does make you smarter.'[91] However, it's important to address Nuthall's research in the context of expertise and empowerment. In his book, *The Hidden Lives of Learners*,[92] Nuthall showed how 80% of the feedback students receive is from their peers, but found 80% of this student-student feedback is wrong. Wiliam's reply to this is: 'There is a huge amount of well-grounded research that shows that helping students improve their self-assessment skills increases achievement.'[93] For many of us, all of this educational knockabout, using research to beat each other over the head with, can go against the grain of our instincts. In our search for empowering 'the walk toward' a dialogue in which you sense something is actually going on beyond mere 'babble', you and the participants just kind of know when it happens. In many ways, the writer and philosopher, Robert Pirsig, is spot on when he says: 'Quality doesn't have to be defined. You understand it without definition. Quality is a direct experience independent of and prior to intellectual abstractions.'[94] Wiliam sort-of agrees, by quoting Claxton's wonderful soundbite, a shoo-in for our list: 'We should be aiming for "a shared construct of quality" (what Guy Claxton calls a "nose for quality").'[95] However, it might not be enough to talk in terms of instinct, our 'nose for quality', 'you just kind of know....' kind of talk. Wiliam is also right to tell us: 'On those rare occasions when we can spell out the rules for success, we should, of course do so.'[96]

We had arrived at one of those occasions. The students were starting to acquire 'a nose for quality', as well as an empowerment, by also acquiring a way of carrying out 'ordinary thinking' to be 'done well'. Hence, the higher level of thinking in their 'thoughtful' and 'careful' discussions was becoming apparent to them and to me. Had it become part of a 'never-ending' dialogue where they were now fully invested in their own growth? It was too early to call; we had just started.

There's a section in the play where Rosalind explains to Esther and Joe about her research which resulted in Photograph 51. She explains why Crick and Watson's work is flawed:

> '*Rosalind: Where's the water? You're building models and you ignore the hard facts. I distinctly stated that the magnesium ions holding the phosphate groups together have to be surrounded by tight shells of water molecules. Where are they? Are they hiding? No don't tell me – you've got some pretty little theory about where they are hiding, haven't you? No? And you've got the sugar-phosphate backbone going down the centre. That won't work. The sugar-phosphate backbone has to be on the outside. I gave you that deduction in my lecture. You were there, weren't you listening? There's no point in coming to these things if you're not going to pay attention. Unless of course you're just playing. It just doesn't hold up, does it?*
>
> *Maurice: Did you say there was train at twenty to four?*'

I certainly didn't understand the science, but I felt the excitement and urgency in the dialogue. It met David Mamet's requisite for a worthwhile piece of theatre: 'In playwriting, you've got to be able to write dialogue.'[(96)] Miller rightly puts the case that polemics don't make for good theatre: 'I do not believe that any work of art can help but be diminished by its adherence at any cost to a political program... and not for any other reason than that there is no political program – any more than there is a theory of tragedy

– which can encompass the complexities of real life.'[97] Gearing has crafted a piece of theatre rather than a theoretical essay. The students needed to feel 'the wonder' but, unlike me, they needed to also understand the science. So, we decided to invite the students to adopt the mantle of the expert by giving a lecture about the discovery of DNA. This would be a milestone. It would be one of those 'head-hurting' challenges as defined by Hattie:

> 'When you ask students what challenge means to them, they'll tell you, "It's when my head hurts." So I want teachers to think – obviously not about making their students' heads hurt – but about how to get students to that point where there is challenge. Teachers have to do the thinking; they have to reconcile what the student knows with what the student needs to know.'[98]

It would require students, in Berger's phrase, 'to bust a gut'. There were a lot of students in the cohort who lacked resilience when the going got tough. It was going to get tough. In an attempt to persuade our students, we could happily put up on the whiteboard one of Berger's core beliefs about what it takes to create 'beautiful work': 'If you're going to do something, I believe, you should do it well. You should sweat over it and make sure it's strong and accurate and beautiful and you should be proud of it.'[99] But what would the students' motivation be to put themselves through a rigorous drafting process in order to create both, a scientifically accurate lecture as well as a speech capturing the excitement they'd clearly experienced in Gearing's dialogue? If the previous sentence is long, then it's intentionally so. Speaking on behalf of many in the class, one student's response to the task was to cry out, 'That's long, sir!' – an oft used phrase when faced with one of Hattie's 'head-hurting' challenges. Berger is correct; none of this is easy, 'Building and maintaining a positive community takes constant vigilance. It's a job that's never really done.'[100]

I was always uneasy about a public audience being the silver bullet for the creation of 'beautiful work'. It never ceased to move me how much care students took over their work in drama so long as there was ownership. The work was for no-one but themselves. I'm writing this book purely for me; 'for an audience of one'.[101] It really doesn't matter if anyone reads it (Thank you for getting this far). Berger understands it when he says, 'There's no magic bullet towards excellence, it's all cultural, and by building a culture within our schools where our kids feel pressured to do good work and be good people, we succeed.'[102] We felt we'd created such a culture within the privacy of the ensemble in which, 'The peer community sets the tone on how to be. It sets positive peer pressure.'[103] We felt we had a chance.

The science teacher was delighted, as the process would offer her ample opportunity to diagnose each student's level of understanding and their commitment to developing that understanding. It would be about what Lin Tarr, a maths teacher in Colorado, neatly describes as looking for 'brilliant mistakes': 'Our models aren't "products", but ways of thinking. We critique our class exit slips often as models of thinking with the intent of helping students identify common misconceptions. We look for "brilliant mistakes".'[104] However, I wanted to continue to address the disaffection the students were feeling when faced with the rigours of the subject. I could feel them already becoming 'buried' all over again. I also knew the majority of the students had never experienced an academic lecture. One of Berger's requisites for learning was to model; there's good reason why he calls his centre, *Models of Excellence: The Center for High-Quality Student Work, an open-source collection of the nation's best K-12 student work.* He stresses the importance behind this rather grand title: 'For all the correcting we do, directions we give, and rubrics we create about what good work looks like, students are often unclear about what they are aiming for until they actually see and analyse strong models.'[105] By sharing models of excellence or making students' work models of excellence, it would create in students 'an appetite for excellence'.[106] I really like the way Berger describes himself as 'an historian of excellence, an archiver'. Berger is in search of 'models of beautiful work, powerful work, important work'.

He creates a library of excellence 'on the walls, on the counters, in boxes'. It's part of a 'never-ending' dialogue in which both the teacher and the students together 'critique and discuss what makes work powerful: what makes a piece of creative writing compelling and exciting; what makes a scientific or historical research project significant and stirring'. I, too, am a believer in the modelling of excellence, simply because 'excellence is a better teacher than mediocrity. The lessons of the ordinary are everywhere. Truly profound and original insights are to be found only in studying the exemplary.'[107]

I knew the science teacher was becoming disaffected with teaching. She was in danger of losing her passion: 'I don't know any more if I am finding that song or if I am that song.'[108] In our discussions, she was very moved by the Galileo quote Franklin cites in the play: 'For anyone who had ever experienced just once the perfect understanding of one single thing, and had truly tasted how knowledge is accomplished, would recognize that of the infinity of other truths he understands nothing.' It was returning her to why she became a science teacher in the first place. Her engagement with Franklin had ignited something within her. So, I asked her to model an academic lecture that would both explain DNA in the most accessible, interesting but rigorous way, as well as conveying her passion for science. First and foremost, I wanted her to speak to herself about what science really meant to her. If she could articulate this, then perhaps 'the song' could begin 'to sing' once more. It would offer the students a 'model', not of a dead scientist from the past but a living, breathing woman who has committed her life to conveying her passion for science to young people. It would be her stand, a declaration of who she be. She's the teacher I quoted earlier on when she reflected on the experience in a postcard she sent to me:

'My first big thanks comes from the INSET. It gave me a new look at my life and affected me in a profound way. I don't know if I've found my stand or if I even know what a stand really is but it has helped me to re find myself... before working on this project I was seriously thinking of leaving the profession... it is so easy to allow yourself to be caught up in the business of life that you forget why you're there. Now I feel like I'm back and I know where I am (although not sure about where I'm going yet)... I owe this to you, there are so many times we can change another's life without ever knowing it.'

It was a triumph. The majority of the students had caught 'the vibratory qualities' in her lecture. It was proof of what Hattie articulates about the teacher learner: 'The remarkable feature of the evidence is that the greatest effects on student learning occur when teachers become learners of their own teaching.'[109] They were further inspired by a whole range of clips from lectures I discovered on YouTube. There are many ways to deliver a lecture. I've listed them for you, so have a watch; don't be put off by the titles, you'll be fascinated.[110] In the spirit of Berger, we critiqued these lectures as well as the science teacher's passionate lecture discovering what made them compelling. We created a long list. Due to the empowerment their oracy curriculum had given them, the pupils noticed a lot.

Play away; when you've watched the clips on YouTube did you notice all of this? Are you as expert as the students? Next time you're listening to a lecture try using this lens:

✓ The visual
✓ Eloquence
✓ Technical language
✓ Poetic language
✓ Different rhythms and patterns of language, metaphors, similes, imagery, alliteration; rhetorical techniques (The Linguistic strand)
✓ Autobiographical
✓ Humour
✓ Building an argument (The Cognitive strand)

- ✓ To speak with passion
- ✓ Connecting to your own experience
- ✓ Researched
- ✓ Wide range of references
- ✓ Expertise
- ✓ Making the complex simple for the non-specialist
- ✓ Raising questions then answering them
- ✓ Lots of 'what if...'
- ✓ Tell the audience what we don't know
- ✓ Tease and intrigue
- ✓ Anecdotes
- ✓ The hook/setting up the proposition
- ✓ An intriguing title as well as motifs that repeat
- ✓ There's a through line
- ✓ Telling it as a story
- ✓ Contact with the audience (The Emotional strand)
- ✓ Use of props
- ✓ Use of video
- ✓ Highlighting a problem then knocking it down
- ✓ Formal/informal – a balance
- ✓ Balance between the personal/subjective and the non-personal/objective
- ✓ Let your personality shine through
- ✓ Be controversial/provoke your audience to think
- ✓ The physical – hands; face; appropriate movement; voice; the pause (The Physical strand)
- ✓ The speech is full of shades, tonal shifts
- ✓ There's a climax
- ✓ The speech is bookended; the start and end reference each other
- ✓ Characterisation
- ✓ Recreating
- ✓ Demonstrating
- ✓ Performing
- ✓ Form and content to demonstrate expertise

The first phase for the students was to write an academic essay. At one level, it was to ensure the scientific content was accurate, and that all aspects of what DNA is and how it was discovered were covered. At another level, it was about what the educationalist, Seymour Papert, is talking about here:

> 'So the model that says learn while you're at school, while you're young, the skills that you will apply during your lifetime is no longer tenable. The skills that you can learn when you're at school will not be applicable. They will be obsolete by the time you get into the workplace and need them, except for one skill. The one really competitive skill is the skill of being able to learn.'[111]

A requisite for this kind of ability to learn required the creation of multiple drafts. It's inherent in Hattie's discussion of what challenge involves: 'By knowing what we do not know, we can learn; if we were to make no errors, we would be less likely to learn (or even to need to learn) – and we probably are not involved in challenge if there is not an element of being wrong and not succeeding.'[112] We invited the English department to teach formal essay writing, the stages this would involve as well as the formal language needed. Jeffrey had his class analyse two essays he'd written on his blog demonstrating the richness of playing away; of course he did. He kept the passion for expertise and empowerment burning: 'A comparison of *Never Let Me Go*, the book, and *Never Let Me Go*, the film'; 'A critical analysis of Frisco's verse from the song *Too Many Man* (featured in Skepta's album, *Microphone Champion*).'[113] My role was to be vigilant, to use lots of the willpower strategies we've explored earlier on, to keep the more challenged students on task. The second phase was to flip the academic essay into a lecture of expertise. Heavily influenced by the diverse range of lectures in the film clips, the students had synthesised their choice of form to these possibilities. The lecture could be delivered in one of these styles:

- Charming
- Impact

- Anecdotal
- Storytelling
- Teasing/playful
- Performance poetry
- Demonstration
- Formal lecture
- Provocative
- Passionate

There was plenty of 'latitude for personal choice and artistry'. Once more the students went into a drafting process. The range of different models had given the students 'the nose for quality' they could apply to their own speech. The criteria were clear, because they'd come to it by themselves when analysing the clips of film. For the students, to 'ignite' the audience with their expertise, they were asked to consider these elements:

- ✓ The Hook
- ✓ Visual
- ✓ Informative
- ✓ Making the complex understandable
- ✓ Humour
- ✓ Building an argument (The Cognitive strand)
- ✓ Balance between the personal/subjective and the non-personal/objective
- ✓ Wide range of references
- ✓ Use research
- ✓ Let your personality shine through (The Emotional strand)
- ✓ Anecdotes
- ✓ Connect it to your own experiences
- ✓ Characterisation
- ✓ The balance between formal and informal language
- ✓ Beautiful language – try to be clever, original, playful using different patterns and rhythms, metaphors, alliteration, different tones, rhetorical techniques (The Linguistic strand)

- ✓ Be controversial/provoke
- ✓ Demonstration
- ✓ Passion – fire in your voice; face; body; language (The Physical strand)
- ✓ Raise questions and then answer them
- ✓ Knock down the counter-arguments
- ✓ See the speech as a painting full of shades (tonal shifts)
- ✓ Have a title, a motif that repeats
- ✓ The climax – the main action of the speech
- ✓ Book end the lecture; the beginning echoes the ending

We took on board Dylan Wiliam's five key strategies for assessment for learning, as well as for formative assessment :[114]

1. Clarifying and understanding learning intentions and criteria for success.
2. Engineering effective classroom discussions, questions and tasks that elicit evidence of learning.
3. Providing feedback that moves learners forward.
4. Activating students as instructional resources for each other.
5. Activating students as owners of their own learning.

Wiliam emphasises it's the teacher who's responsible for the choice of strategies that 'are grounded in deep cognitive principles about learning'.[115] We chose to focus on the latter two of Wiliam's strategies. We wanted to actively teach the academy of critiquing, which Wiliam defines as pedagogy of 'engagement': 'because the students have to get involved.... as owners of their own learning.'[116] But it also allows for what he calls a pedagogy of 'contingency', which allows 'the teacher to be responsive to the students' needs'. Wiliam calls upon Aristotle's highest intellectual virtue, 'phronesis', sometimes translated as 'practical wisdom'. He draws from this: 'In education, "what works?" is not the right question because everything works somewhere and nothing works everywhere, so what's interesting, what's important in education is: "Under what conditions does this work?".' We felt

291

the conditions were right for a type of critiquing where the students would become owners of their own learning to 'ensure that feedback causes a cognitive rather than an emotional reaction – in other words, feedback should cause thinking.' Berger also stresses the need, when critiquing, to keep the focus on the cognitive rather than the emotional, the work rather than the person. 'Be tough on the content but kind on the person' is the mantra we like to use. We felt the students had 'acquired sufficient surface knowledge'. This is the stage when, for Hattie, 'cooperative learning is most powerful'.[117] It allows for the students to be 'involved in discussion and learning with their peers – usually in some structured manner'. Wiliam goes so far as to assert that 'cooperative learning' is 'one of the greatest success stories of educational research'.[118] Hattie puts it very simply in another of his soundbites which needs to be pinned up on the wall: 'If you want to increase student academic achievement, give each student a friend.'[119]

> Play away; change the word 'student' to suit where you work and see what this does to the dynamics of the social capital.

The students were used to having meaningful one-to-ones with their tutor. They could understand the answer lay with the mentee, rather than the mentor simply saying what he/she liked and didn't like; the Orwellian school of feedback, 'Four legs good, two legs bad'. As Galileo had featured in the play, they were open to explore what he meant by, 'All truths are easy to understand once they are discovered; the point is to discover them.' It would be through questioning that the writer would come to an understanding about the qualities of certain parts of the speech and therefore would keep. Through questioning, the writer would also come to an understanding about why moments needed developing. It met Robin Alexander's (more of him later) 'bottom line', captured in two quotes he often cites for their epigraphic force:

- 'If an answer does not give rise to a new question from itself, it falls out of the dialogue.'
- 'What ultimately counts is the extent to which teaching requires pupils to think, not just report someone else's thinking.'[120]

The students had come across Bloom's taxonomy for deeper thinking, so they were equipped to make the attempt to move up the scale of higher-level questioning.

Play away; when might this intentionality of questioning be of use to you? What might be the different contexts?

- To ask questions to *clarify and explain* (Can you explain what this phrase means? Can you clarify what made you use this word at this point in your lecture?)
- To ask questions to *predict* (Can you predict how the audience might feel at this point? Can you predict what the science teacher might say about this sentence?)
- To ask questions to *compare* (Can you compare your explanation of Photograph 51 with the explanation in the play? Can you compare your ending with an ending in one of the lectures we watched?)
- To ask questions to *justify* (Can you justify what made you start the lecture in this way? Can you justify what was going on in your mind when you chose this for your third paragraph?)
- To ask questions to *create* (Can you create what Crick and Watson might have felt at this moment? Can you create what Franklin might have felt at this moment?)

We avoided 'why' questions in this context, as they become loaded with judgement. The aim is to encourage what is often described as 'open' questioning'. Dare I mention what Nystrand prefers to call these kinds of open questions? Shoot me down, but he prefers to call them 'authentic questions'.[121] These are questions without 'prespecified' answers; the opposite of recitation or what Mehan calls 'known information questions'.[122] For Nystrand, 'authentic questions' are 'about figuring things out – in class, face-to-face, teacher and students together'.[123] If you want to kick out the word 'authentic', then you might prefer 'substantive conversations'.[124] In these kinds of 'substantive conversations', the questioning empowers a collaborative interpretation and construction of an improved understanding, by interacting with ideas together. Not only were the students familiar with Blooms, but they'd also been used to categorising questions across the curriculum in an attempt to show them a question always needs an intention. Here are some of the categories they had explored:

- Probing (Can you talk to me about what is meant when you wrote...? Please can you show me where your research opened up a new area of understanding?)
- Provoking (What would you say to someone who found this moment confusing? What would you say to the science teacher if she told you this was lacking in evidence?)
- Challenging (Would there be any place for an anecdote? Might there be room for a piece of characterisation?)
- Essential (In which places do you think the lecture gets to the heart of the matter? What are the moments that ignite your audience with your expertise?)
- Subsidiary (Which pieces of language do you feel demonstrate the passion you have felt for what you are writing about? Could you explain a moment where you really have worked hard at making the complex understandable?)
- Hypothesising (What if you decided to change the order of these two paragraphs? What if you added an extra paragraph?)

- Strategic (What research might you need to add to strengthen this opinion? How might you reorganise this paragraph?)
- Sorting and sifting (Would you say this information is relevant? How reliable do you think this source is?)
- Elaborating (Could you say a little more about...? Could you find two more pieces of evidence to...?)
- Inventive (Can you think of a more visual way of expressing this? How might you be more provocative at this moment?)

We focused on bite-sized moments such as their hook, or a moment of research, or a moment where they raised a question only to knock it down. They did a lot of walking around the drama studio with a pen, reading aloud their own work, so they could hear what they'd written before making any alterations. I wanted them to hear it the way Albee hears his writing, 'like music':

'When I'm writing a play I hear it like music. I use the same indications that a composer does for duration. There's a difference, I tell my students, between a semi-colon and a period. A difference in duration. And we have all these wonderful things, we use commas and underlining and all the wonderful punctuation things we can use in the same way a composer uses them in music. And we can indicate, as specifically as a composer, the way we want our piece to sound.'[125]

(Now go back; read Albee again, but this time aloud and feel the difference. You'll also start to understand how Albee constructed his paragraph – a synthesis of form and content.)

The students carried out a lot of peer-to-peer mentoring using the questioning I've outlined. I demonstrated a lot of modelling of the critiquing models I wanted the students to use by torch-beaming on one piece of writing in front of the whole class. I spent time demonstrating the need for open, sensitive body language rather than closed, aggressive, body language. Adults and students do like to jump to what needs improving straight away. Of course we do, but we'd be better off heeding Gladwell's advice: 'Criticism is a privilege that you earn – it shouldn't be your opening move in an interaction.'[126] Scaffolding of specialist, critiquing language was used endlessly, even if it got in the way of their train of thought at times. Keep your nerve. It's a vital part of the process. In support of this approach, Bruner describes the deal you have to strike: 'The steps taken to reduce the degrees of freedom in carrying out some task so that the child can concentrate on the difficult skill she is in the process of acquiring.'[127] I restricted them to just using the sentence stems of mentoring such as:

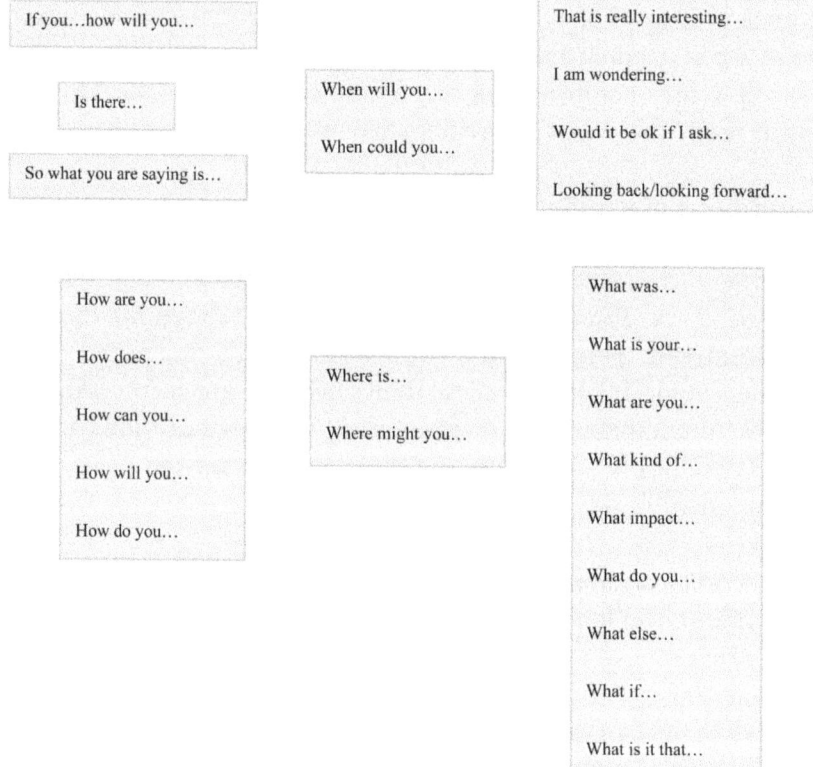

If you...how will you...

Is there...

So what you are saying is...

When will you...

When could you...

That is really interesting...

I am wondering...

Would it be ok if I ask...

Looking back/looking forward...

How are you...

How does...

How can you...

How will you...

How do you...

Where is...

Where might you...

What was...

What is your...

What are you...

What kind of...

What impact...

What do you...

What else...

What if...

What is it that...

It was offering a 'negotiated scaffold'[128] they could use in collaboration with each other. It certainly made for awkwardness and a stilted kind of conversation, but it was asking for everyone to focus on the kind of dialogue that was required. Keep your nerve. Wiliam supports this approach as well, because it helps 'students develop the habits of mind that define the discipline and coming to terms with the "official" language is part of that process'.[129] We were all in a deliberate process of what Hattie likes to call 'visible learning', when there is 'deliberate practice aimed at attaining mastery of the goal, when there is feedback given and sought, and when there are active, passionate, and engaging people (teacher, students, peers) participating in the act of learning'.[130]

Alexander places Bruner's scaffolding in a process in which 'the baton of reasoning and enquiry is passed from one person to another – teacher to child, one child to another child – and "handover", when the transition is achieved from existing understanding to new'.[131] However, before any 'handover' could happen, we knew the timing of feedback, particularly any teacher intervention, was crucial. Soderstrom and Bjork warn:

> 'One common assumption has been that providing feedback from an external source (i.e., augmented feedback) during an acquisition phase fosters long-term learning to the extent that feedback is given immediately, accurately, and frequently. However, a number of studies in the motor and verbal domains have challenged this assumption.'[132]

Here's the kicker: like most things in life, it's all about the timing:

> 'Empirical evidence suggests that delaying, reducing, and summarising feedback can be better for long-term learning than providing immediate, trial-by-trial feedback. However, the very feedback schedules that facilitate learning can have negligible (or even detrimental) performance effects during the acquisition phase... Numerous studies – some of them dating back decades – have shown that frequent and immediate feedback can, contrary to intuition, degrade learning.'

Hattie and Timperley agree, pointing out the complexities of providing feedback: 'Simply providing more feedback is not the answer, because it is necessary to consider the nature of the feedback, the timing, and how the student "receives" this feedback (or, better, actively seeks the feedback).'[133] The students first needed to finish critiquing each other's work, in what was starting to take on the character of a 'substantive conversation'. It was only now the teacher could enter the process, providing specific, appropriate feedback to match the students' needs. Because the challenge had been rigorous and because the peer critiquing had created an eagerness of purpose, commitment, and aspiration in many, it was more likely the student would seek and need feedback. If you buy into this argument, then it's vital at this point 'that there is a teacher to provide feedback and to ensure that the learner is on the right path to successfully meet the challenges'.[134]

> Play away; is there transference in Hattie and Co's theories about feedback in other settings outside of the classroom? Conversely, could teachers learn a great deal about how other organisations offer feedback for long-term impact? Or are children simply too messy, not quite fitting into any other boxes? It might be worth the search.

What were we to do with all of these lectures of varying expertise? We were tempted to find a 'real world' context for the pupils to deliver their speeches. The science teacher had strong connections with the science PGCE course at the nearby university – a rich possibility for an audience. However, we heeded Hattie's advice about the 'effect size', where he studies the impact of various interventions. We had to weigh up the time implications if we went down that road, and what we would lose in the final 'product'. So, we made a choice to place both the critical spirit we believed we'd fostered, as well as a foundation of knowledge we'd built together – however shaky for some – in the context of the outside world. We wanted to put the students in a place with people outside of the school or home environment so they could engage in dialogue based on a depth of knowledge and inquiry. To return to Papert's single purpose of school, the ability to learn, we wanted to see if the students would 'know how to act when they're faced with situations for which they were not specifically prepared'.

We also took into consideration Nuthall's research that 'learning takes time'.[135] He estimates for complex concepts to be retained, it takes at least three encounters. For the science teacher, the retention of knowledge was paramount. To put it plainly: 'If nothing has changed in long-term memory, nothing has been learned.'[136] So, we created another encounter, another 'shock'. We decided to invite three very different people to have 'an encounter' with our students. There was a woman who worked for 'Jeans for Genes'; there was a female priest who used to be a doctor (a gift for us in this context); and there was Adam Pearson, who along with his twin brother, at an early age, were both diagnosed with neurofibromatosis (type one). Incredibly for his brother, Neil, the tumours didn't grow on his face. For Adam, noncancerous tumours grew on the nerve endings on his face, leading to startling disfigurement. Google him; he's a remarkable person. He's an actor (he appeared in *Under the Skin* with Scarlett Johansson, refreshingly not as a villain or as an isolate; shame on you, Walt Disney, and your portrayal over many years of people with disability), a presenter and campaigner (studies show nine out of ten people have an unconscious bias against people with a facial disfigurement; good on you, Dreamworks, the makers of *Shrek*). In a documentary for the BBC called *The Ugly Face of Disability Hate Crime*, Pearson documents what his life's been like, from dealing with bullying at school to serious hate crime: 'I had a guy in a club in Brighton once think I was wearing a mask and tried to rip my face off and say "what kind of person gives birth to something like this?" ...He even received a comment from one woman, saying he "should have been burned to death at birth".'[137]

We gave the students the full background of each person, and asked them to create questions drawing on all of the previous work in the spirit that 'if the questions are not causing students to struggle and think, they are probably not worth asking'.[138] The hope was the students would be able to use their acquired metacognition about the intentionality of questioning, as well as the cognition about DNA developed in their lectures, to create a meaningful dialogue with the visitors. In their search to create such a dialogue, it would satisfy Professor Robert Coe's criteria: 'Learning happens when people have to think hard.'[139] It would be a milestone in their 'walk toward', working out what all of this meant to them.

The arts understand the importance of giving the student space to practise their responses rather than giving them little time to develop their thinking. One might call it drafting a response. Professor Galton is one of the few academics in this field who makes the connection with the expertise of arts practitioners in relation to talk: 'How they instinctively allow wait/thinking time and share control of exchanges: Creative practitioners seem more comfortable with silence... [and frequently] reverse roles so that the pupils and not the adult asks the questions.'[140] So, we created a 'wait/thinking time' by offering the students a space to practise what Resnick calls a 'culture of argumentation', in which 'the students challenge one another, call for evidence, change their minds and restate their claims, just as adults do in virtually every discipline of knowledge in the world outside of school'.[141] However, I wanted the science teacher to experience this, but in a different kind of 'encounter' with the students. Alexander suggests Resnick's 'culture of argumentation' creates a belief in the students he calls 'I can learn'. But he goes on to say: 'The "culture of argumentation" embraces teachers no less than students, and "I can learn" is most likely to convince the students when their teacher believes "I can teach" (dialogically). After all, it takes two, at least, to dialogue.'[142] I wanted the science teacher to let go of the 'control of the trajectories of both lesson content and student behaviour', because 'exposure to the consequences of publicly and perhaps incorrectly answering "test" questions is highly risky for students, and some teachers prefer to keep things that way'.[143] Perhaps this kind of constant 'exposure' to a testing culture was one of the sources for the disaffection of the students in their science lessons. For Alexander, it creates a risk adverse 'counter-culture':

> 'The well-documented student counter-culture of classroom risk-avoidance... and the tactics that students adopt in response to their teachers' view of "communicative competence" – by, for example, bidding to answer questions in a way that "balances the risks of not being noticed against the risks of being ignored as too enthusiastic".'[144]

We needed to take some risks. I proposed the science teacher and I adopt the role of each of the visitors, inviting the students to ask their questions as well as respond to our answers. Not only would it provide an opportunity for the students to think through their responses, but would create a meaningful arts experience. Galton captures the impact of such an experience:

> 'Creative practitioners gave pupils more time to think when planning and designing activities... extended questioning sequences so that classroom discourse was dialogic rather than... the more usual "cued elicitations"... offered more precise feedback... tended to extend rather than change pupils' initial ideas... built appropriate scaffolding into the task instead of using teacher-dominated approaches such as guided discovery... were more consistent in their management of learning and behaviour.'[145]

Alexander rightly states that what Galton describes only happens 'if the teacher makes them happen'. Again, he perhaps identifies further sources of disaffection:

> 'But what is particularly striking about Galton's observations and interviews is how students felt about the talk encouraged by the visiting arts practitioners. Contrasting it with fear of

boredom and making mistakes in mathematics lessons, they found these arts sessions engaging and stimulating, and the talk far less likely to be imbued with negative comment or dominated by procedural niceties and time-watching.'[146]

Salute, Mr Alexander and Mr Galton. The advantage of being in role was to allow us to stretch, to challenge, to provoke, to probe, to seek clarification and justification in a live interchange. The science teacher would experience what an empowering position she was about to be put into: 'When the teacher, as well as the students, enters into the world of the drama he or she can speak from the position of any character in a story, any historical figure, or re-express any students' views in order to recontextualize, amplify, extend, or question ideas'.[147] Alexander doesn't choose to live in the world of drama, but rather spends his time exploring dialogic pedagogy and classroom discourse. He would probably classify the kind of 'hot-seating' we'd chosen to make happen as 'enacting dialogue'; it's a powerful definition that rewards the more time you revisit it:

'Enacting dialogue – to help children grasp that learning is an interactive process and that understanding builds through joint activity between teacher and pupil and among pupils in collaboration, and thereby to develop pupils' increasing sense of responsibility for what and how they learn. To help children recognise that knowledge is not only transmitted but also negotiated and recreated; and that each of us in the end makes our own sense out of the meeting of knowledge both personal and collective. To advance a pedagogy in which dialogue is central: between self and others, between personal and collective knowledge, between present and past, between different ways of making sense.'[148]

However, drama teachers might add that what's also happening in this kind of 'enacting dialogue' has its roots in theatre. The relationship being created between the teacher and student is a relationship between artists: 'The way the teacher initiates, builds, empowers, challenges, and perceives what is happening is as a theatre artist and as colleague to the other artists, the students.'[149] We were really stretched as teacher artists. Many of the encounters were intense and absorbing; it would've been easy to have got carried away revelling in our roles. It's not often I get to play a priest who was a doctor. What a role for a good Jewish boy! However, we also had to be mindful we needed to be 'objective and reflective, since experience alone without reflection will not lead to learning'.[150] We were in a powerful position to hold the quality of talk to account. 'Accountable talk' is based on three principles that were being met in the hot-seating:

- Accountability to the learning community: the talk should 'attend seriously to and build on the ideas of others'.
- Accountability to standards of reasoning: the talk should 'emphasise logical connections and the drawing of reasonable conclusions' on the basis of premises and argumentation.
- Accountability to knowledge: the talk should be 'based explicitly on facts, written texts or other... information that all... can access. Speakers make an effort to get their facts right and make explicit the evidence behind their claims and expectations. They challenge each other when evidence is lacking or unavailable.'[151]

Within this kind of talk is the further challenge of 'cumulation' where, as teacher artists, we needed to hold the talk to account. We needed to ensure the dialogue didn't just go around in circles but rather push the students to build, 'critically and discriminatingly', on what was being said, 'interrogating evidence, of moving discourse and understanding forward'.[152] We were engaged in a process that was complex and rigorous; it certainly wasn't the case of doing 'a bit of hot-seating'. The difference now was I had a pedagogy which could fully articulate what was going on, to not only the science teacher but to myself.

Due to the students' ever-increasing empowerment and expertise, as teachers, we concurred with Nystrand: 'A single authentic question or a single student question significantly increased the measured probability of a subsequent dialogic spell.'(153) The subsequent probability of a 'dialogic spell' was realised in their encounters with the visitors. For me, this was a moment of 'beautiful work'. We split the cohort into three groups, spending time with each visitor. We were privileged to witness an encounter which met Alexander's criteria for dialogic teaching, the five principles being:

- Collective (the classroom is a site of joint learning and enquiry)
- Reciprocal (participants listen to each other, share ideas and consider alternative viewpoints)
- Supportive (participants feel able to express ideas freely, without risk of embarrassment over 'wrong' answers, and they help each other to reach common understandings)
- Cumulative (participants build on their own and each other's contributions, and chain them into coherent lines of thinking and understanding)
- Purposeful (classroom talk, though open and dialogic, is structured with specific learning goals in view)(154)

So, let me share a couple of moments of a 'substantive conversation' that were significant and meaningful. Isaiah was a challenging student due to severe mental health issues, as well as being dyslexic, which made accessing the curriculum very difficult. His frustration would often boil over into confrontation with teachers and an unwillingness to carry out any work. However, verbally he was very sharp, reflecting a highly inquisitive mind. Again, we turned to Berger. He's right to say, 'the apathy, disconnection, or lack of self-esteem' that had caused Isaiah to disengage, 'to stop caring', is 'not inherent. It's learned behaviour'.(155) It'd been learnt over many years, which was why it'd become so deep-rooted. Our only chance was to believe it would be through the work that we might be able to start to change how Isaiah viewed himself. Berger believes this, too: 'We can't first build the students' self-esteem and then focus on their work. It is through their own work that their self-esteem will grow.'[156] Isaiah's self-worth had indeed grown. The way of working in this project had begun to give him Daniel Pink's three drivers of motivation:

- Autonomy – Isaiah was beginning to gain more of a sense of control and an ability to make meaningful decisions.
- Mastery – Isaiah was slowly getting better at something, developing skill and expertise.
- Purpose – Isaiah was starting to connect to something meaningful and larger than himself.[157]

Berger captures how it works for the students and indeed, for us all:

Play away; see if motivation is like this for you:

'The most important assessments that take place in any school building are seen by no-one. They take place inside the heads of students, all day long. Students assess what they do, say, and produce, and decide what is good enough. These internal assessments govern how much they care, how hard they work, and how much they learn… All other assessments are in service of this goal – to get inside students' heads and raise the bar for effort and quality.'[158]

Isaiah had made such an assessment and decided to hang in there with the scientific content, just as I had. For both of us, both 'inefficient (Scientific) learners', we'd found it'd been better for the science teacher 'to provide elaborations through instruction than to provide feedback on poorly understood concepts'.[159] But even this had been enough to enter into a dialogic relationship between language and thought that had enhanced Isaiah's cognitive development. Alexander articulates what had happened:

'Studies of classroom communication indicate that certain patterns of interaction – exploratory talk, argumentation and dialogue – promote high-level thinking and intellectual development through their capacity to involve teachers and learners in joint acts of meaning-making and knowledge construction.'[160]

The memorable moment, it's never left me, 'the shock', was when Isaiah asked the priest whether she had, and I quote, 'an ethical dilemma concerning DNA, being a priest who had once been a doctor'. Was he challenging? Probing? Provoking? Getting to the heart of the matter? Whatever his intentions were, the priest was now in an encounter. She was faced with one of Papert's situations for which she was 'not specifically prepared' – an exchange 'not completely scripted or controlled'.[161] She had to work out a position. This was deep questioning, eliciting deep thinking.

The encounter with Adam Pearson was equally memorable; it too has never left me. Alexander and Wolfe quote Gibbons' thesis that the best pedagogic tasks 'involve some kind of information gap – that is a situation whereby different members within a group, or individuals in a pair hold different or incomplete information, so that the only way that the task can be completed is for this information to be shared'.[162] When faced with Adam Pearson's face and his highly humorous approach to life, there was indeed an information gap the students wanted to close. Alexander makes claim this kind of dialogic exchange has wider aspirations: 'The dialogue in dialogic teaching is not just between teacher and child or child and child, as the official "speaking and listening" formulation has it; it is also between the individual and society. It is about cultural and civic interaction, not just classroom interaction.'[163]

The students wanted to ask lots of things about what his life had been like; about his twin brother; about his life as an actor. The memorable moment was when Adam let it be known he had a girlfriend. After a prolonged pause, as they took in 'the shock',

Isaiah cracked the silence by asking whether Adam would consider having any children. Again, deconstruct the intentionality of his question to get inside his head. Where was he 'walking toward'? Here was another encounter, a 'shock', which the students had to think through, 'to use their minds well'. Adam confronted them with a challenging answer, that of course he would have a child if the opportunity arose, that if the child inherited his genes then the child would have to develop the same resilience he had growing up. This was active citizenship, as the students wrestled with the moral implications long after Adam had left the school. If we may be so bold, it was 'about trying to use pedagogy to support the quest for the good society'.[164]

The climax of the play was reflected in the climax of the scheme of learning. My colleague, Jeffrey, questions the validity of the 'neatly packaged scheme of work', calling it, in one of his classic soundbites, 'a safety blanket for that daunting walk in the woods that is teaching'.[165] He provocatively quotes academic and stand-up comedian, Kevin McCarron, who believes: 'Excessive preparation is done to protect themselves from their students.'[166] Some are not so polite about these things we call schemes of work: 'There will be a scheme of work and it will meet school policy.'[167] However, a meaningful scheme of learning isn't about 'mechanically working your way through a recipe book' but 'can be a thing of beauty'.[168] Jeffrey, in his inimitable way, describes 'preparation' as something closer to 'living': 'We don't plan the moment-by-moment experiences of our lives, but we continually prepare for them, through the process of living. We plan through our experiences, our various moments, our conversations of the past that inform our present.' In other words, designing a scheme of learning is a craft.

Richard Sennett has much to say about craft.[169] However, like Jeffrey, Sennett links craft with living, taking us back to our early experiences of play. It's an apt metaphor for the craft of creating a scheme of learning. The child, by playing, is experimenting with a world he/she is deeply immersed in. Given time and the right conditions, the child slowly but surely gains a control over that world just as 'in craftwork people can and do improve'. It's not linear. Skills build 'by moving irregularly, and sometimes by taking detours'.[170] Jeffrey agrees, likening teaching to a conversation that demands 'reflexiveness, spontaneity, agility and cooperation'. He uses McCarron to make his point, comparing the stand-up comedian's use of mental agility to a teacher's ability 'to respond to and work with audiences (students) towards a shared outcome':

> '...just as comedians can move material around in the set, or drop it completely, depending on the response they are getting, or spontaneously improvise on something somebody has said, so too teachers should be able to shift their material, or drop it, depending on the response of their students.'[171]

The child often works with 'a will' which Sennett believes is 'the craftsman in him (her)'. It's a space of freedom where experimentation with ideas and techniques can take place, mistakes can happen, and where the child can lose him/herself. It returns us to Csikszentmihalyi's 'flow'; note the emphasis on infinite possibilities:

> 'The best moments usually occur when a person's body or mind is stretched to its limits in a voluntary effort to accomplish something difficult and worthwhile. Optimal experience is thus something that we make happen. For a child, it could be placing with trembling fingers the last block on a tower she has built, higher than any she has built so far... For each person there are thousands of opportunities, challenges to expand ourselves.'[172]

Sennett describes it as the 'interplay between tacit knowledge and self-conscious awareness'. In other words, both the child and the scheme of learning, create a space that fosters 'the special human quality of being engaged'.

> Play away; consider Sennett's leap when he observes this kind of 'good citizenship found in play, is lost at work'. Is this true in your setting?

He sets out a challenge for all of us: 'This is a condition for which people will have to fight in modern society.'

> Play away again; consider what it is Sennett is asking us to fight for. Is he offering us a series of requisites to develop craft? Read and discuss the following at your next faculty meeting or training day; it may tease out the passion, energy and genuine interest in learning so often lacking in those settings:
>
> - You don't have to be a genius to be highly skilled. Craft can be improved.
> - Imagination develops technical understanding.
> - To develop skill isn't easy. It requires experiment and questioning.
> - Craft is about problem-finding as well as problem-solving: 'The probing craftsman does more than encounter problems; he or she creates them in order to know them.'[173]
> - The slow process of craft, taking your time to do something well that isn't easy, centres the individual creating a high level of self worth.
> - The objective standard of craft is quality for its own sake.
> - In craft there will always be things left unresolved, 'never-ending', which is what keeps the work alive.
> - There's progression to craft. When craft is first being developed it works at the mechanical

> level of getting things to work. However, as craft deepens to a high degree, 'people can feel fully and think deeply about what they are doing, once they do it well'.[174]
> - The craftsman 'anticipates each time that something important is about to happen'.[175]
> - Crafting provides new insight and discovers 'an unknown reality latent with possibility'.[176]
> - It's often through metaphor and narrative that craft is developed.

Each of these propositions is framed by a search; 'a walk toward'; a 'never-ending dialogue' that underpins the planning process. So, how does all of this translate? What is it I do when I craft a scheme of learning? In a multiple drafting process that's not looking for 'quick transactions or easy victories',[177] I have learned, over a long period of time, to create richly-layered, textured and contoured journeys, full of metaphor and narratives. They are journeys where we create problems 'in order to know them'; where we discover 'an unknown reality latent with possibility'; where we anticipate 'each time that something important is about to happen'. Over the years, some of the journeys have been far too arduous or have ended in quite spectacular car crashes (confess, we've all experienced them!), but Sennett's insight is that craftwork is an art which can be improved, 'to become better at, and more involved in'.[178] Over the 'slow tempo' of time, a level of expertise can be achieved, empowering people to 'feel fully and think deeply about what they are doing'.[179] Rather than producing the anxiety and fear of the door being opened only for you to be found wanting – a charlatan after all – the searching actually creates self-worth and 'is profoundly stabilizing to individuals'.[180]

One important insight I've gained along the way is that these crafted journeys require an arc. The arc mirrors the construction of any powerful play, or film, or piece of music, what Aristotle called 'the artistically made plot'.[181] We were reaching the climax. The students were now fully immersed in the world of Gearing's play, arriving at the lessons brimming with anticipation, eager to experience the next twist and turn. Towards the end of the play, Gearing has written Rosalind a strikingly beautiful monologue using the metaphor of a mountain. Before we attempted to decode the cognitive argument running through the speech, we needed to feel its emotional power by physically getting inside the language.

> Play away; see for yourself how useful the four strands are (The Cognitive; The Emotional; The Linguistic; The Physical) when applied to something worth getting inside of.

We got inside Gearing's text by playing; by digging; by experimenting with; by making connections; by asking different kind of questions; by feeling. It's a process beautifully captured by Natalie Diaz, a Mojave American poet, activist, and educator. Significantly, she also played professional basketball, that most physical of sport. For her, 'text is a happening' (just let this hang in the air for a moment, then read aloud Diaz's prose):

'Text is a way of voice, a speaking to the ear and to the eye. Letters were once bodies, are bodies now. They are not symbols, are not static. Nothing is static; nothing is unmoving. Not ink, not thread. Everything is energy. Text is a happening. In some moments, letters become an extension of my physical body: when I am writing them, or thinking them, or when I am pressing my eyes over their dark bodies on the page. A page, like a letter, has a sound. It speaks. It moves. Once spoken, once touched with the eye, it is loose – an energy from a cage to which it cannot be returned. It goes on forever and will outlast its maker.'[182]

Rosalind's speech had now been let loose; released from its cage, it made a deep impression on many of the students. I asked them to make connections with the work they'd done on creating their own stands (flick back to Chapter 3 to remind yourself what's meant by a 'stand'). Could they 'encounter' the words through a new lens, seeing it not as a speech in a play but as Rosalind's stand? An animated discussion ensued about how flawed a 'stand' it actually was. If 'education is the kindling of a flame, not the filling of a vessel',[183] then it was clear their critical spirit had been lit. There was a Socratic quality to the debate: 'The awakening of the mind to the need for criticism, to the uncertainty of the principles by which it supposed itself to be guided.'[184] Because an 'uncertainty', an ambiguity had been created, I was able to put before them a provocation: 'The really important thing is not to live, but to live well. And to live well meant, along with more enjoyable things in life, to live according to your principles.'[185] Using the framework of Philosophy for Children, which they'd been trained in since entering the school, to nurture 'strong minds' able to 'discuss ideas', they explored Rosalind's 'obsessional energy', her 'work story',[186] and the dangers of an approach that repeatedly says, 'I had my eye on the work. Only that. Only that.'[187] From conversations with many of their tutors, I knew they and the students had found it hard to create stands that were meaningful. However, we'd arrived at one of those moments Sennett captures so succinctly, the anticipation that 'something important is about to happen'. It was now about how they showed up in relation to Rosalind's 'stand'. Also in relation to the fictional protagonist, Esther, who was discovering what it was she stood for:

> *'Everyday there's something new, something big, something momentous. It's going so fast now – I don't know where to start, where I am going to jump on the roller coaster, where I am going to go. I just know I have to be a part of it. More than anything I want to be a part of it.'*

Here was an opportunity to revisit, redraft, in order to create a 'stand' as resonant, as beautiful as Rosalind's, if they so wished.

We'd collectively created a 'space of freedom', in which the students could discover Sennett's 'unknown reality latent with possibility'. They would be as empowered as they wished to be. In the text, Esther was telling them this: 'It is all down to me.' As was Socrates: 'To find yourself, think for yourself.'[188] So, they created new stands. For some, this was huge, because here was 'the shock' of sensing something of his/her own vast and untapped resources, which is a rather dry way of expressing it. Maybe for some of these disaffected students, it was actually 'an act of optimism, an act of creation, a demonstration that creativity holds back the forces of destruction'.[189] For Sennett, there's no finished end to craft; it's all about the process of participation. Life would come to them in good time; they would find their audience at some point in the future. It's the Bakhtinian notion of unending dialogue: 'When dialogue ends, everything ends. Thus dialogue, by its very essence, cannot and must not come to an end.'[190]

However, the 'Grand Exhibition' was soon upon on us, and was placing the kind of pressure which can result in the process becoming lost. 'The product' would need to avoid any sense of a 'product-ion', there would certainly not be proper time for it 'to flower'.[191] Through a process of cumulation and argumentation, Alexander's 'enacted dialogue', students had moved from their initial 'babble' – based on what they knew – to a depth of knowledge and mastery of ideas. We'd certainly asked the students to think carefully. For the cognitive scientist, Willingham, thinking carefully means this:

'Given that you cannot store everything away, your memory system lays its bets: if you think about something carefully (and repeatedly) you'll probably have to think about it again, so it should be stored. If you don't think about something very much, then you probably won't want to think about it again, so it need not be stored. Your memory is a product of what you think most carefully about. What students think about most carefully is what they will remember.'[192]

The science teacher was keen to test the students to see if this was true. There's evidence to suggest this kind of dialogic approach increases test scores:

> 'Students who had experienced this kind of structured dialogic teaching performed better on standardised tests (i.e. tests that the investigators did not control) than similar students who did not have discussion experience. The data also showed that some students retained their learned knowledge for two or three years. More surprising, in some cases students even transferred their academic advantage to a different domain (e.g. from Science instruction to an English literature exam).'[193]

However, the science teacher was disappointed, as her results were inconclusive. I pointed her to Berger: 'The strategy most often employed to create pressure for high standards is assigning grades to work. Ideally the promise of good grades and the threat of bad ones will keep everyone working hard. In reality, it doesn't always work this way.'[194] 'The Grand Exhibition' might show us what was actually at work.

Alexander adds to Resnick's three criteria for accountable talk, the accountability to language.[195] This accountability to language underpinned the teaching of a small unit on verbatim theatre, including a workshop run by the Almeida Theatre – experts in the genre. In the role of commissioned researchers, Heathcote's 'mantle of the expert', we asked them to assume the responsibility of collecting language from the widest range of sources to ensure rigour. The language could come from the play; their family interviews; video clips; the discussions with the visitors; quotes from us, the teachers; quotes from other students; quotes from themselves; from their independent research; from their science textbooks. Responsibility and rigour are two of the requisites of Heathcote's 'commission', as well as a built-in time structure. The commission element is important. It might be going too far to believe we were meeting Heathcote's wonderful vision for the commission:

'The perfect model I keep before me of a commission engaging students and staff, and serving the world community, is the one in the science department of the school which tracked and identified the first Sputnik in space before even N.A.S.A. knew. Let that encourage us.'[196]

However, as well as rigour and responsibility, the third requisite for Heathcote's 'commission', realisation, is crucial. She cites this as the 'factor often missed out of schooling'. However, it's this vital part of the process that allows both student and teacher to realise 'what we have learned, can understand, and put to use in our lives, that previously we had not recognised'.[197] With this in mind, in the first year we ran the project, we challenged them to construct a piece of verbatim drama focusing on an aspect of DNA. In the second year, the challenge was to deliver a lecture on a particular aspect of DNA, just using the verbatim language they'd gathered. The inquiry question, 'Is it ever right to play God?', was still the driving force for their verbatim pieces. However, we used the language of Rosalind in the play to set them a subsidiary question that we felt would keep the newly-lit engagement in scientific inquiry alight.

Play away; consider for a moment how challenging a task this is:

'How might you construct a piece of verbatim theatre/ scientific lecture entitled, 'Is it ever right to play God?' that gives your audience, at 'The Grand Exhibition', a sense of your own interpretation of Rosalind's words:

'Half the brilliance of science is in asking the right question-- that's what steers you to the heart of the problem'

As well as a sense of Esther's statement:

'I love science – you find the solution to one problem and a whole new set of problems appears'?

The rigour of the process would force them into an encounter with the cognitive content expressed in the subject specific language that students find so difficult in science. For some, 'robust student learning'[198] lies in the cognitive. Others go further, believing if the impact of dialogic talk 'is not primarily cognitive then the prospects for learning – and indeed the value of what is communicated – are greatly diminished'.[199] The danger is to reduce this kind of cognitive learning to 'test' talk. Berger is right to warn once again: 'If tests are the primary measure of quality, the majority of schools feel compelled to have students spend much of their time memorising facts and preparing for tests.'[200] Alexander points us to continental Europe, where curriculum and pedagogy work hand-in-hand, where 'the relationship between "what" and "how" is always pursued as a matter of course'. 'German, Dutch, Czech or Swedish educators, for example, would be somewhat puzzled by the notion that it is possible to set down requirements for the science curriculum which avoid saying or implying anything about how it should be taught.'[201] So for us, the 'what' and 'how' had indeed been pursued relentlessly. However, the chosen form of verbatim theatre would ensure that 'students put artistic care into everything that they do'.[202]

Part of this 'artistic care' is to think very carefully, but not in a context of memorising facts and figures for a test. The process of creating would involve selection, interpretation, sequencing, editing, discussing, suggesting, challenging, moving from page to the stage. Interestingly, it seldom involves learning lines. The students of all abilities rarely say they've spent hours memorising the script, nor do they say it's a problem. The process allows for the language to organically go into the child. This interplay between the conscious and the subconscious, each time the student experiences the words, allows for new insights and discoveries. It's more akin to when we view sculpture. Each time we revisit it from a different angle, in a different light, in a different mood, our perceptions change. Therefore, it follows: 'If you can change your perception, you can change your emotion and this can lead to new ideas.'[203] So it is with our engagement with text, Diaz's urgent 'happening' where 'nothing is static; nothing is unmoving... Once spoken, once touched with the eye, it is loose – an energy from a cage to which it cannot be returned.'[204] Way back in 1975, Bullock named his report, *A Language for Life*; Diaz wouldn't disagree. Nor would I disagree; in the process of creating and performing a piece of verbatim theatre, we were fully aware of the power of Bullock's insight that 'the mental processes' we sought to nurture 'are the outcomes of a development that originates in speech':

> 'A curriculum subject, philosophically speaking, is a distinctive mode of analysis. While many teachers recognise that their aim is to initiate students into a particular mode of analysis, they rarely recognise the linguistic implications of doing so. They do not recognise, in short, that the mental processes they seek to foster are the outcome of a development that originates in speech.'[205]

I wanted this process, in some way, to reflect the process Rosalind experiences in Gearing's play. So, when she expresses her frustration with Watson and Crick, it's because 'I'm surrounded by people who are not serious. By men who are playing... It's infuriating. It is exhausting me.' For the students, too, it would be about holding each other to account because 'the overall quality of the work that emerges is a concern for every member in it... there is a sense of peer pressure to keep up with the standard'.[206] To fall short, by failing to be reliable, or work with the sufficient effort needed, would show the students not only how exhausting and frustrating that can be, but also how damaging to relationships it inevitably is. By the end of the play, Rosalind has learnt 'progress is a joint effort'. If their group piece was to have integrity, they needed to live by Rosalind's belief.

We also wanted to give a sense of the community of learners we'd become, by joining together as an ensemble so they could feel they were part of something bigger than themselves, that 'they belonged to something'.[207] They would be offered the opportunity to experience what Rosalind had felt in her relationship with Esther: 'When you get to work with a good team, you'll see – it's the most satisfying thing in the world.' We created a verbatim script for the whole ensemble. It was a chance to place each pupil, 'not for their abilities but for their human qualities... to build a theatre where each feels he has his or her own place in our little society'.[208] Many had arrived at the start of the project feeling disempowered, incapable of becoming experts in science. They were now prepared to advocate for their own learning in front of an outside audience, willing to say at the end of the exhibition, 'We were a good team today.' It's certainly about creating a sense of infinite possibilities: 'The first task in teaching for creativity in any field is to encourage young people to believe in their creative potential, to engage their sense of possibilities and to give them the confidence to try.'[209] There's good cause to say it's also about beginning to show them what it was going to take if they weren't to live in Alinsky's 'valleys of a dreamless day-to-day existence'. It had started to build 'the independence, critical thinking skills, perseverance, and self-reflective understanding students need for college and careers',[210] and yet it's bigger. It goes to the heart of expertise and empowerment. Berger's evocative phrase speaks to me and catches what it's fundamentally about: 'Shepherd(ing) students toward becoming positive citizens and human beings.'[211]

In the second year, we didn't bring them together as an ensemble due to the logistics of the space in the science labs. I felt something important was lost. Nevertheless, on both occasions, many of the students got a sense, some for the first time in their school lives, of what Rosalind feels at one point in Gearing's play: 'That was – exhilarating. Just exhilarating (then she realises) I'm shaking. Look at me, I'm all shaky.' We had watched the students perform their verbatim pieces with controlled passion; eagerly field questions they weren't prepared for with developed answers grounded in their acquired knowledge; engage in debate and discussion with adults they'd never met. One such adult was Ben Drew – a worldwide, genuine pop star (before you show your age, look him up aka Plan B). Drew grew up in the same area as the students, spent much of his schooling in Tunmarsh – a Pupil Referral Unit – just down the road from us, and who happened to be visiting. Go watch his TED talk,[212] hear how he began his 'walk toward' empowerment and expertise. The memorable exchange, I haven't forgotten, involved Drew's real-life concerns about having his own children and the issues of genetic inheritance. Unphased by his rock star status and his burly entourage, the students carefully explained the science to him. They patiently answered all of his questions with an expertise leaving Drew lost for words by the end – a rare experience, I should imagine, for the director of *Ill Manors* – the loudest of films. Students of all abilities could explain, analyse, challenge, and justify at a far more expansive level than when they'd started out. In short, their expertise and empowerment had meant their talk had become far more dialogic. We didn't have to imagine what Berger asks us to imagine. We were able to experience at 'The Grand Exhibition' an audience that was encountering the students in terms of their 'work, thinking and character'.

> Play away; as you read what Berger has to say, ask yourself whether you might want this for any workplace.

'Imagine if students were judged instead on the quality of student work, thinking, and character. Imagine an expectation that an adult should be able to enter a school and expect that any child in that school older than seven or eight would be ready to greet him politely, give an articulate tour of a well-maintained, courteous school environment, and present his portfolio of academic accomplishments clearly and insightfully, and that the student's portfolio would contain original, high-quality work and document appropriate skill levels. If schools assumed they were to [*sic*] going to be assessed by the quality of student behaviour and work evident in the hallways and classrooms – rather than on test scores – the enormous energy poured into test preparation would be directed instead toward improving student work, understanding, and behaviour. Instead of working to build clever test-takers, schools would feel compelled to spend time building thoughtful students and good citizens.'[213]

After the exhibition was over, it was important for all of us – teachers and students – to realise 'what we have learned, can understand, and put to use in our lives, that previously we had not recognised'.[214] The project-based learning had the potential to be 'the necessary casting off point of realisation'.[215] It's another requisite for this kind of long-lasting expertise and empowerment to build in time for one-to-one conversations. We created a timetable for each student to have such a conversation, as well as time for the science teacher and myself to engage in the same kind of dialogue. Several profound insights came out of these conversations that are worth sharing:

- ✓ It was apparent many of the students could now reimagine themselves as 'learners', due to the fact that if students 'over an extended period of time, are treated as if they are intelligent, actually become so. If they are taught demanding content, and are expected to explain and find connections as well as memorise and repeat, they learn more and learn more quickly. They think of themselves as learners.'[216]
- ✓ They had learnt 'the skill of being able to learn'.[217]
- ✓ The impact on their self-esteem had come from their (the sound bites are piling up) 'accomplishments, not compliments'.[218]
- ✓ It had crossed all abilities, offering them 'a framework for motivation and a framework for achievement'.[219]
- ✓ Importantly, the students could now appreciate the purpose of gaining expertise: 'Motivation is in fact the most important result of student-engaged assessment – unless students find reason and inspiration to care about learning and have hope that they can improve, excellence

and high achievement will remain the domain of a select group.'[220]

✓ They were on their way to understanding: 'It's a long-term commitment. It's a way of life.'[221]

✓ Our hope for the students (remember, they were only 13 years old) was the same as Berger's: 'I believe that work of excellence is transformational. Once a student sees that he or she is capable of excellence, that student is never quite the same. There is a new self-image, a new notion of possibility. There is an appetite for excellence.'[222]

✓ I also hoped it would have a transformational impact on the way the science teacher would now craft her schemes of learning, because she'd experienced that '"I can learn'... is most likely to convince the students when their teacher believes "I can teach" (dialogically)'.[223] She, too, was in the process of reimagining herself.

✓ For me, I'm not quite the same either. I don't skip over the science section in my Sunday paper, but rather linger on niche articles by the late Mary Warnock entitled, *We Need to Use Gene Editing Wisely but also Embrace its Vast Potential*,[224] feeling rather smug and proud that I can understand most of what I'm reading.

✓ I can now question, as well as provoke, my students to also inquire why there's a much lauded institution called, 'The Francis Crick Institute', which seems to maintain the myth on their website that 'Crick and Watson's work led to the identification of the structure of DNA in 1953, drawing on the work of Maurice Wilkins, Rosalind Franklin and others'.[225] Not true.

✓ I can not only get excited, but can create the same excitement in my students, as we awaited the House of Lords ruling whether Britain was to become the first country in the world to allow 'three person IVF'. (If you've stoically got to the end of the chapter, then I'm sure your new-found appreciation of what it takes, will inspire you to look it up yourself to see if it was passed.) I could also begin to imagine my own grandmother's excitement when I discovered she was right there at one of the greatest breakthroughs in modern medicine. Ethel Florey carried out the clinical trials of penicillin at Birmingham Accident Hospital in 1941 where, after arriving in England, my grandmother worked until she was 80. If you ever happen to be in this hospital, go find the plaque they put up in honour of Olga Muller – an ordinary extraordinary woman.

But I will end (exhale) on what became, for the students and myself, a description that resonated about what it takes to be truly expert and empowered. To hear what we heard, it has to be read aloud. At the end of the day, ultimately, it's all about cracking bones:

'*Rosalind: At the foot of the mountain – at the foot of the mountain you are filled with excitement at the prospect of the journey to the peak. You know – you hope – it will be arduous, precarious, dangerous, stretch you to the very limit. Until your bones crack. But you want to get there – more than anything you want to see the world spread out before you. You want to have made it.*

It's the journey, the effort that counts. To arrive at the summit without the experience of getting there – that would be to arrive without blood pumping through your veins, without the sharper sight of constant wariness, without the sweet pain of overworked muscles. You create it – it's your climb, your own pain, your own victory. As I get nearer to the top – I don't look down, I don't look across to see how the stranger on the nearby rock face is doing. I give my full concentration to the mountain.

It is the mountain and me.

The instant summit – that would be nothing more than a picture postcard – it wouldn't be mine, my own.

In France. It was cold. We set out in cloud. And suddenly, quite suddenly, at sunrise the cloud lifted, just as we were coming out onto the glacier. There were pink summits above a sea of cloud. The light rested so gently on the mountains and on the clouds. I was so happy. I had to weep. The world is so beautiful.'[(226)]

1-Picasso quoted in Picasso, M. 2001: *Picasso, my grandfather:* Vintage Books, London

2-Shakespeare, W: *Macbeth (Act 5 scene 3)*

3-Stone, J.2013: *The Routledge Dictionary of Latin Quotations: The Illiterati's Guide to Latin Maxims, Mottoes, Proverbs, and Sayings*: Routledge

4-Csikszentmihalyi, M. 1996: *Creativity: Flow and the psychology of discovery and invention:* Harper Collins

5-Berger, J. 1972: *G:* Weidenfeld & Nicolson

6-Sehgal, P. 2016: *Fighting "Erasure":* The New York Times Magazine

7-Davis, N. 2014: *Stop female scientists being written out of Wikipedia history:* The Guardian

8-Maddox, B. 2002: *Rosalind Franklin: The Dark Lady of DNA* by Harper Collins

9-Rosalind Franklin: Discovery of DNA: Historyworks: http://www.creatingmycambridge.com/history-stories/rosalind-franklin-discovery-of-dna/

10-Maddox, B. 2002: *Rosalind Franklin: The Dark Lady of DNA* by Harper Collins

11-Emerson, R: 1841: *History Essays ~ first series* in *The Essays of Ralph Waldo Emerson* Edited by Ferguson, A., Carr, J.

12-Mate, G. 2009: *In the Realm of Hungry Ghosts:* Vintage Canada

13-Bernal, J. 1958: In his Obituary for Rosalind Franklin. As given in Brown, A. 2005: *J.D. Bernal: The Sage of Science:* Oxford University Press

14-Widely quoted, source unknown

15-Batty, D., Davis, N. 2018: *Why science breeds a culture of sexism*: The Guardian

16-Watson, J. 1968: *The Double Helix: A Personal Account of the Discovery of the Structure of DNA*: Weidenfeld & Nicolson

17-Levy, R. 2005: *Antisemitism*: ABC-CLIO Inc.

18-Lipton, S. 2014: *Dark Mirror*: Henry Holt and Company

19-Hitler, A. 1925: *Mein Kampf (Book 1 Chap 11)*

20-Johnson, C. 2011: *Thatcher and the Jews*: The Tablet: https://www.tabletmag.com/jewish-news-and-politics/87027/thatcher-and-the-jews

21-Rosenberg, Y. 2017: *Are Jews white? Just ask the white supremacists*: Washington Post

22-Slayton, R. 2017: *When did Jews become white?*: Jewish Currents: https://jewishcurrents.org/writings-grid/when-did-jews-become-white/

23-Ignatiev, N. 1995: *How the Irish Became White*: Routledge

24-Mueller, M. 2017: *Wonder Woman: There IS A Person Of Color In The Lead Role*: comicbook: http://comicbook.com/dc/2017/05/31/wonder-woman-person-of-color/

25-Ibid

26-Watson, J. 1968: *The Double Helix: A Personal Account of the Discovery of the Structure of DNA*: Weidenfeld & Nicolson

27-Conor, S. 2014: *James Watson profile: A human riddle wrapped in a DNA double helix*: Independent

28-Katz, Y. 2017: *It's time to take the "great" white men of science off their pedestals*: The Guardian

29-Coyne, J. 2017: *Now they want to demonize Francis Crick'*: Why Evolution is True: https://whyevolutionistrue.wordpress.com/2017/09/21/now-they-want-to-demonize-francis-crick/

30-Rutherford, A. 2014: *He may have unravelled DNA, but James Watson deserves to be shunned*: The Guardian

31-Moaveni, A. 2017: *How Did Rumi Become One of Our Best-Selling Poets?*: The New York Times

32-As quoted in Ferguson, L. 2011: *Path for Greatness: Spiritualty at Work*: Infinity Publishing

33-Neruda, P.: Ode to a Naked Beauty

34-Franklin, R. 1940: In a letter to her father as quoted in Bush, L. 2010: *Rosalind Franklin and the Double Helix*: Jewish Currents: https://jewishcurrents.org/jewdayo-grid/april-16-rosalind-franklin-and-the-double-helix/

35-Mandela, N.1994: *The Long Walk to Freedom*: Abacus

36-Camus, A. 1975: *The Myth of Sisyphus and Other Essays:* Penguin

37-Klug, A: 1982: Interview Transcript: Nobelprize.org

38-Emerson, R. 1876: *Letters and Social Aims*: Boston: James R. Osgood

39-Watson, J. 1990: *The Human Genome Project: past, present, and future*: Science: American Association for the Advancement of Science

40-Dali, S. 1964: quoted in Playboy Magazine

41-Martin, B: 2003: *Rosalind Franklin: The Dark Lady of DNA*: Medscape: https://www.medscape.com/viewarticle/448302

42-Glynn, J. 2012: *Remembering my sister, Rosalind Franklin*: The Lancet: https://www.thelancet.com/journals/lancet/article/PIIS0140-6736 (12)60452-8/fulltext

43-Maddox, B. 2002: *Rosalind Franklin: The Dark Lady of DNA*: Harper Collins

44-Maddox, B. 2000: *The Dark Lady of DNA?*: The Guardian

45-Shakespeare, W 1601: *Hamlet, Act 3 Scene 1*

46-Laing, O. 2016: *The wild beauty of Georgia O'Keefe*: The Guardian

47-Brown, B.2012: *Daring Greatly: How the Courage to Be Vulnerable Transforms the Way We Live, Love, Parent, and Lead*: Avery

48-Maddox, B. 2002: *Rosalind Franklin: The Dark Lady of DNA*: Harper Collins

49-Belt, H. 2009: *Playing God in Frankenstein's Footsteps: Synthetic Biology and the Meaning of Life*: Nanoethics: https://www.ncbi.nlm.nih.gov/pmc/articles/PMC2837218/

50-Savulescu,J. 2002: *Deaf lesbians, "designer disability", and the future of medicine*: BM: https://www.ncbi.nlm.nih.gov/pmc/articles/PMC1124279/

51-Cairns, D. 2012: *How forensics "solved" Stephen Lawrence murder*: BBC, Newsbeat

52-Bordier, A. 2015: *Experience: I found my identical twin on YouTube*: The Guardian

53-*Significant Strangers* directed by Rothby, K.: http://cargocollective.com/treeleaffilms/SIGNIFICANT-STRANGERS

54-Pratchett, T.1990: *Good Omens: The Nice and Accurate Prophecies of Agnes Nutter, Witch*: Victor Gollancz Ltd.

55-Baron-Cohen, S: 2013: *WHAT *SHOULD* WE BE WORRIED ABOUT?*: Edge: https://www.edge.org/response-detail/23749

56-Google doodle, 2013: *Celebrating Rosalind Franklin: a perfect example of single-minded devotion to research*: The Guardian

57-Klug, A: Nobel speech 1982: Nobelprize.org

58-Letter to her father, Ellis Franklin, undated, perhaps summer 1940 while she was an undergraduate at Cambridge, quoted in Maddox, B. 2002: *Rosalind Franklin: The Dark Lady of DNA*: Harper Collins

59-Rosalind Franklin-Official Report, submitted in Feb 1952 quoted in Sayre, A. 2000: *Rosalind Franklin and DNA*: Norton

60-Berger, R. 2014: *Leaders of Their Own Learning: Transforming Schools Through Student-Engaged Assessment*: Jossey-Bass

61-Edutopia: https://www.edutopia.org/profile/ron-berger

62-Berger, R. 2003: *An Ethic of Excellence*: Heinemann Educational Books

63-Ibid

64-Hattie, J. 2012: *Visible Learning for Teachers: Maximizing Impact on Learning:* Routledge

65-Morton, S. 2017: *Concrete factory plans for Queen Elizabeth Olympic Park withdrawn:* Newham Recorder

66-Newmann, F and Wehlage, G. 1993: *Five Standards of Authentic Instruction:* ASCD, April 1993 | Volume 50 | Number 7

67-Berger, R. 2014: *Leaders of Their Own Learning: Transforming Schools Through Student-Engaged Assessment* : Jossey-Bass

68-Berger, R. 2003: *An Ethic of Excellence*: Heinemann Educational Books

69-Gearing, D. 2006: *Rosalind*: Oberon

70-Berger, R. 2003: *An Ethic of Excellence*: Heinemann Educational Books

71-Larmer, J. and Mergendoller, J. 2010: *Seven Essentials for Project-Based Learning*: ASCD.org: http://www.ascd.org/publications/educational_leadership/sept10/vol68/num01/Seven_Essentials_for_Project-Based_Learning.aspx

72-Gini-Newman, G. 2017: *Inspiring wonder through learning and thinking*: TEDxKitchenerED

73-Letters: *Gove will bury pupils in facts and rules*: 2017: Independent

74-Menon, A and Portes, J. 2016: *You're wrong Michael Gove – experts are trusted far more than you*: The Guardian

75-Livingstone, R. 1941: *The Future of Education*: Cambridge University Press

76-Mergendoller, J.2012: *Teaching Critical Thinking Skills Through Project Based Learning*: Blog: P21

77-Ibid

78-Berger, R. 2003: *An Ethic of Excellence*: Heinemann Educational Books

79-Brook, P. 1972: *The Empty Space*: Pelican

80-Williams, T. 2007: *Notebooks*: Yale University Press

81-Brook, P. in the preface to Grotowski, J. 2002: *Towards a Poor Theatre*: Routledge

82-Ibid

83-Resnick, L., Asterhan, C., Clarke, S. 2015: *Socializing Intelligence Through Academic Talk and Dialogue*: American Educational Research Association

84-Heathcote, D., Bolton, G. 1996: *Drama for Learning: Dorothy Heathcote's Mantle of the Expert Approach to Education*: Greenwood Press

85-Berger, R. 2014: *Leaders of Their Own Learning: Transforming Schools Through Student-Engaged Assessment* : Jossey-Bass

86-Gearing, D. 2006: *Rosalind*: Oberon

87-Cadwalladr, C. 2016: *How to bump off Holocaust deniers from Google's top spot? Pay Google*: The Guardian

88-Bacon, F. (1597) 1996: *Meditationes Sacrae*: Kessinger

89-Gearing, D. 2006: *Rosalind*: Oberon

90-Mergendoller, J.2012: *Teaching Critical Thinking Skills Through Project Based Learning*: Blog: P21

91-Wiliam, D. 2011: *Embedded Formative Assessment*: Solution Tree Press

92-Nuthall, G. 2007: *The Hidden Lives of Learners*: NZCER Press

93-Wiliam, D. 2014: *Dylan Wiliam's defence of formative assessment*: Didau, D. Blog: The Learning Spy

94-Pirsig, R. 1991: *Lila: an inquiry into morals*: New York, Bantam

95-Wiliam, D. 2014: *Dylan Wiliam's defence of formative assessment*: Didau, D. Blog: The Learning Spy

96-Lair, J. 1997: *David Mamet, The Art of Theatre, No 11: The Paris Review*

97-Miller, A. 1957: *Collected Plays*: Viking Press

98-Interview with Hattie, J. 2013: *Know Thy Impact: Teaching, Learning and Leading*: In Conversation: Spring 2013 vol4 issue 2 (PDF)

99-Berger, R. 2003: *An Ethic of Excellence*: Heinemann Educational Books

100-Ibid

101-Interview with Lee, H. 2013: *To Kill a Mockingbird* Turns 50: www.thebluegrassspecial.com

102- Berger, R. 2003: *An Ethic of Excellence*: Heinemann Educational Books

103-Ibid

104- Berger, R. 2014: *Leaders of Their Own Learning: Transforming Schools Through Student-Engaged Assessment* : Jossey-Bass

105-Ibid

106-Berger, R. 2003: *An Ethic of Excellence*: Heinemann Educational Books

107-Bennis, W., Biederman, P. 1997: *Organizing Genius: The Secrets of Creative Collaboration*: Perseus Publishing

108-Grotowski, J. 2002: *Towards a Poor Theatre*: Routledge

109-Hattie, J. 2012: *Visible Learning for Teachers: Maximizing Impact on Learning*: Routledge

110- Here's a Library of Lectures, enjoy:

-Diebedo Francis Kere: *How to build with clay... and community* https://www.youtube.com/watch?v=eJDvFLQuMeg

-Jack Horner: *Building a dinosaur from a chicken* https://www.ted.com/talks/jack_horner_building_a_dinosaur_from_a_chicken

-Miranda Wang and Jeanny Yao: *Two young scientists break down plastics with bacteria* https://www.ted.com/talks/two_young_scientists_break_down_plastics_with_bacteria

-Beau Lotto + Amy O'Toole: *Science is for everyone, kids included*
https://www.youtube.com/watch?v=0g2WE1qXiKM

-Kelvin Doe: *Persistent Experimentation*:

TEDxTeen: https://www.youtube.com/watch?v=wQigsI3xsHw

-Dylan Vecchione: *Passionate Questioning*:

TEDxTeen: https://www.youtube.com/watch?v=IO_k8qx2Ook

-Denise Herzing: *Could we speak the language of dolphins?* https://www.
ted.com/talks/denise_herzing_could_we_speak_the_language_of_
dolphins

-Andras Forges: *Leather and meat without killing animals* https://www.
ted.com/talks/andras_forgacs_leather_and_meat_without_killing_animals

-Carvens Lissaint: *Put the financial aid in the bag* https://www.ted.com/
talks/put_the_financial_aid_in_the_bag

-Kevin Allocca: *Why videos go viral*

https://www.ted.com/talks/kevin_allocca_why_videos_go_viral

-Maurice Ashley: *Working backward to solve problems* https://www.
youtube.com/watch?v=v34NqCbAA1c

-David Fasanya and Gabriel Barralaga: *Beach bodies*

https://www.youtube.com/watch?v=nVnPQw0f8Qc

-Luis von Ahn: *Massive-scale online collaboration*

https://www.youtube.com/watch?v=-Ht4qiDRZE8

-Daniel Linehan: *BMW Tate Live: Performance Room*

http://www.tate.org.uk/context-comment/video/bmw-tate-live-performance-
room-daniel-linehan

Alan Cumming presents a quick-fire guide to Pop Art

http://www.tate.org.uk/context-comment/video/unlock-art#open290575

Palace x Tate: Palace Skateboards inspired by John Martin

http://www.tate.org.uk/context-comment/video/palace-x-tate-palace-skateboards-inspired-john-martin

-Vi Hart : *twelve tones* https://www.youtube.com/user/Vihart?desktop_uri=%2Fuser%2FVihart&app=desktop&disable_polymer=true

-Logan LaPlante: *Hack schooling makes me happy*

https://www.youtube.com/watch?v=h11u3vtcpaY

-Henry Dotson: *Confessions of An All-Night Dancer, Ignite Phoenix #15* https://www.youtube.com/watch?feature=player_embedded&v=H7XsONXtgwc

-Clay Richardson-: *How to Build and Enjoy a Wood Fired Pizza Oven* https://www.youtube.com/watch?feature=player_embedded&v=jXG70Y71deM

111-Papert, S. 1998: *Child Power: Keys to the New Learning of the Digital Century*: This speech was delivered at the eleventh Colin Cherry Memorial Lecture on Communication on June 2, 1998, at the Imperial College in London: http://www.papert.org/articles/Childpower.html

112-Hattie, J. 2012: *Visible Learning for Teachers: Maximizing Impact on Learning*: Routledge

113-https://unseenflirtspoetry.wordpress.com/

114-Wiliam, D. 2006: *Excellence in Assessment: Assessment for Learning* (paper delivered at Assessment for Learning Seminar, Cambridge): University of Cambridge

115-Wiliam, D. 2011: *Embedded Formative Assessment - practical strategies and tools for K-12 teachers*: Solution Tree

116-Wiliam, D. 2006: *Excellence in Assessment: Assessment for Learning* (paper delivered at Assessment for Learning Seminar, Cambridge): University of Cambridge

117-Hattie, J. 2012: *Visible Learning for Teachers: Maximizing Impact on Learning*: Routledge

118-Wiliam, D. 2014: *Dylan Wiliam's defence of formative assessment*: Didau, D. Blog: The Learning Spy

119-Hattie, J. 2012: *Visible Learning for Teachers: Maximizing Impact on Learning:* Routledge

120-Alexander, R.2010: *Speaking but not listening? Accountable talk in an unaccountable context:* UKLA: Literacy Volume 44 Number 3 November 2010

121-Nystrand, M., & Gamoran, A. 1991: *Instructional discourse, student engagement, and literature achievement:* Research in the Teaching of English, National Council of Teachers of English

122-Mehan, H. 2009: *'What time is it, Denise?': Asking known information questions in classroom discourse:* Theory Into Practice

123-Nystrand, M. et al 1997: *Opening Dialogue: Understanding the Dynamics of Learning and Teaching in the English Classroom:* New York: Teachers College

124-Newmann, F. & Wehlage, G. 1993: *Five Standards of Authentic Instruction* ASCD: April 1993 | Volume 50 | Number 7: Authentic Learning

125-Albee, E. 1998: An interview with Daniel Stern 1998-from Dircks, P. *Edward Albee, a Literary Companion:* McFarland and Company, Inc., Publishers

126-Gladwell, M 2014: Interview 'LIVE from the NYPL' series

127-Bruner, J. 1978: *The role of dialogue in language acquisition,* In Sinclair, A., Jarvella, R. & Levelt, W.: *The child's conception of language:* New York: Springer-Verlag

128-Daniels, H. 2001: *Vygotsky and Pedagogy:* NY: Routledge/Falmer

129-Wiliam, D. 2011: *Embedded Formative Assessment - practical strategies and tools for K-12 teachers:* Solution Tree

130-Hattie, J. 2012: *Visible Learning for Teachers: Maximizing Impact on Learning:* Routledge

131-Alexander, R.2010: *Speaking but not listening? Accountable talk in an unaccountable context:* UKLA: Literacy Volume 44 Number 3 November 2010

132-Soderstrom, N. and Bjork, A. 2015: *Learning versus Performance*: Perspectives on Psychological Science Vol. 10: Sage

133-Hattie, J. & Timperley, H. 2007: *The Power of Feedback*: Sage

134-Hattie, J. 2012: *Visible Learning for Teachers: Maximizing Impact on Learning*: Routledge

135-Nuthall, G. 2002: *The Cultural Myths and Realities of Classroom Teaching and Learning: A Personal Journey*: New Zealand Annual Review of Education, 11

136-Kirschner, P., Sweller, J. & Clark, R. 2006: *Why Minimal Guidance During Instruction Does Not Work: An Analysis of the Failure of Constructivist, Discovery, Problem-Based, Experiential, and Inquiry-Based Teaching*: Educational Psychologist, 41, Lawrence Erlbaum Associates, Inc

137-Mitchell, L.2015: *"They tried to rip my face off"*: *Actor with facial tumours victim of horrific hate crime*: The Daily Star

138-Wiliam, D. 2014: *The Right Questions, The Right Way*: Volume 71 | Number 6, *Using Assessments Thoughtfully*: ASCD

139-Coe, R. 2016: *Improving Education: A triumph of hope over experience Revisited Three Years On*: The Telegraph Festival of Education, Wellington College: CEM, Durham University

140- Galton, M. 2008: *Creative Practitioners in Schools and Classrooms*: Cambridge: University of Cambridge Faculty of Education quoted in Alexander, R. 2017: *Developing Dialogue: Process, Trial, Outcomes*: 17th Biennial EARLI Conference, Tampere, Finland

141-Resnick, L. 2015: *Talking to Learn: The Promise and Challenge of Dialogic Teaching*, in Resnick, L., Asterhan, C. and Clarke, S. (ed) 2015: *Socializing Intelligence Through Academic Talk and Dialogue*: American Educational Research Association

142-Alexander, R. 2017: *Developing Dialogue: Process, Trial, Outcomes*: 17th Biennial EARLI Conference, Tampere, Finland

143-Ibid

144-Ibid

145-Galton, M. 2008: *Creative Practitioners in Schools and Classrooms*: University of Cambridge Faculty of Education

146-Alexander, R. 2017: *Developing Dialogue: Process, Trial, Outcomes*: 17th Biennial EARLI Conference, Tampere, Finland

147-Wilhelm, J.& Edminson, B. 1998: *Imagining to Learn: Inquiry, Ethics, and Integration Through Drama*: Heinemann

148-Alexander, A. 2010: *Children, their World, their Education: final report and recommendations from the Cambridge Primary Review*: Routledge

149-Bolton, G. in Heathcote, D. and Bolton, G. 1995: *Drama for Learning: Dorothy Heathcote's Mantle of the Expert Approach to Education*: Heinemann

150-Johnson, L. and O'Neill, C. 1984: *Dorothy Heathcote: Collected Writings on Education and Drama*: Hutchinson

151-O'Connor, C., Michaels, S. & Resnick, L. 2007: *Deliberative discourse idealized and realized: accountable talk in the classroom and civic life*: Studies in Philosophy and Education 27, Springer Netherlands

152-Alexander, R.2010: *Speaking but not listening? Accountable talk in an unaccountable context*: UKLA: Literacy Volume 44 Number 3 November 2010

153-Nystrand, M., Wu, L., Gamoran, A., Zeiser, S. & Long, D. 2003: *Questions in Time: Investigating the Structure and Dynamics of Unfolding Classroom Discourse*: Discourse Processes 35, Routledge

154-Alexander, R. 2017: *Developing Dialogue: Process, Trial, Outcomes*: 17th Biennial EARLI Conference, Tampere, Finland

155-Berger, R. 2014: *Leaders of Their Own Learning: Transforming Schools Through Student-Engaged Assessment* : Jossey-Bass

156-Berger, R. 2003: *An Ethic of Excellence*: Heinemann Educational Books

157-Pink, D. 2009: *The Surprising Truth About What Motivates Us*: Riverhead Books, New York

158-Berger, R. 2014: *Leaders of Their Own Learning: Transforming Schools Through Student-Engaged Assessment* : Jossey-Bass

159-Hattie, J. & Timperley, H. 2007: *The Power of Feedback*: Sage

160-Alexander, R. & Wolfe, S. 2008: *Argumentation and dialogic teaching: alternative pedagogies for a changing world*: Beyond Current Horizons, Futurelab

161-Newmann, F. & Wehlage, G. 1993: *Five Standards of Authentic Instruction*: ASCD: April 1993 | Volume 50 | Number 7: Authentic Learning

162-Gibbons, P. 2002: *Scaffolding Language: Scaffolding Learning. Teaching Second Language Learners in the Mainstream Classroom*: Heinemann

163-Alexander, R.2010: *Speaking but not listening? Accountable talk in an unaccountable context*: UKLA: Literacy Volume 44 Number 3 November 2010

164-Ibid

165-Boakye, J. 2017: *Underplanned and Fully Prepared: Let's Teach*: https://unseenflirtspoetry.wordpress.com/category/teaching-2/

166-McCarron, K. 2007: *Stand-Up or Fall Down: Pedagogic Innovation, the Comedy Club and the Seminar Room*: Paper delivered at a conference organised by the University of Wales Institute, Cardiff, in collaboration with the Higher Education Academy

167-Edwards, D 2012: as quoted in: Didau, D: *The best laid schemes of work & learning*: The Learning Spy: http://www.learningspy.co.uk/learning/the-best-laid-schemes-of-work/

168-Ibid

169-Sennett, R. 2008: *The Craftsman*: Yale University Press

170-Ibid

171-McCarron, K. 2007: *Stand-Up or Fall Down: Pedagogic Innovation, the Comedy Club and the Seminar Room*: Paper delivered at a conference organised by the University of Wales Institute, Cardiff, in collaboration with the Higher Education Academy

172-Csikszentmihalyi, M. 2002: *Flow: The Psychology of Optimal Experience*: Rider, Random House

173-Sennett, R. 2008: *Labours of love*: The Guardian

174-Sennett, R. 2008: *The Craftsman*: Yale University Press

175-Ibid

176-Ibid

177- Sennett, R. 2008: *Labours of love*: The Guardian

178-Ibid

179-Ibid

180-Ibid

181-Aristotle: *Poetics*: Penguin Classics (1996)

182-Diaz, N. 2017: *Natalie Diaz on the physicality of writing*: Poetry, Process, Inspiration: From a conversation with Brandon Stosuy : The Creative Independent: https://thecreativeindependent.com/people/natalie-diaz-on-the-physicality-of-writing/

183-Socrates-Widely quoted, source unknown

184-Anderson, J. 2008: *Socrates as an educator*: Australasian Journal of Psychology and Philosophy, 9:3: Routledge

185-Socrates-Widely quoted, source unknown

186-Sennett, R. 2008: *The Craftsman*: Yale University Press

187-Gearing, D. 2006: *Rosalind*: Oberon

188-Socrates-Widely quoted, source unknown

189-Almond, D. 2015: *The Kind, the Cruel, and the Physicality of Reading and Writing*: Signature, Penguin Random House: http://www.signature-reads.com/2015/10/under-the-influence-the-kind-the-cruel-and-the-phsyicality-of-reading-and-writing/

190-Bakhtin, M. 1929 tr. Emerson, C.1984: *Problems of Dostoevsky's Poetics (1929)*: Minneapolis University Press

191-Robinson, K. 1999: *All Our Futures: Creativity, Culture and Education*: NACCCE report

192-Willingham, D. quoted in Kirby, J. 2013: *Why don't students remember what they've learned?*: Pragmatic Education: https://pragmaticreform.wordpress.com/2013/11/16/memory/

193-Resnick, L. 2015: *Talking to Learn: The Promise and Challenge of Dialogic Teaching*, in Resnick, L., Asterhan, C. and Clarke, S. (ed) 2015: *Socializing Intelligence Through Academic Talk and Dialogue*: American Educational Research Association

194-Berger, R. 2003: *An Ethic of Excellence*: Heinemann Educational Books

195-Alexander, R. 2013: *Improving Oracy and Classroom Talk in English Schools: Achievements and Challenges*: Primary First, Vol.10

196-Heathcote, D. 2000: *Contexts for Active Learning*: In: Lawrence, C. (ed.) 2000: Drama Research. 1. London: National Drama. 2000:14

197- Heathcote, D. 2013: *Four models for teaching & learning*: Blog from Mantle of the Expert (MoE): http://www.mantleoftheexpert.com/blog-post/dorothy-heathcote-four-models-for-teaching-learning/

198-Resnick, L. 2015: *Talking to Learn: The Promise and Challenge of Dialogic Teaching*, in Resnick, L., Asterhan, C. and Clarke, S. (ed) 2015: *Socializing Intelligence Through Academic Talk and Dialogue*: American Educational Research Association

199-Alexander, R. 2017: *Developing Dialogue: Process, Trial, Outcomes*: 17th Biennial EARLI Conference, Tampere, Finland

200-Berger, R. 2003: *An Ethic of Excellence*: Heinemann Educational Books

201-Alexander, R. 2013: *Improving Oracy and Classroom Talk in English Schools: Achievements and Challenges*: Primary First, Vol.10

202-Berger, R. 2003: *An Ethic of Excellence*: Heinemann Educational Books

203-De Bono, E. Quoted in Balakrishnan, A. 2007: *Edward de Bono: Iraq? They just need to think it through*: The Guardian

204-Diaz, N. 2017: *Natalie Diaz on the physicality of writing*: Poetry, Process, Inspiration: From a conversation with Brandon Stosuy: The Creative Independent: https://thecreativeindependent.com/people/natalie-diaz-on-the-physicality-of-writing/

205-Bullock, A. 1975: *A Language for Life*: Report of the committee of inquiry appointed by the Secretary of State for Education and Science: DES, HMSO

206-Berger, R. 2003: *An Ethic of Excellence*: Heinemann Educational Books

207-Ibid

208-Roose-Evans, J. 1970: *Experimental Theatre-from Stanislavsky to Peter Brooke*: Routledge

209-Brahmachari, S. & Landon-Smith, K. 2001: *Time 2001-Placing teachers' voices at the centre of intercultural debate*: in Drama 8.2(Summer 2001)

210-Berger, R. 2014: *Leaders of Their Own Learning: Transforming Schools Through Student-Engaged Assessment* : Jossey-Bass

211-Ibid

212-Drew, B. 2012: *Youth, music and London*: Plan B at TEDxObserver

213-Berger, R. 2003: *An Ethic of Excellence*: Heinemann Educational Books

214-Heathcote, D. 2013: *Four models for teaching & learning*: Blog from Mantle of the Expert (MoE): http://www.mantleoftheexpert.com/blog-post/dorothy-heathcote-four-models-for-teaching-learning/

215-Ibid

216-Resnick, L. 1999: *Making America Smarter*: Education Week

217-Papert, S. 1998: *Child Power: Keys to the New Learning of the Digital Century*: This speech was delivered at the eleventh Colin Cherry Memorial Lecture on Communication on June 2, 1998, at the Imperial College in London

218-Berger, R. 2003: *An Ethic of Excellence*: Heinemann Educational Books

219-Berger, R. 2014: *Leaders of Their Own Learning: Transforming Schools Through Student-Engaged Assessment* : Jossey-Bass

220-Ibid

221-Berger, R. 2003: *An Ethic of Excellence*: Heinemann Educational Books

222-Ibid

223-Alexander, R. 2017: *Developing Dialogue: Process, Trial, Outcomes*: 17th Biennial EARLI Conference, Tampere, Finland

224-Warnock, M. 2018: *We need to use gene editing wisely but also embrace its vast potential*: The Guardian

225-https://www.crick.ac.uk/news/press-releases/francis-crick-portrait/

226-Gearing, D. 2006: *Rosalind*: Oberon

CHAPTER 11: CREATING EXPERIENCES TOGETHER

Play away; techniques; strategies; concepts in this chapter that can be used in different contexts:

Visual anthropology

The pedagogy of Paulo Freire

The pedagogy of Mikhail Bakhtin

Monologism

Internalisation

Conscientização

Self-actualisation

'Banking'

Praxis-action/reflection; verbalism; activism

Problematizing

Depositing

'An act of knowing, a political act, and an artistic event'

Boal's 'Theatre of the Oppressed'

Forum Theatre

The poetics of the oppressed

Polyphony

Thematics

Co-investigators

Incompleteness

The requisites for transformational dialogue when building experiences:

- *A love for the world and for people*
- *Hope*
- *Faith*
- *Humility*
- *Trust*
- *Critical thinking*

The custodians of the knowledge

Defamiliarization

Collective writing

Rituals

'Roll up, roll up for the greatest show on earth…'

> Play away; what are the emotional memories provoked by the call to the circus tent?

The circus has always had an allure through the ages, prompting more than a few people to sometimes ask themselves, 'Why the hell shouldn't I run away with the circus?'[1] Perhaps Hemingway exaggerates when declaring, 'The circus is the only fun you can buy that is good for you.'[2] For those of us of a certain generation, it's the world conjured up in the film about P.T. Barnum, *The Greatest Showman*. Hugh Jackman, the star of the film, makes the case for Barnum as a symbol of the outsider: 'what makes you different makes you special'.[3] All fine and dandy, except it all comes with a health warning: 'Hugh Jackman's new film celebrates PT Barnum – but let's not airbrush history'. Sadly, the romantic bubble has been pricked. Trump has been compared to Barnum, Samuel L. Jackson using it as an insult when he called him 'more P.T. Barnum than politician'.[4] Trump tweeted back (of course he did): 'I don't know @SamuelLJackson, to best of my knowledge haven't played golf w/ him & think he does too many TV commercials—boring. Not a fan'.[5] Trump went on to embrace it. In an appearance on *Meet the Press* in January 2016, he was asked, of all the people he'd been likened to, which one did he consider as a compliment. He replied, 'P.T. Barnum. Look, people call you names. We need P.T. Barnum, a little bit, because we have to build up the image of our country.'[6] It's not really surprising when you consider both men wrote books: Barnum called his *The Art of Money Getting*, Trump naming his *The Art of the Deal*. If you're interested to see the similarities between the owner of a circus and the President of the United States of America, it's all there in Schmidt's article I've cited; you couldn't make it up. But we know Trump isn't really a reader: 'I like bullets or I like as little as possible. I don't need, you know, 200-page reports on something that can be handled on a page. That I can tell you.'[7] So, he'll be unaware of the verdict on the life and times of 'the greatest showman on earth', best summed up here: 'Barnum and his colleagues were the problem, not the solution. They created and perpetuated ethnic stereotypes and cordoned off a swath of humanity as "different". To really do Barnum's story justice, they would be better off making a horror movie.'[8]

Let's turn to Dickens and the role of the circus in *Hard Times*. In a scholarly article, *The Circus in Hard Times*,[9] Lillian M. Young makes a compelling case that the circus is more than the lisping Sleary's belief it's essentially about amusement: 'People mutht be amuthed... they can't be alwayth a working, nor yet they can't be alwayth a learning.'[10] Dickens conjures up a chaotic, diverse world where you find people who 'dance upon rolling caskets, stand upon bottles, catch knives and balls, twirl hand-basins, ride upon anything, jump over everything, and stick at nothing'. In response to the Gradgrindian view that circus is no more than 'wonder, idleness, and folly', Young argues Dickens 'consistently describes the circus as a craft and a trade. It is difficult and skilled work that people have to train at for a long time'. Essentially, in the industrial revolution that was taking place, when skilled craftsmen were being replaced by untrained labour, the circus performers needed 'the institution of apprenticeship to learn their skills'. People built relationships and experiences together in a caring and nurturing environment:

'For Dickens the value of the circus is in its relations. The circus people have "an untiring readiness to help and pity one another" (Dickens 31) that is missing from the worldview of Bounderby and Gradgrind. This is the crux of the matter for Dickens. They are good people whether or not they participate in the system of production. This is why they "deserve, often of as much respect, and always of as much generous construction, as the every-day virtues of any class of people in the world" (Dickens 31). It is their compassion that Dickens consistently puts forward as their primary trait... This is Dickens's purpose for the community of circus people and the trait that he values most.'

But Dickens doesn't pull his punches. Circus life is brutal: 'It requires balms and oils and broken bones and occasionally drives a man to abandon his daughter.' However, ultimately Young's conclusion is Sleary's:

> "There ith a love in the world, not all Thelf-interetht after all, but thomething very different" (Dickens 218). Gradgrind recognizes this in the form of "Faith, Hope, and Charity" (Dickens 221). These, not facts, were always the things that were needful in order to counter the problems of the industrial city. The circus, in depositing its best qualities into the industrial world, has made the place human.'

'The gentle compassion', as Young calls it, that Dickens found in the circus was brought into sharp focus in 1861 when he, with thousands of others, went to see the renowned Funambulist – the French tightrope walker, Chevalier Blondin – perform at the Crystal Palace (those personal connections once again). Blondin had made his deserved reputation in 1859 when, at the age of 35, he'd crossed the Niagara Falls, a distance of about 1,100 feet, just using a tightrope. His was an incredibly daring act of bravery and skill considering 'the tightrope was 50 metres (160 feet) above the water, nearly half a kilometre (over quarter of a mile) long and just 7.5cm (three inches) in diameter'.[11] However, Blondin, the 'hero of Niagara' – his self-appointed name – wanted to experience more. Incredibly, he carried out a further 16 crossings, making each more daring than the last. He walked it blindfolded pushing a wheelbarrow; another time he crossed it carrying a stove, stopping halfway to fry himself an omelette; once he performed the act on stilts. So the myth goes, after watching Blondin cross the Niagara Gorge, the Prince of Wales was asked by Blondin if he would like to be carried on his back on the return journey. Unsurprisingly, the Prince of Wales politely declined the offer. Apparently Blondin was paid what was then a huge sum of money, £1,200, for 12 performances at the Crystal Palace. He didn't disappoint; it was some performance. When he walked across the tightrope, high in the air, with his five-year-old daughter sat in a wheelbarrow scattering rose petals on the ground, the Home Secretary was moved to intervene. In a rare act of child protection, he stopped the performance. Indeed Dickens was meant to have proclaimed: 'Half of London is here eager for some dreadful accident'.[12] But clearly, this was half the fun, as Dickens goes onto quip, 'It is so delicious to see a man risk his life, without being in danger oneself.'[13] However, the author and journalist Jaqueline Banerjee places Dickens' remarks in context, reminding us of the moral ambivalence attached to the spectacle of the circus act:

'The quotation comes from an early biography of Blondin. Had Simon gone to the original source in *All the Year Round*, she would have seen just how Dickens struggled with his scruples as he jostled with the rest to see the spectacle. The circus is life pushed to its extreme, a metaphor for life, affording thrills for the masses and opportunities for reflection in the more sensitive.'[14]

The experiences created in the world of Barnum, Dickens, and Blondin are ones of brutality and abuse as well as excitement, skill, and community. It's in this context we can now travel to Nepal to view the experiences created by Circus Kathmandu. A remarkable film has been made about Circus Kathmandu, *Even When I Fall*,[15] which certainly supports Banerjee's depiction of the circus: 'life pushed to its extreme'. I went to see the film. Afterwards, in a fascinating Q and A with two of the film-makers, Sky Neal and Kate McLarnon, they mentioned the genre of 'visual anthropology' which I'd never heard of. This experience led me on a search taking me back to 1973 and the controversy over a 12-part fly-on-the-wall documentary shown on American television called, *The American Family*. Pat Loud, one of the main participants, scathingly reflected on her experience:

Play away; how relevant are the questions asked by Loud in relation to today's television shows and print media? Which ones spring to mind?

345

'Like Kafka's prisoner, I am frightened, confused... I find myself shrinking in defense, not only from critics and detractors, but from friends, sympathizers and, finally, myself ... The truth is starting to dawn on me that we have been ground through the big media machine and are coming out entertainment. The treatment of us as objects and things instead of people has caused us wildly anxious days and nights. But I would do it again if, in fact, I could just be sure that it did what the producer said it was supposed to do. If we failed, was it because of my family, the editing, the publicity, or because public television doesn't educate? If we failed, what role did the limitations of film and TV tape play? Can electronic media really arouse awareness and critical faculties? Did we, family and network alike, serve up great slices of ourselves – irretrievable slices – that only serve to entertain briefly, to titillate, and diminish into nothing?'[16]

Even When I Fall was premiered in Nepal on November 4th, 2017. I can only take Neal and McClarnon's word for it, as well as the smiling faces of Sheetal, Saraswoti, and the other people featured in the film, as they give their initial reactions on seeing the film for the first time,[17] that what Loud describes wasn't their experience; far from it. Neal and McClarnon give some insight into their process. They worked with performers of Circus Kathmandu over a six-year period, starting when they were children, some from the moment of their actual rescue from their traffickers in an Indian circus. The film follows them from childhood to adulthood, to the formation of the circus company. Here's how Neal and McClarnon describe their long and complex 'walk toward'– a process that would have integrity at its core; it's worth quoting in full:

'We chose to follow a process of filmmaking which had collaborative storytelling at its heart.

Early on we came across the challenge of how unfamiliar documentary filmmaking was, and how difficult it was for the young people to articulate their feelings to us, even though the desire to share was there. It was important for us to find a method they could relate to – that included them.

As they discovered that performance could be their medium for both personal and political change, the film inevitably followed suit. Together, we looked at ways we could harness their skill and expression to help us to tell their story. The switch between the fantastic and the mundanity of daily life is one they make quite naturally as circus performers, and one we've tried to capture in the film.

As we got to know Saraswoti and Sheetal, the two main protagonists, we decided together that we didn't want to create a documentary that focused only on the problems faced by poverty-stricken Nepalis or the graphic horrors of victimhood, but instead to tell a story of resilience and transformation. We felt the story more rarely told is about the aftermath of trafficking in a survivor's life and the barriers to surviving it with dignity. There is the collateral damage visible within families and communities – the stigma, the loss of childhood and education – but also the insidiousness of trafficking in the midst of so many problems and the way it hides itself in plain sight – offering safety, salvation and promise to desperate parents. We wanted to be able to show and understand the pain and guilt we saw carried by a mother who sent her daughter away with an aunt – only hearing her harrowing story 10 years later.

Saraswoti and Sheetal are inspiring, funny, brave and full of strength. It is thanks to their trust and patience that this is a film that portrays the impact of modern slavery on the lives of a small handful of individuals, in the microcosms of family and friendship.

The story of trafficking is complex and the road to tackling it is the same. The film we've made is not black and white but it gives us a glimpse into the changing lives of some amazing young men and women, whose skill and resilience we found incredible to witness. Instead of great declarations we have awkward silences, undercurrents of memory and distress, the slow building of trust and resolve. And the occasional gravity-defying back flip.'[18]

The American anthropologist, Sol Worth, urged us to think critically about what we view on the screen in these terms:

'Treating film (the camera and celluloid) as a copy of the world, rather than as materials with which to make statements about the world, forces us into the impossible position of asking whether performance is true. Understanding that photos and films are statements rather than copies or reflections enables us to look explicitly, as some of us are now doing, at the various ways we have developed of picturing the world.'[19]

If we agree with Worth's thesis that Neal and McClarnon's film is a 'statement' enabling us to view a picture of a world, then in our search we might discover something important about building experiences together. In this spirit, it might be useful to explore this remarkable film through the work of the Brazilian educator Paulo Freire and the Russian philosopher Mikhail Bakhtin.

The social and political background to the film is the trafficking of people, particularly women and children from Nepal. The UN report: '10,000-15,000 persons (mostly women and children) are trafficked every year for commercial sex and forced labour.'[20] This may not surprise you. However, what I was unaware of was the trafficking of children from Nepal directly to Indian circuses. In Chapter 8, we heard about Rushdie's attachment to India's tradition of travelling entertainers. It not only produced the storytellers he so admired, but resulted in the creation of the very first circus in 1880. It's a proud tradition; still today, there are ethical circus troupes, such as 'The Great Bombay Circus', who practise the craft Dickens describes in *Hard Times*. However, reports[21] suggest the circus tradition of India has indeed hit hard times. In spite of this, there are thought to be more than 100 circuses operating in India today, but only 12 are registered with the Indian Circus Federation – a nongovernmental organisation responsible for ensuring lawful and humane

CHAPTER 11: CREATING EXPERIENCES TOGETHER

standards of employment. It's an enormous task. According to 3 Angels Charity, a rescue charity set up to intercept trafficked children:

'The border between Nepal and India is 1,000 miles long with just 14 checkpoints along the route. This makes it easy to smuggle over 30,000 women and young girls (mostly aged between 12 and 25) from Nepal to India every year. In recent times, some girls as young as 8 have been rescued from traffickers. Every day more than 54 young girls and women are trafficked out of Nepal and into India to enter a life of slavery.'[22]

The film-makers were working in the Kathmandu valley. It's an environment where women and children are 'disappeared' for the purposes of labour and sexual exploitation.[23] Nepali children, in particular young girls, are sold into the circus industry for as little as 1,000 rupees (£10) for their fair skin and malleable bodies. The attraction for Nepali girls in particular is explained: 'Some circus owners have said... that genetically the Nepalese have a very flexible body to perform, so they prefer those children... [and] the girls from Nepal are considered to be more exotic.'[24] According to the Esther Benjamin Foundation, the rescue charity featured in the film: 'It is estimated that 500 children under the age of 14 years are trafficked to Indian cities for the purpose of using them in circus. Of them, 233 children were rescued and brought back to the country and reunited to their families by the same organization. Among the rescued children, 217 were girls and 16 were boys.'[25] The majority of the children come from the most vulnerable groups in Nepalese society, particularly in the rural districts close to the porous Indian border. Many of the children are sold with the parents' silent consent. It's easy to judge.

Back in Brazil, Freire documents a conversation he had with a worker when giving a lecture on why parents shouldn't use corporal punishment. The worker questioned his certainty by articulating how it was for some families: 'If people hit their kids, and even "go beyond bounds", as you say, it's not because people don't love their kids. No, it's because life is so hard they don't have much choice.'[26] However, even though these desperate Nepali parents do 'go beyond bounds', the majority of them are unaware about what happens to their children once they're living at the circus.[27] Chhotu is one of the children we see rescued in the film. His father features in a prequel to *Even when I Fall* that Sky Neal made for Al Jarzeera called, *People & Power – Nepal's lost circus children*. The father explains why he sold his son for 50 dollars: 'I let him go for the sake of food, for the sake of the family and I thought his future would improve. I bought two goats; I butchered one of them and sold it for 1200 rupees ($26). I used this money to pay off all of my debts.'[28] What he and many of the parents were unaware of was that the children are trapped in squalor, unable to leave the circus compound. They are regularly beaten if their acts fail to meet the required standard or as a cruel method to teach them the demanding physical routines. Abuse is widespread. Bijaya, now a star performer with Circus Kathmandu, bears witness: 'We were forced to train for long hours. It was difficult. Sometimes, we were beaten and abused. It was like a prison and I thought of running away from that circus on many occasions. Luckily, I was saved.'[29] It becomes even more complex, as many of the circuses operate in 'lawless' states where powerful mafia-style operations are in force, including gun-running, gambling, prostitution, and drugs. Corruption is rife, with police and local government collusion being commonplace. It's very easy to disappear girls if any of the rescue charities get close. I would direct you to Sky Neal's prequel, which vividly documents many of these harrowing experiences.

In the Q and A, the film-makers explained why they made the two women, Saraswati and Sheetal, the main protagonists of *Even when I Fall*. They were keenly aware of the kind of controversies Pat Loud and her family provoked concerning the issues surrounding the filming of real people. As far back as 1936, Margaret Mead states in her book, *Growth and Culture*, how the community she was filming in 'very cautiously, but quite definitely, they gave us permission to live among them'.[30] Neal and McLarnon also talked about a long process of gradually building trust with the community. Heeding Mead's advice when making a film about the Navajos, Sol Worth also understood the importance of first seeking 'their permission and then acknowledging their great contribution. They were in their own films and they wanted to be seen.'

The challenge for the visual anthropologist was 'to find ways to study how people can and do depict mankind, oneself, and others in all their diversity'. Ultimately, Worth concludes it's 'how you tell a story'.[31] 'How you tell a story' has become a central theme for film-makers from Errol Morris's 1988 film, *The Thin Blue Line*, to Joshua Oppenheimer's 2012 *The Act of Killing*, to Bart Layton's 2018 *American Animals*. While for the film-maker true stories are the attraction as they speak of bigger themes, their films are a mix of fact and fiction. This wasn't how Neal and McLarnon were going to tell 'the story'. They set about a process of 'collaborative storytelling', but due to erratic funding they had reels and reels of film in need of translation. They felt as overwhelmed as Worth did when he returned in 1967 from the field with '12,000 feet, 480,000 single frames of exposed film, and 7 movies made by Navajo Indians. I was looking for patterns, but I was overwhelmed (as so many researchers are when they return from the field) by the masses of observations and possible data I had collected. The patterns were far from clear in my mind.' Worth tells a great story about Mead:

'I was tired. Dr. Mead asked me to show some of the films and talk about my research to her class. I did. The next day after breakfast, she quietly set up the projector, pulled up her typewriter, and asked me to start going over the footage with her. I had worked with this material for over a year. Margaret Mead began to teach me how to find patterns in it. When I finally said something like, "I know that, why do we have to keep going over it?" she replied somewhat tartly, "Sol, you begin with intuition, but you can't rest your case upon it. You must build upon it and make clear to others the patterns that seem clear to you.'"(32)

Neal and McLarnon found the patterns Mead insisted upon in Saraswati and Sheetal. Early in the film, we witness the rescue of Saraswati from an Indian circus, led by the fearless Shailaja CM, the director of the Esther Benjamin's Memorial Foundation. Listen to Philip Holmes, the founder of the charity set up in honour of his wife, Esther Benjamin, who tragically killed herself. His experiences are worthy of a chapter in itself. (The connections are extraordinary. Esther spent her life helping Holocaust survivors and had written a dissertation, *Things That Do Not Pass Away: Anti-Semitism, Racism, Discrimination and Persecution*, and here we are in Nepal.) It's important to understand a little about the kind of person Shailaja is. When recommending her for an international humanitarian award, Holmes wrote this about her:

'She has travelled widely within the trafficking prone areas of Nepal, motivating field staff and interacting with the communities and their children. She is a "people person" and never more comfortable than when operating in this kind of role. Shailaja has shown typical courage, herself going on rescue missions where "no" is never taken for an answer. She has been directly involved in the counselling of teenage girls who have been intercepted on the trafficking routes and has managed to convince them to give evidence against the traffickers (no small undertaking). As a consequence agents are now behind bars. And just a couple of weeks ago she was the one who personally confronted a lady at her Kathmandu home in a bid to rescue a ten-year-old girl from domestic slavery. The lady tried to intimidate Shailaja by telling her how important she was; Shailaja responded by filing a case with the police which is ongoing.

Shailaja now lives in the midst of 120 children, mainly trafficking victims and their "at risk" siblings at the EBMF refuge in Godawari to the southeast of Kathmandu. It is hard to overstate how fatiguing this must be, day in, day out, with little time taken by Shailaja for holiday. However, she manages with her ready grin. Go to most Kathmandu orphanages and you'll find grim Dickensian facilities, and idle staff. Visit the EBMF one and you will see the model of how things should be. I called in there last week, totally unannounced, and found a volleyball competition underway with Shailaja in the middle of the cheering children, dressed in her Manchester United strip.

I venture to suggest that you will find within this part of Asia few examples of commitment to social service and child welfare as strong as Shailaja. On the back of her motorbike she has a sticker reading "Catch me if you can". I expect that few ever will.'[33]

What was surprising was how reluctant Saraswati was in wanting to leave the circus. It was only because of Shailaja's approach, 'where "no" is never taken for an answer', did she finally agree to leave with her three children. Saraswati describes how she ended up in the circus at the age of nine:

'I had four sisters and two brothers. We lived in a remote part of Nepal, and it wasn't easy to go to school… Some girls in my village were getting married before they'd even had their first period, so when this neighbour said he would take care of me, I didn't even go home to tell my parents… For the first few days, everything was new and I liked it, I was so happy… All I could see were these beautiful girls in dresses and makeup, doing the splits. I asked them, "Are you dolls?" …I dressed up, put on the sparkly outfits and the makeup and then, when the training began, I would just cry and cry for home.'[34]

At 14, she married the circus owner's son, within 12 months she'd given birth to twins, by 17 she had a third child, and by 20 she was a widow. What had I done by the time I was twenty? Despite the severity of her life, she still didn't want to leave. Bakhtin's theory of 'monologism' is useful to explain why this was so. In a monological world, the person is reduced to an object. This is because the circus owners are the dominant perspective, reducing Saraswati to the status of a non-being, her rights to autonomy being denied. Bakhtin's definition pretty well sums up Saraswati's existence in the circus as a trafficked child:

> 'Monologism, at its extreme, denies the existence outside itself of another consciousness with equal rights and equal responsibilities... With a monologic approach (in its extreme pure form) another person remains wholly and merely an object of consciousness, and not another consciousness. No response is expected from it that could change anything in the world of my consciousness. Monologue is finalized and deaf to other's response, does not expect it and does not acknowledge in it any decisive force. Monologue manages without the other, and therefore to some degree materialises all reality. Monologue pretends to be the ultimate word. It closes down the represented world and represented persons.'[35]

Freire describes it as 'the theme of silence', 'a structure of mutism in face of the overwhelming force of the limit-situations'.[36] The limits of her situation had been prescribed by the oppressors, whose interests lay in 'changing the consciousness of the oppressed, not the situation which oppresses them'.[37] The oppressor's aim was for Saraswati to be passively 'domesticated'. As a result, she believed the circus was her 'ultimate world'. 'The fear of freedom' had led her 'to erect defence mechanisms and rationalisations',[38] but deeper than that, she suffered from an internal oppression. According to Freire's theory of 'internalisation', the 'boss' was inside her which meant she had crucially 'internalised the image of the oppressor and adopted his guidelines'. Even though the oppressor wasn't there anymore, she carried this 'internalisation' back to the refuge in Nepal.

Neal describes it like this: 'This was not a happy reunion... This amazing, bewildered young woman was catapulted back to an alien life after 14 years in captivity. She was angry and scared and in the midst of shattered relationships.'[39] It was the same for Sheetal. After her mother had drowned in front of her, her grandmother sent her away to the circus. She, too, was rescued by the foundation, ending up living with Saraswati in the refuge. She has no idea of her actual name, her age, her caste: 'It says on my passport that I'm 25 and Nepali, but I don't know when or where I was born... I may actually be Indian. I don't know.'[40] As we watch Saraswati peel the onions; sit staring into space; looking after her children, there's a moment where she becomes animated. It's when she's telling the other girls why she was happier in the circus. In the psychologist Edith Eger's phrase, 'the opposite of depression is expression'.[41] Saraswati describes what it was like to throw knives and all the other skilled and exciting things she was able to do in front of the admiring crowds. From the fire in her eyes and in her voice, there's an ignited passion in the telling of it. It's quickly extinguished as she returns to her monotonous routine.

However, the process of what Friere called 'conscientização', started when the refuge had the insight to introduce the girls to people like Ali Williams, the founder and creative director of NoFitState Circus, who brought in volunteer trainers, including Felipe Salas from Colombia. Felipe had an empathy with the children, having been a street child from the age of three before joining Circocolombia – 'the first professional circus school in the world specifically for disfavoured kids and youths'.[42] Friere is never easy to read, but he's always worth unpicking; try his definition of 'conscientização':

'Humankind emerge from their submersion and acquire the ability to intervene in reality as it is unveiled. Intervention in reality – historical awareness itself – thus represents a step forward from emergence, and results from the conscientizacao of the situation. Conscientizacao is the deepening of the attitude of awareness characteristic of all emergences.'[43]

The girls hadn't been living 'outside' society but rather 'inside' the structures of the oppressor; in other words, 'beings for others'. 'Conscientização' is the process where they stop identifying themselves as an object (a thing) but rather as a subject (a human being); in other words 'beings for themselves'. It's the start of a process for the girls to begin to be aware of their own agency, where they begin to 'emerge from their submersion and acquire the ability to intervene in reality as it is unveiled'. Most importantly for this chapter, it was the building of new experiences together that started this process of 'self-actualisation'. For Friere, 'self-actualisation' is what freedom is: 'The indispensable condition for the quest for human completion.'[44]

A dialogue had now been created. For Bakhtin, dialogue creates 'self-actualisation' where the girls placed themselves and their perspective in relation to the artists, such as Williams and Salas, who worked with them. It was in relation to the different experiences they'd all lived, new meanings were given to the art form of circus. Crucially, as we have seen in the previous chapters, it's in what Bakhtin sees as 'the dynamic interplay and interruption of perspectives', which then produces 'new realities and new ways of seeing. It is incommensurability which gives dialogue its power.'[45] It then follows the power of such dialogue importantly meant the girls – just like many of the people we've met in our search – couldn't 'fail to become an active participant in social dialogue'.[46]

The circus artists had created the relationship and the kind of dialogue with the children that we have been exploring throughout this book. It's very much aligned with Freire, who defines the relationship where a space is created for the person to be who they wish to be: 'The teacher is of course an artist, but being an artist does not mean that he or she can make the profile, can shape the students. What the educator does in teaching is to make it possible for the students to become themselves.'[47] For Freire, the relationship to the past is important, as it would allow the girls to understand 'more clearly what and who they are so that they can more wisely build the future'.[48] Equally for Bakhtin, the past is an essential part of this kind of dialogue if new contexts are to be created, a core theme in our search: 'There are immense, boundless masses of forgotten contextual meanings, but at certain moments of the dialogue's subsequent development along the way they are recalled and reinvigorated in renewed form (in a new context).'[49] The complexity of this argument suggests none of this is an easy process. Neal was shocked at the hidden shame and guilt the girls carried with them:

'It was horrifying to learn that something I loved so dearly – that the world is so enchanted by – could have such a dark side... These young girls, many more skilled than some of my colleagues, were ashamed of their skills, and were deeply stigmatised, often rejected by their families and communities.'[50]

But she discovered what she calls these young women's 'secret weapon' – 'their breathtaking skills as circus artists'.[51] As a skilled arts practitioner, Neal knew about the power that building collaborative experiences could have:

'Over the course of a few weeks we ran a social circus project for 25 kids, which was very much based on the therapeutic use of theatre and circus. It was a very gentle process and we used a lot of trust games where the performers would have to rely on one another to achieve their acts. We also had lots of fun and silly activities that allowed them as children to use their own creativity within performing arts, something they had never done in their previous experiences.'[52]

However, the internalisation of oppression was dominant, resulting in the children being heavily reliant on Freire's 'banking' method of teaching, where they sought the safety of being told what to do. It's a method that turns students into 'containers' to be 'filled' by the teacher, treating 'students as objects of assistance'.[53]

> Play away; where have you witnessed the 'banking' method of teaching? What are the factors that have brought this about? How difficult is it to adopt a different approach with students who have been 'banked'?

Robyn Simpson, co-founder of Circus Kathmandu and also an internationally acclaimed aerial, dance and circus choreographer and performer, describes the impact the oppression had made on the young people when she first started to work with them:

'They had previously been instructed to perform so it was something they just carried out mechanically... When we first started working with them it was a little like working with robots rather than the energetic, wonderful, enthusiastic young people that they are today. The real challenge at that time was to give them enough confidence and to make them feel safe enough to explore and to carry out an idea without being instructed on what to do and how to do it.'[54]

For Freire, the challenge in creating a dialogical relationship is fundamentally about faith.

> Play away; as you read Freire's core belief, what would it mean if this was your institution's purpose for building experiences together, a 'vocation to be more fully human'?
>
> > 'Dialogue further requires an intense faith in humankind, faith in the power to make and remake, to create and recreate, faith in their vocation to be more fully human.'[55]

Simpson and her fellow artists had this faith: 'They were 25 individuals who looked after themselves so we trained them to work together through games like lifting each other up, sharing circus materials and props and suddenly putting them in positions where they had to rely on each other and build trust. That played a really substantial role because without realising, they were letting each other in.'[56] With a world of experiences Neal and Simpson could offer the young adults, they invited them to build an experience together – a live performance to be performed to an outside audience. All those things we've detailed in earlier chapters when creating a piece of art happened. The film captures the exhilaration as they come off the stage at the end of their first show. Simpson recalls the moment: 'It was how they learned during the first three week creation period with us, and then performed, in January 2011 that revealed their potential. They were vibrant and excited and glowing with happiness during the first evening show – and the audience was in tears, standing up, applauding.'[57] The search for a new conversation with themselves and with each other had begun. For both Bakhtin and Freire, it's not a search. Interestingly, they both use the same word. For them transformation is a 'quest': 'The way in which I create myself is by means of a quest.'[58] Bakhtin gives us the purpose of this quest for self-discovery; just let Bakhtin's words hang in the air for a moment, it strikes at the heart of this book:

'I go out into the world in order to come back with a self.'[59]

Neal and Simpson were now on a quest. Such was their faith in what building further experiences could have on these young people's lives, they decided to create a circus vocational training project for the original performers in the first show. Out of this experience, Circus Kathmandu was formed. Knowing how easy it could be for the young women to fall back into bonded labour, it was important for Simpson that they continued to create further experiences: 'Circus Kathmandu is underpinned by social circus... Yet it's also about creating jobs and a sustainable industry. We therefore have to keep raising their skill levels and educating the market about high-quality ethical entertainment. We've provided the opportunities, but it's them that – against the odds – have turned their lives around and now do what they choose to as a job.'[60] But alongside this, within the process of 'conscientizacao', there were other transformative experiences being built. The film shows a human rights activist working with the group. At one point, he asks them what their most powerful agency is. 'Our stories,' is the unanimous response. However, the telling of those stories involved remembering. Ingrid Betancourt, the French-Columbian human rights activist, was held hostage for six-and-a-half years by FARC. She has described the process of what happens when people, who have suffered terrible trauma, tell their stories:

> 'Remembering is painful. And telling your story involves submerging yourself deeply and intensely in your own past, bringing forth a flood of uncontrolled emotion. You become conscious of your most glaring vulnerabilities. But sharing is also your way out. Every time you tell your story, you can distance yourself from it, take a step back. You learn to remember without reliving, and begin to recover.'[61]

Edith Eger understands this when she says, 'The opposite of depression is expression.' Eger isn't only a psychologist but also a Holocaust survivor. Dealing with her own trauma has shown the healing that can happen when we are empowered to express what has previously been submerged. As part of the process of their recovery, the group could now see how powerful their experiences could be. They were no longer prepared to be silent, living testimony to Freire's fundamental belief powerfully expressed:

> 'Human existence cannot be silent, nor can it be nourished by false words, but only by true words, with which men and women transform the world. To exist, humanly, is to name the world, to change it. Once named, the world in its turn reappears to the namers as a problem and requires of them a new naming. Human beings are not built in silence, but in word, in work, in action-reflection.'[62]

The experiences now being built together were giving the young people a growing sense of their own and each other's worth, as well as a sense, for the first time in their lives, that they could be the makers of their own destinies.

> Play away; think back to some of the children we've met on our journey through the book – Hashim, Chantelle, Alisha, Isaiah – and how they discovered their self-worth. Have you found this in your own life? Have people you're close to discovered their own self-worth? What's been the process? Does it involve a reimagining of the self?

It's an essential part of the process of 'conscientizacao' when people 'come to feel like masters of their thinking by discussing the thinking and views of the world explicitly or implicitly manifest in their own suggestions and those of their comrades'. For Freire, it 'starts with the conviction that it cannot present its own program but must search for this program dialogically with the people, it serves to introduce the pedagogy of the oppressed, in the elaboration of which the oppressed must participate'.[63] Bakhtin also points out that the search has to be built together within a dialogic relationship: 'Truth is not born nor is it to be found inside the head of an individual person, it is born between people collectively searching for truth, in the process of their dialogic interaction.'[64]

> Play away; think back again to the premise in the book that this kind of education is about a dialogical search to discover anything meaningful.
>
> It lies in the relationship between our private and public selves. Has this been the transformative process for you when you've discovered anything long-lasting?

For the young adults, this feeling of growth and autonomy was being reflected physically. Because the film spans over six years, we witness the young people slowly changing into artists. The haircuts and the clothes start to cut a dash; they wouldn't look out of place in any dance or theatre youth company. It was evident they were now in a process of 'Praxis'. If the young adults had just talked about their experiences within the workshop, Freire calls this 'verbalism'.

> Play away; how often do we practice 'verbalism'?

Had the young adults rushed out and taken lots of action, without much direction or reflection, Freire calls this 'activism'.

> Play away; how often have we impulsively done this?

However, the sweet spot, the 'Praxis', is when the young people would be able to participate in 'reflection and action on the world in order to transform it'.[65] In order to hit this sweet spot, Freire proposes a process of 'problematizing'. It wasn't about going out into the wider world with messages that met their view of the world but perhaps not the view of the people they were talking to. It wasn't about 'winning people over'. Dialogue 'cannot be reduced to the act of one person's "depositing" ideas in another'. To do so would reduce it 'to a simple exchange of ideas to be "consumed" by the discussants'.

> Play away; how often are we in danger of 'depositing' or being on the end of 'depositing'? Watch carefully at what's going on at the next meeting you attend or the next class you teach, to see if there really is dialogue or mere 'consumerism'.

'Problematizing' showed the young people that 'to liberate and be liberated with the people'[66] required an understanding that things are uncertain and not clear cut. They had to be prepared to 'walk toward' any notions of certainty. The teachers and the young people were now seeing the kind of education they were all involved in was 'simultaneously an act of knowing, a political act and an artistic event'.[67]

> Play away; what happens if you start to frame your own practice in these terms? What happens to the design of a scheme of learning if it becomes an act of knowing, a political act, and an artistic event?

You can see what happened in this context. The new insight resulted in taking the form of circus and filling it with the content of their lives, their experiences, their stories. The form fused, as it inevitably does when it starts to break out of its limitations, into new experiences of dance and theatre. The film now shows them out in the field. Neal explains the aims: 'They take powerful awareness raising campaigns to villages and deliver a show and social circus-based workshops where they work with young people and families to raise awareness and empower people to know where to go for help and where to report trafficking activities.'[68] But this doesn't quite convey the experiences the young people created which we witness in the film. In a remarkable sequence, we watch the group in a rural community 'problematize' in order to promote dialogue and critical analysis in the praxis of action/reflection. (If you don't understand the previous sentence, and I wouldn't blame you, just go back a few paragraphs and read them again.) The power of their knowing, the political content, and their raw art engages both the local audience as well as the viewers of the film. They use forum theatre straight out of Augusto Boal's pedagogy, *Theatre of the Oppressed*.

A fellow Brazilian, Boal was heavily influenced by Freire. Forum Theatre is widely used nowadays. However, it was invented by

Boal in a politicised tradition in which he sees theatre as nothing less than 'a rehearsal for the revolution'. For Boal, theatre is 'a means of transforming society. Theatre can help us build our future, rather than just waiting for it.'[69] It was Boal's belief that 'we are all actors' because: 'Being a citizen is not living in society, it is changing it.'[70] It then follows the aim of Forum Theatre was to change the 'spect-actor', who passively observes, to someone who acts. So, in one devised role play, we see the young people create a powerful piece in which a father is demanding of his daughter to be sent away to domestic service in another country. It's important to emphasise that the point of this kind of theatre is about infinite possibilities. It's definitely not 'to show the correct path, but only to offer the means by which all possible paths may be examined.'[71] To support this, the action stops at heightened moments, 'the problematizing' of experiences that are uncertain and not clear cut. The audience is invited to enter the space and act out or ask the actors to act out alternative courses of action. It's a process Boal defines, in a nod towards Freire, as 'the poetics of the oppressed': 'The poetics of the oppressed is essentially the poetics of liberation: the spectator no longer delegates power to the characters either to think or to act in his place. The spectator frees himself; he thinks and acts for himself! Theatre is action!'[72]

For Bakhtin, the value of this kind of experience is in the plurality of voices which he calls, 'polyphony'. For him, the power of Dostoevsky is the submergence of the dominant authorial voice so that multiple voices, all with different perspectives, can appear: 'A plurality of independent and unmerged voices and consciousnesses, a genuine polyphony of fully valid voices is in fact the chief characteristic of Dostoevsky's novels.'[73]

Play away; wouldn't you like 'polyphony' to describe your classroom, or your workplace, or your family, where an environment, a 'habitus', has been created in which 'a plurality of independent and unmerged voices and consciousnesses, a genuine polyphony of fully valid voices' thrive?

However, for Freire, 'a genuine polyphony of fully valid voices' can only occur if the 'thematics' are in place. Follow his argument – as always dense but so interesting – because it can offer us a frame to articulate not only what was happening in this experience between the villagers and the young people but also in other contexts. Freire believed that to fully release the 'polyphony' of voices, one has to enter a problematic dialogue:

> 'The task of the dialogical teacher in an interdisciplinary team working on the thematic universe revealed by their investigation is to 'represent' that universe to the people from whom she or he first received it – and 're-present' it not as a lecture, but as a problem.'[74]

Play away; you may find 'problematizing' is a way of releasing the plurality of valid voices where you work or within your own family.

The 'walk toward' begins because the people then become the 'investigators in the search for their own meaningful thematics'.[75] This is exactly what we see in the film. A group of women almost storm the space, proving Boal's assertion that 'theatre can be done anywhere'.[76] They have suspended their disbelief, now seeing the father not as an actor but as a real person. They challenge him to hear their voices, to tell him what it's really like for them. Like Boal, the viewer cannot help but see 'empathy is the most powerful weapon'.[77] This new experience has clearly stimulated the villagers. Friere helps us to understand what follows: 'Once participants are stimulated by the "previous perception" and "knowledge of the previous knowledge", decoding stimulates the appearance of a new perception and the development of new knowledge.'[78] Freire might call this collective interaction, 'the investigation of thematics'. The emphasis is on the collective experience. For me, what follows is a powerful analysis of what happens when a group of people build experiences together in any setting:

'It involves the investigation of the people's thinking – thinking which occurs only in and among people together seeking out reality. I cannot think for others or without others, nor can others think for me. Even if the people's thinking is superstitious or naive, it is only as they rethink their assumptions in action that they can change. Producing and acting upon their own ideas – not consuming those of others – must constitute that process.'[79]

The women from the village had become 'co-investigators'. The more active the women became in exploring their 'thematics', the more they deepened 'their critical awareness of reality and, in spelling out those thematics', it importantly led them to taking 'possession of that reality'.[80] A woman confides in Saraswati and Sheetal, telling them how dissatisfied she is in her life, divulging how she too had been in a circus in the past. She thanks the girls for giving her a sense of her self- worth and a renewed purpose to make changes in her life. Of course, it's impossible to say if this woman's or any of the other women's perception of reality changed enough to enable them to take action. However, the point is that the dialogue is never-ending. Bakhtin talks about a 'boundless past' and a 'boundless future' in which 'there is neither a first nor last word'.[81] Boal asks:

'When does a session of The Theatre of the Oppressed end? Never – since the objective is not to close a cycle, to generate a catharsis, or to end a development. On the contrary, its objective is to encourage autonomous activity, to set a process in motion, to stimulate transformative creativity, to change spectators into protagonists. And it is precisely for these reasons that the Theatre of the Oppressed should be the initiator of changes, the culmination of which is not the aesthetic phenomenon but real life.'[82]

Freire also joins in, talking about a lifelong process where 'no-one is born fully-formed: it is through self-experience in the world that we become what we are'.[83] Simpson expresses the process in terms of therapy, believing it helped the young adults 'deal with their own trauma because as kids in Nepal they have very little access to therapy so being able to make sense or have a purpose for their own past in helping prevent others undergo what they did is a really positive way of managing their histories'.[84]

The film takes place when the Nepalese earthquake happened in 2015. Circus Kathmandu was in Australia at the time. They immediately flew back to Nepal, thankfully to find all of their loved ones were safe. However, their belief in the importance of their work was now never stronger, with many children left orphaned by the disaster. They were acutely aware of the risks and what was at stake. Unicef reported, within four months of the earthquake, that its partners had intercepted 793 people, of which 455 were women and girls – all at risk of being trafficked into India.[85] Without doubt, these young people would agree with Freire that the 'fundamental theme of our epoch' is one of 'domination' and its opposing 'theme of liberation'.[86] By building experiences together, the film shows them eliminating 'dehumanising oppression' by surmounting 'the limit-situations' which had reduced them to 'things'. They had been 'out into the world' and now can be seen in the film taking themselves to those areas of high risk. Silence was not an option. They'd come such a long way.

At the start of the film, Freire's critique would be a fair summing-up of their emotional state: 'In the face of a problem whose analysis would lead to the uncomfortable perception of a limit-situation, their tendency is to remain on the periphery of the discussion and resist any attempt to reach the heart of the question.'[87] But now these young people clearly viewed these 'limit-situations' as 'obstacles' to be overcome. Therefore, they were empowered to engage in 'limit-acts' in 'a climate of hope and confidence'. Simpson proudly tells us, 'Now they are standing tall, they are vibrant, engaged young people.'[88] Their quest wasn't going to stop there. Neal realised 'that this could become something else'. Both the young people and the educators were acknowledging their 'incompleteness' – a dialogue that's 'never-ending'. Freire again brilliantly articulates this core requisite:

'It is in our incompleteness, of which we are aware, that education as a permanent process is grounded. Women and men are capable of being educated only to the extent that they are capable of recognising themselves as unfinished.'[89]

> Play away; if we reimagine ourselves as incomplete, seeing this as something essential for our growth, how might it open up limitless possibilities? Why is this an optimistic way of living our life, rather than something to fear or hide?

Their experiences went global. They travelled to festivals and events. As Neal explains, 'We knew they had the potential to become international performers and we recognised they had the skills to help set up the industry in Nepal and tap into potential European markets. We wanted to offer them a package that could determine their future and their jobs under their own terms.'[90] They appeared on national television:

'At the end of last year we performed at a large conference attended by some of the world's richest entrepreneurs and the former Prime Minister of Nepal. Suddenly these 13 kids who had been so scared of talking about their circus background were proud to be performing at this incredibly high-profile event and a month later they performed on national TV.'[91]

They performed in Dubai:

'The reception from the Dubai audience had such an impact on their confidence... They felt the impression they made. It was very obviously a significant milestone and since then they are all posting on Facebook about their profession and are proud of what they're doing.'[92]

But probably the collective experience that made the deepest impact was when they went to Glastonbury, interacting with the most incredible circus artists from around the world, many of them women. If you watch a video of their performance, the evolution of their craft is immense. It had truly become 'simultaneously an act of knowing, a political act and an artistic event'.[93] Go watch it;[94] everything that's been discussed is in the performance. They have used the art form of circus to explore their stories, imbuing their consummate physical skills with an emotional power, further enhanced by the stunning visual imagery and design.

The impact on their lives is captured by Saraswati: 'I've often complained to my mother that she named me after the goddess of wisdom and knowledge, but I stopped school when I went to the circus... People look down on me because I come from the circus, but it's not something to be ashamed of, it's a talent to be a performer and the circus is entertainment. People here are slowly starting to realise that.' The power in her own agency is in her conclusion: 'I think now I do have my own wisdom to share.'[95] Their openness and the ability to fully articulate their emotions is a marked feature of their journey. The space for conversations, which has been built by collective experiences, is never more evident than the intimate, vulnerable, and sometimes painful rooftop conversations we see Saraswati and Sheetal engage in. In their listening to each other, being present, and the trust the film-makers had built over a long period of time, it allowed both women to be who they wished to be. Freire called this 'authentic humanism' (we'll let him have that one) in which permission is given for 'the emergence of the awareness of our full humanity'.[96]

However, at the start of the film, that permission hadn't been granted by both Saraswati and Sheetal in their relationship with their families. Over time, the film-makers managed to create relationships not only with the two women but also with their families. They were gradually granted the privilege of slowly witnessing the 'emergence' where people seek to become 'complete human beings' through 'communication with others'.[97] Early on we see Saraswati visiting her family, during which she expresses some of the painful feelings she carries around within her. They make her frustrated and angry to the point where she confides she doesn't really love them. But she keeps visiting.

Freire may have captured the complexity of how a daughter felt about her mother whom she believes abandoned her. The experiences she is exploring in her new world in the refuge are bringing her to the discovery that 'without freedom' she 'cannot exist authentically'. Although she desires 'authentic existence', she fears it. She is 'at one and the same time', herself, 'and the oppressor whose consciousness' she has 'internalized'. For Saraswati, 'the conflict lies in the choice between being wholly' herself or 'being divided; between ejecting the oppressor within or not ejecting them; between human solidarity or alienation; between following prescriptions or having choices; between being spectators or actors; between acting or having the illusion of acting through the action of the oppressors; between speaking out or being silent'.[98] It's why early in the film Saraswati, in her relationship with her family, chooses to remain silent. She is stuck in Bakhtin's 'monologism' – 'a kind of discursive "death" of the other'.[99] It would have been easier for her to rely on her self-sufficiency that had been established in her world outside of her family. It would have been easier to hold onto her naïve thinking which only sought to hold onto a 'guaranteed space and adjust to it', to maintain a status quo which doesn't want to 'rock the boat'.[100] Both Saraswati and her mother could easily have turned the past into what Freire terms as 'mythicized', which then establishes 'a climate of irrationality and sectarianism', resulting in oppressive resentment, anger, and a lack of communication.

> Play away; have you ever 'mythicized' the past? I have; it didn't end well.

But both Saraswati and her mother avoid this. As we see Saraswati mature, gaining a sense of her own self-worth, it allows her to begin to create a new relationship with her mother. This in turn starts to give her mother a sense of her own self-worth. A dialogue is slowly established. In Bakhtian terms it is: 'The process of coming to know one's language as it is perceived in someone else's language, coming to know one's belief system in someone else's system.'[101] Both Saraswati and her mother have 'gone through something', the result of which verifies and establishes 'their identity, their durability and continuity'.[102] They both begin 'to be heard', which 'is itself a dialogic relationship. The word wants to be heard, understood, it wants to be an answer and again to reply, a question and so on ad infinitum'.[103] They have both been able to reimagine their relationship.

Freire identifies a series of requisites for transformational dialogue. I have played away searching for places and people where transformation is clearly happening, particularly in the toughest environments with young people. In any dialogue, what emerges so clearly is how the people embody Freire's requisites for transformation. I recently talked to a coach at Brixton Top Cats – a grassroot basketball club that has been impacting on the lives of young people since 1984. One of the coaches is now in his 40s. He'd played professional basketball in Germany, got a degree, and qualified as a social worker. He'd attended the club in his youth, when he openly admits he was at risk of going down the wrong path, as many of his contemporaries had. It's his lifelong relationship with the inspirational founder of the club, Jimmy Rodgers (look him up, a remarkable man) that had led him back to volunteer at the club as a coach after a long day at work. He wasn't the only one. There was another coach who now worked as a teacher, but she too gave up her time voluntarily. She'd attended the club when she was 16. When they both spoke, it was evident it's their love and faith in this community which inspires the young people. Their optimism, humility, and creativity – they are skilled coaches – create a trust which has brought about transformation in so many people's lives. The coaches and the young people had come 'to know one's belief system in someone else's system'.[104] It's these Freireian requisites that transformed Saraswati's relationship with her mother:

- *A love for the world and for people*

For both Saraswati and her mother, love is a massive 'act of courage' rather than fear. Their love is defined by a commitment to each other. This commitment, 'because it is loving, is dialogical'. They both realised what the consequences would be if they chose not to love: 'If I do not love the world – if I do not love life – if I do not love people – I cannot enter into dialogue.'[105]

- *Hope*

Her experiences had certainly not turned Saraswati into someone 'crossing one's arms and waiting'. She's a fighter and, therefore, is 'moved by hope'. For Freire, if one fights with hope, then one can wait. But the waiting isn't a form of hopelessness in which there's 'silence', a 'denying of the world and fleeing from it'.[106] It's rather rooted in Sarawati's 'incompleteness'. She'd been out 'into the world' and had 'come back with a self'.[107] For her, it's now about the 'constant search', but she's aware it's a search which 'can be carried out only in communion with others'.[108]

- *Faith*

For Saraswati, to keep visiting also implies a faith in her 'vocation to be more fully human'. For Freire, 'faith in people is an *a priori* requirement for dialogue', even before she meets her mother 'face-to-face'. But this faith 'is not naïve'. It is 'critical and knows that although it is within the power of humans to create and transform,

372

in a concrete situation of alienation individuals may be impaired in the use of that power'.[109] How many of us would've turned away from someone who we felt had betrayed us so deeply? But Saraswati's experiences had taught her that 'far from destroying' her 'faith in the people', it was actually 'a challenge to which' she 'must respond'. For her experiences had convinced her 'that the power to create and transform, even when thwarted in concrete situations, tends to be reborn'.[110] As a result, we witness the rebirth of a relationship between mother and daughter.

• *Humility*

Both Saraswati and her mother show the humility essential in a dialogue where two people 'are attempting, together, to learn more than they now know':

> 'Someone who cannot acknowledge himself to be as mortal as everyone else still has a long way to go before he can reach the point of encounter. At the point of encounter there are neither utter ignoramuses nor perfect sages; there are only people who are attempting, together, to learn more than they now know.'[111]

> Play away; when in your private or working life are you in a humble relationship where together you are trying to 'learn more than' you both 'now know'? What would it take to show such humility?

• *Trust*

The natural consequence of love, hope, humility, and faith, is the creation of mutual trust. It takes time, but by the end of the film, there's trust. This isn't a relationship of 'false love, false humility and feeble faith'. It's a dialogue bringing Saraswati and her mother into a 'closer partnership in the naming of the world'.[112]

- *Critical thinking*

Saraswati is now in a process of 'walking toward', in which her experiences have finally developed in her a willingness to engage in critical thinking that 'constantly immerses' her in 'temporality without fear of the risks involved'. She can now see the world, and hence her relationship with her mother 'as process, as transformation, rather than as a static entity'.[113]

I walked out of the film buzzing. The search to make sense of what I'd seen confirmed the belief that the building of experiences is about a 'never-ending' dialogue that is rooted in these requisites of love, hope, faith, humility, trust, and critical thinking. It's a transformative dialogue because it's willing to 'walk toward' uncertainty, and thereby discover in the tensions created by these collective experiences, a context for infinite possibilities.

> Play away once more; where in your life are you part of this kind of collective dialogue? I have certainly discovered it in my drama studio.

Teaching context

'Most people come to know only one corner of their room, one spot near the window, one narrow strip on which they keep walking back and forth.'[114]

The power of the kind of collaborative, intense experiences discussed in this book is to entice the students, the teachers, and maybe the reader, from out of the corner of their room, the spot near the window, the narrow strip on which they keep walking back and forth. The selection of the experience is complex, but has to be bound by the potential of something real occurring. By real, one means experiences where 'we are certain by not being certain of our certainties. To the extent that we are not quite sure about our certainties, we begin to "walk toward" certainties'.[115] The 'walk toward', which I have often referenced, is made up of experiences where the students and the teacher are indeed 'attempting, together, to learn more than they now know', but also where the students need to be made aware: 'We know more than they do, but also that we are knowing.'[116] The 'we' is the teacher, and the experience is one where the teacher is also a learner, immersing him/herself in a process that would allow him/her to see him/herself in a different light. By building on these experiences in other contexts, it would then give it a wider value.

Shakespeare is often put forward as an experience all young people should have an opportunity to explore. Ben Jonson famously declared, 'He was not of an age, but for all time.'[117] Samuel Johnson later wrote about Shakespeare's universality: 'His characters... are the genuine progeny of common humanity, such as the world will always supply, and observation will always find.'[118] Arnold's definition of culture is often wheeled out: 'The acquainting ourselves with the best that has been known and said in the world, and thus with the history of the human spirit.'[119]. It seems to be working. The World Shakespeare Festival[120] tells us, according to the British Council's research, that a staggering 50% of the world's children study Shakespeare, which amounts to over 64 million children worldwide. I do like the Festival's timely reminder: 'While we in Britain like to imagine Shakespeare is ours alone, the reality is that he has long slipped over the border, evaded our grasp, moved on elsewhere, to many places at once.'[121] Akala is someone who very much approves of this sentiment. In his song, *Comedy, Tragedy, History*,[122] he references himself as 'the black Shakespeare':

> 'Akala, Akala, wherefore art thou?
> I'm the black Shakespeare and
> The secret's out now'

He founded the Hip Hop Shakespeare Company; it's got credentials – Sir Ian McKellan is a patron. Akala makes sense of the Bard like this: 'Both hip hop music and Shakespeare's theatre represent energetic and inventive forms of expression. Both are full of poetry, wordplay and lyricism. Both deal with what it is to be human, and issues from people's lives, and of course just like Shakespeare's work, hip hop is all about the rhythmic tension of words.'[123] In short, for Akala, Shakespeare 'was a musician of words'.[124]

But for Freire, all this talk might mean we are in danger of imposing our dreams on our students. Freire believed that 'our task is to challenge' our students, 'to have their own dreams, to define their choices, not just to uncritically assume them'.[125] In a challenge to the kind of Arnoldian elitism dominant in the educational debate, Akala puts it like this when he asks the essential question of his Ted Talk, *Hip Hop & Shakespeare?*[126]: 'Who are the custodians of the knowledge?' The question formed my invitation to the students in Year 9. I followed it up with Akala's challenge of deciding whether they wanted to be the people who 'choose to pick up that baton and run with it'. I told them, if they joined the ensemble, we would build experiences in which 'we are going to educate ourselves and... transmit this knowledge',[127] not through music but through an exploration of *Macbeth*. We would 'unite around it... this proud, intelligent discourse' that would be 'so undeniable', it would 'pull(ed) everybody in'.[128]

The provocation was enough for a group of students to enter the process. They arrived, 'full of spontaneity – with their feelings, with their questions, with their creativity, with their risk to create'.[129] They had an unquestioned desire to 'getting their own words "into their own hands" in order to do beautiful things with them'.[130] Because, ultimately, I'm sure Akala would agree with Freire: 'The basis for critical reading in young children is their curiosity.'[131] Read that again; imagine this is the premise all educators might hold before embarking on a 'walk toward' the creation of 'beautiful work' with a group of people. The possibilities are infinite.

Using the same universal process Neal and Simpson employed with their ensemble in the refuge of Nepal, I set about building an ensemble and equipping them with new skills they might need. I also checked into their existing knowledge of the text. They'd been studying *Macbeth* elsewhere in their English lessons. Their grasp of the plot was fairly sound. At the 2018 NUT conference, a delegate ridiculed the government's assertion that the new exam system was providing a 'world class' provision, by telling delegates about students 'who do *Macbeth* every year from 7 to 11 because that is what is going to come in their GCSE exams, they don't feel world class either'.[132] Quite so; there were certainly dangers in choosing *Macbeth* as an experience that could evolve into something meaningful.

With this in mind, I wanted to use the sociologist Zygmunt Bauman's concept of 'defamiliarization'. Bauman sought 'defamiliarization', because we limit ourselves with 'a natural propensity to absorb and accommodate new experience into the familiar picture of the world; habitual categories are the main tool of this absorption. New experience does not fit the categories easily.'[133] If we could create a process of 'defamiliarization' of this familiar text, a reimagining, the potential was as wide as Bauman places on it. For Bauman, 'defamiliarization' examines (as does reimagination) – it's big so take your time:

'That which is taken-for-granted, it has the potential to disturb the comfortable certitudes of life by asking questions no-one can remember asking... it may open up new and previously unsuspected possibilities of living one's life with others with more self-awareness, more comprehension of our surroundings in terms of greater self and social knowledge and perhaps also with more freedom and control.'[134]

Play away; what would happen if we used this process of 'defamiliarization' in the context of schools? In the context of our practice? By reimagining 'that which is taken-for-granted' (our 'comfortable certitudes') by asking questions that had never arisen before, what might happen to our identity as an educator? Who is reimagining education today in a process Bauman outlines?

The start of this process was for the ensemble to choose a context in which to place the play, in order to disturb 'the certitudes' they brought with them about the text and Shakespeare in general. We looked at numerous images from previous productions from across the world –*Macbeth* in a decadent Polish world of raves, binges, transvestites and addicts; *Macbeth* in the Congo; *Macbeth* all suited and booted in the world of modern politics; *Macbeth* in the world of South East Asian gangs; *Macbeth* in the glamorous world of Fitzgerald's1920s America; *Macbeth* in the war-torn Balkans; *Macbeth* in the dystopian world of the blasted heaths of Scotland; *Macbeth* in a psychiatric ward; *Macbeth* as the Bengali Raja, set against the background of the prawn wars (Do you remember Andy's cohort? This was the context for their production); *Macbeth* in a Brick Lane restaurant; *Macbeth* set in a commedia dell' arte circus (Trump might enjoy this one; maybe not); *Macbeth* as Samurai General in Kurosawa's *Throne of Blood*. We tried a few on, but none of them really fitted this ensemble. Then we stumbled upon child soldiers, and it seemed to fit this group of young people. Their curiosity had been fired perhaps by other experiences, such as the human rights project I'd carried out with them in the previous year.[135] It was part of the Bakhtian 'never-ending' dialogue, the Freirean process of 'incompleteness... education as a permanent process'.[136] These students also knew the necessity for knowledge, to start to drop down the 'T' bar we explored in the previous chapter. We all needed to know what we were talking about, including me. They were drawn to the War Lord Joseph Kony, the terrifying leader of the Lord's Resistance Army (LRA), who operated in what was then Uganda in the early 90s. Still being hunted by the International Criminal Court, he is purported to be alive in the Central African Republic.

As we've seen time and again, the power of a story can give the unimaginable some kind of form. For Hannah Arendt, who knew a thing or two about the nature of evil, storytelling 'reveals meaning without committing the error of defining it'.[137] With that in mind, we read Norman Okello's harrowing story;[138] he'd been abducted by Kony's men at the age of 12. His experiences gave us our first insight into the importance of ritual, which was to play a significant part in our 'walk toward' *Macbeth*. Ritual was central in turning the children into human beings capable of killing. It's an extreme extension of the oppression we've explored in the context of the trafficked circus children. The LRA set out to dehumanise the children, creating 'an unjust order that engenders violence in the oppressors which in turn dehumanises the oppressed'.[139] They created a terrifying perversion of the Freirean requisites for becoming human, such as love, faith, hope, trust, humility, critical thinking. The first step was to create the abandonment of hope of ever returning home, often by relentless marching. Such was the trauma, Norman even developed a belief that if he thought of his family, he would become sick and die: 'The moment you think about home, you start getting really thin. You'll get diarrhoea and grow so tiny, you look like a skeleton. If you have it, you will die.'[140] The second step was to create fear. Norman witnessed anyone asking for rest would be taken under a tree and killed. We would refer back to this when trying to understand the climate of fear that prevailed under both Duncan's and Macbeth's rule. Indeed, Macbeth threatens his messenger with exactly the same fate but worse:

'If thou speak'st false,
Upon the next tree shall thou hang alive
Till famine cling thee'[141]

The third stage was to take away any self-worth, treating the children as unclean, forcing them to eat away from the soldiers. Macbeth dehumanises his soldiers, chastising one petrified soul as a 'liar and slave'.[142] Like all tyrannies, human beings are treated as less than human; Macbeth is no different:

'The devil damn thee black, thou cream-faced loon!
Where got'st thou that goose look?'[143]

At this point, an initiation ceremony would occur. Norman recalls one such ceremony and how it left him feeling: 'They mixed shea oil and water and put the sign of the cross on his head, lips, hand and heart. "I was not unclean anymore," he says. "I could even eat with them." Was it a good feeling? "Yes."'(144)

The next step is to carry out a murder for the first time. Arendt offers an explanation of how this could be possible for these traumatised children: 'Under tyranny it is far easier to act than think.'(145) Edward describes the impact of something so unimaginable: 'When you kill for the first time, automatically, you change... Out of being innocent, you've now become guilty. You feel like you're becoming part of them, part of the rebels.'(146) However far removed from our experiences, 'murder most foul' and all that involved psychologically wasn't something we could shy away from in *Macbeth*. When did Macbeth first kill someone? What would make someone slice open another human being 'from nave to the chaps' going onto fix 'his head upon our battlements'? What was the psychological impact of all of the 'bloody execution'? What was the psychology behind his emotional turmoil in murdering the King? These were some of the questions the process of 'defamiliarization' was stirring in the students, 'asking questions no-one can remember asking'.

Further rituals occur. Norman describes what happens during a full blessing ceremony:

> 'Successful children were lined up as their brigade clapped and sang, and handed new weapons sprinkled with holy water. "They do that to bring you and the gun together." They were anointed, once more, with shea oil mixed with egg and a milk-like substance. After the ritual, the boys had to spend three days bare-chested, showing their markings. "You feel very proud," he recalls. "You feel you're now one of the family of the LRA. You are one of them, you are part of them, all you have is them."'(147)

The children now believed this is their 'ultimate world',(148) a new persona has been created: 'When we kill the child in us, we are no longer.'[149] Instead, the oppressed becomes the oppressor: 'Their ideal is to be men; but for them, to be men is to be oppressors. This is their model of humanity.'[150] In such a context, Arendt says, 'There are no dangerous thoughts; thinking itself is dangerous.'[151] Norman describes his dangerous thinking in terms of the rage that had seized him. It's the first mention of the furies: 'More than anything else when recounting, Norman talks of his own possession, not by the spirits but by the furies. "Whenever I saw anything, it was not with a good heart. All my mind was full of destruction."'[152] The furies were to play a vital role in the pupils' interpretation when they finally went to the text.

Norman's complex portrayal of Kony challenged the students. What would turn out to be an important description was this passage, when he struggles to convey what an interaction with Kony was actually like:

'Kony's not scary," he says. "He will talk with you in a friendly manner. He doesn't want you to be afraid of him. He wants you to be a very strong man and look him in the eyes. And he can talk! From morning to sunset about very many things, mostly political. By the way a person behaves, you will recognise they're possessed. When he's talking, he's shouting, his face looks changed. We see that. A common man could not speak from morning until sunset while standing."'[153]

Arendt's analysis can help us understand the psychology in Norman's account: 'Totalitarian rule... the distinction between fact and fiction (i.e. the reality of experience) and the distinction between true and false (i.e. the standards of thought) no longer exist.'[154] So when the students read that Norman believed he was made to view Kony as 'a godly person', they were quick to make the link to the godly Duncan, whose 'silver skin lac'd with... golden blood'[155] embodied the Elizabethan belief of the King being God's representative on earth.

It was also important for the students to consider the effects of the post-traumatic stress for the returning children. Many of the symptoms Norman describes would later be assigned in a different context to both Macbeth and Lady Macbeth. By looking at *Macbeth* through the lens of PTSD, it would offer a process of 'defamiliariza-tion', opening up questions we'd never thought of asking, opening up Beauman's 'new and previously unsuspected possibilities'.[156] We learnt in Acholi, the language spoken by Norman, that those who are suffering from PTSD are named 'ajiji'. There's a belief the furies have entered the body of the 'ajiji', taking over the spirit.

Charles Onekalit, a councillor working with returnees, talks about the importance of telling the community that these traumatised people aren't possessed; the stories they'd been telling themselves over and over again were, in fact, not true: 'If a [returnee] wakes up shouting in the middle of the night, they have not been bewitched by Kony, they are just remembering battle.'[157] In Luo, a dialect of Northern Uganda, there's a word, 'akwiila', which means the whispering of things that can barely be verbalised. The students could hear this notion of 'akwiila' in Lady Macbeth's doctor's explanation:

> 'Infected minds
> To their deaf pillows will discharge their secrets'[158]

Both Lady Macbeth's physician and Onekalit know the terrifying truth why Lady Macbeth cries out:

> 'Here's the smell of blood still. All the perfumes
> Of Arabia will not sweeten this little hand'[159]

It's all to do with trauma. Like Lady Macbeth and her husband, it's almost impossible for the returnees to ever finally be rid of the furies, 'to leave what you've done in the bush'.[160] Even though Norman describes himself as 'normal now... just another member of the community', happily married with a family, like so many 'ajiji': 'The nightmare is there. I dream about someone coming to abduct me.'[161]. It wasn't hard for the students to make the transference to *Macbeth*. They were beginning to understand the difficulties of redemption, in Arendt's phrase, 'the predicament of irreversibility – of being unable to undo what one has done'.[162] The students were now ready to consider the rest of her assertion in the context of *Macbeth*:

'The remedy for unpredictability, for the chaotic uncertainty of the future, is contained in the faculty to make and keep promises. Both faculties depend on plurality, on the presence and acting of others, for no man can forgive himself and no one can be bound by a promise only to himself.'[163]

> Play away; it's complex. Do you agree with Arendt?

The students couldn't find consensus. However, in our discussions it was now clear the students' certainties were not so certain. It was evident 'the walk toward' had begun.

Further rituals of cleansing were described, emphasising the use of water – the link to *Macbeth* once again. Edward, abducted at 12 years old, testifies how they were often assigned to fetch Kony his 'holy water' from a special location. We read his description of a purifying ritual: 'After prayers and songs beneath the shade of a neem tree, each villager lined up before Edward, dipped a branch into a calabash, and sprinkled him with water – symbolising the community cleansing his past.'[164] 'A little water clears us of the deed'[165] turned into a traumatic water ritual based on the cleansing rituals they'd found out about. It was a way of entering Lady Macbeth's over-familiar 'out damned spot' speech.

> Play away; now you've read a little about Norman's and Edward's experiences in Uganda, go to the text. What are you hearing; seeing; touching; smelling; tasting; feeling when you now encounter a line such as 'What, will these hands ne'er be clean?'?[166]

There were details that left an impression. One was how an ex-child soldier 'rolled into a whimpering ball whenever a helicopter passed over the centre'.[167] On hearing the sound of a helicopter we played loudly over our speakers, we would see Macbeth drop to the ground, curling up into a foetal ball in the same way. Another was when we learnt play was an important part of group therapy. Norman recalls how when he played football with his friends – all former child soldiers – it seemed to free them up to share their inner thoughts: 'You say, "I think destructive things. What about you? How do you feel?" They say, "Even me, I feel the same." And, for sure, you feel very good.'[168] When the witches, as child soldiers, 'played', it was this glimpse into their inner feelings that gave the familiar childhood games which the students had chosen to play, a different subtext. I offered them a quote from Martin Dysart, the psychiatrist in Shaffer's *Equus* – an experience they'd later build together in Year 11. It captures what they were aiming for: 'The Normal is the good smile in a child's eyes – all right. It is also the dead stare in a thousand child soldiers.'[169]

The ensemble had enough context to create a back-story for their interpretation of *Macbeth*. In the process of 'defamiliarization', 'the new experiences' they'd absorbed now meant the habitual categories didn't apply. They'd been making their own connections consciously and subliminally. I needed to offer them a form through which they could 'become conscious of the contents that press upward from the unconscious'.[170] I asked them to write a collective journal that recorded the history of the play before it'd begun - Let me remind you of the rules of collective writing: it must be spontaneous without interruption; each person must follow on from whatever the last person has said; any editing can happen afterwards. The collective experience is fundamental because: 'Human learning presupposes a specific social nature and a process by which children grow into the intellectual life of those around them.'[171] Their interpretations would be built upon, challenged, changed in a process of fusion. The element of spontaneity would create possibilities in the moment that could never be cognitively planned for - It was one of those late sessions after school, as a group of people, we wouldn't forget. Project-based learning might call it a milestone. The excitement and challenge we felt about the document we'd created met the thrill Akala describes in his TED talk, about inspiring 'people towards their form of artistic, literary, cultural and societal' forms of expression. The students were now in a process of owning the knowledge. The students had 'slipped over the border' moving *Macbeth* 'to many places', as evidenced in the coherence their back-story was now making of Shakespeare's play. The process of 'defamiliarization' had created this remarkable context in which to place the text:

The back-story

- *Duncan* – Born into a bloodline of War Lords, he's now the ruling War Lord, the leader of an army of brutal rebel soldiers from the West and the North. Having watched Lady Macbeth grow up into one of his fiercest soldiers, he rapes her, resulting in her becoming pregnant with twins. After learning of this, he forces her to endure an enforced caesarean birth in which the babies from the mother were 'untimely ripped'. The children were taken away to be raised as soldiers. One of the children becomes known as Macduff who, being 'from his mother's womb untimely ripped',[172] is able to return at the end to kill Macbeth. Lady Macbeth is left with the most terrible physical and emotional scar. She avoids execution by running away.
- *Macbeth* – In the West in the early hours of Friday morning, the soldiers belonging to the War Lord, Duncan, raid the home of Macbeth – an eight-year-old child. Before he was abducted, he was forced to watch Duncan's soldiers murder his parents and his sister. He becomes one of Duncan's most fierce and loyal soldiers, which results in him being promoted to the highest rank in Duncan's army.
- *Lady Macbeth* – In the North, rebel soldiers also violently barged into the home of an eight-year-old girl. After

committing atrocities Lady Macbeth still has never talked about, the soldiers laughed as they abducted her.

Macbeth and Lady Macbeth grew up as child soldiers beholden to Duncan – two young, traumatised children joined by friendship, turning inevitably into love. Just before Lady Macbeth ran away, she'd left Macbeth a note under his pillow which allowed him to find her. He persuaded her to return, assuring her she would be safe if she married him, secure in the knowledge such was his relationship with Duncan that they'd be protected. Seeking the War Lord's blessing, they were permitted to marry. However, the rape of Lady Macbeth and the atrocities inflicted on their families were the motivation for both of them to find closure in the murder of Duncan, to end the intolerable life of having to serve their tormentor.

- *Banquo* – In the East, a young boy volunteered to join Duncan's army for the sake of his family. His loyalty, bravery, and unflinching willingness to do whatever was required meant he rose quickly in the ranks until he reached almost the same status as Macbeth. Unbeknown to anyone, Banquo had unrequited feelings for Lady Macbeth. This fuelled the rivalry between the two.

We weren't ready to explore who the witches were. There were further collective experiences to be built before an interpretation could be arrived at or before we could start to encounter the text. One was to work with Iroko Theatre Company whose mission is: 'To use traditional African theatre forms as a vehicle for facilitating learning and self-development.'[(173)] I'd been in dialogue intermittently with Alex, the founder, for over twenty years. Long-term partnerships are often more likely to create richer experiences. In the planning we discussed the experiences of the ensemble so far and how Iroko might build further experiences. The students were subsequently immersed in rituals from across the African continent, including the rituals of cleansing; the appeasing of the angry spirits of the dead; of warding off the devil; of greeting and welcome; of celebration; of crowning; of prayer. We also learnt dance/movement and songs/rhythms, as well as lots of different ways of marching.

Alongside this, a friend of mine had pointed me towards the work David Lan, the former artistic director of The Young Vic, had done around this area in his book, *Guns and Rain: Guerrillas and Spirit Mediums in Zimbabwe*. Lan had written about the relationship of the local peasantry and the guerrillas in the context of Zimbabwe's war of independence from 1966 to 1980. Lan found out about the vital role the spirit mediums had played, which he believed turned the war into 'a collaboration between ancestors and their descendants, the past and the present, the living and the dead'.[174] It was a rich lens through which to reimagine the text. So now, before we'd even opened the first page of *Macbeth*, we knew this:

- There are spirits that arise from the earth. In the Shona culture, they're known as 'people of the soil' ('Vanu Venyika'). Banquo also views them as spirits arising from the earth:

  'The earth hath bubbles, as the water has,
  And these are of them'[175]

- 'The Midzimu', the spirits, present the history of the land and act it out, as do Shakespeare's witches.
- The spirits tell the truth only with the wisdom the dead can acquire, which is why Macbeth is so terrified of Banquo's ghost. Think about the resonance this gives to Lady Macbeth's loss of her children, the result of a rape by a murdered War Lord. For the students, it gave credence to their view that Lady Macbeth's suicide was the result of trauma.
- 'Mhondoro' in the Shona culture are the spirits of the past. The 'Mudzimu' are the spirits who know the future before it happens. The witches are all of these things and more.

They're the 'Mweya' – a spirit of breath/air both 'fair' and 'foul'. Macbeth's response to Banquo's description of the witches as bubbles of the earth, is to report:

'Into the air, and what seemed corporal
Melted, as breath into the wind'[(176)]

- The child soldiers would, wherever possible, face forward. To turn behind is to look into what they've seen and done. For child soldiers, this was facing their trauma. To turn behind was also to face the furies which their actions may have let loose. It meant the students' decisions about when to face the audience and when to turn away was a highly considered choice. Lady Macbeth and Macbeth played the whole of the secret aftermath of Duncan's murder facing forward.

Play away; choreograph Act 3 Scene 4 when Banquo's ghost appears; see where it takes you. Before you do, try and reimagine the famous scene by placing it into an unfamiliar context of 'Kutambaguva'. In Shona, it literally means 'to roll up'. In terms of ritual, it's 'to dance the grave', which is to take the spirit from the bush to the home so the living will be protected. The students turned the scene into part terrifying gathering of the soldiers with their new leader and part 'Kutambaguva', the bringing home of a spirit that could never be laid to rest due to being murdered. Another layer to consider, as the students had to, was the idea that the appearance of Banquo's ghost was a perversion of another Shona ritual, 'Kurova guva'. This is a ceremony performed, usually for a married person, a year after death, in order to transform the deceased into an ancestor. That's a lot for you to consider. If you want to have a go, then turn to the extract[(177)].

- 'Nyika' is the spirit realm; the part of the country where the spirits roam. They can be called up in many different ways. The students created, theatrically, powerful rituals based on their experiences with Iroko and what their research had thrown up. Macbeth calls them up with a white and black cloth over his head (read on to understand the symbolic significance of this striking image), placing small coins in clay pots; at other times, a circle of seeds was sprinkled; it was accompanied at times with drumming, as well as rhythmic clapping; the lighting captured the sense of time when the spirits were summoned, either before dawn or after dark.

- When calling up a spirit, the notion of 'Kukonya' is essential. Its root is in the idea of 'cure'. It's therefore the first question, and as such, it's very important to understand the type of spirit being summoned. For the students, Lady Macbeth didn't only want to know what her husband was planning after the death of Duncan, but more fundamentally, the students believed she was seeking to know about 'Kukonya'. What spirits was he now summoning and what would be his first question? Was Macbeth looking for some kind of 'cure' to ward off the furies now threatening 'his bloody stage'?[178] Read the Shakespeare and imagine the kind of scholarly discussions we had over these lines when Macbeth visits the witches once more. It's an example of 'Kukonya':

'How now, you secret, black and midnight hags?
What is't you do?'[179]

- Lightning is punishment if you upset the spirits, whereas rain is purification/healing. The students were able to mine the play for the numerous references to the elements, making decisions about the subtext informed by their acquired knowledge.

- The concept of spirits leaving only to return is captured in the words, 'Aenda-enda' (he/she has gone) and

'Achadzoka' (he/she will return), reflecting the relentless and terrifying torment that not only runs through the play but something Norman still endures today: 'Does Norman believe the evil presences are still with him? He nods. "The spirit is still there."'[180] The students felt Lady Macbeth summoning up the courage to visit the murdered Duncan wasn't to incriminate the guards. Rather, it was a desperate attempt to find closure, by seeing for herself the murdered body of her abuser, in the false hope his spirit was now gone from her forever.

- 'Ngozi' are people who've led unsatisfactory lives, such as a childless couple or a person who never received a satisfactory burial. The students immediately made the connections. Macbeth and Lady Macbeth are 'Ngozi'. A murdered person such as Banquo, such as Lady Macduff and her children, are also 'Ngozi' as they seek revenge until the crime is acknowledged, reparation is made, and the dead are given a proper burial – a ceremony that brings home the spirit.

- Childless couples are often regarded in some rural communities in Zimbabwe as angry; malicious; harmful; destructive; furious; and spiteful. They're often buried with a seedless cob tied to their back in place of the child, in order to calm the spirit. Shakespeare gives us the enigmatic line that seemingly has been discussed forever, as scholars try to work out what Macbeth was feeling, if anything at all, on hearing his wife had killed herself: 'She should have died hereafter.'[181] Our Macbeth takes out a seedless cob, performing the tenderest of rituals. It conveys his painful acknowledgement, after all these years of living with such trauma, that the only person whom he could ever love, such was his life as a child soldier, was now finally at peace. I can't be sure how the audience felt, but I know that for the ensemble, who'd built all of these experiences together, this was a moment they fully owned.

- Colours are highly symbolic. Red is forbidden in Shona culture due to its close association to the Shavi spirit – a malignant force. In the context of the child soldier, it had traumatic connotations, as it does throughout *Macbeth*. Black brings life-giving rain. It's also associated with royalty, as well as the past. It can also be a colour to be feared. White stops the rain, connecting it to cleansing. It's associated with the glow of the moon but also the terror of lightning. The students would find all of these themes in Shakespeare's language. Hence the students' decision to place the black and white cloth over Macbeth's head when calling up the spirits.

It's worth mentioning at this point how the design evolved. Halfway through the process, I offered the ensemble a further experience by taking them to *Liberian Girl* by Diana Nneka Atuona at The Royal Court. Using a powerful 'defamiliarization' device, it explores a girl's experience as a child soldier, having to disguise herself as a male in order to survive in one of Charles Taylor's 'Small Boy Units' during the devastating Liberian civil war (1989 -1996). It was an immersive production. We were all placed in the action amongst these gun-toting, often drug-crazed child soldiers, made utterly terrifying at times, as they lined us up against the wall, moved us across the stage, and made us compliant witnesses to the atrocities performed in front of our eyes. Of the many things we took away from the theatrical experience were questions about the extraordinary cross-dressing the child soldiers adopted as they advanced on Monrovia. The students found out it served multiple purposes:

'According to the soldiers themselves, cross-dressing is a military mind game, a tactic that instills fear in their rivals. It also makes the soldiers feel more invincible. This belief is founded on a regional superstition which holds that soldiers can "confuse the enemy's bullets" by assuming two identities simultaneously. Though the accoutrements and garb look bizarre to Western eyes, they are, in a sense, variations on the camouflage uniforms and face paint American soldiers use to bolster their sense of invincibility (and therefore, immunity) during combat. Since flak jackets or infra-red goggles aren't available to the destitute Liberian fighters, they opt for evening gowns and frilly blouses.'[182]

It goes further than this, and is deeply rooted in Western African rites of passage rituals: 'Rebels dressed in gowns and wigs and adorned with bones, leaves and other "forest culture" trappings are practicing a modern variation on this technique of using symbolic "clothing" to access sources of power far stronger than their own.'[183] It also lies in Liberian initiation ceremonies around a boy's passage to adulthood, which is symbolised by the wearing of female clothes. The students were utterly intrigued by a process that was happening to them, as they too were making the transition into adulthood:

'He must first pass through a dangerous indeterminate zone between male and female identity before becoming a man. A soldier dressed in women's clothes – or Halloween masks, or shower caps, etc. – on the battlefield is essentially asserting that he's in a volatile in-between state. The message it sends to other soldiers is, "Don't mess with me, I'm dangerous."'[184] ('Don't mess with me, I'm dangerous', a universal mantra for many adolescents around the globe!)

The most extreme example was General Butt Naked, a name chosen to incite fear, just like other names adopted by Liberian Generals, such as General Rambo, General Bin Laden. General Butt Naked was infamous for 'fighting completely naked in the war apart from shoes and a gun. This was a ritual that was required of every member of his army and was implemented as the general believed once stripped down, no bullet could affect his body or his men's bodies.'[185] Incredibly, he survived and now prefers to be called, Joshua Milton Blahy. He still lives in what the Canadian journalist Shane Smith describes as a 'post-apocalyptic Armageddon'. According to Smith, Blahy looked him in the eye, telling him bluntly 'that with all of the guns in Liberia, it would take a rebel group no longer than 2-3 hours to completely take over the country'.[186] We watched some clips from a documentary, *The Redemption of General Butt Naked*.[187] After appearing before Liberia's Truth and Reconciliation Commission, Blahy was set free. He claims to have seen an apparition: 'I had a vision where Jesus met me and told me to repent and live or refuse and die – with the bloodstains of the child still in my hands.'[188] Watch the film; see if you believe his redemption to be real or not. Unsurprisingly, the students didn't believe a word of it. Don't stop there, play away; look up some of the startling photographs these damaged children were very willing to pose for. I bought every member of the cast a plastic gun, and the cast did the rest. Their own extraordinary designs captured a sense of the Liberian horror show, as portrayed in the terrifying imagery. However, due to the empathy the process had created, the students were always mindful to convey the vulnerability of these traumatised children.

So, all that you've just read is what the students would bring to *Macbeth* when, after a term of process, we finally turned to the actual text. It was a test of nerve to hang off for so long, but a risk always worth taking. I'd learnt this in Bangkok when putting on *Haroun*. Frank Kermode, who I had read a lot of at University, tried to work out why he was still writing books about Shakespeare. His conclusion was: 'The reason it still seems to me to have been worth doing is simply that it required close attention to the writer's language.'[189] He would have liked Akala's love of Shakespeare for the same reason, 'the musician of words'. Auden would also agree: 'A poet is, before anything else, a person who is passionately in love with language.'[190] Barthes may have gone too far to condemn the author to his death, but he was right when he said: 'A text's unity lies not in its origin but in its destination.'[191] The students and I were able to bring the experiences we'd built together to Shakespeare's love of language. It's because of this that very little needed explaining. The collective experiences when transferred to the language opened up 'new and previously unsuspected possibilities', but importantly with far 'more awareness, more comprehension... more freedom and control'.[192] In short, they were empowered; they were the custodians of the knowledge. Therefore, the language was embraced, rather than feared or dismissed as impenetrable or irrelevant.

A close look at one passage will demonstrate how the students worked in such a process as this. It's Act 1, Scene 6, the entrance of the War Lord, Duncan, to Macbeth's and Lady Macbeth's encampment after a fierce and prolonged but ultimately successful battle. The Porter in *Macbeth* makes a brief and bawdy appearance in the play – a rather obvious device to create a pause in the action. However, we'd found out that children forced into child labour around armed conflict was widespread. They were 'the servants of strife' ;[193] the cooks, the porters, the messengers serving the soldiers. So, in the spirit of Shakespeare's Porter, we created two life-sized puppets that were manipulated by a boy whose home language was Somali and a girl whose home language was Hindi. They were domestic workers in the Macbeths' encampment. They spoke in iambic pentameter wherever possible, folding in home language to highlight how widescale domestic labour was. They served many purposes, from comic interludes, to commenting on the action, to setting the scene, to creating tension. It's why, before the entrance of Duncan, we see them not only preparing for the visit, but also preparing the audience for what was about to take place. Lady Macbeth then takes a call on her satellite phone from her husband, catching up on his great news before hearing, chillingly, that her abuser will be staying the night.

The student who played Lady Macbeth was from Lithuania. Macbeth was played by a Bengali-speaking student who was Muslim. It was a mixed marriage which became an added layer to explore in their relationship. We discovered, while tribal identity was the most important factor in The Central African Republic, for instance: 'Many people marry outside their faith, and it's not uncommon for one partner to retain his or her religion rather than convert.'[194] However, increasingly, religious identity was superseding tribal identity, leading to persecution of the minority religion. By making Duncan a Muslim, as well as most of the soldiers, it added to Lady Macbeth's isolation and insecurity. Because of this, the student playing Lady Macbeth drew heavily on her religious background in her private moments; the notion of 'akwiila', the secret, the whispered, once again. As this traumatised woman determines to kill Duncan, we can see the enormity of the act in how the student lit the incense at a shrine; in how she quietly incants a Lithuanian prayer, intercutting the lines we know so well. Take one of the familiar lines: 'O never shall the sun that morrow see';[195] over time, the student developed an almost instinctive movement towards her stomach, indicating the scar left by the brutal caesarean she'd endured. As she clutches her scar, she faces forward, as to look behind would be to see horrors that have been and will be. She has her back to a huge projected image of a Lithuanian shrine; original Lithuanian church music is underscoring; breaking into her chanted prayer, she speaks the line connecting it to the twinned sons she has never seen, as well as to the enormity of murdering this God-like figure. She's terrified she won't be able to go through with it, and if she does, she'll be haunted by the avenging furies.

Suddenly a loud M.I.A track, *Paper Planes,* comes blasting out of the speakers, shattering the 'akwiila', the inner world Lady Macbeth has just created. M.I.A.'s music became a key component in the production. Most of the cast knew of some of her music but had no knowledge about her, apart from one girl who, like M.I.A., was Tamil. Her family had also escaped the war. Mathangi 'Maya' Arulpragasam, whose stage name is M.I.A. (Missing in Action), was born in England in 1976, but at six months old moved to Sri Lanka. Her father joined the Tamil's fight for emancipation in the Sri Lankan civil war. Eventually, in 1986, her mother decided it was too dangerous, moving back to England to a South London council estate with the young Maya. Her father remained, continuing to fight in a war where 100,000 people were killed by the Sri Lankan military, leaving behind 90,000 Tamil war widows.[196] He rarely saw his family. In an interview in 2005, Maya describes her activism that was very much aligned to our process:

> 'There's so much confusion about what I stand for and what I'm saying that that's the whole point: there have to be discussions; there has to be people talking, and there has to be young people talking about politics if they want. They have to have a chance to hear different opinions. And that's what it's about.'[197]

So, we had discussions, important discussions, not least because there were several Sri Lankan Tamil students in our school. This wasn't something far away – it was right here, now. It was real. By reading about Maya's life, we learnt about the conflict still going on today for the Tamils, and their fight for their human rights. But we also encountered a woman, 'multifaceted and complicated', 'incomplete' and 'unending',[198] who continues to fight for justice. In 2020 she was awarded an MBE. Incredibly after receiving asylum, her mother and her cousin were the only women in the country who actually hand stitched these medals for the last 30 years because when they took the job in 1986 it was the only non English speaking manual labour they could find. Many of the ensemble's parents were earning the minimum wage but not for the Queen! For the Sri Lankan student, it was incredibly affirming. In 'the never-ending' dialogue we'd created, she would go onto fully explore her Sri Lankan roots in her final GCSE piece, another journey that had some of its roots in this experience. In her fascinating Master's Thesis, *Political Elements in the Music of M.I.A*, Irene Lonnblad shows the complexity of M.I.A.'s work and why she was worth placing in our context:

> 'By approaching M.I.A. from different perspectives, from technological to cultural, while not forgetting the meaning of gender and race, this study attempts to examine how she has been able to turn politically inspired material into hit songs,

reached audiences all over the world and managed to avoid the stereotypes attached to women in popular music.'[199]

> Play away; go listen, watch, read about M.I.A. Then think hard before booking that next holiday in Sri Lanka.

We chose *Paper Planes* for its ambiguity. M.I.A invites us to make up our own minds: 'It's up to you how you want to interpret.'[200] We wondered how a War Lord would arrive, recalling some of the pictures from the Liberian conflict of trucks loaded up with massive sound systems. It wasn't so far removed from some of the events these students attend on the weekend. Just listen to the introduction at full volume and imagine a posse of cross-dressed, gun-toting, child soldiers sashaying in, using some of the movement learnt from Iroko Theatre and what they'd taken away from *Liberian Girl*. They were all facing front, 'the good smile' in their eyes and 'the dead stare' at the audience. Lady Macbeth stood utterly still; hand on her inner wound; eyes fixed on the entrance where her abuser would appear; behind her a projected picture of Kony at his most terrifying; gunshots firing off in the crazy mix of the chorus in M.I.A.'s song.

The student playing Duncan had fought his way through the first three years of secondary school, not allowing his autism to prevent him achieving. He liked to sing and had performed publicly. The ensemble threw down the challenge for him to sing some of M.I.A.'s song. We spent many evenings in the music room discussing the subtext of *Paper Planes* that we agreed was both aligned with his character as well as with the 'super objective', the essence, of the scene. We concluded that what we were after was what Lonnblad found in M.I.A.'s music, 'the lyrics of *Paper Planes* are provocative, rebellious and created to cause a stir'.[201]

Duncan's entrance was high up on a block at one end of the traverse, in full military dress, with a bright red beret – a direct reference to the malevolent spirit of power, both dangerous and destructive. His stare, fixed solely on Lady Macbeth, the woman he'd raped, had all the menacing provocation designed to create a 'stir'. There are reasons why there's now a law that doesn't require the victims of rape to face their abusers face-to-face. Not before time, it's about to be extended to all victims of domestic abuse.[202] Duncan jumps down and slowly walks up the long alleyway, singing the chorus but missing off the word 'money' from the original:

'All I wanna do is
And
Take'

He does this three times, until he's almost touching Lady Macbeth's face. Imagine the courage these two adolescent students needed to pull this off. This was real. As was Lady Macbeth's terror. The ensemble, as child soldiers, sings the refrain. Again, Linnbald helps us discover the subtext: 'The harsh and arrogant refrain is also dubbed with children's voices that are backing up M.I.A.s vocals. In general children's voices represent innocence but here with the brutal sound effects the resolutions is rather disturbing and sarcastic.'[203]

In the third verse, there's a sample of the Clash song, *Straight to Hell*. Linnbald is there once more, pointing out the reference to 'already going to hell', 'illustrates how many people living in poverty feel about life in general: it does not matter what one does when nothing can change the situation into which one is born'.[204] For this reason, it was on this line that both Macbeth and Banquo appear physically separated but joined by their impotence to intervene, stopping Duncan's assault on the woman they both love. By using the word 'you' in her lyric, M.I.A is inviting us 'to watch what is going on in the world of the protagonist, "the bona fide hustlers", well appreciated and respected in the ghetto who have gained their reputation by selling guns, selling drugs and/or women'.[205] So we, the audience, can only join Macbeth and Banquo as bystanders while Duncan rapes Lady Macbeth for a second time, not physically but emotionally. Play away before you turn your back on such an extreme interpretation, and examine the text in this context. I certainly couldn't shy away from it, as this was where our 'walk toward' had led us.

When Duncan declares sneeringly, 'This castle (encampment) hath a pleasant seat', he invites Lady Macbeth to sit on his lap. If she wasn't scared enough, he references the spirits, the 'Mweya', when he whispers into her ear:

'The air,
Nimbly and sweetly recommends itself
Unto our gentle senses'

The notion of air in the context of the 'Mweya' is complex. At a surface level, it's the air, the breath, the wind. But it's also the soul, 'the life principle of an individual that survives the death of a body'.[206] Just think how many 'Mweya' are present in the minds of the child soldiers watching Duncan torment not only Lady Macbeth but everyone present. But it's closely associated with the 'Ngozi' – the aggrieved dead, the source of the child soldiers' nightmares. It was an extraordinary discovery for all of us when we found out that these spirits are 'raised by the witches'.[207] It's also Lady Macbeth's fear that if she murders this monster, his 'Ngozi' will come back in the air as a malevolent spirit, as a 'Mweya', to torment her further. There can be no closure. She's as trapped as she is in that moment, sat on his lap, in front of all to see.

He suddenly throws her to the floor and stands to his full height, echoing the tyrants throughout the ages who've ruled in countries where there've been child soldiers. Some of these monsters are now being projected behind him, from Pol Pot in Cambodia to Seko in the Congo. We had discussed why Duncan decides to take the trouble to visit the Macbeths in their own encampment rather than make them travel to him. The students felt this was a pure power play. As he arrogantly stands in the bright light of naked aggression, calling out everyone including Macbeth and Banquo, to 'See, see', it's clear that this is a challenge to see if anyone is brave enough to stop him from doing whatever he likes. It's a reminder that: 'There are stages in the history of nations, perhaps of every nation, when the fanaticism, the arrogance, the ruthlessness, the ambition and the hubris of one individual can plunge millions of men and women into madness, suffering, fear and destruction.'[208] After the repetition, there's a pause; the music vibrates; Lady Macbeth is still on the floor. Duncan slowly stands over her with the disgust of someone who has now reduced another human being to a mere 'object'. Duncan's language is an extreme version of Bakhtin's 'monologism' which,

'denies the existence outside itself of another consciousness with equal rights and equal responsibilities...With a monologic approach (in its extreme pure form) another person remains wholly and merely an object of consciousness, and not another consciousness. No response is expected from it that could change anything in the world of my consciousness. Monologue is finalized and deaf to other's response, does not expect it and does not acknowledge in it any decisive force.'[209]

He finishes the line, exclaiming, 'Our honoured hostess!' No-one is sure what he'll do now as he reaches down. All of sudden, he picks her up by the hand. The music changes to a piece of classical music composed by the anti-Semite, Wagner. It echoes the insanity of Joseph Conrad's *Heart of Darkness* as recreated by Coppola's *Apocalypse Now*. I shared my experiences of visiting the Vietnam village of My Lai, where unarmed civilians were massacred in one of the most terrible episodes of the Vietnam War. We then watched a clip from the scene where Robert Duvall's, Lieutenant Colonel Bill Kilgore declares, 'I love the smell of napalm in the morning', before dropping the bombs from helicopters with speakers attached to them, blasting out Wagner's *Ride of the Valkyries*. 'It scares the hell out of the slopes, my boys love it,' Kilgore explains.[210] I also shared my experiences of my cousin, Kitty Hart-Moxon, who survived Auschwitz as a child. We read some passages from her books,

Return to Auschwitz[211] and *I am Alive*.[212] Classical music was used in the camps by the SS, 'to attack prisoners' identities, certainties and self-conceptions'.[213] Duncan now does exactly that, attacking the certainties of Lady Macbeth as well as the watching brigade of child soldiers, Macbeth, Banquo and the audience, by dancing with her to the sound track of Wagner. He speaks the lines with the almost crazed tone he'd seen Brando's Colonel Kurtz use:

> 'The love that follows us sometimes is our trouble,
> Which still we thank as love. Herein I teach you
> How you shall bid God 'ild us for your pains,
> And thank us for your trouble'

He's asking her to thank him. Her humiliation is complete.

> 'Lady Macbeth: All our service
> In every point twice done and then done double
> Were poor and single business to contend
> Against those honours deep and broad wherewith
> Your majesty loads our house; for those of old
> And the late dignities heap'd upon them,
> We rest your hermits'

She does so by kissing his feet. This is a complex action loaded with significance. For the Christian student playing Lady Macbeth, she told us it's an act of humility, as Christ showed when he kissed the 12 apostles' feet. It's carried out every Maundy Thursday in churches and cathedrals across the world. It's a symbolic act of goodness, as the apostles were meant to go out into the world carrying out selfless acts rather than murder. However, our Macbeth was Bengali. He told us the touching of the parent-in-laws' feet is a sign of respect, especially just before marriage. However, if it's done in a posture of prostration ('sajda'), the Muslim prayer position, but not in the name of Allah, then it's a sin. Yet another layer is in the Islamic belief: 'Paradise is under the feet of mothers.'[214] Remember Macbeth, as an eight-year-old, watched his mother die at the sword of Duncan's men. Duncan was literally rubbing their faces into the ground in an act of utter degradation.

Of course, the washing of the feet before prayer is also a 'partial ablution',[215] cleansing the body and soul of all sin. By murdering Duncan, both Macbeth and Lady Macbeth hoped to find 'total ablution'. To mark their intentions, Lady Macbeth takes off her bandana, glancing at Macbeth, and places it under the feet of Duncan before she kisses his feet. This startlingly nuanced act came about when the student taught us that a Lithuanian bride, on entering her home as a married woman, immediately places a red belt or towel onto the stove as a mark of respect for the household spirits in her new home. Further connections were made. The fireplace also plays a central role in Acholi culture. 'Wang Oo' was a gathering of people around the fireplace, a place where stories were told as well as a forum 'for the exchange of ideas and discussion of problems facing the community, was the seat of wisdom where parents and elders taught youngsters good behaviour, traditional norms and gender roles'.[216] Kony's reign of terror had led over two million people to abandon their homes and to live in camps. With this exodus, the campfire culture died out: 'Here, educational activities and cultural norms and values were seriously limited – including parent to child contact – and the children exposed to all sorts of different behaviour.'[217] In this layered context, Lady Macbeth's defiant act by placing her bandana under the feet of Duncan symbolised her desire to begin her marriage properly, untainted by the monster that stood before her. It was another moment the ensemble owned.

I want the building of experiences together to be the final chapter. It works, I hope, as a metaphor for the reading of this book. The power of creating and exploring experiences collectively had been the driving source of something happening in the lives of the women in Nepal and in my students in East London. It arises out of community, context, and a long-term commitment to personalisation. But for 33 years I've been in search of those experiences inside and outside the classroom. It's in all my long-lasting relationships; in my professional and personal life. It's in all that I read, watch, listen, and of course, eat. If I might be so bold as to merge Bakhtin with Rumi, I've gone out into the world allowing the beauty of what I love be what I do in order to come back with a self. We want our students to leave us as people who are creative; inspiring; skillful; confident; agile; articulate; brave; resilient; generous; reflective; comfortable with each other and with themselves; prepared to stand up for what they believe. I wanted that for my own children. Surely this is what we want for ourselves as well.

My final words to my students who are about to leave my Drama Studio for the very last time, are always Apollinaire's. They will also serve to be the last words in this book. However, the 'never-ending' dialogue and 'the walk toward' will continue for those of us willing to engage in the search for something more. The search is always worth it.

> '"Come to the edge," he said.
> "We can't, we're afraid!" they responded.
> "Come to the edge," he said.
> "We can't, we will fall!" they responded.
> "Come to the edge," he said.
> And so they came.
> And he pushed them.
> And they flew.'(218)

1-Gruen, S. 2016: *The Sara Gruen Collection: Water for Elephants – At the Water's Edge – Ape House*: Hachette UK

2-Hemmingway, E. Quoted in: Joyner, C. 2017: *The show mustn't go on*: Campbell Law Observer

http://campbelllawobserver.com/the-show-mustnt-go-on/

3-Rose, S. 2017: *Hugh Jackman's new film celebrates P.T. Barnum – but let's not airbrush history*: The Guardian

4-THR staff, 2016: *Donald Trump Claims He Doesn't Know Samuel L. Jackson After "Hateful Eight" Star Implies He Cheats at Golf*: The Hollywood Reporter

https://www.hollywoodreporter.com/news/donald-trump-samuel-l-jackson-golf-commercials-852214

5-Trump, D. 5th Jan 2016: Twitter

6-Schmidt, S. 2017: *Why people keep comparing Donald Trump to P.T. Barnum, of circus fame*: Washington Post

7-VandeHei, J., Allen, M. 2017: *Reality bites: Trump's wake-up call*: Axios: https://www.axios.com/reality-bites-trumps-wake-up-call-1513299979-3bd3a708-26be-4232-8faa-6970e65c6cf1.html

8-Rose, S. 2017: *Hugh Jackman's new film celebrates P.T. Barnum – but let's not airbrush history*: The Guardian

9-Young, L. 2013: *The Circus in 'Hard Times*: College Digital Repository 115 VernonTrinity's Journals and Serial Publications

10-Dickens, C: *Hard Times* as quoted in Young, L.

11-The Blondin Memorial Trust: *Funambulus/Funambule: Rope Walkers & Equilibrists: A Potted History Using Quotes & Anecdotes Through the Centuries*

From Material Researched by Demoriane, H. 1989: *The Tightrope Walker*: Secker and Warburg

https://www.blondinmemorialtrust.com/funambulus

12-Victoria and Albert Museum: *Chevalier Blondin*: http://www.vam.ac.uk/content/articles/c/blondin/

13-Simon, L.21014: *The Greatest Show On Earth: A History of The Circus*: Reaktion Books

14- Banerjee, J. 2014: *Behind you…*: The Times Literary Supplement

15-*Even When I Fall*: 2017: Directed by Neal, S and McLarnon, K.: Satya Films

16- Loud, P. with Johnson, N. 1974: *A Woman's Study*: New York: Bantam Books

17-http://www.satyafilms.com/press/

18-Ibid

19-Worth, S. 1980: *Margaret Mead and the Shift from "Visual Anthropology" to the "Anthropology of Visual Communication"*: Studies in Visual Communication: Volume 6, Issue 1 Spring 1980 Article 55-1-1980, Penn Libraries, University of Pennsylvania

20-United Nations, Nepal information platform: *Migrant workers and their families*: http://un.org.np/oneun/undaf/migrant_workers

21-2016: *Demonetisation impact: Great Bombay Circus is struggling to survive*: Business Standard

https://www.business-standard.com/article/economy-policy/demonetisation-impact-great-bombay-circus-is-struggling-to-survive-116120300123_1.html

22-Angels Nepal: *Human Traffiking*: https://3angelsnepal.com/human-trafficking/

23-National Human Rights Commission, 2012-2013: *Trafficking in Persons Especially On Women and Children in Nepal*: National Human Rights Commission

'According to the records of Kathmandu Valley Police Commissioners, the four-yearly average (2009/10-2012/13) number of women reported missing was 845 in Kathmandu valley. Nearly four in five women reported missing continue to remain missing. According to the Central Child Welfare Board (CCWB), the total number of missing children recorded was 1453 in 2012/13. Two in 5 missing children continued to remain missing while one out of two missing girls continued to remain missing. This fact provides the nexus of missing children phenomenon with trafficking for sexual exploitation.'

24-Ganotra, K. Of Childline India as quoted in Ayache, A. 2014: *The Circus of hope*: Friday Magazine: https://fridaymagazine.ae/life-culture/the-circus-of-hope-1.1350999

25-Ibid

26-Freire, P. 1998: *Pedogogy of Freedom*: Rowman & Littlefield

27-National Human Rights Commission, 2012-2013: *Trafficking in Persons Especially On Women and Children in Nepal*: National Human Rights Commission

> 'Assessing the awareness level of rural women about the laws related to combating violence, it appears that prevention related programs have yet to reach the needy groups and communities in the country. In a study conducted by the Office of the Prime Minister (2012) among 900 rural women, it was found that the proportion of women reporting heard of laws ranged from as low as 13 per cent for Domestic Violence and Crime and Punishment Act, to 24 per cent for law on sexual harassment of women, to 35 per cent for HTTCA 2007 to 70 per cent for the law that guarantees property rights to daughters. Age, caste/ethnic groups, education and wealth quintile determine the knowledge of laws. While women were enquired about whether or not they were aware of the presence of different support systems for violence survivors, a few women (less than 5%) reported that they had knowledge on such systems in the district.'

28-2011: *People & Power – Nepal's lost circus children*, directed by Neal, S: Al Jazeera English : https://www.youtube.com/watch?v=eRHPmx2McSQ

29-Ethirajan, A. 2014: *Kathmandu youth circus turns tables on human trafficking*: BBC News: http://www.bbc.co.uk/news/world-asia-27989494

30-Mead, M. and MacGregor, F. 1951: *Growth and Culture: A Photographic Study Of Balinese Child-hood:* New York: Putnam Press.

31-Worth, S. 1980: *Margaret Mead and the Shift from "Visual Anthropology" to the "Anthropology of Visual Communication"*: Studies in Visual Communication: Volume 6, Issue 1 Spring 1980 Article 55-1-1980, Penn Libraries, University of Pennsylvania

32-Ibid

33-Holmes, P. 2008: *Shailaja's birthday*: http://philipinnepal.blogspot.co.uk/2008/05/

34-Hodal, K. 2018: *Sold to the circus as children: trafficking survivors showcase their skills in Nepal*: The Guardian

35-Bhakhtin, M. (originally published 1963) 1993: *Problems of Dostoevsky's Poetics*: University of Minnesota Press

36-Freire, P. 1970: *Pedagogy of the Oppressed*: Continuum

37-Ibid

38-Ibid

39-Hodal, K. 2018: *Sold to the circus as children: trafficking survivors showcase their skills in Nepal*: The Guardian

40-Ibid

41-Eger, E. 2017: *The Choice*: Simon and Schuster

42-Sooke, A. 2010: *Circolombia: From street urchins to circus stars*: The Daily Telegraph

43-Freire, P. 1970: *Pedagogy of the Oppressed*: Continuum

44-Ibid

45-Robinson, A. 2011: *In Theory Bakhtin: Dialogism, Polyphony and Heteroglossia*: Ceasefire Magazine: https://ceasefiremagazine.co.uk/in-theory-bakhtin-1/

46-Bakhtin, M. Ed. Holquist, M. 1981: *The Dialogic Imagination: Four Essays*: University of Texas Press

47- Freire, P. & Horton, M: 1990: *We Make the Road by Walking: Conversations on Education and Social Change*: Temple University Press, Philadelphia

48-Freire, P. 1970: *Pedagogy of the Oppressed*: Continuum

49-Bakhtin, M. 1974: *Toward a Methodology for the Human Sciences* in Emerson, C. & Holquist, M. 1999: *Speech Genres and Other late Essays*: University of Texas Press

50-Hodal, K. 2018: *Sold to the circus as children: trafficking survivors showcase their skills in Nepal*: The Guardian

51-Ibid

52-Ayache, A. 2014: *The Circus of hope*: Friday Magazine: https://fridaymagazine.ae/life-culture/the-circus-of-hope-1.1350999

53-Freire, P. 1970: *Pedagogy of the Oppressed*: Continuum

54-Ayache, A. 2014: *The Circus of hope*: Friday Magazine

55-Freire, P. 1970: *Pedagogy of the Oppressed*: Continuum

56-Ayache, A. 2014: *The Circus of hope*: Friday Magazine

57-Kavanagh, K. 2014: *Trafficking and Trapeze: Meet Circus Kathmandu:* This is Cabaret: http://www.thisiscabaret.com/trafficking-trapeze-meet-circus-kathmandu/

58-Clark, K and Holquist, M. 1984: *Mikhail Bakhtin*: Harvard University Press

59-Ibid

60- Kavanagh, K. 2014: *Trafficking and Trapeze: Meet Circus Kathmandu:* This is Cabaret

61-Brodzinsky, S. & Schoening, M. 2012: *Throwing Stones at the Moon: Narratives From Colombians Displaced by Violence*: McSweeney's

62-Freire, P.1970: *Pedagogy of the Oppressed*: Continuum

63-Ibid

64-Bakhtin, M. 1984: *Problems of Dostoevsky's Poetics*: University of Minnesota Press

65-Freire, P.1970: *Pedagogy of the Oppressed*: Continuum

66-Ibid

67-Freire, P. 1985: *Reading the World and Reading the Word: An Interview with Paulo Freire:* Language Arts, Vol. 62, No. 1, Making Meaning, Learning Language, National Council of Teachers of English

68-Ayache, A. 2014: *The Circus of hope*: Friday Magazine: https://fridaymagazine.ae/life-culture/the-circus-of-hope-1.1350999

69-Boal, A. 1992: *Games for Actors and Non-Actors*: Routledge

70-Boal, A. 2009: *World Theatre Day Message*, Geneva, Switzerland

71-Boal, A. 1979: *Theatre of the Oppressed*: Pluto Press

72-Ibid

73-Bakhtin, M. 1984: *Problems of Dostoevsky's Poetics* : University of Minnesota Press

74-Freire, P. 1970: *Pedagogy of the Oppressed*: Continuum

75-Ibid

76-Appleseed, J. quoted in Weber, B. 2009: *Augusto Boal, Stage Director Who Gave Voice To Audiences, Is Dead at 78*: The New York Times

77-Boal, A. 1995: *The Rainbow of Desire*: Routledge

78-Freire, P. 1970: *Pedagogy of the Oppressed*: Continuum

79-Ibid

80-Ibid

81-Bakhtin, M. 1974: *Toward a Methodology for the Human Sciences* in Emerson, C. & Holquist, M. 1999: *Speech Genres and Other late Essays*: University of Texas Press

82-Boal, A. 1992: *Games for Actors and Non-Actors*: Routledge

83-Friere, P. – widely quoted but unable to find source

84-Ayache, A. 2014: *The Circus of hope*: Friday Magazine: https://fridaymagazine.ae/life-culture/the-circus-of-hope-1.1350999

85- Jones, S. 2015: *Nepal earthquakes leave bitter legacy as children become quarry for traffickers*: The Guardian

86-Freire, P.1970: *Pedagogy of the Oppressed*: Continuum

87-Ibid

88-Ayache, A. 2014: *The Circus of hope*: Friday Magazine: https://fridaymagazine.ae/life-culture/the-circus-of-hope-1.1350999

89-Friere, P. 2000: *Pedagogy of Freedom: Ethics, Democracy, and Civic Courage*: Rowman & Littlefield Publishers

90-Ayache, A. 2014: *The Circus of hope*: Friday Magazine: https://fridaymagazine.ae/life-culture/the-circus-of-hope-1.1350999

91-Ibid

92-Ibid

93-Freire, P. 1985: *Reading the World and Reading the Word: An Interview with Paulo Freire*: Language Arts, Vol. 62, No. 1, Making Meaning, Learning Language, National Council of Teachers of English

94-*Khatmandu Circus, Glastonbury*, Free: 2012: Jack In The Box Films

https://www.youtube.com/watch?v=569ABlh8M6w

95-Hodal, K. 2018: *Sold to the circus as children: trafficking survivors showcase their skills in Nepal*: The Guardian

96-Freire, P.1970: *Pedagogy of the Oppressed*: Continuum

97-Ibid

98-Ibid

99-Robinson, A. 2011: *In Theory Bakhtin: Dialogism, Polyphony and Heteroglossia*: Ceasefire Magazine

100-Freire, P. 1970: *Pedagogy of the Oppressed*: Continuum

101-Bakhtin, M. Ed. Holquist, M. 1981: *The Dialogic Imagination: Four Essays*: University of Texas Press

102-Ibid

103-Ibid

104-Ibid

105- Freire, P.1970: *Pedagogy of the Oppressed*: Continuum

106-Ibid

107-Clark, K and Holquist, M. 1984: *Mikhail Bakhtin*: Harvard University Press

108-Freire, P.1970: *Pedagogy of the Oppressed*: Continuum

109-Ibid

110-Ibid

111-Ibid

112-Ibid

113-Ibid

114-Rilke, R. 2011: *Letters to a Young Poet*: Penguin Classics

115-Freire, P. 1985: *Reading the World and Reading the Word: An Interview with Paulo Freire*: Language Arts, Vol. 62, No. 1, Making Meaning, Learning Language, National Council of Teachers of English

116-Ibid

117-Jonson, B. 1623: In the preface to the First Folio, *Mr. William Shakespeare's Comedies, Histories, & Tragedies*: British Library

118-Johnson, S. 1765: In the preface to, *The Plays of William Shakespeare In Eight Volumes*: J. and R. Tonson

119-Arnold, M. 1873: *Literature & Dogma*: Macmillan and Co.

120-worldshakespearefestival.org.uk

121-Dickson, A. 2012: *World Shakespeare festival: around the globe in 37 plays*: The Guardian

122-Akala, 2007: *Comedy, Tragedy, History* (Official video): https://www.youtube.com/watch?v=pT8m3w9j8Y0

123-Taylor, K. 2018: *Akala, the new Shakespeare? Where unfathomable worlds collide*: I am Hip hop urban lifestyle magazine: http://www.iamhiphopmagazine.com/akalashakespeare/

124-Lewis, H. 2017: *Akala interview: Artists are an alternative source of power*: Skiddle: https://www.skiddle.com/news/all/Akala-interview-Artists-are-an-alternative-source-of-power/30005/

125-Freire, P. 1985: *Reading the World and Reading the Word: An Interview with Paulo Freire*: Language Arts, Vol. 62, No. 1, Making Meaning, Learning Language, National Council of Teachers of English

126-Akala, 2011: *Hip Hop and Shakespeare*: TED x Aldeburgh

127-Ibid

128-Ibid

129-Ibid

130-Ibid

131-Freire, P. 1985: *Reading the World and Reading the Word: An Interview with Paulo Freire*: Language Arts, Vol. 62, No. 1, Making Meaning, Learning Language, National Council of Teachers of English

132- George, M. 2018: *Reality of GCSE reform is pupils studying Macbeth for five continuous years*: TES

133-Bauman, Z. 1982: *Memories of Class: The Pre- History and After-Life of Class*: Routledge &Kegan Paul

134-Bauman, Z. & May, T. 2001: *Thinking Sociologically, 2nd Edition*: Oxford: Blackwell

135-Strudwick, P. 2014: *Pupil protests – teaching children to campaign*: The Guardian

136-Friere, P. 2000: *Pedagogy of Freedom: Ethics, Democracy, and Civic Courage*: Rowman & Littlefield Publishers

137-Arendt, H. 1968: *Men in Dark Times:* Harcourt, Brace & World

138-Storr, W. 2014: *Kony's child soldiers: 'When you kill for the first time, you change'*: The Daily Telegraph

139-Freire, P. 1970: *Pedagogy of the Oppressed*: Continuum

140-Storr, W. 2014: *Kony's child soldiers: 'When you kill for the first time, you change'*: The Daily Telegraph

141-Shakespeare, W.: *Macbeth*, *Act 5 Scene 5*

142-Ibid

143-Ibid, *Act 5 Scene 3*

144- Storr, W. 2014: *Kony's child soldiers: 'When you kill for the first time, you change'*: The Daily Telegraph

145-Arendt, H. 1958: *The Human Condition*: The University of Chicago

146- Storr, W. 2014: *Kony's child soldiers: 'When you kill for the first time, you change'*: The Daily Telegraph

147-Ibid

148-Freire, P. & Horton, M: 1990: *We Make the Road by Walking: Conversations on Education and Social Change*: Temple University Press, Philadelphia

149-Ibid

150-Freire, P.1970: *Pedagogy of the Oppressed*: Continuum

151-Arendt, H. 1978: *The Life of The Mind*: New York: Harcourt Brace Jovanovich

152- Storr, W. 2014: *Kony's child soldiers: 'When you kill for the first time, you change'*: The Daily Telegraph

153-Ibid

154-Arendt, H. 1951: *The Origins of Totalitarianism*: Schocken Books

155-Shakespeare, W.: *Macbeth*, *Act 3 Scene 3*

156-Bauman, Z. & May, T. 2001: *Thinking Sociologically, 2nd Edition*: Oxford: Blackwell

157-Mark, M. 2013: *Joseph Kony child soldier returns to terrorised boyhood village*: The Guardian

158-Shakespeare, W.: *Macbeth*, *Act 5 Scene 1*

159-Ibid

160- Storr, W. 2014: *Kony's child soldiers: 'When you kill for the first time, you change'*: The Daily Telegraph

161-Ibid

162- Arendt, H. 1958: *The Human Condition*: The University of Chicago

163-Ibid

164-Mark, M. 2013: *Joseph Kony child soldier returns to terrorised boyhood village*: The Guardian

165-Shakespeare, W.: *Macbeth*, Act 1 Scene 2

166-Shakespeare, W.: *Macbeth*, Act 5 Scene 1

167-Mark, M. 2013: *Joseph Kony child soldier returns to terrorised boyhood village*: The Guardian

168- Storr, W. 2014: *Kony's child soldiers: 'When you kill for the first time, you change'*: The Daily Telegraph

169-Shaffer, P. 1973: *Equus, Act 1 Scene 19*

170-Jung, C. 1973: *Memories, dreams, reflections*: Random House

171-Vygotsky, L. 1978: *Mind in Society: The Development of Higher Psychological Processes*: Cambridge, MA: Harvard University

172-Shakespeare, W.: *Macbeth*, Act 5 Scene 8

173-irokotheatre.org.uk

174-Lan, D. 1995: *Guns and Rain: Guerrillas and Spirit Mediums in Zimbabwe*: London: James Currey, Ltd and Berkley: University of California Press

175-Shakespeare, W.: *Macbeth*, Act 1 Scene 3

176-Ibid

177-We staged the whole play in the traverse, the audience either side of the space, so there would be no hiding places for the spectators. They would have the same choice, to look ahead or to look away. At one end was a cyclorama, a white wall, on which we projected images throughout the production.

The GHOST OF BANQUO enters, and sits in MACBETH's place

MACBETH

Facing forward or behind?
Here had we now our country's honour roof'd,
Were the graced person of our Banquo present;
Who may I rather challenge for unkindness
Than pity for mischance!

ROSS

His absence, sir,
Lays blame upon his promise. Please't your highness
To grace us with your royal company

MACBETH

Facing forward or behind?

The table's full.

LENNOX

Here is a place reserved, sir.

MACBETH

Facing forward or behind?

Where?

LENNOX

Here, my good lord. What is't that moves your highness?

MACBETH

Facing forward or behind?

Which of you have done this?

LORDS

What, my good lord?

MACBETH

Facing forward or behind?

Thou canst not say I did it: never shake
Thy gory locks at me.

ROSS

Gentlemen, rise: his highness is not well.

LADY MACBETH

Facing forward or behind?

Sit, worthy friends: my lord is often thus,
And hath been from his youth: pray you, keep seat;
The fit is momentary; upon a thought
He will again be well: if much you note him,
You shall offend him and extend his passion:
Feed, and regard him not.

Facing forward or behind?

Are you a man?

MACBETH

Facing forward or behind?

Ay, and a bold one, that dare look on that
Which might appal the devil.

LADY MACBETH

Facing forward or behind?

O proper stuff!
This is the very painting of your fear:
This is the air-drawn dagger which, you said,
Led you to Duncan. O, these flaws and starts,
Impostors to true fear, would well become
A woman's story at a winter's fire,
Authorized by her grandam. Shame itself!
Why do you make such faces? When all's done,
You look but on a stool.

MACBETH

Facing forward or behind?

Prithee, see there! behold! look! lo!
how say you?
Why, what care I? If thou canst nod, speak too.
If charnel-houses and our graves must send
Those that we bury back, our monuments
Shall be the maws of kites.

GHOST OF BANQUO vanishes

LADY MACBETH

Facing forward or behind?

What, quite unmann'd in folly?

MACBETH

Facing forward or behind?

If I stand here, I saw him.

LADY MACBETH

Facing forward or behind?

Fie, for shame!

MACBETH

Facing forward or behind?

Blood hath been shed ere now, i' the olden time,
Ere human statute purged the gentle weal;
Ay, and since too, murders have been perform'd
Too terrible for the ear: the times have been,
That, when the brains were out, the man would die,
And there an end; but now they rise again,
With twenty mortal murders on their crowns,
And push us from our stools: this is more strange
Than such a murder is.

LADY MACBETH

Facing forward or behind?

My worthy lord,
Your noble friends do lack you.

MACBETH

Facing forward or behind?

I do forget.
Do not muse at me, my most worthy friends,
I have a strange infirmity, which is nothing
To those that know me. Come, love and health to all;
Then I'll sit down. Give me some wine; fill full.
I drink to the general joy o' the whole table,
And to our dear friend Banquo, whom we miss;
Would he were here! to all, and him, we thirst,
And all to all.

Lords

Our duties, and the pledge.

Re-enter GHOST OF BANQUO

MACBETH

Facing forward or behind?

Avaunt! and quit my sight! let the earth hide thee!
Thy bones are marrowless, thy blood is cold;
Thou hast no speculation in those eyes
Which thou dost glare with!

LADY MACBETH

Facing forward or behind?

Think of this, good peers,
But as a thing of custom: 'tis no other;
Only it spoils the pleasure of the time.

178-Shakespeare, W.: *Macbeth, Act 2 Scene 4*

179-Shakespeare, W.: *Macbeth, Act 4 Scene 1*

180- Storr, W. 2014: *Kony's child soldiers: 'When you kill for the first time, you change'*: The Daily Telegraph

181-Shakespeare, W.: *Macbeth, Act 5 Scene 5*

182-Scheffler, M. 2003: *Scare Tactics, Why are Liberian soldiers wearing fright wigs*: Slate

183-Ibid

184-Ibid

185-Logan, C. 2014: *Cannibal Warlords of Liberia*: Borgen Magazine: http://www.borgenmagazine.com/cannibal-warlords-liberia/

186-Ibid

187-*The Redemption of General Butt Naked*: 2011: directed by Daniele Anastasion, Eric Strauss: part2pictures

188-Gaffey, C. 2017: *General Butt Naked and Other Former Warlords Roam Free in Liberia. Will a New President Prosecute Them?*: Newsweek

189-Kermode, F. 1999: *Writing about Shakespeare*: Vol. 21No. 24: London Review of Books

190-Auden, W. 2002: *The complete works of W.H. Auden Volume 11: Prose, 1939-1948*: Princeton University Press

191-Barthes, R. 1977: *Image-Music-Text*: Fontana Press

192-Bauman, Z. & May, T. 2001: *Thinking Sociologically, 2nd Edition*: Oxford: Blackwell

193-Somavia, J. 2003: *The unbearable fate of child soldiers*: The International Labour Organisation: https://www.ilo.org/global/about-the-ilo/newsroom/features/WCMS_075611/lang--en/index.htm

194-Raqhavan, S. 2014: *Christian-Muslim marriages are latest casualty of religious strife in Central African Republic*: The Washington Post

195-Shakespeare, W.: *Macbeth, Act 1 Scene 5*

196-Healey, J. 2013: *The Real M.I.A. In Sri Lanka: Basic Human Rights*: Huffington Post

197-Wheaton, R. 2005: *London Calling-For Congo, Columbo, Sri Lanka*: http://www.popmatters.com/music/interviews/mia-0505062.shtml

198-Lonnblad, I. 2012: *Political Elements In The Music of M.I.A*: Masters thesis, Department of Philosophy, History, Culture and Art Studies, University of Helsinki, Musicology

199-Ibid

200-Ibid

201-Ibid

202-Dearden, L. 2018: *Domestic abuse survivors will not have to come face-to-face with perpetrators in court under Government proposals*: The Independent

203- Lonnblad, I. 2012: *Political Elements In The Music of M.I.A*: Masters thesis, Department of Philosophy, History, Culture and Art Studies, University of Helsinki, Musicology

204-Ibid

205-Ibid

206-Nhemachena, A. 2017: *Relationality and Resilience in a Not So Relational World?: Knowledge, Chivanhu and (De-)Coloniality in 21st Century Conflict-Torn Zimbabwe*: Langaa RPCIG

207-Ibid

208-Schapiro, L. 1972: *Totalitarianism: Key Concepts in Political Science*: The University of Michigan

209-Bakhtin, M. 1984: *Problems of Dostoevsky's Poetics* : University of Minnesota Press

210-Marshall, C. 2013: *Apocalypse Now's "Ride of the Valkyries" Attack*: The Anatomy of a Classic Scene': Open Culture: http://www. openculture.com/2013/10/ride-of-the-valkyries-attack.html

211-Hart, K. 1981: *Return to Auschwitz*: Atheneum

212-Hart, K. 1962: *I Am Alive:* Corgi

213-Brauer, J. 2016: *How Can Music Be Torturous?: Music in Nazi Concentration and Extermination Camps*: Volume X, Issue 1, Winter 2016 , *Music and Politics*

214-Hadith 142

215-Surah 5

216-IRIN, 2007: *Traditions eroded by years of war*: http://www.irinnews.org/report/72267/uganda-traditions-eroded-years-war

217-Ibid

218-Apollinaire, G.: Widely quoted, source unknown

SELECT BIBLIOGRAPHY

Alexander, A. 2008: *Towards Dialogic Teaching: Rethinking Classroom Talk*: Dorchester Publishing Company, Incorporated

Alexander, A. 2010: *Children, their World, their Education: final report and recommendations from the Cambridge Primary Review*: Routledge

Alexander, R.2010: *Speaking but not listening? Accountable talk in an unaccountable context*: UKLA: Literacy Volume 44 Number 3 November 2010

Alexander, R. 2017: *Developing Dialogue: Process, Trial, Outcomes*: 17th Biennial EARLI Conference, Tampere, Finland

Alexander, R. 2018: *Developing dialogic teaching: genesis, process, trial*: Routledge

Alinsky, S. 1989: *Rules for Radicals: A Pragmatic Primer for Realistic Radicals*: Vintage

Arendt, H. 1951: *The Origins of Totalitarianism*: Schocken Books

Arendt, H. 1958: *The Human Condition*: The University of Chicago

Arendt, H. 1963: *Eichmann in Jerusalem: A Report on the Banality of Evil*: Viking Press

Arendt, H. 1968: *Men in Dark Times:* Harcourt, Brace & World

Bakhtin, M. 1974: *Toward a Methodology for the Human Sciences* in Emerson, C. & Holquist, M. 1999: *Speech Genres and Other late Essays*: University of Texas Press

Bakhtin, M. 1974: *Toward a Methodology for the Human Sciences* in Emerson, C. & Holquist, M. 1999: *Speech Genres and Other late Essays*: University of Texas Press

Balfour, M; Bundy, P; Burton, B; Dunn, J; Woodrow, N: 2015: *Applied Theatre: Resettlement: Drama, Refugees and Resilience*: Methuen Drama

Barba, E; Savarese, N. 2011: *A Dictionary of Theatre Anthropology*: Taylor and Frances

Bauman, Z. 1982: *Memories of Class: The Pre- History and After-Life of Class*: Routledge &Kegan Paul

Bauman, Z. & May, T. 2001: *Thinking Sociologically, 2nd Edition*: Oxford: Blackwell

Berger, R. 2003: *An Ethic of Excellence*: Heinemann Educational Books

Berger, R. 2014: *Leaders of Their Own Learning: Transforming Schools Through Student-Engaged Assessment*: Jossey-Bass

Boakye, J. 2019: *Black, Listed*: Dialogue Books

Boal, A. 1979: *Theatre of the Oppressed*: Pluto Press

Boal, A. 1992: *Games for Actors and Non-Actors*: Routledge

Bolton, G. and Heathcote, D. 1995: *Drama for Learning: Dorothy Heathcote's Mantle of the Expert Approach to Education*: Heinemann

Bourdieu, P. 1984: *Distinction: A Social Critique of the Judgement of Taste*: Routledge

Brook, P. 2008: *The Empty Space*: Penguin Classics

Brown, B. 2012: *Daring Greatly: How the Courage to Be Vulnerable Transforms the Way We Live, Love, Parent, and Lead*: Avery

Cain, S. 2012: *Quiet: The Power of Introverts in a World That Can't Stop Talking*: Crown Publishing Group/Random House, Inc

Chambers, C. 2011: *Black and Asian Theatre In Britain: A History*: Routledge

Claxton. G. And Lucas. B. 2013: *What Kind of Teaching For What Kind Of Learning*: SSAT

Csikszentmihalyi, M. 1996: *Creativity: Flow and the psychology of discovery and invention*: Harper Collins

Dweck, C. 2017: *Mindset: How You Can Fulfill Your Potential*: Little, Brown Book Group

Dodgson, D. 1984: *Motherland*: Heinemann

Eddo-Lodge, R. 2017: *Why I'm No Longer Talking to White People About Race:* Bloomsbury

Edward, C. 2012: *The Hundred Languages of Children: The Reggio Emilia Experience in Transformation*: Praeger

Freire, P.1970: *Pedagogy of the Oppressed*: Continuum

Galton, M. 2008: *Creative Practitioners in Schools and Classrooms*: University of Cambridge Faculty of Education

Gearing, D. 2006: *Rosalind*: Oberon

Gibran, K. 2015: *The Prophet*: Wisehouse Classic Edition

Gladwell, M. 2008: *Outliers: The Story of Success*: Little, Brown and Company

Goss, T. 1995: *The Last Word on Power*: Rosetta Books

Grotowski, J. 2002: *Towards a Poor Theatre*: Routledge

Hattie, J. & Timperley, H. 2007: *The Power of Feedback*: Sage

Hattie, J. 2012: *Visible Learning for Teachers: Maximizing Impact on Learning*: Routledge

Holt, J.1989: *Learning all the time*: Perseus Books

Holt, J. 1995: *How Children Fail: De Capo Press:* Perseus Books

Ignatiev, N. 1995: *How the Irish Became White*: Routledge

Lan, D. 1995: *Guns and rain: Guerrillas and Spirit Mediums in Zimbabwe*: London: James Currey, Ltd and Berkley: University of California Press

Lipton, S. 2014: *Dark Mirror*: Henry Holt and Company

Livingstone, R. 1941: *The Future of Education*: Cambridge University Press

Maddox, B. 2002: *Rosalind Franklin: The Dark Lady of DNA* by Harper Collins

Manson, M. 2016: *The Subtle Art of Not Giving a F*ck: A Counterintuitive Guide to Living A Good Life* : Harper

Mate, G. 2009: *In the Realm of Hungry Ghosts*: Vintage Canada

McGonigal, K. 2011: *The Willpower Instinct: How Self-Control Works, Why It Matters, and What You Can Do to Get More of It* : Avery

Newmann, F and Wehlage, G. 1993: *Five Standards of Authentic Instruction*: ASCD, April 1993 | Volume 50 | Number 7

Nuthall, G. 2007: *The Hidden Lives of Learners*: NZCER Press

Nystrand, M. et al 1997: *Opening Dialogue: Understanding the Dynamics of Learning and Teaching in the English Classroom*: New York: Teachers College

Oida, Y. 1992: *An actor adrift*: Methuen Drama

Palacio, R. 2012: *Wonder*: Knopf

Pearson, C. 1986: *The Hero Within: Six Archetypes We Live By*: Harper Collins

Prochaska, J.,DiClemente, C. 1982: *Transtheoretical therapy: Toward a more integrative model of change*: Psychotherapy: Theory, Research & Practice, Vol 19 (3)

Putnam, R. D. 2000: *Bowling Alone: The collapse and revival of American Community: New* York: Simon and Schuster

Resnick, L. 2015: *Talking to Learn: The Promise and Challenge of Dialogic Teaching*, in Resnick, L., Asterhan, C. and Clarke, S. (ed) 2015: *Socializing Intelligence Through Academic Talk and Dialogue*: American Educational Research Association

Robbins, T. 2007: *Awake The Giant Within*: Simon and Schuster

Robinson, K. 1999: *All Our Futures: Creativity, Culture and Education*: NACCCE report

Roose-Evans, J. 1970: *Experimental Theatre-from Stanislavsky to Peter Brook*: Routledge

Sawyer, K. 2012 (second edition): *Explaining Creativity: The Science of Human Innovation*: Oxford University Press

Seligman, M. 2011: *Flourish: A Visionary New Understanding of Happiness and Well-being*: Simon and Schuster

Sennett, R. 2008: *The Craftsman*: Yale University Press

Sokolove, M. 2013: *Drama High*: Riverhead Books

Stanislavsky, C. trans. Hapgood, E. 1986: *An Actor Prepares*: Methuen

Wacquant, L. 2004: *Body & Soul: Notebooks of an Apprentice Boxer*: Oxford University Press

Wiliam, D. 2011: *Embedded Formative Assessment*: Solution Tree Press

Worth, S. 1980: *Margaret Mead and the Shift from "Visual Anthropology" to the "Anthropology of Visual Communication"*: Studies in Visual Communication: Volume 6, Issue 1Spring 1980Article 55-1-1980, Penn Libraries, University of Pennsylvania

ACKNOWLEDGEMENTS

To all the numerous students who went on the five-year 'walk toward' with me. You always gave so much of yourself. It's been such a privilege. I thank you more than you'll ever realise.

There have been many people who've helped and influenced me over the years. I'm sure you know who you are. I thank you, too. However, there are some relationships that are transformational. Simon, Cara, Swanlea School and School21 – life has never been the same. Thank you.

A huge shout out to my faithful readers, Rayne, Ehpriya, Clare, always so wise, kind and generous.

Big thanks to Jo Shindler for the initial proof reading and to Rosa Shindler for the cover design. Thank you Ellie Shindler for suggesting Jeffrey write the foreword to the book, inspired.

Lastly, there's my family – Jo, Ellie and Rosa, my angels. Thank you for being you and the life we've created together. My love for you is beyond words.

ABOUT THE AUTHOR

Daniel Shindler was a teacher of drama, wellbeing, oracy and project-based learning for 33 years. He worked in a range of settings in the UK and overseas, including rural, inner city, and international schools. He spent much of his career in Whitechapel in the East End of London. He was also a founding teacher of the innovative School21 in Stratford, East London, and the architect of their groundbreaking oracy curriculum. He's now reinvented himself as an ethical cook, retaining the core values that underpinned his teaching career. He also works as a freelance trainer of teachers, trying to find ways of exploring what it means to be an educator.

Contact: terama95@gmail.com or Instagram @wastechefdan

Lightning Source UK Ltd.
Milton Keynes UK
UKHW010653310720
367482UK00002B/494